The Taste of Yiddish

The Taste of Yiddish

A Warm and Humorous Guide
to a Fascinating Language

by Lillian Mermin Feinsilver

South Brunswick and New York.
A. S. Barnes and Company
London: Thomas Yoseloff Ltd

© 1970 by Lillian Mermin Feinsilver

Library of Congress Catalogue Card Number: 70-88260

REPRINTED 1980

A.S. Barnes and Co., Inc.
Cranbury, New Jersey 08512

Thomas Yoseloff Ltd
Magdalen House
136-148 Tooley Street
London SE1 2TT, England

ISBN 0-498-02515-2 (cloth)
ISBN 0-498-02427-X (paper)

Printed in the United States of America

To the memories of
five unknowing contributors
to this book:
Charles and Nechame Mermin
and their first-born, John,
and Morris and Rachel Feinsilver,

ז״ל

Publisher's Note

Acclaimed both here and abroad when originally published, this landmark book is back in print by popular demand. The first comprehensive analysis of the unique qualities of Yiddish, it also presents the first classified and annotated listing of popular Yiddish terms, phrases, and proverbs. In addition, it contains the most systematic and authoritative treatment to date of the colorful ways in which Yiddish and English have affected each other.

Lillian Mermin Feinsilver offers her insightful theories on the origins of such terms as "shmegegge," "mockie," "snide and shine," "tocker," "shnook," etc., and presents a fascinating discussion of the "shm-" sound as seen in terms such as "fancy-shmancy," "shmo," and "shmoo." Particularly intriguing is her treatment of bilingualism, including bilingual puns.

Along the way there are expositions of the distinctive features of Yiddish humor, vulgarity, endearment, and invective, and a wealth of spirited comment on Jewish character and experience—from the Jews' traditional familiarity with God to the "problem" of Christmas and Chanukah, from acrostics in the Bible to the Jewish attitude toward sex, from the sociology of Bar Mitzvah to the cultural impact of the bagel—all part of the bubbling exuberance bursting through every page of this robust book.

An extra treat is the selection of books and records for further enjoyment. And don't forget the notes—they're as captivating as the text—or the two efficient indexes, designed to keep you from BLONJE-ing.

Contents

Preface

SHOLEM ALEYCHEM. Peace be with you.

That's the Yiddish way of saying "Howdy." And you're expected to reply lightly, in reverse, ALEYCHEM SHOLEM. May *you* have peace.

The hearty friendliness of SHOLEM ALEYCHEM made it a delightfully homey pen-name for the Yiddish writer Solomon Rabinowitz, who became known the world over as the Yiddish Mark Twain. His stories about the everyday trials and joys of the European Jewish "little man," and the language he wrote in, are being rediscovered and relished by the children, grandchildren and great-grandchildren of his generation, as well as by plenty of GOYIM, the outsiders who want to know what all the fun is about too.

The free rein being given to Yiddish these days is really something to see and hear. Not only the marketplace (as we shall have occasion to see later) but every nook of the entertainment world has been invaded. The Jewish writer has an almost limitless pantry shelf of description and quip to draw on. Can he blame everybody else for wanting in? Magazine and newspaper ads—to say nothing of hard-hacking novelists—are trying so desperately to get with it, that they're malapropping all over the place.

This book can help you avoid such faux pas. It can brief you on the basic terms you are likely to encounter in conversation with Jews or in comedy routines, in books and comic strips, in the supermarket and the theatre. It can make of you A SHTIKEL MEYVEN (a bit of a connoisseur). At the same time, I hope it will give you some appreciation of the varied ingredients making up the Yiddish TAM or flavor and convey some insight into the unique character and experience of the Jews as a cultural group. It will also provide a systematic account of a process I have been documenting for a number of years, the variegated influence of Yiddish on the English language. In addition, the effects of English on Yiddish are briefly summarized, and there are suggestions for "where to go from here," in case—as I hope will be true of many readers—you want to know much more.

But before we proceed to the feast, let me tell you a little about this fascinating language called Yiddish. First of all, it is not correct to call it "Jewish." We do not "speak Jewish," even though the word YIDDISH does mean "Jewish"; we "speak Yiddish."

Yiddish is one of several Jewish languages that developed in different historical periods. It arose among the Jews of the Rhineland, who migrated from France and Italy in about the ninth century. These settlers spoke vernaculars of Old French and Old Italian tinged with Hebrew and Aramaic, to which they and their descendants added chunks of the local German dialects. As the Jews moved eastward across Europe in the wake of continual persecutions, they picked up other bits of language from the Slavic tongues and added them to the polyglot German they carried with them. In this process, four major dialects developed. Of these, the one spoken by so-called Litvaks, the Jews of Lithuania, White Russia and Northeastern Poland, is essentially "standard" or literary Yiddish (chiefly because the first Yiddish writers and public speakers in the United States were from those areas).

In the late nineteenth and early twentieth centuries, pogroms in Russia and Poland impelled masses of Jews to move back to the West. Some settled in Central and Western Europe; some went on to the New World or other parts of the globe. The results were an intermingling of dialects and the exposure of Yiddish to new influences. In the United States, Yiddish has picked up elements of American English, in South America of Spanish and Portuguese, in Israel of modern Hebrew.

Yiddish uses the Hebrew alphabet—just as Jews used Hebrew characters in earlier centuries for writing Arabic, Spanish and other languages, and just as we in this book will be using English letters for Yiddish. But Yiddish is clearly an independent language, different from either Hebrew or German. In the early

decades of this century, American Jews often derided it as
JARGON (jargon or vernacular). Although there was a body of
Yiddish literature—not only Biblical commentaries and prayerbook translations, but also fiction, nonfiction and poetry—Yiddish was looked down upon by Hebraists, who felt the sacred
idiom of Scripture to be more worthy.

The past twenty-five years have made a difference. The mass
murder of European Jewry destroyed the central source of
Yiddish culture, and the loss of that community to world Jewish
civilization is being freshly apprehended by a generation of
American Jewry that has new status. The holocaust itself—by
the perverse logic that has characterized Jewish history—served
to stimulate Jewish loyalties, which were solidified in the establishment of the State of Israel. The existence of the State since
1948 has helped to effect both outer and inner Jewish acceptance. These have been further aided by the critical reassess-
ments of the Nazi period, as well as by the churches' increasing
recognition of their Jewish roots. Also involved is the process
of coming-of-age of the American Jewish community, which is
no longer a mere agglomeration of German, Russian, Polish
and other Jewries not fully at home on these shores.

We have as a result been witnessing a rediscovery of Jewish
identity, with an avalanche of books on Jews and Judaism, in
hardcover and paperback; new translations of prayerbook,
Torah and Talmud; new magazines of Jewish content; and a
new emphasis on Jewish education, including both Hebrew and
Yiddish.

Indeed, at a time when by earlier forecasts Yiddish should
be quietly dying, there are signs of a possible rebirth—or at the
very least, as in certain trees, a last dramatic blooming before
death. Scholars have been tracing the origins and development
of Yiddish more clearly and no longer speak of it as mere
"Judeo-German." Grammar and spelling have been standard-
ized, largely through the efforts of the YIVO Institute for
Jewish Research (formerly the Yiddish Scientific Institute—
YIVO). A pioneer study at Columbia University has devoted
years to recording the versions of Yiddish spoken in New York
and in Israel, for an ambitious *Language and Culture Atlas of
Ashkenazic Jewry*. A mammoth new etymological dictionary,
entirely in Yiddish, is available in several volumes, with more
still to come. Sponsored by a wide variety of Jewish organiza-

tions and individuals, the work is being assisted by City College's new Yiddish Lexicological Institute. Two modern concise English-Yiddish Yiddish-English dictionaries are also off the press. A new history and several grammars have been produced, and college courses in Yiddish are being offered on a growing number of campuses. Yiddish literature in translation is being studied in English departments as well.

On other levels, Yiddish folk schools are still operating in various parts of the country, and some Jewish parochial schools (where Hebrew has been dominant in the curriculum) are beginning to give new thought to Yiddish. In addition, new English-Yiddish magazines have been launched, one by a long-established commercial press. The Yiddish theatre has been revived (again!), and many thousands of New Yorkers (over 25,000 in 1969) have thronged to Central Park for the Summer Yiddish Music Festival inaugurated in 1968. Informal Yiddish circles and study groups have been springing up in many places, including so unlikely a one as Albuquerque, New Mexico (where the stimulus came from a converted spouse!). Philadelphia has a new Yiddish Youth Theatre as well as a Yiddish Literature Group and a Sholem Aleichem Club, the last having even published a book. To top it all, a national Society of Yiddish-speaking Gentiles has been reported in New York, some two-thirds of its members being Negro!

In Israel, too, the attitude has changed, partly because of an emergent recognition of Yiddish as the language of the martyred six million, partly because of the settlement of new groups of Yiddish-speaking Jews such as the Rumanians. Today Yiddish language and literature are being taught on the college and university levels, where Yiddish scholarship equals that of the United States. Even the high-school curriculum has been penetrated, and will doubtless become increasingly hospitable to Yiddish as time goes on. Tel Aviv has a Sholem Aleichem Museum, and plans are in process for a Leivick House to honor the Yiddish poet. The Yiddish theatre has half a dozen acting companies, some going abroad on tour, and there are Yiddish radio programs, concerts and recordings. As of 1965 there were not only a thriving Yiddish daily newspaper, but six different weeklies, a fortnightly, two monthlies (one in Hebrew and Yiddish), a bi-monthly and two quarterlies (one of the last being considered by many to be the world's finest Yiddish periodical).

Indeed, Tel Aviv has enough good Yiddish writers around—
their numbers being increasingly augmented by new settlers
attracted by the current mood of receptivity—for a lively Yiddish writers' organization, in a home of its own. It is fascinating
that in 1968, when the late Itzik Manger gave a Yiddish poetry
reading, the police had to be called to control the overflow
crowd. Most significant, perhaps, is the fact that President
Shazar has inaugurated an annual Manger Prize for Yiddish
Literature. Dr. Sol Liptzin, writing in the *Jerusalem Post* on
July 4, 1969, noted that in so doing President Shazar "pointed
out that the struggle against Yiddish belonged to a distant past
but not to the present. Today Tel Aviv has become the chief
centre for Yiddish literary creativity."

Though slightly outdistanced by the output in Israel, and
about equaled by that in Argentina, Yiddish literature in the
United States is still creative. Not only prose (history, demog-
raphy, folklore, fiction, literary criticism, etc.) but poetry and
drama continue to be published, even if usually at the authors'
expense. The category which usually has the longest list, interestingly enough, is poetry. Moreover, as has been true in the
past with writers like Sholem Aleichem and Sholem Asch, translations of Yiddish fiction at times attract notice in the general
literary world. Isaac Bashevis Singer, whose Yiddish stories
deal with obscure European Jews of a world that is past, holds
an award of the National Academy of Arts and Letters.

True, the average American Jew has but a limited acquaintance with the language (fewer than a million, out of more than
five and a half million American Jews, may be presumed to be
Yiddish-speaking, and even among these knowledge varies con-
siderably). But there exists a widespread affection for Yiddish
expressions, which this book is meant to serve.

It has seemed wise to classify the various terms and phrases.[1]
Some, it will be seen, could fit under more than one category.
The choice has sometimes had to be arbitrary. In certain instances, a term may be discussed in more than one place. However, cross-referencing has been generous, to help the reader in
understanding the background surrounding many terms. The
cross-referencing also makes it possible, if desired, to dip into
the material at any point.[2]

I should mention that adjectives, articles and some nouns
take different endings according to gender and to their use as

subject or object, nominative or predicate adjective, etc. Verbs also take different endings according to tense, person and number, and there are both formal and familiar forms for the second person singular. These facts explain why the form of a particular word may not be the same every time it appears. (They also explain why the current use of Yiddish as an advertising gimmick is so often botched!) Occasionally the language quoted is "unladylike." I hope it will be accepted in the same spirit in which it is offered—with an objective view of its pertinence to the discussion.

I apologize for whatever errors and inconsistencies are present. I have tried to adhere to the "standard" forms but have wavered when others seemed more common. As in any language, colloquial speech may make its own rules. With respect to spelling, precision has often been sacrificed for clarity —sometimes quite difficult to achieve. While the results may at times disturb the expert, I believe they make for better readability and may help more readers feel at home.

May I encourage those inclined to send on corrections and comments—addressed to me care of the publisher—for the benefit of any future edition.

A book of this kind owes much to the work of others—books and articles on Yiddish, English and language in general, on Jews and Judaism, on folklore and humor; conversations and correspondence—all too numerous for listing. One debt, however, must be acknowledged: to the late Dr. A. A. Roback of Cambridge, Massachusetts, psychologist, linguist and Yiddishist, rare mind and human being. His innumerable observations— some written in Yiddish to demonstrate his loyalty to the language and his faith in its future—have enriched my thinking at almost every turn. It was Dr. Roback who suggested to me the preparation of a book based on my published articles on Yiddish, and I regret that I did not act on the suggestion soon enough to gain the benefit of his generous criticism. I can only hope that he would not have found too many flaws in the manuscript.

Another very helpful person at the start was Dr. Sol Liptzin, former Chairman of the Department of Germanic and Slavic Languages at the City College of New York, now Professor of Comparative Literature and Head of the Language and Literature Division of the American College in Jerusalem. His kind hand-written letters from Israel encouraged me to forge ahead and provided useful advice on Yiddish sources. Miss Dina Abramowicz, Librarian of the YIVO Institute for Jewish Research, was of assistance in the compilation of Chapter V, as were Charles A. Madison, editor and writer, author of a recent survey volume on Yiddish literature; Dr. Joseph C. Landis, Professor of English at Queens College, New York, a translator and spirited champion of Yiddish literature; and Yudel Mark, Chairman of the World Bureau for Jewish Education of the Congress for Jewish Culture and Editor of the *Great Yiddish Dictionary*. The last-named also graciously answered miscellaneous questions. (These consultants are not, however, responsible for my judgments.) Editor David Redstone made several useful suggestions. Further details for improvement were offered by Alvin A. Mermin and Myer D. Mermin, who lent their critical minds to galley proofs.

Many courtesies were extended, over a period of years, by the libraries of Yale and Harvard universities, YIVO, Hebrew Union College—Jewish Institute of Religion, Lafayette College and Temple Covenant of Peace in Easton, Pennsylvania, as well as by the public libraries of Easton, New York, New Haven and Milford, Connecticut.

The process of writing was greatly helped at various stages by the cordial havens of retreat provided by Dr. and Mrs. Harry Klein of New Haven, Connecticut, and Mr. and Mrs. Harrison D. Horblit of Ridgefield, Connecticut.

Thanks also must be expressed to those relatives, friends and readers of my articles who over the years, both consciously and unconsciously, have fed my files on Yiddish in the American scene. It is impossible to name them all. Some are mentioned in the text and notes. However, special mention should be made of the warm residents of Easton, Pennsylvania, both Jewish and Christian, whose spoken and written words have often provided windfalls of precious research. Perhaps my most deliberate and enthusiastic informant was Cantor Morris Siegel of Easton. My son David, through his warm attachment to certain expressions, did much to insure their inclusion. My daughter Ruth developed a fine aptitude for spotting and recording for me instances of Yiddish borrowings on TV, in the comics and in other reading. My husband, Rabbi Alexander Feinsilver, assisted in checking Hebrew and Yiddish spellings and in numerous other ways—the most important, perhaps, being the act of marrying me over two decades ago. Without the rewarding years of sharing his life, I could not have written this book.

A final word of gratitude to my Maker and to His medical helpers for the gift of continued life. In the opportunity to resume and complete my interrupted labors, I have won a new appreciation of the brilliant Yiddish irony contained in "Cancer, shmancer, ABI GEZUNT."[3]

—L. M. F.

Pronouncing Guide

a as in "ma"
ay as in "aye" or "bye"
e as in "bet"
ey as in "hey"
i as in "bit"; at times as in "Fiji" or "grandiose" (mostly at
    end of word and before another vowel)
o as in "or"
ō as in "go"
oy as in "toy"
u as in "full"; at times as in "Zulu" (chiefly at end of word)
uh as in "but"
ch as in German *ach* or Scottish *loch*
zh as in "z" of "seizure"
tsh as in "tch" of "watch"
g always hard, as in "get" or "leg"
Other consonants as in English, except that "r" is closer to the
    French "r," being half-gargled, and in "kn" each letter is
    pronounced.
Now and then, the spelling may depart slightly from this scheme.
    Ex.: "h" is sometimes added after a final vowel, as in TAKEH,
    to distinguish it from English "take." Names or terms which
    have become widely known in other spellings have usually
    been kept in the popular forms: Sholem "Aleichem" instead
    of "Aleychem" (the latter being used for the greeting); "hoo-
    ha" instead of "hu-ha"; "Chanuka" instead of "Chanike";
    etc. In Hebrew spellings, the Ashkenazic pronunciation is
    given unless the Sephardic rendering is common.

When two vowels appear together, pronounce each one separately, as in "siesta"—with the exception of HOO-HA.

Accent the next-to-last syllable of most Yiddish words.

In words with case or gender endings, or with long suffixes, apply the rule to the root of the word (SHÉNEREN, MISHÚG-GENE, KÉPELDIKER).

In words with long prefixes (OPGE-, OYSGE-, ARIBER-,etc.), accent the next-to-last syllable of the prefix (OPGEKUMEN, OYSGEVEPT, ARÍBERGEYN); but with ARAYN-, AROYS-, and ARUM-, accent the second syllable (ARÚMSHLEPPEN).

In words of two syllables containing the prefix GE-, FAR-, or DER-, accent the second syllable (GENÚG, FARSHÉMT, DERFÁR).

There are other exceptions (ABÍ, CHÁNUKA, OREMÁN, etc.), but for the most part these guidelines will help you get by.

Acknowledgments

Thanks are hereby expressed for permission to use material previously published, as follows:

Excerpt from "Yossel Rakover's Appeal to God" by Zvi Kolitz. Reprinted by permission of Zvi Kolitz.

Excerpt from *The Source* by James Michener. Copyright © 1965 by Random House, Inc. Reprinted by permission of Random House, Inc., New York.

Excerpt from "The King" by Isaak Babel, translated by Walter Morison in *Russian Humorous Tales,* edited by Janko Lavrin. Copyright © 1946. Reprinted by permission of Sylvan Press Limited, London.

Excerpts from *The World of Sholom Aleichem* by Maurice Samuel. Copyright © 1943 by Maurice Samuel. Reprinted by permission of Alfred A. Knopf, Inc., New York.

Excerpts from *Little Did I Know* by Maurice Samuel. Copyright © 1963 by Maurice Samuel. Reprinted by permission of Alfred A. Knopf, Inc., New York.

Excerpts from Heinrich Heine, "In Praise of Schalet"; Moritz G. Saphir, "The Gastronomy of the Jews"; Der Tunkeler, "The Gift"; translated by Nathan Ausubel in *A Treasury of Jewish Humor,* edited by Nathan Ausubel. Copyright © 1967 by Nathan Ausubel. Reprinted by permission of Doubleday & Company, Inc., New York.

Excerpt from Sholom Aleichem, "Reb Yozifl and the Contractor," translated by Isidore Goldstick, in *Inside Kasrilevke.* Copyright © 1948 by Schocken Books Inc. Reprinted by permission of Schocken Books Inc., New York.

Excerpt from *A Dictionary of the Underworld* by Eric Par-

The Taste of Yiddish

"O let me approach the joy of the Yiddish word . . . ."

—Jacob Glatstein

I. The Yiddish TAM

On a recent tour of Israel I heard a guide ask how many people wanted explanations in English and how many in Yiddish. About half of the passengers—including some from England, France, South Africa, the United States and other places—asked for Yiddish.

"Ah!" the guide responded. "Yiddish! It's the most beautiful language in the world, for in it you can truly express your feelings!" This man, I learned later, was fluent in five languages. But he saw in Yiddish certain qualities that set it apart. And many of his passengers shared his appreciation of this unique tongue, delighting in his having offered it.

What *are* these qualities that make Yiddish so endearing?

Let me begin the answer, in good Jewish fashion, with a story. The Russian-born writer Chaim Nachman Bialik, who became world-famous for his Hebrew poetry, once ran into a little store in what was then Palestine and asked for a box of matches—in Yiddish. "Why Bialik," the proprietor exclaimed, "you, the poet laureate of the Jews, a master of Hebrew, speak to me in Yiddish?" "Yes," said Bialik, "I'm in a hurry. Yiddish is faster."

Another time, Bialik was entertaining at home and speaking to his guests in Yiddish. When one of the company asked about his choice of language, he explained that at home he liked to relax and speak Yiddish—that it was like putting on a pair of comfortable old slippers!

The point is that in Yiddish there is intimacy—a quality lacking in Hebrew, and for which modern Hebrew is constantly borrowing expressive Yiddish terms. As the Israeli writer

23

Aharon Megged has put it, "All the wrinkles of sorrow and of laughter to be found on Jewish faces are engraved on Yiddish words, sentences, and intonations."

Just how these "wrinkles of sorrow and of laughter" have been engraved is a fascinating subject for study. Let's examine the process one step at a time.

INTONATION

A generation ago, two young men in sneakers approached the tennis courts of the Hebrew Union College in Cincinnati. Rackets in hand, they stopped at the gate, puzzled by a new sign, which read:

PRIVATE
NO VISITORS ALLOWED

These boys were not students at the Reform Jewish seminary and therefore turned to go away. As they did so, a passing professor stopped and asked, "What's the matter, boys? Aren't you going to play?" "We wanted to," they replied, "but there's a new sign there that says we can't." "Really?" the professor asked. "What does it say?" "See," they pointed, "it says: 'Private; no visitors allowed.'" "Oh, no, no," said the professor, "I can see you boys have never studied Talmud. Let me tell you how that sign should be read." And he proclaimed for their benefit:

"Private?
No! Visitors Allowed!"

Obviously, the professor had inserted some punctuation in the sign. But more than that, he had supplied a very definite intonation. His Talmudic sign-reading could actually have been put to musical notation, as:

Pri- vate?   No -o!   Vi- si- tors Al- lowed!

That same musicality—which characterized the Hebrew and Aramaic of the Talmud—has also been an outstanding characteristic of Yiddish. Indeed, a number of Yiddish jokes point up the ambiguity that is often involved with this intonation. One old story deals with an innocent Jew who has been brought into court on a charge of stealing a chicken. The poor man exclaims ironically, "*I* stole a chicken!"

I   stole a   chicken!

(Preposterous!) But the non-Jewish judge, insensitive to the irony of the intonation, interprets this as an admission of guilt.

There are even other versions of this story which supply a "super-climax." For instance, after the defendant's exclamation, the judge asks why he stole the chicken, and the Jew, still protesting innocence, exclaims ironically, "AF KAPORES I needed it!" (For sacrifice I needed it!—equivalent to "I needed it like a hole in the head"), and the judge again misinterprets his answer. (Involved in the joke is the fact that literally KAPORES *would* make use of a chicken. See Chap. II, Rel. and Cul.)

Intonation is so striking in Yiddish because the traditional Jew spent a good deal of time in prayer—much of it being chanted rather than spoken. Various sections of the Bible had their own NIGUN or cantillation, so that even the study of Scripture was interlaced (not to say "interlarded"!) with melody. The time-honored discussions of Torah and Talmud had a certain cadence, punctuated by gestures. The mood of such discussions has been captured by a number of famous paintings, in which you can almost hear the intonation suggested by facial expression and hand motion.

This emphasis in tone and gesture must have been partly an effort to interpret the text of the Torah scroll, which contains no vowels and no punctuation. Traces of this effort at expressiveness can still be heard in the speech of American Jews and have even influenced American slang, as we shall see later.

FAMILIARITY WITH GOD; IRONY

Involved with intonation are a number of other characteristic features. Two of these are the Jew's familiarity with God and his very special brand of irony. Let's look at them for a moment.

The lot of the East European Jew was hard. He reacted to this reality in various ways. He not only stated the fact in popular dicta: A YID IZ IN GOLES (A Jew is in exile); 'SIZ SHVER TSU ZAYN A YID (It's hard to be a Jew); ME MUTSHET ZICH (One suffers). He also learned to express it with a shrug and to go about his business.

But in the process, he was not simply resigned. He bellyached with ironic comments (which have in translation invaded American slang) like VER DARF ES? (Who needs it?); ICH DARF ES ZEYER HOBN (I need it very badly); NOR DOS FEYLT MIR (That's all I need); TSU A HUNT ZOL ES NIT TREFN (It shouldn't happen to a dog).

And he didn't hesitate to complain to his God, with Whom he was on quite familiar terms, well aware of the precedent for such intimacy. Had not Abraham presumed to question God's threat to destroy sinful Sodom, and had he not talked the Almighty out of His expressed intention, bargaining with Him step by step? (Genesis 18: 23-32.) Had not the Psalmist been so CHUTZPADIK as to tell God that He should save him for His own sake, reminding Him that "in death there is no remembrance of Thee: in the grave who shall give Thee thanks?" (Psalm 6:5.) Surely it was not unusually presumptuous, then, for the Yiddish-speaking Jew centuries later to protest familiarly in rhyme: OY, GOT,/FARZICH MAYN COMPOT,/VESTU VISN VOS A TAM ES HOT! (O God, try my compote and you'll know what a taste it has!)

An old *New Yorker* cartoon by William Steig epitomizes this attitude. Two women are outdoors, one looking up at an oncoming downpour and complaining, "Who asked for rain?" This makes use of the ironic Yiddish idiom VER HOT GEBETN . . . ? (Who asked for . . . ?). The constant asking of God's help and the certainty of His response were a basic assumption; therefore displeasure with actual occurrence wryly acknowledged that someone else may have asked for this!

Sholem Aleichem's famous character Tevye the Dairyman (or Milky One[1]) goes beyond such philosophical dissatisfaction.

After continual prayers and continual misfortunes, he asks God please to forget that there is a Tevye in the world—as though he were using the ironic interpersonal jibe, TU MIR NISHT KEYN TEYVES (Don't do me any favors! Just forget about me!).

In this process, God was addressed in a variety of informal ways: OY, GOT (O God); OY, GOTTENYU (O God, Dear); OY, REBOYNE-SHEL-OYLEM (O Master of the World); GOTTENYU ZISSER (God Dear, Sweet One); OY, TATTENYU (O Father Dear); and the like. And God was personified in descriptions of the height of luxury: VI GOT IN FRANKRAYCH or VI GOT IN ODESS (like God in France; like God in Odessa). A typical Sholem Aleichem description is: GANTS FRI—VEN GOT ALEYN SHLOFT NOCH (Really early—when God Himself is still sleeping)![2]

The Torah, too, was humanized, as the bride of Israel. A number of Yiddish folk songs sing of the courting of the Torah as the daughter of God, and the men honored with the reading of certain holiday Torah portions were known as bridegrooms of their portions.[3] (The Hebrew word *Torah* is feminine, and Proverbs 3:18 is often translated literally: "She is a tree of life to them that lay hold upon her.") Even the Sabbath was spoken of as the "Sabbath bride" or the "queen of days," and the festive meal served at the conclusion of the Sabbath was known as MLAVEH MALKE (Escorting the Queen).

The same informality extended to important names in the people's past. Moses was spoken of as Moyshe Rabbeynu (Moses our Teacher), and a number of later distinguished personalities were known popularly by pet names, as we will see in the discussion of acronyms. Intriguingly enough, the name of Jesus too had an intimate form, Yeyzel.

Despite a basic piety, nothing was really sacred. There are numerous ironic quips about God—from GOT IZ AN ALTER KUNTSENMACHER (God is an old Joker) to MIT GOT TOR MEN ZICH NIT SHPILEN—ERSHTNS TOR MEN NIT, UN TSVEYTNS LOZT ER NIT (We'd better not fool around with God—in the first place, we must not, and in the second place He doesn't let us). In the same vein is the expression AZ GOT ZOL VOYNEN AF DER ERD, VOLTN IM DI MENTSHN DI FENSTER OYSGESHLOGN (If God lived on earth, the people would break His windows). Perhaps the most fascinating is the following ironic expression of faith: GOT VET HELFN—VI HELF NOR GOT BIZ GOT VET

HELFN! (God will provide—if only God would provide until God provides!)

The MEGILLE, or scroll, of Esther which is read aloud on Purim, and which takes some time to read, gave rise to the humorous description of a long story as A GANTSE MEGILLE (a whole MEGILLE). Jokes were made about other portions of the Bible, about the Talmud and the Midrash, about various holidays, about Moses, the angels, even the Messiah. A typical Yiddish story has three men debating whether the Messiah will come. The believer says, "Of course he will come!" The agnostic says, "I don't know; maybe he will, and maybe he won't." And the nonbeliever says, "Not on your life! He won't come!" The situation is projected that the Messiah *does* come, and the believer says to his two friends, "You see? He has come!" The agnostic replies, "TAKEH (true), he has come." The nonbeliever, still recalcitrant, exclaims, "KAM GEKUMEN! (About time!)"[4]

It was only logical that the rabbi too should come in for his share of jest, and that his wife should attain a special designation, the affectionate and slightly disrespectful title of REBBITZEN. Indeed, it might be said that the Jew's familiarity with God may be the ultimate explanation for CHUTZPA: If you can argue with God, what else can't you do?

Oddly enough, all this characterized a people with a tradition of awesome reverence for an all-knowing God, Whose very name was not spoken directly in prayer! The Hebrew *Adonoy,* Lord, was an intentional misreading of God's name, *Yhvh.*[5] Even the substitute *Adonoy* was avoided by using *Adoshem* or *ha-Shem,* The Name.[6] (The practice has carried over into English, many Orthodox Jews circumventing the spelling out of "God" with the form "G-d.")

In spite of philosophical rebellion, there was usually conformity with expected religious practice. The fact is beautifully illustrated by an old story about two Jews who meet on the street and start talking about God. They are both skeptical and agree that there's very little reason for believing that God exists at all. Whereupon one of them looks up and sees that the sun is getting very low, and he comments, NU, KUM SHOYN, ME DARF GEYN DAVENEN MINCHE (Come on, let's go; it's time for the MINCHE service).[7] When worship was inconvenient, the synagogue-goer might grumble in rhyme, ICH VEL DOS NIT FAR-

DINEN IN SHIL/VOS ICH VEL FARLIREN IN MIL[8] (I won't earn
in the synagogue what I'll lose at the mill). But he went. And
after going, he might voice the sardonic thought, VEN ES ZOL
HELFN GOT BETN, VOLT MEN SHOYN TSUGEDUNGEN MENTSHEN
(If it did any good to pray, they'd be hiring people to do it).

Still he *went*—partly, perhaps, because it was the expected
thing in a tightly knit community where public opinion mattered
greatly; partly, perhaps, out of habit; yet partly, too, because
of an underlying faith. The famous Yiddish song of protest to
God about Jewish fate, "Eyli, Eyli," demonstrates the point.
Building on the Biblical Hebrew *Eyli, Eyli, lomo azavtoni* (O
God, my God, why have You forsaken me?),[9] it expounds on
the injustice yet nevertheless ends with the *Sh'ma*, the affirmation of faith. In keeping with this tradition, Zvi Kolitz (co-
producer of the stage play *The Deputy* in New York) wrote a
moving appeal to God in the name of Yossel Rakover, a Hasidic
Jew who died in the Warsaw ghetto in 1943, ending with the
declamation, "And these are my last words to You, my wrathful
God: nothing will avail You in the least. You have done everything to make me renounce You, to make me lose my faith in
You, but I die exactly as I have lived, a *believer!* . . . 'Hear,
O Israel, the Lord our God, the Lord is One . . .' "

Rakover's testament and "Eyli, Eyli" both show the same
mixed emotions of the loving child toward his father that appear
so often in the Bible. Job's defiant outcries give way to ". . . I
abhor my words, and repent . . ." The exasperation of Psalm
13: "How *long*, O Lord? Wilt Thou forget me *forever?*" dis-
sipates with: "But I have trusted in Thy mercy; my heart shall
rejoice in Thy salvation." And Psalm 22, on which "Eyli, Eyli"
was based, itself concludes with: "All the ends of the earth shall
remember and turn unto the Lord. . . . They shall come and
shall declare His righteousness . . ."

No wonder that the same pattern appeared in the famous
Kaddish by the eighteenth-century Rebbe Levi-Yitschok of Berditshev, who defiantly told God, "I shall not stir from here! An
end must come to all this! Israel's sufferings must end!" and
then followed with the first line of the mourner's prayer, "Mag-
nified and sanctified be the name of the Lord!" It is not at all
surprising that the process should show itself today in the first
five books of Elie Wiesel, the great chronicler of the holocaust,
whose initial volume, *Night*, ends with an anguished denial of

God, and whose fifth offering, *The Gates of the Forest*, concludes with a deliberate recital of the *Kaddish,* as a mark of the hero's acceptance of life as it must be lived, with both agony and affirmation. Indeed, the *Kaddish* itself is the epitome of this duality: a prayer in memory of the dead, it devotes itself to extolling God's Name!

CONCERNS ABOUT LIFE AND HEALTH; DESTINY

As you can see, the Jew was concerned about fate. This concern expressed itself very directly in a spate of idioms dealing with life and health—from the famous Hebrew toast *l'chayim!* (to life!)[1] to the planning-qualifier AZ GOT VET HELFN UN MIR VELN LEBN (If God helps and we live). A satisfied clucking over a child is A LEBN AF IM! (A life on him!) or AF LANGE YOREN! (May he have long years!). Even notice of the passing of time involves thanks to God for having survived: 'SIZ SHOYN GOT-TSU-DANKEN ELEF AZEYGER (It's already God-be-thanked eleven o'clock). This has a certain lightness of touch, and the second generation often adds the time in English: " 'SIZ SHOYN GOT-TSU-DANKEN eleven o'clock"—equivalent to "My, it's getting late; we've been at this some time!"

To the question "Is everybody well?" American Jews often respond with a pious "Thank God" (GOT TSU DANKEN). This is as natural for some people as "Fine, thanks." I remember the time I asked the question of a woman who answered automatically, "Thank God"—and then stopped herself with, "What am I saying? My mother is in the hospital . . . went in on Monday."

Gentile Americans are sometimes taken aback when Jewish friends may chance to say "Be well" or "Stay well" on parting; the answer is often a puzzled "I'm feeling fine." They are unaware of the emphasis on health in Yiddish idiom which is carried over into American Jewish speech. Witness ZAY GEZUNT (Be well) and its variants ZAYT MIR GEZUNT (Be well for me—for which my husband sometimes uses a playfully literal rendering: Be me well) and ZAYZHE MIR GEZUNT (So be well for me). Notice also GEY GEZUNT UN KUM GEZUNT (Go well and come back well) and even ZAYT MIR DERVAYL GEZUNT, which is the equivalent of "See you later" but means literally "Meantime stay well."

This emphasis on health in partings has been spoofed in the story about the prosperous American Jew who settles in Israel and donates several million dollars to a philanthropic foundation. He is rewarded with a government post, that of Minister of Transportation and Health, whose duty it is to see off all departing planes and ships with the hearty wish: FORT GEZUNTERHEYD! (Travel in good health!).

There are other health-conscious expressions: TSU GEZUNT! (to health!) and GEZUNTHAYT, the counterpart of German *Gesundheit!*—with the statement GEZUNTHAYT IZ BESSER VI KRANKHAYT (Health is better than illness); A GEZUNT IN DI BEYNER! (Health in the bones!—approval of a child); and A GEZUNT AF . . . (Health on . . .) for anything well done, as in A GEZUNT AF IR PISKELE (Health on her dear mouth) for someone who has spoken well. There is also the popular expression of good wishes to someone who has acquired new clothing, TROG ES GEZUNTERHEYD (Wear it well, or Wear it in good health).

Indeed, the exclamation GEZUNTERHEYD! (In good health!) may be used in the sense of "Don't blame me!"—i.e., All right, go ahead, if that's what you want, but leave me out of it!"

Conversely, annoyance at someone's not having done something may be put ironically, BIST KRANK TSU . . .? (Are you sick to . . .?—Are you sick so that you can't . . .?), and poverty or bad luck is symbolized by A MAKEH (a boil) or KADOCHES (malaria).[2]

Talk of the future may be qualified twice. The idiom quoted earlier was merely "If God helps and we live." A different expression puts it, AZ MIR VELN LEBN UN ZAYN GEZUNT (If we live and are well). I know of a family in which this latter qualification is such a byword that the daughter (third generation), when away at school, always used it in alphabetical form in writing home of her plans; "a.m.v.l.u.z.g." A certain New England rabbi is so concerned about GEZUNT that he chose for his automobile license plate the letters GZNT! (As a rabbi, he's used to reading the Torah without vowels.)

Though neither life nor health is taken for granted, there is always hope for more. Embarking on a new venture evokes the wish, ZOL ZAYN MIT GLIK (*or* MAZEL): May it be with

happiness (*or* luck). When rabbi-archaeologist Nelson Glueck
was elected president of the Hebrew Union College in 1947, his
students sent him a telegram saying, "ZOL ZAYN MIT Glueck!"

If things should go well, there is the happy MIR HOBN ES
DERLEBT! (We have lived to see it!) and the generous hope,
MIRTZISHEM BAY DIR! (If God wills it, may it be true of you!).

Plans and hopes do not always work out, NEBBECH,[3] but there
is the reminder of the overriding value of health: ABI GEZUNT
(As long as you're healthy).

Superstition

Popular Yiddish implies that we must not dwell on good
fortune: why tempt fate? Delight over destiny is accompanied
by KEYN EYN HORE (no evil eye). And profuse congratulations
may be cut short with GIB MIR NISHT KEYN GUT OYG! (Don't
give me a good eye!). Here even the mention of "evil eye" is
avoided, by the use of its opposite. The expression can also be a
retort to the pessimist who is noting the things that may go
wrong with your expressed plans.

Or you might combine two antidotes in PFUI, PFUI, KEYN
EYN HORE—making the sound of spitting, which was to scare
away evil influences, in addition to the direct exorcising of the
evil eye. (Second-generation American Jews sometimes quote
this with a laugh—usually as "poo-poo kinahora"—to accen-
tuate their feelings about something we "shouldn't know from.")

Another act surrounded by superstition—which, like the preceding two, is shared by other cultural groups—is sneezing.
GENOSN AFN EMES! (Sneezed to confirm the truth!) attributes
approval to whatever has just been said. (This is the opposite
of the American allusion in "That's nothing to sneeze at.") If
the conversation had anything to do with death, the companion
might pull at the sneezer's ear lobe as a form of negation.
OPSHPRECHERIN (de-hexers) were thought capable of obliter-
ating evil influences, and there was even the professional OP-
SHPRECHER. (My maternal grandmother is supposed to have had
some such powers. Family members recall that if she yawned
after going through her routine, it was a sign that her OPSH-
PRECH would "take.")

Further, a compliment about the physical appearance of a
child might be buttressed with counter-superstition: ER KUKT
OYS VI ZAYN TATTEN, ZOL ER LEBN UN ZAYN GEZUNT (He

looks like his father, may he live and be well). This is often heard in translation.

Indeed, children were sometimes given names intended to ward off evil. The Hebrew word for "life" was a common boy's name, Chayim—leading to American variations like "Hyam," "Hyman" and "Hime." Women who had lost babies by miscarriage or illness might name a son Selig (Blessed) or a daughter Alte (Old One). In the United States, the latter name is sometimes encountered as "Alta" or, in the masculine, as "Alter" or "Alton."

If a child fell and hurt himself, the mother would say, GUTTE MELOCHIM AF DIR! (Good angels attend you!). There is an inverse Gresham's Law involved here: it takes good angels to drive out the bad!

Counter-superstition was also evident in the phrases used when a person's age was mentioned. If that of a child, the response might be UMBASHRIEN! (No harm come to him!) or UMBARUFEN! (No evil hurt him!). If that of an adult, the response was usually BIZ (or, in the case of the elderly, IBER) HUNDERT UN TSVANTSIK YOR! (Till—*or* Over—a hundred and twenty years!). This derives from the age projected for man by God in Genesis 6:3 (" . . . his days shall be a hundred and twenty years") and which Moses was supposed to have attained (Deuteronomy 34:7). The practice has sometimes created problems in American courtrooms. A generation ago, the story was reported of an elderly Jewish woman who, on being asked her age, replied, "ZIBETSIK YOR, BIZ HUNDERT UN TSVANTSIK YOR" (seventy years, till a hundred and twenty years). The judge and jury were confused, and the interpreter thought of an ingenious strategem to get a direct reply. He smilingly asked the witness, "BIZ HUNDERT UN TSVANTSIK YOR, how old are you?"

In Israel, a recent quip has it, they now invoke only a hundred and eight. Why? Because ten percent goes to the government!

The same fear of attracting bad luck was evident in the reply to the question VOS MACHT IR? (How are you?). A DANK AYCH FAR A NOCH FREG (Thank you for an inquiry) was the frequent indirect answer. If you further asked about other members of the family, the reply would usually be, A DANK AYCH (Thank you). I recently heard this in translation—i. e., a simple "Thank you" in reply to my "How are you?"

Similar uneasiness was seen in the Old World manner of counting persons in a group: NIT EYNS, NIT TSVEY . . . (not one, not two . . .), and this usage is often laughingly employed in family gatherings of second- and third-generation American Jews. Even cussing-out of a child was often put in the negative, as in DER SHLAK ZOL IM NIT TREFN! (May he not get apoplexy!)—as though one were to say in English, "Oh, don't go to the devil!" Also, expressed intentions might be followed up with BALENEDER (not making any vow), to allow for the eventuality of not carrying through and to absolve oneself of guilt on that account.

The abhorrence of expressing some dire possibility was evident in the statement ICH VIL ES FARN MOYL NIT BRENGEN (I don't want to bring it to my mouth)—presumably for fear it might thus be encouraged to take place (reminiscent of "I don't even want to think about it"). If something gloomy or unkind had already been spoken, an effort was made to annul it with NIT OYSGEREDT ZOL ES ZAYN (May it not be spoken) or NIT MIT MAYN MOYL REDENDIK (Not speaking with my mouth).[1] After an uncomplimentary reference to the dead, one might say NIT IM MEYN ICH DOS, NOR DI VANT (I don't mean him by that, just the wall), lest the departed suffer in the afterlife or even cause the speaker harm. One did not trifle with the dead.

According to Rabbi Immanuel Jacobovits in his famous *Jewish Medical Ethics*, superstition among Jews has usually reflected the magical and occult beliefs prevalent in the surrounding cultures; Jewish literary sources have given little credence to it. In contrast to the popular fear of the power of words, for instance—particularly with respect to talk of death—a medieval Jewish code, reflecting earlier Talmudic opinion, advises that a gravely ill person should be encouraged to settle his affairs "and he should not be afraid of death on this account"—for "words cause neither life nor death."

Such wholesomeness of course won out. In spite of the fears, death was the subject of bantering, as in the phrase NIFTER, PIFTER, ABI GEZUNT (Departed, deshmarted, as long as he's healthy) or in observations like ZINT 'SIZ OYFGEKUMEN DOS SHTARBN, IZ MEN NIT ZICHER MITN LEBN (Since dying was invented, life hasn't been safe). The same bantering note is evident in various humorous tales about the MALECH HAMOVES, the

Angel of Death. Though one might want to avoid his influence, one could still feel free to joke about him!

REALISM

Concerned though they were with destiny, Jews were not really fatalistic. True, the coming of the Messiah and the rebuilding of the Temple were awaited by some with simple faith; an acceptance of tragedy was 'SIZ BASHERT (It's destined) and even the term for a "beloved" was DER BASHERTER (the destined one). An old story tells of a Gentile who asks a Jew, "If your God created the whole world in six days, what has He been doing all the time since then?" and the answer is, "Arranging marriages." This is a charming thought, of course, but Jews did not sit back and wait for God to do it all by Himself. They employed the services of a SHADCHEN,[1] to help God along! Judaism views man as a "partner of God": God rules the world and sets the guidelines, but man has to do his share!

Accordingly, Yiddish responses to the exigencies of fate—far from the Spanish *Que sera sera* (Whatever will be, will be)—stressed positive action: ME DARF ZICH INTERGARTLEN (You have to gird yourself); AZ ME VIL, KEN MEN IBERKEREN DI GANTSE VELT (If you want to, you can turn over the whole world); AZ ME MUZ, KEN MEN (If you have to, you can); ME GEFINT ZICH AN EYTSE (You find a way out).[2]

After complaining to God and arguing with Him, one forced oneself to face facts: A B'REYRE HOT MEN? (Does one have a choice?); ES TREFT ZICH (These things happen); VOS IZ GEVEN IZ GEVEN IZ NISHTO (What has been has been, is no more); and one found consolation in health (ABI GEZUNT), in work (MACHST A LEBN?—Do you make a living?) and in the notion that the loss has been a good, clean sacrifice (A SHEYNE, REYNE KAPORE). Further, in the process of daily living, one learned to be cautious and conserving: ME VARFT NIT AROYS DI UMREYNE VASSER EYDER ME HOT REYNES (You don't throw out the dirty water until you have a clean replacement). A man's job might be unsatisfactory, but he would be unwise to quit before he had another.

Despite the many regulations involved in Orthodox Judaism, Yiddish reflected a healthy realism about religion, too. Take the matter of an individual's defiance of ritual, for instance. Yiddish had the worldly observation, BESSER A YID ON A BORD VI A BORD ON A YIDN (Better a Jew without a beard than a beard without a Jew)—that is, better that a man be true to the essentials of his faith while ignoring minor rules than to conform in appearance and be wanting within. The same idea appears in GUTSKAYT IZ BESSER FUN FRUMKAYT (Goodness is better than sanctimony). This defiance of ritual goes back at least to Isaiah, who taunted those that fasted on Yom Kippur but did not follow the ethical imperatives of their faith.[3]

Another popular saying put it, AZ ME FREGT, IZ TREYF (If you ask, it isn't kosher). In other words, there are times when you might be better off not asking; what you don't know won't hurt you. Why look for trouble? But, suppose you have broken a rule. Well, you might as well relax and enjoy it: AZ ME EST CHAZER, ZOL RINNEN FUN'M BORD! (If you eat pig, let it drip from your beard! Go whole hog!)

IMPRECATION

A truly fatalistic people could not have produced the rich vocabulary of imprecation that is to be found in Yiddish. Swearing is at least an effort to affect the fate of others! ZOL DIR CHAPN A CHALERYE! (May a cholera catch you!) or its shorthand A CHALERYE! are not expressions of passive submission. Neither are A SHVARTZ YOR! (A black year!); A MISE MESH-INNE AF DIR! (A horrible death to you!); IN D'RERD ARAYN! (Into the ground!); ZOLST VAKSEN VI A TSIBILE—MITN KOP IN D'RERD! (You should grow like an onion—with your head in the ground!).

Yet in spite of their forceful expression, Yiddish imprecations do not, as a rule, profane the name of God or of any honored forebear. There seem to be almost no parallels in Yiddish for the common English blasphemies.

Theoretically, IN D'RERD ARAYN is a less direct expression than "Go to hell" or "The devil take you." However, in both languages, the tone of voice or the sensitivity of the hearer may modulate or intensify the meaning. There is an old story about a Jewish mother who hears her child sneeze and says, TSU GE-ZUNT, MAYN KIND! (To your health, my child!). At the second sneeze, she responds, TSU GEZUNT, MAYN TAYERE! (To your health, my dear one!). At the third sneeze, she exclaims, AY, IN D'RERD ARAYN, HOST SHOYN GECHAPT A KALT! This is literally "Ah, into the ground, you've already caught a cold!" But the tone is perhaps better translated as: "Oh, the hell with it, you've gone and caught a cold!" It is not to be taken seriously. Yet, some years ago when my husband was addressing a group of women, one of whom sneezed several times, he was reminded of this story and interrupted his talk to tell it, only to discover that the sneezer was insulted rather than amused!

ENDEARMENT

As a balance to invective, Yiddish had a precious storehouse of endearment. Pet terms like FISHELE (little fish), KROYNELE (little crown), BUBELE (sweetie-pie) decorated the speech addressed to young children, as did loving phrases like MAYN KLEYNER (my little one), MAYN SHEYNER (my pretty one), MAYN FEYGELE (my little bird).

These are not too different, of course, from the American counterparts of "pet," "darling," "sugar-plum," "baby-doll," "honey-child," "my little chickadee." The really distinctive form of endearment in Yiddish is the diminutive suffix. English provides the endings of "-y" or "-ie" or "-kins" as in "Billy" or "Blondie" or "babykins." But Yiddish has a rich garden of endings to pick from, as detailed in Chap. II, and tacks them onto almost any kind of word.

I once heard an entertainer give an amusing demonstration in sound and motion of the different kinds of beard that can be described in Yiddish: A BORD (forceful, with a long hand motion, suggesting a most dignified and lengthy beard); A BERDEL (lighter tone, with hand stopping a few inches below the chin, suggesting a medium-length growth); A BERDELE (smiling, with fingers suggesting a closer crop); with still other degrees of style and stubble in A BERDINKE, A BERDINKELE, A BERDINYUNKELE, A BERDINYUNTSHIKEL![1]

Notice how such suffixes can also embellish other parts of speech, as in the warm and affectionate "Good night"—A GUTSHINKE NACHT—or the directions to children such as ZINGENYU (Sing, my sweet) or PAVOLYINKE (Slowly, dear). The process even carries over into adopted English terms. In the United States "hello" may sometimes become "helloele,"[2] and in England a sixpence may be a "sixpencel." (British and American parallels are "good-by-ee," "all righty" and "yes indeedy.")

This affectionate note is seen in still other expressions. A recognition that it is getting late, for instance, might be 'SIZ HALB NUCH TSVELEF, A BISSELE (It's 12:30, a little bit). And a siblingless offspring is not just an only child: he is AN EYNSIKEL (an only little one) or AN EYN-EYNSIKEL (a one and only little one). An only son is A BEN YUCHIDEL, a Hebrew-derived term meaning "an only little (*or* dear) son," carrying the connotation of "privileged character." An especially doting designation combines the two foregoing terms in AN EYN-EYNSIKEL BEN YUCHIDEL. An only daughter also has a special term: BAS YECHIDELE.

As you may have gathered, a Yiddish diminutive suffix often connotes more than just a simple "little" or "dear." A classic example is the name by which the famous twentieth-century cantor Joseph Rosenblatt was known the world over, Yossele Roznblat. This conveys a certain admiration and respect along with the intimacy, something like the feeling of "Our own dear Joseph Rosenblatt."

WORD-CONSCIOUSNESS

Impact of Scriptural Study

The warmth of Yiddish word-endings is only one aspect of the word-consciousness that has so strikingly characterized the Jewish group. Going back to the revelations of God's Word, this word-consciousness was nurtured by the tradition of study of Holy Writ—in which one puzzled over word meanings and sentence structure (made difficult by the lack of vowels and punctuation mentioned earlier), sifting ambiguities, comparing commentaries of different authorities. It is intriguing to realize that Maimonides, back in the twelfth century, recognized and expounded the problem of what we today call semantics in his analysis of Biblical texts.

It is understandable too that so many Yiddish proverbs should deal with wisdom and folly (discussed under Learning below) and with the power of the tongue. Just as Solomon's and Ecclesiastes' concerns about wise men and fools were assimilated, so did the latter's "A time to speak and a time to keep silent" father many an admonition on the importance of weigh-

ing one's words or restraining them: A PATSH FARGEYT,/A VORT
BASHTEYT (A slap subsides,/A word abides); A VORT IZ AZOY
VI A FAYL;/BEYDE HOBN GROYSSE AYL (A word and an arrow
are the same;/Both can take sharp aim); AZ ME REDT A SACH,
REDT MEN FUN ZICH (Talk a lot, and you talk about yourself).
These are capped by the sardonic observation, AZOY LANG ME
LEBT, TOR MEN NIT REDN; AZ ME SHTARBT, KEN MEN NIT
REDN (In our lifetime we dare not speak; in death we cannot).

Impact of Continual Migrations

The Jews' history of enforced migrations also contributed to
their sensitivity to words: they had constantly to learn new
languages. Long before the beginning of the Christian era,
Jews were already widely dispersed outside of ancient Palestine,
and they have been bilingual for some twenty-five hundred years,
since the Babylonian exile. The philosopher Philo, for example,
in the first century, wrote in Greek. Maimonides wrote in Arabic. Spinoza, in the sixteenth century, wrote in Latin. Indeed, a
fascinating fact of Jewish history is the development in different
places of special languages of the Jews, which were essentially
dialects of the languages of their adopted countries, written in
Hebrew characters: Ladino, Judeo-Arabic, Judeo-Persian, Yiddish.

The intriguing thing is that the cosmopolitan touch was not
restricted to the literati. It was the usual thing. My father's
experience was typical of his time. Living in Russia, where he
was a salesman in a department store with a well-to-do Christian
clientele, he knew Russian and French (the latter being spoken
by the Russian upper classes) in addition to the Yiddish, Biblical Hebrew and Talmudic Aramaic in his Jewish background.
When he came to the United States and started peddling, later
opening a store, he learned to function in English as well as in
Polish and Italian, the languages spoken by many immigrant
customers. Language, to the Jews, was not only the key to their
own culture, a highly literate one, but also the key to contact
with the world.

Punning

In addition, of course, word-play is free fun. Wry humor
finds easy expression in the manipulation of words. Take the
Yiddish story that is told of the tourist in Israel who calls the

Megiddo Hotel in Haifa and gets, by mistake, the Collector of Internal Revenue. When he asks, "Megiddo?" the reply is, NO, ME NEMT DO. (ME GIT DO means " We give here" and ME NEMT DO means "We take here.")

Or witness the old riddle, FAR VOS EST MEN SHEVUES NOR MILCHIKS UN NIT KEYN FLEYSH? (Why do we eat only dairy food on Shevuoth and no meat?) Answer: VAYL DI BEHEYMES ZAYNEN GEGANGEN NEMEN DI TOYRE (Because the cattle—or fools—had gone to take the Torah). In this pun we find some of the same familiarity and skepticism about sacred matters that were noted before. Shevuoth is the spring festival which commemorates the giving of the Law to Moses at Mount Sinai. After all, the acceptance of the Torah was the taking on of moral responsibility. Who in his right mind, the folk humor asked, would deliberately assume such a burden? Who needed it? Since the fools, or cattle, had gone to do this, there naturally was no meat, and therefore MILCHIKS was the menu for Shevuoth!

Punning among the Jews goes way back. We know that in the time of the Maccabees, in the second pre-Christian century, they called the tyrant Antiochus Epiphanes "Antiochus Epimanes," using the Greek word for "fool." In the second century, when Bar Kochba, the great Jewish military leader whom many believed to be the Messiah, did not produce the expected deliverance from the Romans, his name—which meant "Son of the Star"—was resentfully twisted into "Bar Kozeba," meaning "Son of Deception."

Later puns were even more outspoken. Notice the partially rhymed Hebrew-Yiddish folk saying, *"Lo mimidbor horim"*— FUN ZOGN/VERT MEN NIT TROGN ("Nor yet from the wilderness cometh lifting up"—From mere speech/You don't pregnancy reach). The first half is a quotation from Psalm 75:7. The second half, which supplies a homely application for the quotation (suggestive of "Saying is one thing; doing is another"), builds on the fact that the root of *midbor* (desert or wilderness) may also mean "to talk"—probably suggesting words empty as the desert—and that the root of *horim* (mountains) may mean "lifting up" or "child-bearing." ("Lifting" can of course be related to the physical appearance of pregnancy.)

As you can see, sex could be joked about intellectually, despite the rules governing sexual conduct. Sex, we should remember, was treated matter-of-factly in the Bible. Witness the simile in Psalm 19, which is read during Yom Kippur and in Sabbath services during the year: "The heavens declare the glory of God; and the firmament showeth His handiwork. . . . He set a tabernacle for the sun, which is as a bridegroom coming out of his chamber." The radiance of the sun and the radiance of the bridegroom—a charming, if earthy, comparison!

Or witness the famous passage in Deuteronomy concerning Moses in his old age: "His eyes were undimmed and his vigor unabated" (literally, ". . . and his vital fluids had not departed"). As a Jewish character comments in James Michener's *The Source,* "A man who had known God, who had created a nation, and who had laid down the law that all of us still follow. And when he dies you say of him, 'He could still function in bed.' Ours is a very gutsy religion, Cullinane."

This fact has been all too little recognized by modern investigators in the field of sex, who have tended to see only the Hebrews' proscriptive attitude toward adultery and fornication, falsely interpreting this as a denial of sexuality. "A man may have sexual relations with his own wife," the Talmud tells us, "in any manner he prefers." And the twinkling comment is added: "It is the same as in eating meat; some like it salted, some roasted, some sodden." Significantly, in recommending different frequencies of coitus for men in varying occupations, the Talmud urges the scholar to cohabit on the eve of the Sabbath. The Zohar saw divine meaning in the sexual relationship and even observed that wisdom cannot come to the virgin. Indeed, the Talmud has the fascinating opinion that in the World to Come we will be held accountable for every pleasure we declined on earth without good reason.

True, not all the authorities, either in the Talmud or afterward, were equally uninhibited. Maimonides centuries later took a pretty dim view of sex. But Nachmanides took him to task for his attitude. Some sexual self-discipline was generally required even within marriage,[1] and in certain periods the tone of moral pronouncements was quite strict—though I suspect the latter tendency was usually due to influences from the outer environment (either the example of licentious behavior, which created a negative reaction, or the Christian association of sex with sin). It is significant, I think, that for engaged couples the prevailing standards were at various times—as in the beginning of the Christian era and during the Middle Ages in some parts of Europe—quite permissive.

The basic thread of the tradition was a wholesome acceptance of sex as part of life. How could it have been otherwise, when the symbol of a male baby's covenant with God was the foreskin of his sex organ, and when the offering of that symbol was the occasion for family celebration;[2] when the little boy started his Hebrew instruction with—of all books in the Bible —Leviticus, containing specific sex regulations; when later study of Talmud covered commentaries on such material; and when synagogue services included, among other passages, not only the outspoken Psalm quoted earlier but the erotic Song of Songs read every Passover? It is probably understandable that sex scientist Dr. Alfred C. Kinsey over twenty years ago found his Jewish respondents were able to talk more freely about their sex experience than the others surveyed.

It should be borne in mind that even for the period of the exodus from Egypt, the Bible notes that if a man takes a second wife, he must not diminish what he gives his first wife in "food, clothing and conjugal rights." (Exodus 21:10.) What more enlightened recognition can one ask of the sexual needs of woman? These needs are just being "discovered" in the twentieth century!

The Talmud went much further, noting that a man with more than one wife should not only distribute his sexual attention equally among his wives, but should limit the number of his wives to four, so that each would be satisfied at least once a month! (This rule, by the way, was later borrowed by Islam.) And just as it held that a man whose wife denies him sexual relations is entitled to a divorce, so did it recommend a similar right for a wife after certain periods of neglect. Indeed, the Talmud showed an awareness of the psychology of sex, warning a man not to force cohabitation on an unwilling wife, noting warmly the outcome of an opposite situation: "Any man whose wife asks him for sexual relations will have sons the likes of whom have not been seen!"

Intriguingly enough, a frank prescription for the begetting of sons was for the husband to help a wife reach her climax before he reached his own. This reflects the view that the birth of sons was cause for rejoicing, such happy results being predicted for what was recognized as a joyful variety of sexual encounter. (The formula has been offered for less exalted motives in a recent paperback guide to seduction.) The Talmud also offered other "modern" specifics, such as the advice that a couple should not separate too quickly after the sex act.

In fact, the Talmud even had its own Dr. Masters. An amusing incident is related of one rabbi who hid under the bed of a colleague to eavesdrop, all in the name of science!

It is intriguing too that the Talmud—which is for the most part a legalistic compendium of comment on the Bible—contains occasional puns, including some of a rather broad nature. Rashi, for instance, explains the meaning of *zono* (prostitute) through the literal meaning of a phrase which is equivalent to *a fortiori* (i.e., the legal principle which assumes that a judgment in a minor matter will be even more applicable to a major matter of the same kind). The phrase is *al achas kamo v'chamo,* which means literally "on one, many and many."

It is hardly surprising, then, that the very statement ALLES SHTEYT IN TALMUD (Everything is in the Talmud) was the subject of an off-color pun in a joke told by seminary students over a generation ago.[3]

The Hebrew-Yiddish pun—such as the one which led into this discussion of sex—is not widely understood by American Jews, who have not been exposed to Scripture from the age of three as were their forebears. The knowledge of modern Hebrew, too, is limited. Occasionally a joke from Israel puns on Yiddish and modern Hebrew, and entertainers who tell such stories find they usually have to translate the Hebrew—even as some of their listeners are busily translating the Yiddish for their neighbors! One such story deals with a new settler who is sent to the Negev and exclaims in his newly learned Hebrew, *Ani ba'aretz!* The Israelis who are assisting him take this as an exultant "I am in The Land!"—but he mutters to himself in Yiddish, ICH BIN IN D'RERD! (I'm in the ground! I'm done for!). As he sees more of the uninviting desert, he exclaims, *Tōv ba'aretz!*—which the Israelis understand as "It is good in The Land!" But he again renders his thought in Yiddish, ICH BIN GUT IN D'RERD! (I'm good and buried!). Becoming more discouraged the more he sees, he wails, *Oti shalchu ba Negev!*—which his guides understand as an exuberant "They've sent me to the Negev!" But he puts it in the ironic Yiddish, PUNKT MIR, DARF MEN SHIKN IN

NEGEV! (Me—of all people—they have to send to the Negev—
of all places!). (This is also an example of a joke with two
"super-climaxes.")

A more common type of Hebrew-Yiddish pun is the one I
heard from a disc jockey on New York's Yiddish station WEVD,
when he introduced the popular Hebrew record *Tsena, Tsena*
with the comment, "I guess we'll dedicate it to the dentists in the
audience." (In Yiddish, TSEYN or TSEYNER is "teeth.") Other
popular multilingual puns are in the same class, like the simple
Latin-Yiddish "TyrannaTSORES Rex" (troubles) or the French-
Yiddish dubbing of a Hasidic section of Brooklyn: "Rue de la
PEYES" (earlocks), or the English-French-Yiddish "potatoes au
GREPSin" (belch). These are somewhat reminiscent of the pseu-
do-French and Yiddish rhyme created by high-school students of
an earlier generation: "Chevrolet coupé,/A VU TUT DIR VEY?"
(Where does it hurt you?). Of the same type was the old pseudo-
French and -English line, *Pas de leur on que nous* (Paddle your
own canoe).

Chinese and Yiddish are punned on, too. A resort-hotel entertainer tells of a Chinese chef named Fang Un (which in Yiddish
means "begin" or "start in"), whose father is named Un Fang
(UNFANG, beginning). There is some problem about food preparation, and inevitably one hears Un Fang advising his son, FANG
UN FUN UNFANG, FANG UN (Begin from the beginning, Fang
Un—i.e., start all over again). The Jewish Community Center
director in my Pennsylvania community recalls an excursion to
Chinatown many years ago, on which the guide took the group
into some kind of warehouse studded with figurines and gongs
and announced with a straight face that they were going into a
Chinese temple and that they should recite with him the Chinese
prayer for "beginning": FANG SHOYN UN! (Begin, already!).
Apparently the Chinese sound of FANG UN has been recognized
for a long time.[4]

In touring Mexico, many a Jewish tourist has smiled on seeing
the traffic sign *Curva Pelaprossa* (Dangerous Curve), mindful
that in Yiddish CURVE means "whore."[5] And in Pennsylvania,
Jews who know Yiddish are often startled during the Christmas
season by ads inviting the public to some company's "putz,"
particularly when its size is heralded. This German word for
decoration means, in Pennsylvania Dutch, a Nativity scene, but

in Yiddish (pronounced slightly differently) it is also a taboo term for the male organ, used pejoratively.[6]

There is of course an endless succession of puns on Yiddish and English. Take the jocular statement, "My favorite brand of cigarettes is YENEMS (someone else's)." Or take the story told by entertainer Emil Cohen: A man isn't feeling well and goes to see a doctor. After examining him, the doctor says, "I think it's from a virus." "What do you think?" the patient replies, "from MITSVES (good deeds) you get sick? AVADE (certainly) from AVAYRES (sins)!" (This is the Galician pronunciation of AVEYRES.) A similar type of punning occurs in the smiling statement, ZI PREGELT, for "She is pregnant." PREGLEN means "to fry" and here capitalizes on its resemblance to "pregnant," giving the idea of "She's got something cooking."

Could it be twins?

Twin Forms

Aside from punning, other kinds of word-play abound in Yiddish. Perhaps the most colorful, and the one which has become very popular in American slang, is the deprecating formula which states a word and then repeats the root with the addition of the particle SHM- as in VAYB, SHMAYB (wife, shmife) or KLIGER-SHMIGER (smart one—shmart one). It gave rise to new words like SHMOYGER (ne'er-do-well) from TOYGER (a good one, an effective fellow), SHMENDRIK (sap) from the name Hendrik, etc.

The process is fun to play around with, but watch out that you don't do what a certain young lady did who was dating a fellow named Edgar. Handsome, brilliant, and aware of his charm, this escort was spoken of outside his presence as "Edgar-Shmedgar." Inevitably, in introducing him to another visitor, the young lady found herself saying, "This is Edgar-Shmedgar"! The deprecation is often followed by ABI GEZUNT, as in the famous bilingual line, "Cancer, shmancer, ABI GEZUNT."

The formula has other varieties too. One of these makes use of SHT-, as in GRAM-SHTRAM (rhyme-shtryme), a derogation directed at a would-be poet. This is reminiscent of an old expression in my family, GROM, SHTROM, MACH MIR A LYETNIK (Wide, shmide, make me a spring coat), which was used to refer to a ludicrous comparison: What has one to do with the other? I can imagine someone asking a tailor to make a spring coat from some material, the tailor noting that there is too little to work with, that it isn't wide enough, and his client commenting, GROM, SHTROM . . . with the same ironic incongruity of "Cancer, shmancer . . ."

Another deprecation uses the sound of P- for the second half, as in the discounting of death noted earlier, NIFTER, PIFTER, or the deriding of Irving in the old nonsense jingle: ITZIK, PITZIK, NUDEL TASHEN,/FORT IN SHTOT KOYFEN KASHEN (Irving, Pirving, needle pockets, rides to town to buy grits). Other popular forms are ICHEL-PICHEL (nausea-pausea), IPSI-PIPSI (fancy-shmancy), SHIHI-PIHI (a mere nothing). The pattern also shows up in jocular bilingual comments like the old "Vat's di mattre, vat's di pattre?"—in which the English is purposely mispronounced and the effect is equivalent to the joking "So what's the matter, so?" (English has a similar use of "p" in "hocus-pocus" or the nursery rhyme "Georgie, Peorgie, puddin' an' pie,/Kissed the girls and made them cry.")

Yiddish is prone to other rhyming doublets, like HANDEL UN VANDEL (wheel and deal); UMZIST UN UMNISHT (free and for nothing); ES SHNEYT UN ES DREYT (It's snowing and blowing). Beyond these, there is an interesting variety of twin forms. Simple repetition appears in SOF KOL SOF (lit., end all end—eventually, finally) or SAY VI SAY (Be that as it may). There also are several charming variations of repetition which appear in expressions used to emphasize an extreme degree of something: A SHLIM-SHLIMAZEL (a very unlucky person); DER SHPITS ASHPITS FUN GROBKAYT (the tip of the top of uncouthness); AF PITS PITSLACH (into teeny tiny bits) or AF SHTIK SHTIK-LACH (into tiny bits of pieces); A CHOCHEM M'CHUCHIM (a sage of sages); KIFFEL KIFLAYIM (double upon double).

Then too, synonyms may be put together in apposition, as in A SHOYTE A TIPESH (a fool, a dolt). Those two words, as Maurice Samuel has pointed out, are both from Hebrew. Sometimes the words of such phrases are from different languages, as in AN EYN-EYNSIKEL BEN YUCHIDEL, an expression already mentioned under Endearment, which comes from German and Hebrew, or AN UMGLIK, A MALYERE! (a misfortune, a tragedy!), from German and French. The same process is seen in the affectionate term for the Yiddish writer Mendele Mocher Sforim —DER ZEYDE, SAVA—which uses two terms for "Grandfather," one of Slavonic origin, the other Hebrew. (Mendele was considered the grandfather of modern Yiddish literature, Peretz the father and Sholem Aleichem the grandson.) In the United States, too, bilingual repetition showed up in the old playful "EFSHER, maybe" (perhaps)—which I recently heard a lecturer use smilingly in triple form: "perhaps, EFSHER, maybe." (Non-Jewish Americans sometimes use simpler redundancies like "maybe, perhaps" or "ample enough," but without the consciousness of humor.)

In addition, Yiddish sometimes has bilingual repetition in a single word, as in FISNOGA (feet), a comic combination of Yiddish FIS and Russian *noga*. The uncomplimentary nickname for an Irishman, BEYTSEMER, combines two terms for "eggs"—both of which may also mean "testes": Hebrew *beytsim* and Yiddish EYER or AYER, the latter including the ghost of a pun on "Ire."[1]

Alliteration, also, is common in twin forms: KIND UN KEYT (child and chain); GEZOGT UN GETON (declared and done—equivalent to "no sooner said than done"); etc. English does this too in "kissin' cousins"; "dry as dust"; "through thick and thin." In other instances, the alliterative words are almost synonymous and emphasize each other, as in A BRI UN A BREN (a burn and a blaze); PROST UN PUSHET (coarse and common); MIES UN MOES (ugly and unpleasant). In English there are similar forms like "kith and kin" (another translation for KIND UN KEYT above); "dribs and drabs"; "tit for tat." It may be, as one writer has suggested, that the tendency toward repetitiveness was influenced to some degree by the style of the Hebrew Psalms, in which the second line often repeats the idea of the first line. Certainly the use of alliteration has good precedent in the Hebrew of the prophets and the religious poetry of the Middle Ages.

Finally, in some appositional phrases, the second noun has a different meaning and gives the first an extra descriptive force. Notice, for example, A CHEVREMAN, A YID (literally, a hail-fellow-well-met, a Jew; hence, an engaging fellow of a Jew) or A MAMZER, A GANEF (a bastard, a thief; hence a dirty crook). English approaches this, perhaps, in repetitive phrases like "a snare and a delusion" or "a prince of a fellow" or "you bastard, you." But in Yiddish the series of appositional terms can be endless. Witness the delightful description of a versatile character: A SHADCHEN A BADCHEN A GANEF A LAMDEN A YID. This is literally "a matchmaker, a wedding jester, a crook, a scholar, a Jew," and Maurice Samuel offers what he considers a less than equivalent English: "a rascally son-of-a-gun of a scholarly matchmaking Jew."

Rhyme

Word-play also shows up in the frequent use of rhyme. Not only is there rhyme in many of the twin forms discussed above or in the intimate rhymed complaint to God mentioned earlier. There also is rhyme in a host of descriptive terms and observations on life, from SHACHER-MACHER (finagler) to IR SHMEY UN IR DREY (her wink and her wiggle) to OPGELEBT UN OYSGEVEBT (lived out and wept out). Eggnog is dubbed GOGEL-MOGEL. Even the serious phrase spoken after the name of the departed —OLEV HASHOLEM—becomes familiarized in the rhyme OLEM B'SHOLEM.

Similar rhymed doublets appeared in the Bible. Genesis 1:2, for instance, speaks of the earth as being *tōhu vovōhu* (formless and shapeless). At the other extreme, I recall an old risqué joke which combines alliteration and rhyme in its contrasting references to RIVKE DI REBBITZEN (Rivke the Rabbi's Wife) and RAVKE DI NAVKE (Ravke the Prostitute).

More, there are rhymed comments on destiny, like VOS GOT TUT/IZ MISTOME GUT (What God doth dispose/Is good, I suppose) and GOT IZ EYNER;/VOS ER TUT ZET KEYNER (God is One;/What He does is seen by none). There are worldly observations like ALEH Y'VONIM/HOBN EYN PONIM (All military men/Have one mien; all brutes look alike) or YEYDER VOREM/ HOT ZAYN DOREM (literally, every worm has its own intestine: Every worm/Can plan confirm).

There's the humorous twist on the reply to "How are things?" when ME DREYT ZICH (One manages) becomes ME DREYT ZICH/ UN ME FREYT ZICH (You stand the gaff/And learn to laugh). And there are blunt descriptions like the one of a thin and unattractive person, DAR UN HEYACH,/SHTINKT MIT REYACH (Skinny and high,/Stinks to the sky). There are even vulgar rhymed jokes like the one about the father who tries to explain what kind of work his son the poet does and offers: MENDEL, MENDEL,/KAKT IN FENDEL (Arbuthnot/Craps in pot), his friend asking, UN FUN DOS MACHT ER A LEBN? (And from that he makes a living?—This is also an example of a joke with a "super-climax.")

Rhyme was used to spice up learning, too. East European schoolboys built rhyme on the letters of the alphabet[1] and also enjoyed spoofing their Talmud assignments in bilingual verse. A typical passage, presenting views of different rabbis, was parodied thus: *"Omar Rabi Eliezer,*/AZ ME TSUBRECHT DI GLEZER . . . ; *Omar Abaye,*/KOYFT MEN NAYE." (Said Rabbi Eliezer, If your glasses you shatter . . . ;/Said Abaye, Get new ones, no matter.)

Rhyme appears in modern bilingual jokes as well. There's the quip about the tourist who visits a synagogue in Ireland and asks a worshipper, "How are things in Glocca Morra?" and is told: "Very good, thanks, KEYN E' HORE." Or witness the greeting the rabbi gave the Pope on Yom Kippur: "GUT YONTIFF, Pontiff" (GUT YONTEF, Good holiday) and the one he used on another occasion: "VOS IZ NAYES, Pius?" (What's new?). Even political matters are subject to bilingual rhyme, as in the punning jingle about Egyptian leader Nasser: ARAYNGEFALEN IN VASSER/UN AROYSGEKUMEN A NASSER (Fell into the H_2O/And came out drenched from head to toe.—In Yiddish NASSER means "wet one.") Note also the TV feature "MEGILLA Gorilla" and the description that a comedy writer has given to the current popularity of Yiddish in American usage: "a mad rushin'/to MAMME LUSHEN."[2]

The intriguing variety of such rhymes can be seen in almost every category of expression discussed in this and other chapters.

Onomatopoeia

As is true of most languages, many popular terms in Yiddish convey by their sounds the actual process being described. Take POFN (to hit the sack). This is reminiscent of the sounds made in sleep, when the expelled breath fills up the cheeks and blows out through the lips. Or take TARERAM. Isn't that a worthy equivalent of "hubbub"? (It usually means a commotion in the sense of "fuss.") Then there's CHVALYE (wave). Next time you're in the ocean and see an enormous wave approaching, think of this word. It has all the sound and look and feel of it.

A number of other Yiddish terms that have a special hold on American Jews are also onomatopoetic. Many, it seems, use guttural, hissing, and related sounds. Notice, for instance, PLYUCHEN (to pour—rain), CHRAKEN (to force up mucus), CHROPEN (to snore), GRIZHEN (to gnaw), ZHLOKEN (to slurp).

Indeed, even several taboo terms have been shown to be highly onomatopoetic.[1]

The sound of SHM, which we discussed under Twin Forms, seems particularly striking in Yiddish. This sound, it has been pointed out, is as characteristic of opprobrium in Yiddish as *ps* is in Greek (*pseudo,* false; *psogos,* shame; etc.). Witness SHMODDER (slob); SHMOCHTES (tatters); SHMONTSES (trifles, folly, worthless talk); SHMAYSEN (to whip); etc. According to A. A. Roback, this combination of letters may be unconsciously related to the sucking process. What to make of this? "It is possible that in the collective Jewish psyche, the oral libido has burst through the dam . . . perhaps more so than in most ethnic groups." Could it be that the well-known Jewish interest in food is a similar indication, and that both may be a reaction to the highly disciplined, mental environment in which Jewish children were raised in the Old World? (But see the introduction to Food and Drink in Chap. II.)

Acronyms and Other Short-cuts

Another kind of word-handling deserves comment. The average Jew, as already pointed out, had a familiar feeling for distinguished brethren and developed popular pet names for them. It is intriguing that a number of such pet names took the form of acronyms, that is, names developed out of leading initials—the process used so commonly today for governmental and other agencies in the United States.

For instance, the popular nineteenth- and twentieth-century Yiddish writer Isaac Loeb Peretz was spoken of as Yal Peretz. The "Yal" comes from the initials of his given name, Yitschok Leybush. (A similar Hebrew pet-naming in modern Israel is that of S. Y. Agnon, Nobel Prize-winning author, known as "Shay," from Shmueyl Yosef—Samuel Joseph.)

More striking was the earlier pet-naming of the eighteenth-century founder of Hasidism, Israel ben Eliezer. This Polish REBBE was known first by the Hebrew honorific, "Baal Sheym Tōv" (Master of the Good Name). This was then reduced to the Yiddish nickname, "Der Besht" (The Besht), utilizing the initials of the Hebrew words.

Two of the most famous Scriptural commentators were given acrostic pet names. Rabbi Solomon ben Isaac of eleventh-century France, whose classic commentaries are included in all editions of the Talmud, was dubbed "Rashi," from the Hebrew Rav Shlomo ben Itschok, and is always thus referred to. Maimonides, great physician-philosopher and codifier of twelfth-century Spain and Egypt, was nicknamed "Rambam," from Hebrew Rav Moshe Ben Maimon, and was known by that designation as well as by "Der Rambam."

As you can probably gather, such playing around with letters had well-established precedent in Hebrew, going back to ancient Scripture. Twelve of the Psalms, for instance, contain what is known as abecedarian acrostics: the first letter of each line or stanza is a different one, in "a-b-c" sequence. Psalm 119 is the prime example, containing the entire Hebrew alphabet in sequence in the first letters of its twenty-two stanzas. Even the Hebrew word for the Bible, *Tanach*, is an acronym from the initial letters of the three major divisions of the Great Book: *Torah* (Law), *Nebiim* (Prophets) and *Kethubim* (Writings). (In Hebrew the sounds of "K" and "Ch" are the same letter.)

The process showed up in Greek and Latin too. An old acrostic from the Greek phrase for "Jesus Christ, the Son of God, the Savior" made the word *ichthys*, "a fish," which was of course a symbol of the early Christians. And the well-known crucifixion inscription, "INRI," is a Latin acrostic, from *Iesu Nazarensis Rex Iudaorum* (Jesus of Nazareth, King of the Jews).

For the Jews over the centuries, acrostics were a convenient device for remembering the proper order of religious rituals. For the Passover seder ceremony, for example, there is a Hebrew phrase built out of the initials of the terms for the ten plagues that beset the ancient Egyptians, all of the plagues being recited in the Orthodox Haggadah in the order so expressed. Indeed, there is a fascinating combination of acronym and pun associated with Passover and other holidays. The term *yaknehaz* comes from the initials of the Hebrew words *yayin* (wine), *kiddush* (sanctification), *ner* (light), *havdalah* (separation, or end of the Sabbath) and *zeman* (return of the festal season), indicating the order of the blessings to be recited when a holiday begins on a Saturday night. Well, somewhere along the line some joker transformed *yaknehaz* into the similar-sounding *yagt den has* (hunt the hare), and the quip took hold. As a result, many old manuscripts—including the Haggadah and festival prayerbook—contain illustrations of a hare hunt!

A somewhat similar situation could conceivably arise in the United States if the joking "pig-in-the-pen" for PIDYENABEN (Chap. II, Rel. and Cul.) were to become widespread and if the ritual used for the occasion were then to be illustrated with a penned pig! This is unlikely of course, for a number of reasons, particularly the character of the animal!

The acrostic process was used in making nouns, too. Notice the word B'TSEDEK, from BIZ TSU DER KESHENE (up to the pocket). This was used in an ironic description of the "blowhard," who promises a lot but doesn't come across: ER IZ A GUTER B'TSEDEK, He's a good giver up to the pocket. (This also contains a pun, since Hebrew *b'tsedek* means "in charity.")[1]

More modern alphabetical play has used English letters for Yiddish words, as in the old earthy description of a bootlicker, "T.L." (TOCHES LEKER—Arse Licker) or the perennially popular "A.K." (ALTER KAKER—Old Crapper).[2] A newer usage of the same type is the rendition of the academic degree of Ph.G. as PAPA HOT GELT (The father has money). One in which the letters stand for both Yiddish and English is "A.M." (Able MAMZER—Able Bastard).

Aside from such alphabetical bilingualisms, English letters have also been used for in-group English, as in "M.O.T." for Member of the Tribe, a fellow-Jew. And Yiddish expressions have been cut down to a word or two, as in the retailers' quick and private warning about shoplifters, TSVEY-AF-TSEN (two-on-ten, for "Keep two eyes on ten fingers").

Special Names

With all this emphasis on words, it is not surprising that names were given special treatment. Not only did many given names come from Hebrew and Yiddish words—boys' names like Baruch (Blessed) or Chayim (Life); girls' names like Nechame (Comfort), Sheyne (Pretty One; encountered today as "Shayna") or Eydele (Genteel One; sometimes spelled "Adla"). But very often the names by which people were known included a descriptive phrase to make the designation more specific. Witness Yankel der Krumer (Jake the Cripple); Leye di Almone (Leah the Widow); and even Sheylik, Mottel dem Chazens an Eynikel (Charles, Our Motte the Cantor's Grandson—as my father was known in his Russian home town). The pattern is seen in many character-names of Sholem Aleichem,

Peretz and Mendele: Pertshik the Cigarette-maker's Son; Davey the Crook; Heikel the Stammerer; Benjamin the Martyr; Zelda the Deserted.

Beyond that, there was a certain playfulness about fictional names, often conveying characterization. In Peretz, a meek soul is named Bontshe Shvayg, the latter term being the root of the verb to be silent. In Sholem Aleichem, a spirited young man is named Feferel (Peppercorn) and a sweet girl Brochele (Little Blessing), while a SHAMMES named Israel is nicknamed Nozel (Nosey) because of the nasal quality of his voice. In Isaak Babel (who wrote in Russian), there's a character with two nicknames: Jew-and-a-Half and Nine Holdups—the explanation for the first being that "no one Jew could contain so much insolence and so much money . . ." and the basis for the second being the fact that his business had been held up nine times. (Such characterization has of course been common in English and American writing, too, from Shakespeare's "Snug the Joiner," to Sheridan's "Mrs. Malaprop," to Cartoonist Webster's "Caspar Milquetoast.")

The same playfulness appeared in the names of fictional towns: Mendele's GLUPSK (from Russian *glup*, stupid) and TUNEYADEVKE (Droneville); Sholem Aleichem's YEHUPETS (from Hebrew *yechupats*, It will be desired) and KOPELISHEL (from two words: Kopyl, the name of the town in which Mendele was born, and KAPELUSHEL, little hat, Jews being people who wear little hats). The famous KAZRILEVKE of the same author played on both German and Hebrew: *Kaz*, the German for "cheese," and *kazrieyl*, Hebrew for "My crown is God"— which he ironically used as the name of a coach driver, Reb Kazriel.

Finally, it is striking how many writers used pen names, and how many of these pseudonyms involved word-plays. Solomon Rabinowitz's Sholem Aleichem is of course the most famous. Sholem Jacob Abramovich, the famous Mendele, dubbed himself Mendele Mocher Sforim (Little Mendel the Book Peddler). Isaac Reiss became Moishe Nadir (Moses Here-You-Are). Chaim Gutman wrote under the name of Der Lebidiker (The Lively One); Jacob Adler under that of B. Kovner (Man-from-Kovne). Joseph Tunkel became Der Tunkeler (The Dark One); and S. Charney, punning on English "char," became S. Niger. Pinches Kahanovitsh signed himself Der Nister (The

Hidden One), playing on a term from the Kabalah (the Hidden One being contrasted with the Revealed One—see Chap. II, Rel. and Cul., LAMEDVOVNIK). Even the famous Max Nordau, who wrote in French and German, played on his family name of Suedfeld, *sued* being German for south, and *nord* being German for north.

TASTE

To eat regularly and well was the unattained dream of many a European Jew struggling on the outskirts of subsistence. Food was consumed with relish whenever it was available, and was freely shared with others. There was the religious injunction to take in the stranger—"for ye," as the Passover Haggadah puts it, "were strangers in Egypt." And there was the honor (KOVED) of providing board to Yeshiva students—even though that often meant the sharing of a pitifully frugal diet. (See Chap. II, Food and Drink, ESSEN TEG.)

The tradition of hospitality was carried to these shores. The immigrant Jews, like the immigrant Italians, found compensation for the difficulties of making their way in a strange land in setting a bounteous table, when they could, to share with family and friends. Like the food of the Italians, much so-called Jewish food is hearty and spiced. And the emphasis on taste is reflected in a number of Yiddish terms. Something good, for instance, is GESHMAK (tasty), or it has MAMMELES TAM (dear mother's flavor) or A TAM GAN EYDEN (a Garden-of-Eden taste). Anything unsatisfactory has MAYN BOBBE YENTES TAM (my Grandma Shrew's taste) or A TAM FUN FLOMEN YUCH (a taste of prune juice). Obviously, such a thing HOT NIT KEYN YIDDISHEN TAM (has no Jewish, hence authentic old-time flavor)!

And lest we forget, people too should have seasoning: ES FEYLT IM EPPES (He lacks something; there's something missing); ER IZ ON TAM (He's tasteless); ER IZ EPPES ON ZALTS (He's somehow without salt)[1]—further emphasized in the comic rhyme, ON ZALTS/UN ON SHMALTS (without salt and without fat).

In a figurative sense, taste is also stressed in the widely heard ES PAST NIT (It isn't proper; it doesn't look right). This concern for appearances—inevitable in a closely knit community with a strong sense of social responsibility—also showed up in questions like VOS FAR A PONIM VET ES HOBN? (What kind of face will it have? How will it look?). (English has the related figure of "face-saving.")

The taste of propriety is part of what goes into the making of a MENTSH, literally a "person" and connoting the attributes of "lady" and "gentleman" and "a fine human being." This is extended in the word MENTSHLECHKAYT, true humanness. With Yiddish ZAY A MENTSH! we are told: Be a real person! Be a someone!

The terms that weighed relative merits in this direction range from the bottom of the scale, A PROSTER (a coarse one) and A GROBER YUNG (a boor) to A YID FUN A GANTS YOR (literally, a Jew from a whole year, hence a constant Jew, a Jew every day of the year, a Jewish "man for all seasons"), to A SHEYNER YID (a fine Jew) and AN EYDELER MENTSH (a fine person, a beautiful or sensitive spirit).

LEARNING

Another characteristic seen in Yiddish terminology is the Jewish emphasis on learning. This shows up in favorable descriptions like A GEZUNTER KOP AN AYZENER (literally, a good head, an iron one; equivalent to "a wonderful head on his shoulders") and A YID A LAMDEN (a Jew a scholar—reminiscent of "a gentleman and a scholar"), and in terms like YESHIVE BOCHER (seminary student; hence an unworldly type), LERNER (one who spends all his time in study), TALMID CHOCHEM (student of a sage, one wise in the Talmud), GOD'L B'TOYRE (an authority on Torah), etc.

This emphasis on learning dramatizes the contrast between the wise man and the fool, perhaps explaining the multiplicity of terms for the latter (SHLEMIEL, SHMENDRIK, CHAYIM YANKEL, etc.)[1] as well as the numerous observations about fools (A NAR/IZ A GEZAR—A fool is a misfortune; A NAR GEYT TSVEY MOL DORT VU A KLIGER GEYT NIT KEYN EYNTSIK MOL—A fool goes twice where a bright person doesn't even go once—reminiscent of "Fools rush in where angels fear to tread"; etc.).[2] But even this customary contrast of the clever and the foolish is spoofed in the saying, AZ A NAR HALT DI KU BAY DI HERNER, KEN ZI A KLIGER MELKN (If a fool holds the cow by the horn, a clever man can milk her).

More importantly, learning is reflected in a variety of popular folk sayings which build on religious and historical knowledge. And it is intriguing to see how many of these have ironic or humorous overtones. Take the complaint about Jewish destiny: *"Ato v'chartonu mikol hoamim"*—LIBER GOT, VOS HOSTU FUN UNZ GEVOLT? ("Thou hast chosen us from among all peoples"—dear God, what did you want from us? That is, what did you have against us? What did you pick on us for?) This takes a passage from Scripture—and a very important one, at that, containing the concept of the Chosen People, which is a part of the Sabbath blessing over the wine and of the blessing recited before reading from the Torah—and gives it intimate running commentary, in line with good Talmudic practice.

The same procedure is seen in another ironic comment on fate, based on Psalm 2:4: *"Yosheyv bashomayim yitschak"*— IM IZ GUT TSU LACHEN! ("He that sitteth in Heaven laugheth" —it's easy for Him to laugh! That is, if He lived as we do He'd have little to laugh about!).

The epitome of such literate complaint was offered by Sholem Aleichem when he had Tevye stop his horse and dismount to say his prayers, rendered by Maurice Samuel as: " 'Blessed are they that dwell in Thy house' (Right! I take it, O Lord, that Thy house is somewhat more spacious than my hovel!) . . . . 'I will extol Thee, my God, O King' (What good would it do me if I didn't?) . . . . "

And when his horse suddenly starts galloping away with him, poor Tevye continues in breathless, truly "running" commentary: " 'Thou feedest all things in mercy, and keepest faith with the sleepers in the dust.' (Stop! Indecent creature! Let a Jew say his prayers, will you? If ever there was a sleeper in the dust, O Father, it's me, Tevye, the father of seven. Did I say dust? In the mud, O Lord, in the filth of life!) . . . . 'Look Thou upon our poverty' (No one else cares to look upon it—Stop!). . ."

Scripture and prayer were popularly used in other joking ways. Note the observation, AZ DER SOYNE FALT, TOR MEN ZICH NIT FREYEN—OBER ME HEYBT IM NIT OYF (When your enemy falls, you mustn't gloat—but you don't have to pick him up either). This makes light of the Biblical injunction, "Rejoice not at thine enemy's fall" (Proverbs 24:17). Or note the frivolous comment on man's mortality: *"Odom yesōdō mey'ofor v'sōfō l'ofor"*—BEYNE-LE-BEYNE IZ GUT A TRUNK BRONFN ("For dust thou art, and unto dust shalt thou return"—betwixt the two, a shot of brandy's pretty good).

Or witness the old riddle which asked why it was necessary to have sixty men guarding King Solomon's bed. Reply: Because the text (Song of Songs 3:7) refers to *migibōrey Yisroeyl*, "of the mighty men of Israel." ("Behold his bed, which is Solomon's. Three score mighty men are about it, of the mighty of Israel.") If the guard were Gentile, the reply explains, one man would have been enough, but since it was Jewish, sixty men were needed! (These mental gymnasts knew they were no athletes![3] Needless to say, this kind of joke has become obsolescent since 1948 and even more so since June, 1967. More typical today is the story about the two Israelis discussing the danger of attacks from France and Russia. "Don't worry," says one. "If it took six days to beat a hundred million Arabs, we can handle fifty million Frenchmen in three days. As for two hundred million Russians, we can figure on twelve days!")[4]

Notice further the way in which a person might turn down a panhandler: *"Ovinu Malkeynu,* BAYTL *meyoleynu"* (Our Father, Our King, remove the purse from us). This builds on the High Holyday prayer, *Ovinu Malkeynu* (Our Father, Our King), *bateyl meyoleynu* (remove from us) *kol gezeyrōs koshōs* (all severe decrees). As you can see, Yiddish BAYTL, purse, provides a pun on Hebrew *bateyl,* nullify. It's striking that not only the Jewish man-in-the-street who cited this, but the panhandler himself, would be so familiar with the prayer.

This kind of familiarity with sacred texts is no longer general among Jews. In the United States, popular jokes of this type are more often in the category of the one about the young men discussing a blind date, in which one fellow remarks that he heard the other's date was a doll. "Yeah," replies the other, *"Yisgadal,"* quoting the opening (Aramaic) word of the well-known mourner's prayer.

PSYCHOLOGICAL INSIGHT

One thing you'll notice about many Yiddish expressions: they show a good deal of understanding about human nature. They all originated long before the development of modern psychology and show an impressive amount of natural insight.

Take the matter of guilt. AFN GANEF BRENT DOS HITL (On the crook, the cap is afire) means, The culprit is self-conscious and shows his guilt. Similarly, we are told, DER VOS FILT ZICH, DER MEYNT ZICH (He who feels guilty applies the reference to himself; i.e., He's got a guilty conscience; apparently the shoe fits).

Or take the matter of self-acceptance: AZ ICH VEL ZAYN VI ER—VER VET ZAYN VI ICH? (If I'm to be like him, who will be like me?). Note also the recognition of the need to accept others as *they* are: YEYDER HOT ZICH ZAYN MISHUGAS (Everyone has his own wackiness—often heard as "We all have our own MISHUGAS").

Or witness the awareness of the lingering effects of unpleasant experience: AZ ME BRIT ZICH OP AF HEYSN, BLOZT MEN AF KALTN (When you're burned by heat, you blow on cold, i.e., you become overcautious). In English we say, "Burned once, twice shy," but the Yiddish goes beyond being careful the second time and speaks of extending the caution to something that does not even warrant it, of overdoing it, the unconscious phenomenon of "overcompensation."

The effects of *conscious* habit are appreciated in VOS M'IZ GEVEYNT AF DER YUGEND, AZOY TUT MEN AF DER ELTER (The habits we develop in youth are what we follow in old age). And the *un*conscious effects of habit are recognized in this ironic comment on twice-married partners: ME SHLOFT FIR IN A BET (They sleep four in a bed), which perceives the presence of "ghosts" that may stand in the way of an ideal marital relationship.

In the area of mental health, old Yiddish observations seem amazingly pertinent today. The power of suggestion was well recognized. Witness AN AYNREDENISH IZ ERGER VI A KRENK (A delusion, or a neurosis—literally, a talking-into—is worse than a disease); RED MIR NISHT ARAYN KEYN KRENK (Don't talk a disease into me); or the corker, ZI REDT ZICH ARAYN A KIND IN BOYCH (She's talking a kid into her belly). We know that this last situation can happen quite literally. Doctors are familiar with the patient who is so anxious to have a baby that she imagines herself to be pregnant, experiencing all the physical symptoms. (And many a physician can report the expectant

father who experiences morning-sickness out of sympathy.) Dr.
Allan F. Guttmacher has written of a woman who was so concerned about *not* having a child that she imagined herself
pregnant and became so distraught she killed herself, a post-
mortem examination confirming that it was all in her mind.
Indeed, it is well known in medical circles that a certain number
of women who obtain illegal abortions are not pregnant at all,
their fears having affected the endocrine function.

There are other striking insights, like the description MIT A
GEZUNTEN KOP IN A KRANKEN BET (With a healthy head into
a sickbed)—of someone in fine shape who gets himself involved,
as might be said of a handsome and bright young man who
marries a divorcee with teen-age children, or of a person with
masochistic tendencies who goes out of his way to find trouble.
Further, notice TSU GUT IZ UMGEZUNT (Too good is unhealthy). This observation has been echoed by child-guidance
experts, in suspecting the complete absence of mischief in a
child, or in deploring the too permissive and indulgent home
which leaves children without proper responsibility.

Even a good social conscience, it was recognized, can be over-
done: AZ DER MAN IZ TSU GUT FAR DER VELT, IZ ER TSU
SHLECHT FARN VAYB (If a man is too good to the world, he's
too bad to his wife). Limits are necessary for thinking, too.
Many counselors have believed this of certain patients: They
think too much (ME KLERT TSU FIL) and even told them so:
Too much probing is unhealthy (TSU FIL KLEREN IZ UMGE-
ZUNT).

The psychological disadvantage of being "too close" to people is pointed out in MIT A YIDN IZ GUT KUGEL TSU ESSEN, OBER
NIT FUN EYN TELER (It's good to eat pudding—i.e., feast—
with your fellow, but not from one plate). This is consistent
with modern mental-health advice, which advocates respect for
individual privacy, using the model of the porcupine: that creature must keep a sensible distance from other porcupines, or
else it will get hurt and hurt others.

Even the meaning of dreams was partly recognized: VOS
EYNER VOLT GEREN GEHAT, DOS CHOLEMT ZICH IM IN BET
(What one would like to have, he dreams of in bed—a simple
statement of "wish-fulfillment") ; VOS ME REDT BAY TOG, CHO-
LEMT ZICH BAY NACHT (What one talks of by day one dreams
of at night). And "displaced aggression" was recognized in

such observations as: AZ DER MELAMED KRIGT ZICH MITN VAYB,
'SIZ AZ ACH UN VEY TSU DI TALMIDIM (When the Hebrew
teacher quarrels with his wife, it's woe and wail for the pupils)
and AZ M'IZ BAROYGES AFN CHAZEN, ENTFERT MEN NIT KEYN
'OMEYN' (When you're mad at the cantor, you don't respond
with the 'Amen').[1] This last covers beautifully the illogical
behavior seen so often in temple and church organizations when
a member resigns because someone in the group has hurt his
feelings!

Still further, there was an awareness of psychological association in a number of admonitions like A GESHLOGENEM HUNT
VAYST MEN KEYN SHTEKEN NIT (You don't show a cane to a
beaten dog); and VER ES HOT A GEHANGENEM IN DER MISH-
POCHE, FAR DEM TOR MEN KEYN SHTRIK NIT DERMONEN (Don't
speak of a rope to someone who's had a hanging in the family).[2]

The fact that inhibitions have their effect was recognized in
ironic sayings like ALEH SHTUMEH VILN A SACH REDN (All
mutes have a lot to say) or ALEH BEZHDETNITSES HOBN LIB
KINDER (All childless women love children). Finally, the tendency of an inhibited sense to stimulate "compensation" by
another sense is observed in such statements as A BLINDER HOT
LIB TSU HEREN ALEH VUNDER (A blind man loves to hear all
sorts of wonderful tales) or VOS A TEYBER DERHERT NIT, DOS
TRACHT ER ZICH OYS (What a deaf man doesn't hear, he imagines for himself).[3]

VULGARITY

What shall we say of vulgarity? In Yiddish, it has an almost
wholesome quality. Bodily functions are accepted as part of life.
How could it be otherwise?—when the Hebrew tradition gives
thanks to God for creating the openings of the body and even
expresses wonder at their marvelous design, noting that if any
one opening were closed and any closed part open, life could
not go on. How else explain the pet term for a male infant,
PISHEREL (little pisser—used as the name of an angel in a fan-
tasy by Itzik Manger!) and its variations like PISHERKE and
PISHEREVITSH, or the good-naturedly defiant RUF MICH PISHER,
which has been perpetuated in the bilingual "Call me PISHER"?
Most second-generation American Jews recall being told as
children at bedtime, GEY, PISH ZICH OYS (Go, piss yourself

out), and as adults they may on occasion with indulgent humor give the same advice to their spouses. "She still has two PISHERS at home" is a common colloquialism that makes its point: she has two offspring still in diapers, or two preschoolers. A charming Yiddish lullaby by the Polish poet Mordche Gebirtig has a mother looking at her infant in his cradle and musing that he will soon be going to Hebrew school, that he will then soon be studying the prayerbook and the Talmud, and that he will then soon be an authority on Talmud; so how can it be, she ironically asks, that this little boy who is progressing in all these wonderful ways should keep his mother up all night and should lie there so wet as in a river?[1]

Blunter are expressions like ZEY BEYDE PISHEN IN DER ZELBER GRIB (They both piss in the same pit—a mocking statement that one is never without the other; they're thick as thieves) or ME VISHT OYS EYN OYG UN PISHT OYS DI ANDERE, UN 'SIZ GOR-NIT (They wipe out one eye and piss out the other eye, and it all adds up to nothing—a sardonic comment on "crocodile tears"). I heard the latter statement quoted recently with reference to the Germans, who, it was pointed out, responded with great sympathy to the dramatization of Anne Frank's diary (which recorded the tragedy of a Jewish family in Nazi-occupied Holland) yet are today steadily putting former Nazis and neo-Nazis into positions of political power.

However, I don't think there is an equivalent in Yiddish for the American vulgarism "He hasn't got a pot to piss in." Yiddish puts it, ER HOT KADOCHES (He has malaria), ER HOT A MAKEH (He has a boil—suggesting the affliction of Job); or ER IZ NEBBECH A KABTSEN (He's—a pity—a pauper). The tradition of mercy (RACHMONES) as well as the constant alertness to vagaries of fate discouraged the belittling of another's bad luck: one might tomorrow be in his shoes.

Although defecation is suggested by the adjective UNGE-MACHT (made on), the word is sometimes used almost synonymously with UNGEPATSHKET (patted up, overly handled), to mean too ornate, gingerbready. The same root appears in the proverbial rhyme FRIER TRACHT MEN,/UN NURDEM BAMACHT MEN (First you think and then you mess yourself up—or, to preserve the rhyme, First you think/And then yourself bestink, i.e., make a real boo-boo.[2] The verb is several shades less vulgar than the English "to besh-t oneself"—which appeared in at

least one colorful eighteenth- and nineteenth-century phrase[3]—
and also less vulgar than "becrapped." There *is* the earthy bit
of advice, KAK IM UN (Crap on him), which is a bit stronger
than "Spit in his eye" though less objectionable than the stronger
English form.[4] Too, there is reference to defecation in the
rhyming joke about Mendel quoted earlier, as well as in the
long-lived "A.K.," discussed in Chap. IIIB.[5]

A common vulgarism which uses Hebrew and Yiddish is
"*chay* KAK," a good-naturedly belittling term meaning "eighteen crap," or a bunch of nothing. It's supposedly a corruption
of the Hebrew *chay tsal*, roughly eighteen cents.[6] (A striking
parallel in English showed up in the recent statement by Australian actress Zoe Caldwell: "I don't give a tuppence of crap for
being a star.")

In addition, there are the numerous uses of the word TOCHES.
This can itself convey shadings of the many synonyms in English:
ass, arse, rump, cheek, behind, rear end, etc. It can at times
seem obscene, as in the angry KISH MIR IN TOCHES (Kiss my
a--), or can be earthily apt as in A KALTER TOCHES (a cold bottom, a cold fish) or in the description of two bosom pals: AZOY
VI TSVEY TECHESER IN EYN POR HOYZN (like two behinds in one
pair of pants). It can at other times be innocently playful, as
in the current bilingual double joke "It TOCHES a long time to
figure it out."[7] And of course it has given rise to the children's
terms "tushie" and "tush" as well as "tough TUKIS"—the last,
equivalent to the ironic "too bad." Witness further the bilingual
pun "TSORASS" for TSORES (troubles) with reference to rectal
operations.

In the area of sex—as already noted in the discussion of
punning—Jews and Yiddish have been rather outspoken, without intending to be either crude or lewd. Note, for instance,
how the popular Yiddish writer Mendele Mocher Sforim de-
ferred to Hebrew writers: ". . . whose little fingers are broader
than my loins! . . ." Isaak Babel, in Russian, exhibited the
same naturalness: "The newlyweds spent three months on the
fat lands of Bessarabia, three months flooded with grapes, rich
food and the sweat of love's encounters."

In earlier times, two superstitious hand motions recommended by the Talmud to ward off evil had frankly sexual
symbolism: the so-called "fig" gesture, in which the fist was
clenched and the thumb placed between two fingers; and the

other in which the thumb was placed within the closed fist. These represented the sexual act and pregnancy, as protective forces.

Earthiness is of course to be distinguished from obscenity. Yiddish does have some obscene sex terms, but occasionally even these are used with descriptive force. Notice, for instance, the blunt appraisal of a certain short man that was made by a famous twentieth-century rabbi: ER IZ TSU KLEYN TSU ZAYN A MENTSH UN TSU GROYS TSU ZAYN A SHMOK (He's too small for a person and too big for a prick). This was unkind, coming from a man himself blessed with stature and whose religious ideals should have prevented such derogation of another, yet as description it is certainly effective.

Other contexts, however, create other judgments. In recent years that same word (from which slang "shmo" derives—see Chap. IIIA) and others like it have been used quite indiscriminately in fiction and the theatre by American Jewish writers, and even by non-Jews. Notice, for instance, the line in the Broadway show *Luv!* by Murray Schisgal: "I knew that shmuck last night was wrong!" There the term had no real justification and was merely crude. (Indeed, the pronunciation used would seem to suggest a direct association with the well-known English four-letter word, in a perhaps unconscious use of the SHM- formula.) It is surprising that even a noted compiler of Jewish folklore and humor has included among a number of neutral words for "fool" one which has definitely suggestive qualities.[8] This same word was used by *Time* in its obituary on Lee Harvey Oswald's killer Jack Ruby, "who yearned to be a *mensch*, a pillar of the community, but always remained a *schwanz*."[9] Part of the difficulty arises from the fact that many Yiddish terms have found their way into compendiums of American slang, where they are at times included in lists of synonyms without proper distinction, giving some a false look of acceptability. The more the process goes on, of course, the more the original Yiddish connotations are becoming diluted—just as has been true with many slang terms picked up from Negro and Army usage.

HUMOR

Two outstanding characteristics of Yiddish humor, as we have seen, are the ever-present irony and word-consciousness.

Both were the Jews' defense against fate and the result of their unique history. The irony was directed at everything and anybody, seen and unseen, including the God with Whom they had a covenant, and not excluding themselves. It helped them to unload their frustrations and to gird themselves for more.

The word-consciousness grew out of the covenant with God and His Torah, which they often considered a burden, but a blessed burden which they were pledged to carry. In studying God's Word for centuries, and in their enforced migrations, the Jews developed a special linguistic ability. They were alert to sounds and meanings, and made the inevitable puns.

Punsters are used to hearing the judgment that their means of laughter is the lowest form of humor. Well, there are all kinds of puns, as I think has been shown. Literate, and even racy, punning is an age-old Jewish custom—which Shakespeare also freely followed. After all, how much did the Jews have to laugh at, anyway? They tried to find humor in every possible situation, sometimes straining a bit to find it in language. As Sholem Aleichem once said, if he did not laugh, he would cry.

The "super-climax" already referred to is another distinguishing mark of Yiddish humor and of Jewish humor generally. As Immanuel Olsvanger has delightfully explained, most ordinary jokes have a single punch line, but Jewish jokes go beyond this "pseudo-climax," adding one or more "super-climaxes."

I think of a story that I first heard in simple form: a Sunday School teacher asks a boy in her class, "Who knocked down the walls of Jericho?" and he replies heatedly, "*I* didn't!" Other versions of the story quoted in Jewish circles are not content with this one punch. One version has the teacher speak afterward with the boy's father, who says, "If my boy says he didn't do it, he didn't do it!" Still another version piles on a whole series of additional laughs: the inquirer is a Jewish education director who drops in on a class and asks the question of a student, who denies having had anything to do with the incident. The director then speaks to the teacher, and is told that the teacher knows this young man and can be sure that if he says he didn't do it, he didn't! Horrified, the expert goes and talks to the religious-school principal, and he too says that he knows the young man and his family and is certain that he cannot be guilty of a falsehood. In desperation, the education director speaks to the president of the synagogue, who says, "All right; so get it fixed and send us a bill!"

This is a wonderful example of ironic self-criticism, a beratement not only of American Jewish religious education but of those dispensing it, including the officers of synagogues.[1]

Freud, in his *Wit and Its Relation to the Unconscious*, notes that the Jews more than any other people have been able to laugh at themselves. This ability is generally considered a mark of maturity. And it would seem to be tied up with the Jews' notable sense of realism, which we discussed earlier. Indeed, one observer has expressed the view that Jewish humor itself represents a supremely analytical facing up to reality—noting that this same achievement is the goal of psychoanalysis—and hence contributed significantly to the Jews' survival.

This ready humor can be seen in every category of expression presented here and in the next chapter. Combined with the other distinctive flavors of Jewish life and language, it reveals the "peculiar treasure" of a people.

Yiddish does have a special TAM. If you have found the appetizers tempting, proceed to the main course. ESS, ESS—GEZUNTERHEYD!

II. Popular Terms and Expressions

ADVICE

A DAYGE HOSTU. (ironic)

Lit., A worry you have. You should worry. Don't let it bother you.

A summer resort in New York State is named "Camp Nitgedaiget"—i.e., Camp Carefree.

AF KAPORES DARFST ES HOBN! (ironic)

For sacrifice you need it!

See last joke quoted in Chap. I, Intonation.

AF MORGN/ZOL GOT ZORGN.

About tomorrow/Let God sorrow. "Sufficient unto the day is the evil thereof."

AF "VOLT-ICH" UN "ZOLT-ICH" BORGT MEN NIT KEYN GELT.

On "I would" and "I should" you can't borrow money. Intentions are not collateral. (You'd better get down to work.)

ALEH MAYLES IN EYNEM/IZ NITO BAY KEYNEM.

All virtues in one/Occur in none. Nobody's perfect.

ALLES VET ZICH OYSGLAYCHEN (*or* OYSPRESN).

Lit., Everything will straighten (*or* iron) itself out. Reminiscent of "It'll all come out in the wash."

MIR KENEN ES OYSGLAYCHEN. We can straighten it out. We'll iron it out; the situation isn't beyond repair.

A MAYSE MIT A TSIG.

A story about a goat.

This refers to the tale about a woman who comes to the

rabbi full of woe: her tiny home is overcrowded and she and her husband and children are getting on one another's nerves. The rabbi advises her to get a goat and keep it in the house, and to come back after a week. She gets the goat, and of course finds her problems multiplied. She comes back to the rabbi and tells him that things are just unbearable. He advises her to get rid of the goat and come back the following day. She follows his advice, and then joyfully reports how wonderful things are without the goat!

The obvious moral is that she didn't know how well off she was until she took on a worse problem. The tale is applicable to many family situations and is often cited by American Jews. It came through in slightly different form in the comic strip *Miss Peach* in the summer of 1966: A man walks into an office mopping his brow and exclaims at the intolerable heat, asking the office girls why the heating system is turned on. They reply that he has no idea how wonderful it is when they turn it off!

AN OPGESHEYLTE EY FALT OYCH NIT ALEYN IN MOYL ARAYN.

Even a shelled egg won't fall into your mouth by itself. (After all! Lift a finger!)

A SHO IN GAN EYDEN IZ OYCH GUT.

An hour in the Garden of Eden is good too. Even a little bit of heaven is worth while; take what you can.

AZ A LEYB SHLOFT, LOZ IM SHLOFN!

When a lion sleeps, let him sleep. "Let sleeping dogs lie." Don't look for trouble.

AZ ME EST NIT KEYN KNOBL, SHTINKT MEN NIT.

If you don't eat garlic, you won't smell; i.e., If you don't like the results, don't bring them on. Know the consequences of your own behavior.

AZ ME GIT NIT YANKEVN, GIT MEN EYSOVN.

If we don't give to Jacob, we give to Esau.

This can mean, By not helping a cause, we help defeat it. But it's also commonly used to indicate, If you don't spend it on one thing, you'll have to spend it on another; you might as well get what you want.

AZ ME HENGT BAY EYN FUS, HENGT MEN BAY TSVEY.

If you hang by one foot, hang by two; i.e., If you're in for trouble anyway, make it pay. "You may as well hang for a murder as for a theft."

See also Chap. I, Realism, AZ ME EST CHAZER. . . .

AZ ME HOT A SACH TSU TON, LEYGT MEN ZICH SHLOFN.

If you have a lot to do, it's best to go to sleep.

Said with a smile, this may encourage procrastination, but it's based on the practical notion that a good rest makes any list of chores seem easier.

AZ ME KEN NIT ARIBERGEYN, GEYT MEN ARUNTER.

If you can't climb over, you tunnel under. (You find a way.)

This proverb pinpoints one of the keys to Jewish survival—never say die! A story that was going the rounds of Christian clergymen several years ago concerns a second worldwide flood: it has engulfed Europe and Asia and is heading toward the United States. The Catholic and Protestant clergy all call their people together for Communion, baptism and last rites. The rabbis and Jewish lay leaders, on the other hand, call a conference on How to Live Under Water!

A similar comment on Jewish resourcefulness is seen in the current story about an explosion which takes place in a synagogue on Yom Kippur and kills off the entire membership. The members all go up to heaven, but are stopped by the keeper of the pearly gates, who notes that the place is overcrowded. He calls down to ask help of Satan, who says he has plenty of room—what's more, he has a good cha-cha band, a Chinese restaurant, and a fine mahjongg game going. So the Jews go down to "his place." But it isn't long before Satan calls up to heaven to complain. It seems that the Jews didn't care for the temperature down there, and before Satan knew what was happening, they had had a drive, raised $10,000 and installed air conditioning![1]

See also AZ ME KEN NIT VI ME VIL, . . . *and* ZOG NISHT KEYN MOL AZ DU GEYST DEM LETSTN VEG.

AZ ME KEN NIT BAYSEN, ZOL MEN NIT SH'TSHIREN MIT DI TSEYN.

If you can't bite, don't bare your teeth. "Don't start anything you're not prepared to finish."

AZ ME KEN NIT VI ME VIL, TUT MEN VI ME KEN.

If you can't do what you want, you do what you can.

Also, AZ ME KEN NIT VI ME VIL, MUZ MEN VELLEN VI ME KEN. If you can't do what you like, you must like what you can do.

AZ M'IZ FOYL,/HOT MEN NIT IN MOYL.

If you'll nothing do,/You'll nothing chew. The reverse of "He who works, eats."

AZ TSVEY ZOGN SHIKKER, ZOL DER DRITTER GEYN SHLOFN.

When two say a man is drunk, he ought to go to bed.

Italian has a similar expression.

BIST DOCH OYCH A MENTSH!

After all, *you're* a person, too! *You* have needs, yourself!

A thoughtful husband may thus encourage his conscientious wife to take an afternoon off.

BIST OYCH GERECHT! (ironic)

You're right, too!

This is a famous punch line of an old tale about a rabbi who is asked to settle a dispute. To each of the two complainants he listens and comments, "You're right." When a third person exclaims that they can't both be right, he nods, "You're right, too." The implication is that no one is ever wholly right or wholly wrong. (The situation has been used on TV.)

BIZ DEN IZ GOT A FOTER.

Until then, God is a father. "You've done what you can. Now put yourself in God's hands."

CHAP ES ARAYN!

Grab it while you can! Pack it in!

Also, ME DARF ES ARAYNCHAPN. You have to grab it while the grabbing is good.

See Exclam., ARAYNGECHAPT!

CHAP NISHT!

Don't grab! *Also,* Take your time! Take it easy!

CHAP NIT DI LOKSHEN FAR DI FISH. Don't grab the noodles before the fish. "Don't jump to conclusions."

DER RICH'L IM NIT NEMEN!

Lit., The devil won't take him! Don't worry; he won't get hurt! He can take care of himself!

DI LETSTE HEMD FARKOYFN, ABI RAYCH TSU ZAYN!

It's worth selling your last shirt, just to get rich!

DI LIBE IZ ZIS, NOR ZI IZ GUT MIT BROYT.

Love is sweet, but it's good with bread. An ironic version of "You can't live on love."

DING DIR A MESHORES UN TU ES DIR ALEYN.

Hire a servant and do it yourself.

As any homeowner can tell you, this is the only way to get things done!

DREY ZICH NIT KEYN KOP MIT. . . .

Don't bother your head with . . . ; don't get involved with. . . .

Also, VOS DREYSTU ZICH A KOP? What are you getting involved for?

DU VEST ZICH NIT OYSVILYEN FUN DER TSORE.

You won't wish yourself out of the problem. (You'll have to *do* something about it.)

See also Ann. and Arg., VEN DI BOBBE VOLT GEHAT A BORD. . .

ES PAST SHOYN GORNIT!

It isn't suitable at all; it's very much out of place.

ES PAST VI A CHAZER. *Lit.,* It's suitable as a pig. It's very bad taste. (*See* Food and Drink, CHAZER.)

FAR DI ZELBE GELT. . . .

For the same money; while you're at it. . . .

Cf. Ann. and Arg., VOLT ES DIR EPPES GECOST TSU . . . ?

FAR GOT HOT MEN MEYRE; FAR MENTSHEN MUZ MEN ZICH HITN.

Fear God; beware of people.

FLI NIT TSU HEYACH!

Don't fly too high! (You'll have less distance to fall.)

See also KRICH NIT.

FOLG MICH.

Mind me. Do as I say.

Cf. Exclam., FOLG MICH A GANG!

FREG AN EYTSE YENEM, UN HOB DAYN SEYCHEL BAY DIR.

Ask for advice, and use your own head.

See ROT MIR GUT; . . . .

FREG NIT DEM ROYFE, NOR DEM CHOYLE.

Ask the patient, not the doctor.

FUN DEM BER IN VALD ZOL MEN DOS FEL NIT FARKOYFN.

Don't sell the skin off the bear when he's still in the woods. (Wait till you've got him trapped.)

See also ME HALT NOCH NIT DERBAY.

FUN EYN OKS TSIT MEN TSVEY FELN NIT AROP.

You don't take two hides from one ox. (Have a heart!)

GEY NIT ARUM BORVES.

Don't go around barefoot.

What immigrant mother's child never heard this?

GEY NIT MIT GETSEYLTE GELT.

Don't go with counted money (to someone leaving on a trip): i.e., Allow yourself something for emergencies.

GEY SHLOFN.

Go to sleep.

More than twenty years ago in Georgia, I heard a college student try to quiet a group of midnight gabbers at a week-end retreat with the delightful "Y'all GEY SHLAFN!"[2] This has ever since symbolized for me the bi-cultural nature of Jewish existence. I was reminded of it recently when I heard the Manischewitz radio commercial in which the "Jewish Cowboy" wished his listeners "a Happy and Kosher Passover" and then followed with, "Come back an' see us, y'hear?"

GEY VAYTER.

Keep going; continue.

HALT ZICH AYN!

Restrain yourself! Take it easy!

HERST?

You hear?

HIT ZICH!

Be careful! Look out!

HOB KEYN YISURIM NIT.

Lit., Have no sufferings or pains. Don't be upset; don't worry. *See also* ZORG ZICH NISHT.

HOB NIT KEYN MEYRE/VEN DU HOST NIT KEYN ANDER B'REYRE.

Don't be afraid/When no other choice can be made.

HOB NISHT MIT IM KEYN GESHEFT.

Don't have anything to do with him.

HOST ES GEDARFT? (ironic)

You needed it? (Didn't I tell you?)

ICH'L DIR GEBN AN EYTSE.

I'll give you a suggestion.

ICH ZOG DIR. . . .

I tell you . . . ; I'm telling you. . . .

IZ NISHT GEFERLECH!

It's not so terrible! It isn't a tragedy! *Cf.* Resig., NU, IZ NISHT.

KAMANDEVE NIT!

Don't "carry on," don't let loose; behave yourselves! (the last word from Papa when visiting cousins were left with us while the grownups gathered in the other room)

KENST ZICH EPPES UNMACHEN.

You can do yourself some harm. (advice to the teenager to stop squeezing those pimples)

KRICH NIT.

    Lit., Don't climb. Have sense enough to know your limits (either mental or social).

    VI KRICHSTU (MIT DI KRIME FIS)? Where are you climbing (with your lame feet)? Do you realize where you're trying to go?

    See also ME SHTIPT ZICH NIT.

KRIG NISHT.

    Don't fight; don't quarrel.

    AZ DU KRIGST ZICH, KRIG ZICH AZOY DU ZOLST ZICH KENEN IBERBETN. If you quarrel, do it so you'll be able to make up; i.e., leave a way open to patch things up.

LEYG DI KLOTZ AF MIR.

    Lit., Put the log, or weight, on me. I'll take the blame. (Just do it my way.)

    Cf. Char. and Des., A POR KLUHTZIM.

LOYF NISHT!

    Don't run! Take your time!

    This is the obvious source of the advice a Pennsylvania host gave to his departing guests: "Don't run with the car!"

LOZ ES UP.

    Let it go; forget it; drop it.

LOZ IM GEYN.

    Let him go. (What do you care? What do you need him for?)

    LOZ IM GEYN TSUM RICH. Let him go to the devil.

LOZ IM UP!

    Let go of him! Leave him alone!

LOZ MIR!

    Let me! (I'll show you!)

LOZ ZAYN AZOY.

    Lit., Let be so. Let's leave it that way.

    This led to the first generation's awkward "Let be like you say"—still quoted good-naturedly by the second generation.

LOZ ZEY VISN AZ MIR ZAYNEN DO!

    Let them know we're here! (urging a family member to perform at a celebration)

MACH A SOF!

    Put an end to it! Finish up! Sew it up!

    Cf. Ann. and Arg., A SOF, AN EK!

MACH NIT CHOYZIK.

    Don't mock.

MACH NIT DERFIN KEYN GANTSEN TSIMMES.

Don't make a whole fuss about it. (*See* Food and Drink, TSIMMES.)

MACH NIT KEYN EYSIK DERFIN.

Don't make a big thing out of it; don't make a to-do over it.

MACH NIT KEYN GANTSEN GESHREY.

Don't raise a holler over it.

MACH SHNEL!

Hurry! (*Lit.*, Make fast. Probably the source of "make it fast," which is common in American Jewish speech.)

MACH ES KURTS UN SHNEL. Make it short and snappy. A drugstore in Brooklyn named Kurtz and Schnall has for years been spoken of as KURTS UN SHNEL.

MACH SHOLEM.

Make peace.

MACH ZICH NIT VISNDIK.

Feign ignorance or unconcern. Pretend you know nothing about it; act casual.

MACHST A LEBN? (*or* A LEBN MACHST DU?)

You're making a living?

The intonation of these can be plotted:

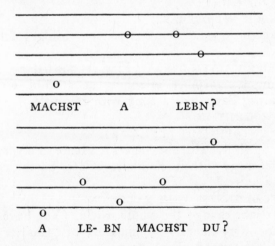

The implication is, don't be concerned; whatever has gone wrong can't be helped or isn't so terrible; you still earn a living, and that's something to be thankful for.

Also, a jesting response of a father to his daughter's details about a new suitor: "Talent, shmalent; handsome, shmand-some—ER MACHT A LEBN? (—he makes a living?).

ME DARF FARKATSHEN DI ARBL.

You have to roll up your sleeves (and get to work).

ME DARF IM FARSHTOPN DEM MOYL.

You have to stuff up his mouth; i.e., Anticipate his criticism and act to avoid it.

See also ME GIT NIT A *pischon peh l'Soton.*

ME DARF IM SHMIREN.

You have to tip him.

See Passing Judgment, AZ ME SHMIRT DI REDER. . . *and* IIIA, "shmear."

ME DARF NOR VELLEN!

Lit., You just have to want to! "Where there's a will, there's a way!"

ME FREGT NIT (KEYNEM).

You don't ask (anybody). Don't start asking questions; go ahead.

See also Chap. I, Realism, AZ ME FREGT, IZ TREYF.

ME GIT NIT A *pischon peh l'Soton.* (*Heb.*)

You don't give a mouth-opening to Satan; i.e., Don't provide an opening for critics.

ME HALT NOCH NIT DERBAY.

We're not there yet. "Don't cross your bridges until you get to them."

LOMIR FRIER HALTEN DERBAY. First let's get there. A Yiddish musical show I remember attending as a child, starring the famous Ludwig Satz, had a song with this title.

See also ZOG NIT HOP . . . .

ME KEN ES UNTAPN (MIT DI FINGER).

You can touch it (with the fingers). Hence, it's very obvious; you can't get away with it. Reminiscent of, "So thick you could cut it with a knife."

ME KEN NIT DI GANTSE VELT FARZORGN.

You can't take care of the whole world. (You have your own problems to worry about.) Reminiscent of "Charity begins at home" and "First tend your own garden."

The famous Rabbi Hillel of the Talmud put it this way: "If I am not for myself, who will be for me?"

See also Chap. I, Psychol. Insight, AZ DER MAN IZ TSU GUT FAR DER VELT. . . .

MENTSHEN VELN DEYNKEN . . . (*or* ZOGN . . .)

People will think . . . (*or* say . . .)

See also V'AZOY VET ES OYSKUKEN?

ME SHTIPT ZICH NIT.

You don't push yourself (where you're not wanted, or where you don't belong).

VI SHTIPSTU ZICH? Where are you pushing yourself?

MISH NIT OYS KEYN KASHE MIT BORSHT.

Don't confuse things. (Lit., Don't mix up KASHE with BORSHT. *Cf.* Food and Drink, KASHE.)

MISH ZICH NIT (ARAYN).

Lit., Don't mix yourself (in). Don't butt in. Don't get into it.

See also Family, VI TSVEY SHLOFN AF EYN KISHEN. . . .

MIT EYN TOCHES KEN MEN NIT ZAYN AF TSVEY YARIDN.

With one behind you can't be at two circuses. (You can't do two jobs at a time and do them both right.)

See Chap. I, Vulgarity.

MIT GEFIL!

With feeling! Now put a little heart into it! (encouragement of a budding public speaker or musician)

MIT GELT KEN MEN NIT SHTOLTSIREN;/ME KEN ES LAYCHT FARLIREN.

Don't be boastful about money; it's easily lost.

See also Chap. III, "Money is round."

MITSHE IM NIT!

Don't torture him! Don't make him suffer so! (Grandma "mixing in" when BUBELE's getting his just deserts)

NEM ZICH DI FIS AF DI PLEYTSES . . . . (good-natured)

Lit., Take your feet on your shoulders . . . . Get going, now!

NEM ZICH TSUM ARBET!

Lit., Take yourself to the job! Get to work!

NU, KRATS ZICH OYS.

So come on, scratch yourself out. (prompting a slow story-teller)

See Ann. and Arg., KAM OYSGEKRATST!

See also RED VERTER! *and* SHPAY AROYS!

OT AZOY!

That's the way (to do it)! *Also,* Attaboy! (if he's doing it right)

RED VERTER!

Lit., Talk words! Speak, man! (to someone who's hemming and hawing)

ROT MIR GUT; NOR ROT MIR NIT OP.

Advise me well; just don't advise me against it. Reminiscent of "A man persuaded 'gainst his will remaineth unpersuaded still."

SHEM ZICH NIT!

Don't be bashful!

SHPAY AROYS!

Spit it out! (mother to a toddler) *Also,* Out with it! (to one who is a long time telling a tale)

SHVAYG.

Be silent.

In Peretz's famous story "Bontshe Shvayg," meekness is satirized in the person of the long-suffering and uncomplaining Bontshe, who goes to heaven. There offered anything his heart may desire, he pathetically asks for a daily warm roll and butter, embarrassing even the heavenly angels. (A Reform rabbi recently did a sequel to the story, in which Bontshe is sent back to earth to play the part of a spiritual and conscientious young rabbi, whose merits of course are little recognized. When Bontshe is recalled to heaven and again allowed to express his deepest desire, he asks please not to be sent back to earth again!)

'SIZ AN AVEYRE AROYSVARFN.

It's a sin to throw it out.

The echo of this in my ears still discourages me from wasting anything—be it food, clothing, or string!

'SIZ DIR NISHT UNGESHPART.

It's no emergency; you don't *have* to do it right now. Relax!

Cf. Ann. and Arg., 'SIZ IM UNGESHPART!

'SIZ NISHT FAR EYBIK.

It's not for eternity. (Stick it out!)

'SIZ NIT NEYTIK.

It's not necessary.

This always comes to mind when I see the name of Natick or North Natick, Mass.

According to the *Jewish Digest,* a horse running in 1967 races was named Zayer Natick—which is an ironic "Very Necessary," *equiv.,* "Who Needs Him?"

TSU BROYT GEFINT MEN SHOYN A MESER.

If you have the bread, you'll find the knife.

V'AZOY VET ES OYSKUKEN?

How will it look? (Think what people will say.)

See also Chap. I, Taste, VOS FAR A PONIM VET ES HOBN?

VEST ZAYN DER ZELBER GVIR (*or* KABTSEN). (ironic)

You'll be the same millionaire (*or* pauper). Live a little! (to someone who doesn't quite FARGIN[3] himself to spend for a personal indulgence)

VET MESHIACH GEBOREN VEREN MIT A TOG SHPETER.

So the Messiah will be born a day later. (discouraging an impetuous act: after all, we've waited so many centuries, we can wait another day!)

VEYS NOR VOS DU HOST TSU TON.

Just know what you have to do. Keep your mind on your purpose.

VILST ZAYN RAYCH? ZAY ZIBN YOR A CHAZER. (ironic)

Do you want to be rich? Be selfish (*lit.,* a pig) for seven years—i.e., keep everything for yourself and give nothing to the community.

This reflects the disdain in Jewish life for the man who can afford to give to charity and does not.

Cf. ZAY NIT KEYN CHAZER.

VOS ART ES DIR?

What do you care? Why should you give a darn?

ZAM ZICH NISHT.

Don't dally; don't delay getting back.

This and KUM BALD AHEYM (Come home soon; come right back) were a popular pair of parental admonitions.

ZAY NIT IBERASHT.

Don't get excited.

ZAY NIT KEYN CHAZER.

Don't be a pig; don't hog it all. Be satisfied with a fair share.

See Food and Drink, CHAZER.

ZHALEVE NIT!

Don't scrimp! (Don't worry about the cost or the calories! Do it right!)

ZITS NIT MIT LEYDIKE HENT!

Don't sit with empty hands! (You can at least mend while you're sitting!)

ZOG GORNIT.

Say nothing. Keep mum.

See also SHVAYG.

ZOG NISHT KEYN MOL AZ DU GEYST DEM LETSTN VEG.

Don't ever say you're traveling your last road.

This is the opening line of the famous "Partisan Song" by Hirsh Glick, a young Polish poet who died in the resistance in 1944, at the age of twenty-four. His song was sung in the underground and in the concentration camps. It epitomizes eternal Jewish determination: Don't give up, even at the point of death.

ZOG NIT HOP/EYDER DU SHPRINGST AROP.

Wait to be delighted/Until you've alighted. Don't anticipate.

ZOL DOS ZAYN DAYN ERGSTE DAYGE.

May that be your biggest worry. (of any problem that is relatively minor)

This is often translated literally as "That should be your biggest worry." It has led to "I hope that's the worst problem you'll ever have," "I hope you'll never have any worse troubles," etc.

ZOL *ER* ZICH FARDREYEN *ZAYN* KOP!

May *he* get *himself* mixed up! Let *him* get involved—*you* don't have to!

ZOL *ZAYN* MAMME ZORGN!

May *his* mother worry! (Why should yours?)

The line is associated with a risqué story about a naïve young lady warned against letting her boyfriend get close to her, so her mother "shouldn't worry," and who therefore gets close to *him,* figuring that she'll let *his* mother do the worrying! It's used humorously in any situation where the speaker feels, "It's not your responsibility; let *them* worry about it."

ZORG ZICH NISHT.

Don't worry.

ZUCH ZICH NIT KEYN GLIKN.

Lit., Don't look for any strokes of luck. Quit looking for miracles. Be realistic.

ANNOYANCE AND ARGUMENT

A BEHEYME!

You fool (*lit.,* cow)! *Equiv.,* You dumb ox!

A CHESOREN, DI KALEH IZ TSU SHEYN! (*ironic*)

A fault, the bride is too pretty! (retort to a complaint about something you consider an advantage)

In the second generation, this is usually heard as "The bride is too pretty!" It showed up in a movie title, *The Bride Is Much Too Pretty,* and even on French TV, where a commentator, noting the burdens which the Gaullists would have to bear for the country's future as a result of their decisive election victory in the summer of 1968, observed, *"La mariée est trop belle."*

A CHOCHME! (ironic)

An expression of wisdom! A real pronouncement!

Cf. Rel. and Cul., VU TOYRE, DORT IZ CHOCHME, under TOYRE; Exclam., ICH VIL NIT VISN FUN KEYN CHOCHMES.

A DANK DIR! (ironic)

Thank you! Thanks a lot!

A DIBBUK!

A she-devil! (exasperation at a shrew)

The DIBBUK in Jewish lore was an evil spirit or soul of a dead person residing in a living individual. The famous play by S. Anski dealt with a girl possessed of such a spirit and with efforts to exorcise it from her. Paddy Chayefsky's Broadway play *The Tenth Man* was a modern variation on the theme, as is Romain Gary's satirical and allegorical novel *The Dance of Genghis Cohn,* which portrays a modern German police commissioner bedeviled by a DIBBUK who is one of the many Jews he shot while a Nazi storm trooper.

There's a suggestion of similar superstition in the English "What's gotten into you?"

Cf. Death, GILGUL.

A GOYLEM!

A dummy!

The GOYLEM in Jewish folklore was a clay person without power of speech. There are many legends of such humanly created beings, some of whom turned into monsters. Though later legends transformed the GOYLEM into a protector of the Jews, the meaning of numbskull is what appears in this expression and in the related A LEYMINER GOYLEM! (a clay dummy!) and GOYLEM, DU! (You clod, you!).

See Passing Judgment, AN OYLEM IZ NIT KEYN GOYLEM *and* TSVEY GOYLIM GEYEN TANTSEN.

A KATS MEG OYCH KUKN AFN KEYSER.

Even a cat may look at a king. (There's no law against looking, is there?)

A KUNTS! (ironic)

A neat trick!

A GROYSER KUNTS! A big deal! Such an achievement!

A LIGN VI DER TSEYLEM!

A lie like the cross!

This reflects the rejection of Christian doctrine. It may also refer to the false attribution of responsibility for the crucifixion.

A MENTSH IZ NISHT KEYN HOLTS!

A person isn't made of wood! (I've got feelings, you know!)

See also MAYN NESHOME IZ NISHT KEYN ROZHINKE.

A MEYVEN AF . . .!

Look who's a judge of . . .!

See also OYCH (MIR) A . . .!, OYCH MIR A MEYVEN!

AN AKSHEN!

A stubborn ox!

OY, IZ DOS AN AKSHEN! Oh, is that a stubborn ox! (This may be followed by FAR AN AKSHEN IZ KEYN REFUE NITO. For stubbornness there's no cure.)

A NAYE CHASINEH! SURKE HOT NOCH NISHT GETANST! Often *abbrev.*, A NAYE CHASINEH!)

A new wedding! Our Sarah hasn't danced yet! (Here we go again!—reaction to the raising of a question which has already been discussed and settled with someone else.)

A NAYE MAYSE!

A new story! That's a new one! (I never heard *those* complaints before.)

A NAYER YIKUM PIRKON!

A new *Yikum Pirkon* (Aramaic prayer in the Sabbath service)!

This suits the same situation as A NAYE CHASINEH!

The prayer appears twice in the service, supplying the basis for the expostulation—i.e., What's it doing here again? An old joke provides the answer: the prayer appears twice to make sure that it doesn't get lost. But, the joke goes on, the MISHEB-EYRACH[1] appears only once; why couldn't the YIKUM PIRKON? And the reply is that this *proves* why you need it twice: one MISHEBEYRACH has already been lost! (This is another example of a joke with a "super-climax.")

ANDERSH BISTU NIT IN DER HEYM GEVEYNT?

I suppose you weren't accustomed to anything different at home? (sarcastic response to a wife's demand for some luxury)

Also, ANDERSH BISTU NIT GEVEYNT BAY DAYN TATTEN? You weren't used to anything different at your father's?

Both are often used good-naturedly.

AN EYSIK!

A business!

Also, AN EYSIK MIT . . .! A business with . . .! (Suppose, for instance, you've gotten involved with a "free gift" offer that turns out to be not so free and you've written to cancel your acceptance, the correspondence then becoming endlessly exasperating, apparently handled at the other end by computers that haven't been programmed for cancellations. You might explode with "AN EYSIK MIT A 'free gift offer'!")

ER MACHT DERFIN A GANTSEN EYSIK. He's making a whole business out of it.

AN UNSHIKENISH!

A dire happening! (exasperation at a person or problem) *See* Chap. IIIA, "oonshick."

A SOF, AN EK!

An end, a conclusion! Stop! (I mean it!)—the stage of exasperation beyond GENUG, SHOYN!

AZ ICH ZOG TOG, ZOGT ER NACHT!

If I say day, he says night! (exasperation at the constant arguer)

AZ ME FARLOZT AF IM! (disgusted)

When you depend on him! (You see what happens!)

AZ ME REDT TSU DIR, 'SIZ AZOY VI ME REDT TSU A TEYTER VANTS!

Talking to you is like talking to a dead bedbug! (Sometimes heard as: "Talking to you is like talking to a TEYTER VANTS!")

A farce by S. N. Behrman, *The Beauty Part*, had a character named "Beno Vants," and *Mad* magazine has used "Mr. and Mrs. Vontz."[2]

See also RED TSUM LOMP!

AZOY REDT MEN TSU A TATTEN?

Is that the way to talk to a father?

The intonation here has a certain pattern:

A- ZOY REDT MEN TSU A TAT- TEN?

and provides special color to the expression when used good-humoredly.

AZOY ZUGST DU!

That's what *you* say! Sez you!

AZ S'KUMT TSUM ARBET, IZ NISHTO KEYNER!

When it comes to work, there's "nobody home." (Sure, a dog is nice, but where is everybody when it has to be fed or walked?)

BIST A GROYSER FERD.

Lit., You're a big horse. You're a big fool.

Also, SHTIK FERD! Hunk of horse! (Sometimes shortened to SHTIK!)

DAYN TSUNG IZ EFSHER IN KIMPET? (sarcastic)

Do I take it your tongue is giving birth (and needs special care)? *Equiv.*, "Has a cat got your tongue?"

See Family, KIMPETORN.

DERFAR!

Because!

DERIBER GEYEN ALEH KETS BORVES. (sarcastic)

Therefore all cats go barefoot. (rejoinder to a poor or pointless explanation)

Also, DERIBER GEYEN DI GENZ BORVES, UN DI KATSHKES IN ROYTE SHICHELACH. Hence the geese go barefoot, and the ducks in little red shoes.[3]

DI GANTSE VELT IZ NISHT MISHUGGE!

The whole world isn't crazy! (*You* could be wrong, you know!)

See Char. and Des., MISHUGGE.

DREY MIR NISHT KEYN KOP!

Lit., Don't spin me a head! Don't get me dizzy with all your talk! Leave me alone!

FARDREY MIR NISHT DEM KOP! Don't get me all mixed up!

See also FARDREY NISHT KEYN SPODIK!

DU BIST TSU MAYNE TSORES!

You're adding to my troubles!

DU FARKIRTST MIR DI YOREN!

You're shortening my years! ("You'll be the death of me!")

This line is punned on in the quip about a man who tells his fractious son that he makes him feel much younger than his age:

DU FARKIRTST MIR DI YOREN!

ER FANGT SHOYN UN!

He's starting in already!

This comment is either addressed to a third person or exclaimed to one's self, though in the latter case it's usually meant to be overheard by *him!* The more direct form is FANGST (*or* HEYBST) SHOYN UN! You're beginning already!

Cf. Chap. I, Punning.

ES BRENT NISHT. (controlled annoyance)

Lit., It isn't burning. It's not that urgent. (It can wait, can't it?)

ES FREYT MICH (ZEYER) TSU HEREN. (sarcastic)

I'm (very) glad to hear it.

ES GEYT MIR IN PUPIK ARAYN! (ironic)

It goes into my belly-button! A lot it hurts me!

See Chap. IIIB, "That doesn't hurt *my* PUPIK!"

See also ES LIGT MIR IN DER LINKER PYATEH.

ES KLAPT IN KOP.

It bangs in the head. It's enough to give you a headache.

KLAP MIR NIT IN KOP ARAYN. *Lit.,* Don't bang into my head. Cut out the yakety-yak. (*See also* HAK MIR NISHT KEYN TSHAY-NIK.)

ES LIGT MIR IN DER LINKER PYATEH. (ironic)

It bothers me in my left sole. A lot I care!

This is a colorful expansion of:

ES LIGT MIR NIT IN KOP. *Lit.,* It doesn't lie in my head. It doesn't concern me; it wouldn't even occur to me.

FARDREY NISHT KEYN SPODIK!

Lit., Don't disarrange a cap! Don't confuse me; keep your bright ideas to yourself! (SPODIK is Polish for "saucer" and denotes the high fur cap trimmed with plush that Polish Jews wore over the YARMULKE on weekdays.)

A Pennsylvania cantor told me about a wedding party he attended at a New York hotel, at which he asked the head-waiter to allow a few minutes following dessert for the singing of after-meal grace, the waiter replying in annoyance, FARDREY NISHT KEYN SPODIK; ICH HOB NOCH A CHASINEH! (Stay out of my hair; I've got another wedding!) To the waiter, the singing of grace meant only delaying preparations for the next crowd!

FARMACH DAYN (CHAZERISHEN) PISK!

Shut your (swinish) mouth!

FARVOS NIT?

Why not? (May be humorous, depending on intonation.)
FREG MIR NISHT KEYN KASHES.

Ask me no questions.
FREY ZICH! (sardonic)

Go ahead and gloat!
FUN VANEN KUMSTU—YEHUPETS?

Where do you come from—Yehupets? (derogatory question to someone who seems ignorant of everyday facts or routines, as though he didn't live here)

Yehupets was the fictional version of Kiev created by Sholem Aleichem.
GEDEYNK!

Remember! (warning)
GENUG, SHOYN!

Enough, already! Come on now, cut it out!
See Chap. IIIA, ". . . already" for ". . . now."
GEY AVEK!

Go away! Scat!

This has been defined by Ruth and Bob Grossman as "Mother, please! I'd rather do it myself!"
HAK MIR NISHT KEYN TSHAYNIK.

Lit., Don't chop me a kettle. Cut out the comedy.

Often heard as, "Don't HAK me a TSHAYNIK" or "What are you HAKing me a TSHAYNIK for?" A letter to the lovelorn column "Dear Abby" was once signed "Hockta Chinik." This is roughly "Has Had an Ear Bent." Though Jews don't often translate the expression fully, it cropped up in the movie *The Eddie Duchin Story* as "I came in to bang a kettle."

See Char. and Des., A TSHAYNIK HAKER.
HOSTU DOS GEHERT?

Did you hear that? (to a third party)
ICH BIN DIR MOYCHL. (ironic)

I forgive you; you're excused. *Also*—with an object—You're welcome to it! (*Ex.*: A couple are splitting up and dividing their worldly goods. The husband might say, "Your framed picture BIN ICH DIR MOYCHL.")
ICH HOB DIR IN BOD!

Lit., I have you in the bath! *Equiv.,* "Go jump in the lake!" Often shortened to ICH HOB DIR! Sometimes humorously used in translation, "I have you in the bathtub."

Some years ago, in a Pennsylvania court, a Jewish litigant

who was displeased with the judge's remarks muttered this Yiddish phrase. The judge asked the man's lawyer what his client had said, and the Jewish attorney had to think fast. He offered the above literal translation, leaving the judge merely confused.

A current story tells of an American Jewish visitor at an agricultural settlement in Israel who hails a worker in the field with a Yiddish dialect pronunciation of English: "Hi there, boddy." The Israeli asks himself, "What's this 'boddy' business? MISTOME HOB ICH IM IN BOD UN ER HOT MIR IN BOD" (Probably he can jump in the lake for all I care and I can jump in the lake for all he cares).

See Char. and Des., ER FIRT IM IN BOD ARAYN.

ICH HOB TSU DIR A TAYNE.

I have a complaint. "I have a bone to pick with you."

ICH KEN ES NISHT FARNEMEN!

I can't take it!

ICH'L DIR BALD GEBN (*or* DERLANGEN)!

Pretty soon I'll give it (*or* hand it) to you! In a minute I'll hit!

ICH'L DIR BALD GEBN (*or* DERLANGEN) A FRASK (*or* A KLAP IN KOP, etc.). In a minute I'll give you a swat (*or* a bop in the head, etc.).

Cf. VILST A PATSH?

See Imprec., concluding portion of introduction.

ICH'L DIR TSUBRECHEN DI BEYNER!

Lit., I'll break your bones. "I'll break every bone in your body."

ICH'L DOS NIT OYS-HALTEN!

I won't be able to stand this! I'm not gonna live through it!

ICH'L IM GEBN A SHMAYS.

I'm gonna give him a wallop.

ME DARF IM SHMAYSEN. He needs a licking. (of a bratty child)

ICH'L IM GEBN VOS S'LIGT MIR IN HARTSN.

Lit., I'll give him what's lying in my heart. (A bit stronger than "I'll give him a piece of my mind.") I'll let him have it.

IN GOTTES VILLEN!

For God's sake!

KAM DERMONT! (sarcastic)

You just remembered! (A fine time to be thinking of it!)

KAM OYSGEKRATST!

You're finally scratched out! About time!

An old movie of Robert Benchley getting up in the morning dramatically illustrates the procedure of "scratching oneself out" before getting started.

See Exclam., EYDER ME KRATST ZICH OYS!

Also, vulgar, KAM OYSGEKAKT! Finally crapped out! (*See* Chap. I, Vulgarity.)

KENST ES HOBN! (defiant)

You can have it!

KLAP KOP IN VANT!

It's like banging your head against a wall! (I can't get anywhere with you!)

This is reminiscent of an old Flemish proverb which was illustrated by Peter Brueghel in the sixteenth century: "I am a sulky and ill-humored man, and in this way I knock my head against the wall."

See Destiny, MITN KOP KEGN DER VANT. . .; Chap. IIIA, note to "Talk to the wall!"

KLAP KOP IN VANT UN SHRAY G'VALD! Bang your head against the wall and yell for help! (to a child complaining that he has nothing to do)

KOP! (ironic)

Head! Nice going! *That's* what I call using your *head*!

KOP, (MAYN) TAYERE! *Lit.,* Head, (my) dear one! Great reasoning, my dear!

KUK MIR NIT IN MOYL ARAYN.

Lit., Don't look into my mouth at me. Don't watch me so closely. "Quit breathing down my neck."

MACH ZICH NIT NARISH (ICH BET DIR)!

Don't make yourself look foolish (I beg you)!

See also RED NIT KEYN NARISHKAYTEN.

MAYN NESHOME IZ NISHT KEYN ROZHINKE.

My soul is not a raisin. (I'm human, after all.)

ME DARF IM HARGENEN.

We ought to kill him. We ought to wring his neck.

MEGST ZICH SHEMEN!

You ought to be ashamed!

Also, SHEM ZICH! (Shame on you! Hang your head!) and, more forcefully, ZOLST ZICH SHEMEN IN VAYTN HALZ (You should be ashamed in your far throat) or MEGST ZICH SHEMEN

IN DAYN VAYTN HALZ ARAYN (You should be ashamed down into your far throat).

ME KEN PLATSEN!

You can just bust (from indignation)!

Cf. Chap. IIIB, "plotzed, plotzing"; Char. and Des., ME KEN TSUZETST VEREN (LACHENDIK).

ME LOZT NIT LEBN!

They don't let you live! *Equiv.*, They'll (*or* he, she or it'll) be the death of me!

NISHT BAY MOTTYEN!

Not by Morty! Not with me! Not to me, you don't! Not with *this* baby!

NOCH A MOL . . . , UN VIDER A MOL . . . !

Again . . . and yet again . . . ! There you go harping on that again!

Repeated requests for a second car might call forth: "NOCH A MOL a second car, and VIDER A MOL a second car!"

See Chap. IIIA, "Again with the. . . ."

NOR ER MACHT KALYE!

All he does is gum things up!

See Char. and Des., A KALYEKER.

NOR ME KRECHTST!

All they do is grunt and groan!

Cf. Tribalism, YIDDISHE KRECHTS.

OT 'OSTU DIR!

Lit., Here you have yourself something! Oh-oh—here's a how d'ya do!

OYCH (MIR) A . . . ! (ironic)

Lit., Also (to me) a . . . ! *Equiv.,* "And that's what passes for a . . . !"

My reaction when I first saw a *Reader's Digest* Condensed Book: "OYCH MIR A book!"

OYCH MIR A MEYVEN! Also a connoisseur! Look who's suddenly an expert! (*See* Chap. IIIA, "maven.")

RED MIR NISHT IN KOP ARAYN!

Lit., Don't talk right into my head! Let up with all the talk!

RED NIT KEYN NARISHKAYTEN.

Lit., Don't say foolish things. Don't talk nonsense.

RED TSUM LOMP!

Talk to the lamp! (Do you get any response from a lamp? That's the kind of response I get from you!)

Also, RED TSUM VANT! Talk to the wall! (As a cartoon in the *Jerusalem Post* ironically noted, before elections posters are plastered everywhere promising everything and "the walls talk to the voters." After the elections, when the politicians are safely in office, the people's wishes are not heeded and "the voters talk to the walls." *See* Chap. IIIA, "Talk to the wall!")

The next stage of exasperation is the resigned RED FUN HAYNT BIZ MORGN . . . (Talk from today till tomorrow . . .), *equiv.,* "Ah, what's the use of talking . . ."

RUF MICH KNAKNISSEL. (casually defiant)

So call me a nut (*lit.,* nutcracker).

See also Chap. IIIB, "Call me PISHER" *and* TU MIR EPPES below.

SHLOG MICH NIT UN LEK MICH NIT.

Hit me not and lick me not. Don't beat me and don't butter me up. (Just leave me alone.)

'SIZ IM UNGESHPART!

It's driving him! He can't wait!

Cf. Advice, 'SIZ DIR NISHT UNGESHPART.

'SIZ NITO MIT VEMEN TSU REDN!

There's no one to talk to! (You just don't understand! There's no point in discussing it!)

STRASHE MIR NIT!

Don't threaten me!

S'TUT MIR TISH! (sarcastic)

I'm very sorry! *Lit.,* It does me table—a pun on S'TUT MIR BANK (I regret it—*lit.,* It does me regret), BANK also meaning "bench."

TU MIR EPPES. (casually defiant)

Lit., Do me something. Make something out of it. Sue me.

See Chap. IIIA, "Do me something!"

Cf. Exclam., EPPES.

VEMEN FREGSTU?

Whom are you asking? (Don't you see you're asking the wrong person? Would you ask a bum on the Bowery for directions to the Waldorf Towers?)

VEN DI BOBBE VOLT GEHAT A BORD, VOLT ZI GEVEN A ZEYDE. (sarcastic)

If Grandma had a beard, she would be a Grandpa.

This is a pointed retort to the person who is unrealistically postulating "if . . ."

See also Advice, AF "VOLT ICH" UN "ZOLT ICH". . . .
VER FARLOREN!

Get lost!

Also, VER FARVALGERT! (Get wandered off!) or, most force-ful, VER FARBLONJET! (Lose your way, but good!). Like so many other Yiddish words, FARBLONJET has a wonderfully expressive sound, which has been taken advantage of by TV comics. Not only did Danny Thomas devote a show to the topic "What Means FARBLONJET?" but the word was even misused in a cartoon movie for kids in the line, "I'll FARBLONJE him." The word can't take an object. That sentence should have been, "I'll make him BLONJE" or "I'll make him get FARBLONJET."

See Chap. IIIA, "Get lost"; Chap. IIIB, "BLONJE time."
VILST A PATSH?

Do you want a slap? (Often heard as "Do you want a PATSH?")

ME DARF IM GEBN TSVEY PETSH. He ought to get two slaps. (of a saucy child)

ME DARF IM OYSPATSHEN 'EM PISK. Someone ought to give his face a good slapping.

Beyond PATSH, there's a FRASK (sock, swat) and a SHMAYS (wallop, whipping).

Notice there's a difference between PATSH, slap, and PATSHKE, fool around with, make a mess. TV star Shari Lewis once got the words twisted when she suggested a pastime for a child: "Just give him a bunch of clay and let him PATSH with it."
VOLT ES DIR EPPES GECOST TSU . . . ? (ironic)

Would it have cost you something to . . . ? Couldn't you have managed to . . . ?
VOS BURTSHEST DU DORTEN? (usually good-natured)

What are you muttering about over there? (Let's have it.)
VOS HOSTU TSU MIR?

What do you have against me?

See Chap. IIIA, "to" for "against."
VOS I' DOS FAR A . . .?

Lit., What's this for a . . .? What kind of goings-on is this? (Often used bilingually, as in "VOS I' DOS FAR A plan? I don't like it.")
VOS NOCH VILSTU?

What more do you want?
VOS TSHEPPEST DU TSU MIR?

What are you picking on me for?

See Char. and Des., TSUTSHEPPENISH.

VOS VILSTU FUN MIR (HOBN)?

What do you want of me? *Lit.*, What do you want (to have) from me?

See Chap. I, Learning, "*Ato v'chartonu . . .*"; Chap. IIIA, "from" for "of."

VU IZ DAYN KOP?

Where's your head? (How could you do such a stupid thing?)

VU SHTEYT ES GESHRIBN . . .?

Where is it written . . .? (Where does Holy Writ say you must . . . ?)

Often shortened to VU SHTEYT ES . . .? (Where does it say . . .?) *Equiv.*, "There's no law that says . . ."

YETST BISTU TSUFRIDN? (sarcastic)

Now are you satisfied?

ZEYER KLIG! (sarcastic)

Very clever!

Also, VI KLIG DU BIST! How smart you are! How brilliant of you!

CHARACTERIZATION AND DESCRIPTION

A DREYER

A maneuverer, one who knows how to pull strings or to get along on credit, an "operator."

See A SHMEY-DREY *and* Greetings and Partings, V'AZOY GEYT ES? ME DREYT ZICH.

A DREYKOP

Lit., a whirl-head. A garrulous pest, a guy who's always trying to interest you in his pet schemes. *Also*, a befuddler, sometimes in the sense of one who confuses to gain advantage. Occasionally used synonymously with A DREYER.

Cf. ER DREYT A KOP.

A FARBISSINER (m.), FARBISSINE (f.)

Lit., a bitten one. A sourpuss.

A FARDARTER (m.), FARDARTE (f.)

A dried-out one. A cheerless type.

A FARSHLEPPENISH

A long drawn-out matter.

A FARSHLEPTE KRENK

A long drawn-out illness; hence, anything that is dragging on
and on (*see* SHLEPPEN).

AF EYN FUS

On one foot; *equiv.,* "on the run."

This derives from Hebrew *al regel achas,* in the famous
story about Rabbi Hillel, who in the first pre-Christian century
was asked by a heathen to explain the meaning of Torah while
he stood on one foot. (*See* Rel. and Cul., HILLEL.)

A FRAYE FEYGEL

A free bird. (the mother whose kids are away at school or
all married off)

FEYGEL is also a girl's name and is the vulgar term for an
effeminate man (*equiv.,* "fairy").

A GANTSE CHALYASTRE

A whole gang. (Mother to teenage daughter: "It's O.K. to
have a few kids over, but I don't want a whole CHALYASTRE.")

A Yiddish literary magazine published in Poland between the
First and Second World Wars was called *Di Chalyastre.* It's
sometimes translated as "The Group."

A (GANTSE) FARDREYENISH (*or* GEDREYENISH)

A (whole) mixup.

A GANTSE GESHEFT

A whole business; a whole production.

A GANTSE GESHICHTE

Lit., a whole history; a whole MEGILLE (*see* Rel. and Cul.,
MEGILLE).

A GANTSE (*or* GROYSE) METSIEH (ironic)

A whole (*or* big) bargain; a real prize (like the girl some
eligible bachelor just married: for this he had to wait so long?).

Sid Caesar used the term on TV in the name of a Japanese
houseboy, "Takeh Metsieh" (Really a Prize), an obvious play
on the name of the well-known Japanese composer Toru Take-
mitsu.

See Chap. IIIA, "metsieh."

A GANTSER KNAKER! (ironic)

A whole man of importance! Such a big shot! (This is the
fellow, we're told, who does crossword puzzles with a fountain
pen.)

A KNAKER GEVOREN! A big shot, he's become!

ER IZ A KNAKER ON A NUN. He's a KNAKER without the
"n." The remaining word is vulgarly critical (*see* Chap. IIIB,

"A.K."). An approximate English would be, "He's a big shot, with an 'i' "—though that seems a bit more vulgar than the Yiddish.

A (GANTSER) MACHER

A (real) bigwig, as in "He's a MACHER at City Hall."

A GANTSER YACHSEN

A privileged character.

A GANTSE TSATSKE

A real chick (*lit.*, a whole decoration) ; a female who's "all made up," a clothes-horse.

See Endearment, TSATSKELE.

A GROYSER M'YICHES (pl. GROYSE M'YICHOSIM)

A person with real status in life, a "V.I.P."

Lovelorn columns of the Yiddish newspapers in New York often present problems occasioned when a person from a family of M'YICHOSIM wants to marry someone of more lowly origin. (*See* Rel. and Cul., YICHES.)

The term is often ironic, as in ER IZ BAY ZICH A GROYSER M'YICHES (He thinks he's pretty important).

A HANDLER

A trader; a dealer.

In American Jewish usage, this connotes a certain cleverness, *equiv.* "smart cookie." A woman recently remarked to me concerning her teenage daughter: "Boy, is she a HANDLER!"

A HEKDESH

A "holy mess" (a teenage girl's bedroom, for instance).

The Hebrew word originally meant something dedicated to a holy purpose, but took on the suggestion of godforsakenness. In Yiddish the term was applied to the community poorhouse, which presumably because of its deplorable condition accentuated the connotation of unholiness and led to the popular meaning of "slum" or "mess." It's interesting that the phrase "holy mess" should be idiomatic in English and fit this situation so perfectly.

A HIPSHE MEYDEL

A hefty, or ZAFTIG, young girl; hence an attractive one. (The older generations' ideal called for some poundage!)

A HUNT MIT OYGN

Lit., a dog with eyes. A mean character.

A KABTSEN, AN OREMAN

Lit., a pauper, a poor man. One who is really down and out,
NEBBECH.

Also, A KABTSEN IN ZIBN POLES   A pauper in seven edges;
a very poor man indeed.

See Passing Judgment, A KABTSEN BLAYBT A KABTSEN.

A KALYEKER (m.), KALYEKE (f.)

One who can be counted on to spoil things.

See Ann. and Arg., NOR ER MACHT KALYE!

A KIND ON A BOYCH VEYTIK (ironic)

A kid without a belly-ache. (Said of a person who identifies
himself with some finished project, as though he had had a hand
in bringing it to life, i.e., as if he had experienced birth-pains
with it.)

A KLEYN GORNISHT (*or* GURNIT)

Lit., a little nothing. A mere trifle; a little nobody.

See Chap. IIIA, "a little nothing" for "almost nothing" *and*
ER IZ A GORNISHT, below.

Cf. 'SIZ A GALEH GORNISHT.

A KLEYN KEPELDIKER

Lit., one with a small bit of head. A person of limited mental
capacity. (This is less harsh than some of the other descriptions. It has a sympathetic note in the diminutive KEPEL in place
of KOP.)

A KRANKER DAYTSH

Lit., a sick German. A guy who's inept at worldly endeavors
—the kind you don't ask to help you out of a business tangle
or to fix a leaky faucet.

A LANGER LOKSH

A long noodle (a skinny person).

See Food and Drink, LOKSHEN.

ALEH MONTIK UN DONERSHTIK

Lit., every Monday and Thursday. Very often. "Every time
you turn around."

Monday and Thursday are the weekdays on which the Torah
is traditionally read at services.

ALTER TERACH

Old fool (from the name of Abraham's old father, who
worshipped idols, perhaps influenced, as suggested by Israeli
scholar Dov Sadan, by ALTER TOYRACH—old burden).

TERACHOVKE (Foolish Place) was the name of a fictional

town created by nineteenth-century Yiddish writer Yachnehoz.[1]

A MENTSH FUN . . . ! (ironic)

A person from . . . ! *Equiv.*, "Some person for . . . !" (Is tongue-tied Sam entering politics? A MENTSH FUN politics!)

A MEYDEL RAYST ZICH.

Lit., A young girl is straining herself. (my father's description of a young opera singer reaching for high notes)

A MOL IN A YEYVEL

Once in a jubilee year. *Equiv.*, "Once in a blue moon."

This refers to the sacred year prescribed in Leviticus—every fiftieth year, in which land was to be returned to its original owners or their descendants, debtor slaves were to be freed, and land was to lie fallow.

AMORETS (Heb. *Am-ho-orets*)

Ignoramus.

A NAKETN HINTN

A bare behind. (what all of us ran around with, between diapers)

See also MUTER-NAKET.

AN OYS NEM (FUN DER VELT)!

Lit., a taking out (of the world)! Someone or something exceptional, "out of this world."

ANTIK (ironic)

A pip, a prize package (from French *antique*).

AN ANTIK FUN FLOMEN YUCH   A pip from prune juice. The expression would seem to be related to the physiological effect of prunes, for which there is a similar euphemism in English: "full of prunes." It must have inspired the name "Montgomery Prunejuice," given to an imaginary temple board member in the satirical *The Life and Letters of Montgomery Prunejuice* (1957), by Rabbi Jacob D. Schwarz. (This character appeared originally, in a series of letters-to-the-editor, as "Montgomery Quetschewasser." That name of course means "Squeeze-water," and seems similar in connotation.)

A POR KLUHTZIM (*or* KLOTZIM)

Lit., A pair of logs (*cf.* Advice, LEYG DI KLOTZ AF MIR). A couple of blockheads.

See Chap. IIIA, "cluck."

A POR KLYATSHES

A pair of mares (two women gabbing away).

A SHEMENDIKER (m.), SHEMENDIKE (f.)

A shy one.

A SHENEREN BAGROBT MEN.

They bury better-looking ones.

Sholem Aleichem suggested this popular comment as the superlative for "pale, paler."

A SHIF ON RIDDER

A rudderless ship. A person or situation without direction.

A SHMEK UN A LEK

A whiff and a lick. "A lick and a promise."

A SHMEY-DREY

A smiling twist; a quick and confident maneuver to "carry it off."

From DREY *and* SHMEYCHEL. *See* Chap. I, Rhyme, IR SHMEY UN IR DREY.

A SHREK

A fright.

As in English, this can apply to a person or thing. (The term has been used on TV.)

'SIZ SHREKLECH. It's frightening.

A SHTIK FLEYSH MIT TSVEY OYGN

A hunk of meat with two eyes. A clod.

Cf. A HUNT MIT OYGN.

A SHTIK LEYM

A piece of loam. A dumb brute.

See also ER IZ A LEYMINER GOYLEM.

A SHTROYENER HELD

A straw hero; a fellow who appears brave but is really a coward.

A SHVARTZ YOR

Lit., a black year. A dire destiny or person, as in ER IZ A SHVARTZ YOR. He's Mr. Trouble (reminiscent of English "blackguard").

See Imprec., A SHVARTZ YOR AF IM! *See also* FINSTER below.

ALEH SHVARTZ YOREN *Lit.,* all black years. Connotes something like "all kinds of stuff," "all sorts of things," as in the sentence from an old story about a sick man: PROFESSOREN UN ALEH SHVARTZ YOREN HOBN IM NIT GEKENT HELFN (Professors and goodness-knows-what-all weren't able to help him).

A TSHAYNIK HAKER

Lit., a kettle-banger. An ear-bender.

See Ann. and Arg., HAK MIR NISHT KEYN TSHAYNIK!

A TSUDREYTER (m.), TSUDREYTE (f.)

A wack, a nut, a MISHUGGENE(R).

A TSUKROCHINE

Lit., a female who is falling apart; one who is full of aches and complaints.

A VELT MIT YOREN

A world of years. A long, long time.

A VINT MENTSH

Lit., a wind person. A will-o'-the-wisp. A person who's here today and gone tomorrow, whose word is unreliable.

-AY

Suffix meaning "stuff," as in CHAZERAY (pig stuff, junk, trash), SHMEKERAY (stuff that smells—joking description of perfume), PATSHKERAY (complicated dish or recipe, one for which you have to PATSHKE), etc. Roughly *equiv.* to English "-ness."

A YUNG MIT BEYNER!

Lit., a young man with bones! There's a young man for you!

BALEBOSTE

A fine housekeeper—the kind you can drop in on at any hour and find presentable, along with the house.

See BERYE; IIIB, "What are you BALEBOSTEvin' about?"

BANDIT

Bandit; a real sharpie; a RICHTIKER GAZLEN (*see* GAZLEN).

BAY IM FLIT DER KOP IN DER LUFTN.

Lit., His head flies in the air. His head is in the clouds. He's impractical.

See LUFTMENTSH.

BENODOM (Heb. *Ben Odom:* Son of Adam)

Guy, fellow, character, upstart.

This is still heard in statements like "So up comes that BENODOM . . ."

BERYE

A domestic marvel, a super-duper BALEBOSTE.

A distinction that's been made between a BALEBOSTE and a BERYE is that the former stores her cans of soup alphabetically, while the latter makes her own soup.

See Chap. IIIB, "Balebairian."

BILLIG VI BORSHT

Cheap as BORSHT.

In its best form, BORSHT is not really cheap, but perhaps

originally it was just a few cow parsnips and seasoned water (*see* Food and Drink). The word is used in other deprecating ways, probably because it was once a peasant's dish. (*See* Chap. IIIB, "not to know from BORSHT.")

BIZ 'EM PUPIK

Up to the belly-button.

If you've had your fill, or can't stomach it, you've had it BIZ 'EM PUPIK. This is often heard as "I've had it up to my PUPIK."

The phrase can also be a humorous description of clothing that is too small, as in "You know how that'll fit me—up to the PUPIK."

Cf. Ann. and Arg., ES GEYT MIR IN PUPIK ARAYN!

BOBBE MAYSE

Lit., Grandma's story. Old wives' tale.

The term derives from *Bovo Buch* (Bovo Book), the title of a Yiddish narrative poem of the early sixteenth century, which dealt with the adventures of a young man named Bovo. It was intended as satire but became very popular among the Jewish masses, particularly women, for its colorful story. Three hundred years later it was rewritten in modern Yiddish prose and renamed *Bovo Mayse* (Bovo Story), and this led to the corrupted name of BOBBE MAYSE—presumably because it was chiefly old or gullible women who took it seriously.

The pun "Buber MAYSES" has been used in some rabbinical circles to disparage the theological ideas of Martin Buber, late Jewish philosopher who popularized the thought and literature of Hasidism (*see* Rel. and Cul., CHOSID) and whose personal approach to God (the "I-Thou" relationship) has strongly influenced many non-Jews.

On a less literary level, a current limerick tells of the pharmacist who "as a gesture of cheer to his grandmother dear" relabeled a drug "bobbemycin."

BRIL'N

Eyeglasses.

VU GEFINEN ZICH MAYNE BRIL'N? Where are my glasses? With all our modern progress, those of us who wear reading glasses are still asking this question. They're never on the right floor of the house or in the right room or in the right pocket or handbag. An old story tells of the rabbi who can't find his spectacles and who decides to be very logical about the problem. Suppose, he muses, someone had pushed his glasses up on his forehead and forgotten about them. Surely that person would later be looking all over for them without success. And, he considers further, would not that person then think of the possibility that they might be on his forehead? The rabbi then gingerly touches his own forehead, and sure enough, there they are! (This is a gentle poking of fun at Talmudic reasoning.)

BULVAN

Bruiser, ape.

On TV, Jan Murray once described a movie actor who plays the part of Tarzan as "a big BULVAN."

BURLAK

Boor.

See also GROBYAN.

CHALOSHES

Weakness, nausea, faintness—often *fig.*, as in:

'SIZ CHALOSHES. It's awful.

CHAYIM YANKEL

Comic name for an undependable character—*lit.*, Hyam Jake. *Equiv.*, Joe Bloke, Joe Zilch.

Also, REB YANKEL Mr. Jake.[2]

See also MOYSHE PUPIK.

CHAZERISH

Piggish, swinish; hence, unsavory, ungrateful, selfish.

See Food and Drink, CHAZER.

CHEYN

Charm.

CHEYNEVDIK Charming.

CHEYSHIK

Enthusiasm, get-up-and-go.

ICH HOB NIT KEYN CHEYSHIK TSU . . . I don't have any enthusiasm for . . .; my heart isn't in the idea of . . .

CHOCHEM

Sage.

A CHOCHEM, A YUNGER MAN! A brilliant young fellow!

Also, ironic:

A CHELMER CHOCHEM A pretentious fool. (*Lit.*, a wise man from Chelm. The Polish town of Chelm was the center of fools in Yiddish folklore.)

A CHOCHEM, A GROYSER! A great sage!

A CHOCHEM FUN DER MA NISHTANO *Lit.*, a sage of the "Why

is this night . . ." This refers to the beginning of the Passover seder ritual, in which the youngest of the family queries his father about the holiday (*see* Rel. and Cul., DI FIR KASHES) and is followed by four older sons, one of whom is the "wise son," who asks about the meaning of the ritual. Since all that is required of the wise son is to read a question in Hebrew, no great wisdom is displayed.

A GANTSER CHOCHEM! A real sage!

ER IZ NIT KEYN GROYSER CHOCHEM, UN NIT KEYN KLEYNER NAR. He's no great sage, and no little fool; i.e., He's not very smart and not a little foolish.

See also Passing Judgment, ZEY ZAYNEN UNZERE CHACHOMIM VAYL MIR ZAYNEN ZEYERE NARONIM, *and* Chap. I, Twin Forms, A CHOCHEM M'CHUCHIM; Learning, TALMID CHOCHEM.

Cf. Ann. and Arg., A CHOCHME!

CHUTZPA

Presumption, crust, nerve, gall, brazenness.

As one wag has put it, CHUTZPA is "reporting your landlord for building violations when you're six months behind in the rent."

Sometimes CHUTZPA is admired, for its utter daring. Jerome Weidman once wrote an ironic story about a Jewish mother who recounted a series of incidents exhibiting her son's impressive CHUTZPA. One observer suggests that such excessive boldness goes back to the exodus from Egypt when the Hebrews, who couldn't swim, plunged right into the Red Sea!

See Passing Judgment, CHUTZPA GILT! *and* Chap. IIIA, "Chutzpa."

DAYN MITVOCH IZ LANGER VI DAYN DONERSHTIK.

Your Wednesday is longer than your Thursday. (to a woman whose slip is showing)

DI GOLDENE MEDINE

The Golden Land (immigrant's preconception of America)

Cf. Imprec., A KLUG AF IM, A KLUG TSU COLUMBUSN!

DI KATS HOT LIB FISH, NOR ZI VIL DI FIS NIT AYN-NETSN.

The cat loves fish but doesn't want to wet her feet. (of someone who knows what he wants but isn't prepared to work for it)

DOS IZ ALLES.

That's all there is.

A woman I know, whose only child is named Ellis, sometimes adds this popular statement when introducing her son, in a kind of bilingual pun.

EK VELT (often ironic)

Edge of the world. A tremendous distance. (What Scarsdale is to Flatbush!)

ER BLOZT (FUN) ZICH.

Lit., He blows from himself. He puts on airs.

See Passing Judgment, DER GVIR BLOZT ZICH. . . .

ER BLOZT TSU FIL. He blows his horn too much. *See also* ER TROMBET.

ER CHRAKET DORTEN.

He's clearing his throat over there.

My father had chronic catarrh, and in seasons when the windows were open, we could tell he was coming when we heard his CHRAKE after he got off the trolley almost a block away!

ER CHROPET.

He's snoring.

ER DREYT A KOP.

Lit., He's making a head whirl. He's being a nuisance.

The expression has special association in my family. One of my older brothers had a friend, Herman Levy, who used to call up frequently. He would engage my brother Myer in conversation when my father thought the latter should be studying and leaving the line free for more important calls. Consequently, when my father answered the phone, he would call out to my brother, "Myer, Levy DREYT A KOP." Since this could be heard on the other end of the phone line, it became a humorous by-word not only in our family but in the vocabulary of Mr. Levy. I had occasion to see him (a Connecticut attorney) not long ago, after many years, and found he still quoted fondly the impolitely frank "Levy DREYT A KOP."

ME FARDREYT IM DEM KOP. They're getting him all mixed up. They're confusing him. (This sometimes carries the implication that they're trying to take advantage of him.)

See also Ann. and Arg., DREY MIR NISHT KEYN KOP.

ER DREYT ZICH A KOP.

Lit., He's whirling himself a head. He's worrying himself, or getting himself involved, unnecessarily.

ER EST AZOY VI NUCH A KRENK.

He's eating as though after an illness (to make up for lost time).

See also Food and Drink, FRESSER.

ER FIRT IM IN BOD ARAYN.

Lit., He's leading him off to the bathhouse. He's duping him. "He's taking him to the cleaners."

This presumably refers to the situation in a public steam bath, where one is stripped of his clothing and can hardly see what is going on through the fog of steam.

Mendele must have been consciously building on this expression when he wrote the delightful sequence in *Benjamin the Third* that deals with his hero being tricked, with his companion, into military service through an invitation to the bath. (Mendele incidentally provides a charming encomium to the public bath and its place in the life of the Jew. The modern "sauna" in many a Jewish Community Center has its cultural forerunner!)

See Ann. and Arg., ICH HOB DIR IN BOD!

ER FONFEVET.

He talks through his nose.

ER IZ A FONFEVATER. He's a fellow who talks through his nose.

ER GEYT IM IN NOZ (*or* IN KOP ARAYN *or* IN TOCHES ARAYN).

Lit., He's going into his nose (*or* right into his head *or* right into his rear end). He's bedeviling him. (Stronger than "He's getting under his skin.")

See also ME KRICHT IM ARAYN IN DI BEYNER.

ER GEYT IM NUCH.

He follows him; i.e., He does what he says; he backs him up.

See NUCHSHLEPPER.

ER GIT IM A SHTOCH.

He's needling him; he's giving him a dig.

ER HOT A KATS IN KOP.

Lit., He has a cat in his head. He has no memory; he can't be depended on to remember anything.

ER HOT A KOP VI A FERD.

He has a head like a horse. He's stupid.

ER HOT ARAYNGEFALEN VI A YOVN IN SUKEH.

He stumbled in like a soldier into a SUKOS tabernacle (Rel. and Cul.).

This connotes a person who is clumsily out of place, reminiscent of "a bull in a China shop."

Cf. Passing Judgment, ALEH YEVONIM HOBN EYN PONIM.

ER HOT AZOY FIL GELT, VI A YID CHAZERIM. (ironic)

He has as much money as a Jew has pigs.

ER HOT GEMACHT DERFIN A KASHE.

He made a mess out of it. (*See* Food and Drink, KASHE.)

ER HOT IM GEGEBN A MISHEBEYRACH.

He gave him a prayer for health; i.e., The second fellow needed a prayer for health when the first one got through with him.

Cf. joke under Ann. and Arg., A NAYE YIKUM PIRKON!

ER HOT KADOCHES.

Lit., He has fever, malaria. He has nothing; he's down-and-out.

A common rhymed reply is: VOS HELFT KADOCHES/TSUM TOCHES? (What good is malaria/To a man's rear area?).

See Chap. I, Vulgarity.

ER HOT LEYMINE HENT.

Lit., He has clay hands. He's inept; he's helpless.

Cf. ZI HOT GOLDENE HENT.

ER HOT NIT KEYN SHTOLTS.

He has no pride.

ER HOT SHPILKES.

Lit., He has pins (said of someone who can't sit still). *Equiv.,* "He has ants in his pants."

ER ZITST AF SHPILKES. *Lit.,* He's sitting on pins. He's waiting impatiently. "He's on pins and needles."

ER HOT TSU ZINGN UN TSU ZOGN.

Lit., He's got something to sing and say. He's got plenty of trouble.

As Dr. Uriel Weinreich noted, this comes down from the Middle Ages, when wandering troubadours recounted, in song and story, moving tales of hardship and adventure.

ER HOT ZEY FAYNT—VI A YID HOT FAYNT CHAZER.

He dislikes them—the way a Jew dislikes pig.

This is a statement from Sholem Aleichem.

ER HOT ZICH TSUGEKLIPT.

He attached himself. (of someone who invited himself and has been hanging around)

See GEKLIPPENISH.

ER HOT ZICH TSUGETSHEPPET.

He made a bothersome pest of himself. *See* TSUTSHEPPENISH.

ER IZ A GORNISHT.

Lit., He's a nothing. He's a nonentity.

I once heard an out-of-town speaker say of a politician: "He's a nothing," and I knew the speaker must be Jewish.

ER IZ A LEYMINER GOYLEM.

He's a clay dummy; he's a numbskull.

Cf. Ann. and Arg., A GOYLEM!

ER IZ A SHTIK FERD.

He's a hunk of horse. He's a clod. (A little more sedate than "He's a horse's a - -.")

ER IZ BAROYGES AF IM.

He's mad at him.

See also ER IZ ZEYER IN KAS.

ER IZ EYNER FUN DI BAAMTE.

He's one of the important people.

Sometimes heard in "He's one of the BAAMTE of the SHUL."

See also A (GANTSER) MACHER.

ER IZ FARKOCHT.

Lit., He's cooked up. He's all steamed up; he's boiling; he's hopping mad.

ER IZ FARMISHT (*or* TSUMISHT).

He's mixed up; he's all confused.

See Chap. IIIB, "FA'MISHT" for "famished."

ER IZ FARSHEMT/UN FARKLEMT.

He is shamed and silenced. (They shut him up.)

ER IZ FARSHMAYET.

He's blitzed; he doesn't know whether he's coming or going.

ER IZ IM SHULDIK DI LOCH FUN A BEYGEL.

He owes him the hole in a bagel; i. e., He doesn't owe him a thing. (*See* Food and Drink, BEYGEL.)

ER IZ MIR A BEYN IN HALZ.

He's a bone in my throat. *Equiv.*, "He's on my back."

ER IZ MIT IM A GANTSER PANI BRAT.

He's a whole Mr. Pal with him. They're real buddy-buddy.

ER IZ ONGEBLOZN.

Lit., He's blown up. He's very much annoyed; he's full of resentment.

ER IZ RAYCH VI KORECH/UN NEMT NISHT KEYN OYRECH.

He's rich as Korach and doesn't take guests. He knows how to hold onto his money; he's a tightwad.

Korach was a Levite who according to Numbers 16 co-sponsored an unsuccessful revolt against Moses and Aaron. The Midrash describes him as very wealthy.

ER IZ SHULDIK GOT DI NESHOME UN DEM KATSEV DOS FLEYSH.

He owes God for his soul and the butcher for meat.

ER IZ UNGESHTOPT.

He's loaded.

A well-known comic comparison, which comes from Sholem Aleichem, is "Rich, richer, UNGESHTOPT."

ER IZ ZEYER IN KAS.

He's furious. (Stronger than BAROYGES, angry.)

ER KEN DIR TSEN MUL KEYFN UN FARKEYFN.

He can buy and sell you ten times over. (He's a man of substance.)

ER KEN IM FARSHTEKN IN GARTL.

He can stick him inside his garter; i. e., He's much superior to him.

ER KLERT, TSI A FLOY HOT A PUPIK. (ironic)

He's meditating—whether a flea has a belly-button.

ER KRICHT AFN KOP.

Lit., He climbs on your head. He gets into your hair.

An old conundrum asks: Why is a barber the most nervy guy around? Answer: ZAYN GANTSER LEBN HENGT AF A HOR, UN ER KRICHT NOCH YENEM AFN KOP (His whole life hangs by a hair, and he gets into other people's hair, yet).

Cf. ZI KRICHT AF DI VENT.

ER MACHT KUTSENYU-MUTSENYU (*or* KUTSHENYU-MUTSHEN-YU).

He's playing footsy; he's getting very friendly.

ER NUDJET.

He's pestering.

In a wrestling telecast in February 1969, the announcer said: "He NUDJes him off the mat." This was not English "nudges" —where the "u" is pronounced differently and the word means merely "pokes"; this used the short Yiddish "u" and connoted a series of offensive movements.

There's a story about two brothers, one of whom was pious and poor, while the other was nonreligious and rich. The poor brother one day went to SHUL and complained to God: "Why, Lord, is it that you let my brother, who never comes to SHUL, get rich, while me you neglect so? Whenever I've had anything on my mind, I have come to you; nothing have I kept back; the good and the bad I have shared with you. When I had to choose a bride, I came here to pray; before every business decision, I have come to consult you. Why then do You punish me so?" There was a loud noise that seemed to come from heaven, and a voice answered, "Because you are all the time NUDJing me!"

"He's such a NUDJ" is commonly heard.

ER REDT AZOY KAY-UN-SHPAY.

Lit., He talks so chew-and-spit. His talk is so meaningless.

ER REDT IN DER VELT ARAYN.

Lit., He's talking right into the world. *Equiv.*, "He's a lot of hot air."

ER SHMEKT NIT UN ER SHTINKT NIT.

He doesn't smell good and he doesn't smell bad; he has neither fragrance nor stench.

See also Chap. I, Taste, ER IZ ON TAM, etc.

ER SHRAYBT *Noach* MIT ZIBN GRAYZN.

He writes "Noah" with seven errors.

This is a colorful description of the fellow who is so inept that he not only will make mistakes when they're most unlikely but will make more mistakes than seem possible. In Hebrew, "Noah" is spelled with just two letters, the *nun* and the *ches*, so you'd think there wouldn't be any chance of error at all. But it is theoretically possible to make about four mistakes: using the wrong forms of the letters (each has two different forms), using a *chaf* in place of the *ches* (like confusing "c" and "k") and using the wrong form of the vowel sign. The fellow who makes seven errors, then, is a genius at getting things wrong!

See Chap. I, Learning.

ER SHRAYT G'VALD.

He's protesting wildly. He's yelling bloody murder.

ER SHLOGT UN SHRAYT G'VALD! He beats you up and *he* yells, "Help!"

ZEY MACHEN A G'VALD. They're raising a hue and cry. They're creating a "big stink."

See also Exclam., G'VALD!

ER SHRAYT, VI DI YIDINE IN BOD.

He's yelling, like the stupid woman in the bath.

This refers to the tale of a woman in a Russian steam bath who was lying on the uppermost level—where the temperature was highest—and screaming that she was being burned, when all she had to do was move down to a lower level. It applies aptly to the person who goes around complaining of his misery, ignoring a simple solution to his problem.

ER TOYG GORNISHT.

He's good for nothing. He's no good for the job.

See Chap. I, Twin Forms, SHMOYGER.

ER TROMBET.

He blows his horn.

A TROMBENIK An egotistical bore; a conceited ass.

ER VET SHOYN KEYN HONIK NIT LEKN. (ironic)

He won't be licking any honey. *Equiv.*, He's got no bed of roses.

This negative form of irony also appears above in the second part of ER IZ NIT KEYN GROYSER CHOCHEM UN NIT KEYN KLEY-NER NAR (under CHOCHEM), as well as in Passing Judgment, 'SIZ SHOYN NISHT FRI! It goes back at least to Paul of Tarsus, who stated: "I am a citizen of no mean city."

ER VEYST FUN BOPKES.

He knows about beans. He knows nothing about the subject.

A recent series of odd little dolls, with names like "Hopeless," "Kwazy Boid," "Lovabull," etc., has been presented as "The BUPKIS Family."

See Exclam., BOPKES!

See also Chap. IIIB, "not to know from BORSHT."

ER ZUCHT A P'GIME AF DER ZEG.

He's looking for a notch on the saw. (ironic comment on the person who's making a production of finding something that's right under his nose)

Cf. ER KLERT, TSI A FLOY HOT A PUPIK.

ES BRENT A FAYER. (ironic)

A fire's burning. (of someone who's very impatient about something)

Cf. Ann. and Arg., ES BRENT NISHT.

ES FEYLT IM GORNISHT.

He lacks for nothing.

ES FIT IR, VI A CHAZER A ZOTL.

It fits her, like a saddle on a pig. (a blunt appraisal of how the new dress looks)

Cf. Advice, ES PAST SHOYN GORNIT, ES PAST VI A CHAZER.

ES GEYT MIR VI A TSADIK AF DER VELT!

Things are going wonderfully for me—as for a saint in this world!

ES GEYT SHOYN TSURIK.

It's going back already. *Equiv.*, "It's coming out of my ears."
See also s'KRICHT IN HALZ.

ES HENGT IN DER LUFTEN.

Lit., It hangs in the air. It's up in the air; it isn't settled.
(Often heard as "It's hanging in the air.")

ES KLAPT IN KOP.

Lit., It bangs in the head. It's making a racket.

ES KLIPT ZICH TSU IM.

It attaches itself to him. "Everything happens to him."
See GEKLIPPENISH.

ES TOYG AF KAPORES.

Lit., It's suitable for sacrifice. It's good for nothing.
(*See* Rel. and Cul., KAPORES.)

ES VARMT OYS DI BEYNER.

It warms up the bones. It's heartwarming. It feels so good.
See also OYSBAKEN DI BEYNER.

ES VERT MIR NISHT GUT.

I feel ill. *Equiv.*, "It makes me sick."
See also CHALOSHES.

EYNER HAKT HOLTS, UN DER ANDERER SHRAYT "AH!"

One chops the wood, and the other grunts.

Is there a better description of the modern carpenter or
plumber and his assistant?

EYN HANT VASHT DEM ANDEREN, UN BEYDE VASHN 'EM PONIM.

One hand washes the other, and both wash the face.

This description of mutual helpfulness is often heard as "One
hand washes the other." The same figure occurs in both Russian
and Italian idiom. Yiddish may have picked up the idea and
added the extra figure of both cooperating to wash the face,
just as it often used a second punch line in its humor. (*See* Chap.
I, Humor.)

FARBRENT

Burnt. *Also*, angry, as in "burned up"; fiery, as in A FAR-
BRENTER ZIONIST, a passionate Zionist.

FARFUFKET (*or* BAFUFKET)

Utterly confused, dizzy, in a whirl.

FARHARGET

Lit., killed up. "Shot."

I recently heard a third-generation American college student say, "The bird cage was so FARHARGET, I left it with the pet-shop man to be thrown out."

Cf. FARSHLOGINER.

FARIKT

Lit., turned back; backward. In the current slang sense, "retarded." Crazy, cracked, "off his rocker."

FARKRIMT

Frowning, glum, as in VOS ZITSTU AZOY FARKRIMT? What are you sitting there so glum about?

FARMISHT (*or* TSUMISHT)

All mixed up.

FARPUTZT (*or* OYSGEPUTZT)

All dressed up, all decked out.[3]

FARSHLOGINER (m.), FARSHLOGINE (f. and n.)

"Beat-up"; a beat-up person or thing; hence, darned, damned, blasted (one). *Mad* magazine is fond of this word, using it in a variety of situations. One issue that supplied elements for a zany do-it-yourself mobile included the term in large letters, spelled FERSHLUGGINER.

FARSHVITST

Sweated up.

I heard this in a recent summer commercial on WNBC radio (announcer, Lee Leonard): "If you've just lugged the groceries and are all FARSHVITST, try cooling off with some Tetley Tea."

See Family, SHVITSER.

FARTUMELT (*or* TSUTUMELT)

Befuddled, confused.

See TUMEL.

FARVORFN

Thrown around, in disorder (what a BALEBOSTE's house is not!).

BAY IR IZ ALLES FARVORFN. Her house is a mess.

FESSEL

Barrel.

Sometimes, as in English, applied to a chubby woman. (*See* Endearment, MAYN FESSEL HONIK.)

FINSTER

Dark, as in FINSTER CHOTSH AN OYG AROYS TSU NEMEN—Dark as though at least to take out an eye. Very dark.

This may also connote bad luck, as in 'SIZ IM FINSTER—It's dark for him; he's had rotten breaks; *or* (reaction to a disturbing turn of events) 'SIZ MIR GEVOREN FINSTER IN OYGN (*or* AFN HARTSN)—Everything went black (*or* My heart went black).

For a people whose kids knew from early childhood that God said "Let there be light," it's understandable that darkness would be abjured. My father, when he came home and found me with only one lamp on, would go around flipping wall switches, as he exclaimed, FINSTER IN HOYZ! FINSTER ZOL ZAYN BAY MAYNE SONIM!—Dark in the house! Let it be dark at my enemies'![4] (*See* Imprec., A FINSTER LEBN AF IM!)

FOLKSMENTSH

Man of the people; one identified with the Jewish people.

Dr. Joseph C. Landis has warmly described the connotations of Jewish group feeling involved in this term, suggesting that Sholem Aleichem's Tevye is a symbol, in his morality, of the East European FOLKSMENTSH.

FUN A SHTETL VERT A DERFL.

A town becomes a hamlet. (comment on the new quiet after most of the guests have departed)

FUN MELECH SOBIESKIS YOREN

Lit., from King Sobieski's years. "As old as the hills."

This refers to the period in Poland when King John Sobieski reigned (1674-96), a time that was "good for the Jews." Sobieski did much to improve the status of Polish Jewry, against the prejudices of the dominant clerical powers. His time and his good works were to the SHTETL[5] Jew "long, long ago."

See Food and Drink, BEYGEL.

FUN YENER ZAYT

Lit., from the other side. In the rear, on the backside, on the rear end.

GANEF

Thief, crook. *Also*, more tolerantly, rascal.

As Vladimir Jabotinsky put it in his memoirs, a GANEF is "a person who would fool you before you could fool him."

FONYE GANEF Vanya the Crook; Russian rascal (applied to someone who's pretty foxy—*see* Chap. IIIB, "very FONYE" ...)

See A MAZIK, A GANEF (under MAZIK); Exclam., AMERIKE GANEF!; Food and Drink, GANEF; Chap. IIIA, "ganef."

GATKES

Underpants.

This has a comic note, like that of "drawers." It's been used on TV, in such a line as "Who's a-wearin' my GATKES?" and in the movies, as in a gangster's advice to his girl: "Stick with me and you'll be wearing GATKES made out of mink."

GAZLEN (pl. GAZLONIM)

Robber.

An entertainer who was enumerating to me the various kinds of Jewish groups he performs for started off with well-known names like Hadassah and B'nai B'rith and then shifted into Yiddish, speeding up his listing with manufactured names. Out of the nonsense verbiage, I remember especially the ironic DI RICHTIKE GAZLONIM—The Real Robbers.

GEFINENE GELT

Lit., found money. A windfall; any unexpected saving, rebate, etc. Something, therefore, to enjoy.

GEFOREN TSU DER CHASINEH UN FARGESN DEM CHOSSEN.

Rode to the wedding and forgot the bridegroom.

This covers beautifully the common boo-boo of going downtown to exchange something and discovering you left it at home.

GEKLIPPENISH

Lit., something or someone that has gotten stuck on; hence, something that has somehow been forced on you.

Cf. KLIPPE.

See also TSUTSHEPPENISH.

GEKNIPT UN GEBUNDEN

Tied and bound. "All sewed up."

See Chap. I, Twin Forms.

GLIKLACH VI DI VELT

Fortunate as the world. Happy as can be.

GOT SHIT OYS DI FIDDERN FUN DEM IBBERBET.

God's shaking out the feathers from the comforter. (It's snowing.)

There may be a similar expression in German, for I heard a Pennsylvania radio announcer comment at the start of snow: "As they say, someone's shaking out a pillow case."

GRAF POTOTSKY (ironic)

Count Pototsky. Someone who's "high and mighty," acting as though he were royalty, as important as the famous Polish count by this name who was a convert to Judaism.

GROBYAN (m.), GROBYANKE (f.)

Rude and insensitive person; A GROBER YUNG.[6]

GUT MORGN, GENNA; RETACH TROG ICH. (ironic)

Good morning, Genna; I'm carrying radish. (comment on any situation in which what the other person says is irrelevant to what has gone before)

Another form is GELYE, VOS MACHSTU? RETACH TROG ICH. Gelye, How are you? I'm carrying radish.

See also GUT SHABBES MIT A GROYEN EK.

GUT SHABBES MIT A GROYEN EK.

Good Sabbath with a gray end.

This comic line derives from the story of a woman who rushes out on the Sabbath to retrieve a chicken that has flown the coop. Running into a friend, she asks her if she has seen a chicken. Her friend interrupts with, "GUT SHABBES." The first woman replies, "GUT SHABBES" and continues, "MIT A GROYEN EK?" The line is quoted to indicate incongruity.

See also Chap. I, Twin Forms, GROM, SHTROM, ...

GUTTE S'CHOYRE

Good merchandise.

See Chap. IIIA, "Good goods!" *and* Rel. and Cul., introduction, *re.* TOYRE IZ DI BESTE S'CHOYRE.

HEYMISH

Homey, friendly, informal.

A character named "Mr. Heymish" has appeared on TV.

HOB ICH FARCHAPT DI FISH FAR A NETS.

I caught the fish before a net. "I beat him to the punch."

HOYCHE (*or* HEYACHE) FENSTER

Lit., high windows. High Mucky-mucks. Powers-that-be.

HULTAY (m.), HULTAYKE (f.)

A dissolute person.

IBERKERENISH

Lit., a turning-over. A situation in which everything's topsy-turvy.

ICH BIN POTER.

I'm free of obligation. I'm off the hook.

ICH HOB ES OYSGEPOTERT. I've gotten it out of the way; I've done my duty.

ICH NISHT FOYL—GIT ER MIR A PATSH.

Lit., I not lazy—he gives me a slap. I lace right into him—and get a sock in the jaw.

INTERSHTIPPER

Lit., an under-pusher. Someone who's horning in.

See NUCHSHLEPPER.

IPPISH

Stench. Hence, *also,* "stinkeroo."

I remember a carton of outdated and shopworn merchandise which sat on the top rear shelf of my father's retail store, boldly marked with black crayon, "IPPISHES."

KAM, KAM

Just barely.

KAM, MIT TSORES   Barely, with difficulties. *Equiv.,* "by the skin of one's teeth."

KLAPER

Banger; hence, a sloppy workman (a nail-banger as against a skilled carpenter). *Also,* a cop (one who bangs with a stick).

Journalist B. Z. Goldberg, reporting in the *Hadassah Magazine* on a recent visit to Moscow, noted that a Jewish cab-driver warned him of the approach of a KLAPER.

KLAVTE

Shrew, "bitch," KLIPPE.

KLIG VI DI VELT

Clever as the world. Bright as a whip.

KLIPPE

Demon, shrew, MARSHAS.

KOCHALEYN

Cook-by-yourself. Summer quarters with housekeeping facilities (usually a shared kitchen) in the Catskill Mountains, near the large resort hotels.

In the old days, the tenants of KOCHALEYNS often quietly "crashed" the hotels at night for the entertainment. Though today the practice is harder to manage, it apparently still presents a problem for the hotel operators. One of these, in desperation, has built his own KOCHALEYNS. That way he at least gets HEYMISHE crashers!

KOCH LEFL

A gossip (*lit.,* a cooking-spoon, which stirs up the pot).

KOLBOYNIK (m.), KOLBOYNITSE (f.)

Know-it-all, smart-aleck.

KOYACH (pl. KOYCHES)

Strength, energy, pep.

ICH HOB KEYN KOYACH (*or* KOYCHES) NIT. I have no energy; I feel weak.

KVETSH

Whiner, complainer, pickle-puss.

This showed up on TV several years ago with Soupy Sales's "The Adventures of Philo Kvetsh."

Cf. Tribalism, YIDDISHE KVETSH (under YIDDISHE KRECHTS).

LANG VI DOS YIDDISHE GOLES

Long as the Jewish exile.

This refers to the almost nineteen hundred years of exile from the Holy Land between the year 70, when the Romans destroyed the Second Temple, and 1948, when the State of Israel was re-established. (GOLES, from Hebrew *galuth*, is commonly spoken of as the Dispersion, and Jews living outside of Israel are spoken of as living in the Diaspora.)

See Chap. I, Famil. with God, A YID IZ IN GOLES.

LEBEYUNGEN

Lively fellows, pleasure-seekers.

Rumanian Jews had this reputation among Jews of other countries.

LEMEL (*or* KUNI-LEMEL), LEMELE, LEMISHKE

Boob, easy mark (*lit.*, lambkin; reminiscent of "lamb waiting for the shearing"). An inadequate or inept fellow.

KUNI-LEMEL, like some of the phrases discussed in Chap. I, Twin Forms, combines two similar ideas. The first half would seem to be influenced by the English term for rabbit, "coney" or "cony"—an older form of which was "cunny." (Though "cunny" has for several centuries had vulgarly sexual uses, these do not seem to have affected KUNI-LEMEL, where the form suggests timidity.)

See also Chap. IIIA, "shnook."

LETZ (pl. LEYTZIM)

A scoffer, a buffoon, a clown.

LEYDIGEYER

A person without a job or responsibilities, with time on his hands (from LEYDIK, empty, and GEYER, goer); hence, *also*, a loafer.

LUFTMENTSH

Lit., an air-person. A schemer and dreamer.

This type has been described by Irving Howe and Eliezer Greenberg as "a trader who dealt in air, exchanging nothing for nothing and living off the profits." The word is supposed to have been coined by nineteenth-century writer Max Nordau. The type has been epitomized by Sholem Aleichem's character Menachem Mendel, who is actually a combination of LUFT-

MENTSH and SHLEMIEL, for his continual bright ideas for making money all end pathetically. Even when he decides to settle down to a regular trade like that of SHADCHEN, he discovers that he has been trying to make a match between two girls! (The author's use of the name Menachem Mendel is ironic, for that was the name of two famous Hasidic REBBES in the mid- and late eighteenth century.)

MARSHAS

Shrew (like KLAVTE and KLIPPE, stronger than YENTE or YACHNE).

MAZIK (pl. MAZIKIM—Aramaic: hurtful spirits)

Scamp (as in English, half-admiringly).

A MAZIK A YUNG! A scamp of a boy! A kid with initiative, all right!

A MAZIK A GANEF! A son-of-a-gun! A smart rascal!

ME FARGINT NIT YENEM.

Lit., One begrudges others. (He, She *or* They begrudge others.)

ZEY FARGINEN ZICH NIT. They don't allow themselves the pleasure; they begrudge themselves.

Cf. Passing Judgment, A NIT-FARDINER IZ A NIT-FARGINER.

ME FLIT!

He's (*or* She's *or* They're) flying! They're dashing around like mad! (Implied is the question, Is it really necessary?)

VOS FLISTU AZOY? What are you rushing for? What's your hurry?

See also ME LOYFT!

ME HULYET!

They're reveling! They're having a ball!

ME KEN IM GETROYEN VI A KATS SMETENEH.

You can trust him like a cat with cream.

ME KEN MIT IM VENT AYNLEYGEN.

You can knock down walls with him. (of a big brute)

ME KEN TSUZETST VEREN (LACHENDIK).

You can split your sides (from laughing). You can split; you can split a gut.

Cf. Ann. and Arg., ME KEN PLATSEN!

ME KRICHT IM ARAYN IN DI BEYNER.

They're climbing into his bones. They're plaguing him.

ME KVITSHET DORTEN.

They're screeching over there. (my father's comment on Saturday afternoon radio opera)

ME LOYFT! (critical)

They run! ("Where's the fire?")

ME MACHT A GANTSEN YONTEF.

They're making a whole holiday; i.e., They're celebrating over it, they're making a big thing out of it.

See Exclam., VOS IZ DER YONTEF?

ME *SHRAYT*!

They're *screaming*!

The second word is almost an octave higher than the first in this disapproving description. The expression is accompanied by a shrug, a partial raising of the eyebrows, and sometimes by a quizzical-pathetic gesture with the palm and a rhythmic shaking of the head for emphasis, all adding up to the implication, "It's so ridiculous; they should know better."

ME TSHEPPET ZICH TSU IM.

They're picking on him. (complaint of the doting mother)

ME TSURAYST IM DI KISHKE.

They're tearing his guts out; they're giving him a hard time.

See Chap. IIIB, "Hit 'em in the KISHKES!"

MIES

Ugly.

MIESKAYT Ugliness. In the first generation, this was sometimes used instead of "beauty" in commenting on a child, as in AZA MIESKAYT—such ugliness—to fool the evil eye.[7]

See Chap. I, Twin Forms, MIES UN MOES (in discussion of alliteration).

MISHUGGE

Crazy, wacky, nutty, cracked.

When Sir Cedric Hardwicke pronounced this adjective in the Broadway show *A Majority of One*, it came out sounding like "My Sugar"!

ER IZ GUT MISHUGGE. He's a real nut.

ER IZ MISHUGGE AF TEYT. He's crazy to death. He's utterly foolish and impractical; he's impossible.

FRISH UN GEZUNT UN MISHUGGE *Lit.*, fresh and healthy and crazy. Hale and hearty and nuts. This is wonderfully descriptive of a normally sensible person who ups and does something crazy, as of me the time I agreed to be neighborhood cookie chairman for the Girl Scouts! I taught the expression at that time to the Protestant professor's wife who had roped me in, and she clutched it to her bosom. She has since been passing it on, in the same way that the deprecating SHM- (Plato, Shmato) was diffused around the country, partly through academic circles.[8] (*See also* Passing Judgment, ME KRICHT MIT A GEZUNTEN KOP IN A KRANKEN BET.)

See Ann. and Arg., DI GANTSE VELT IZ NISHT MISHUGGE!; Chap. IIIA, "mishugge, mishuggene."

Cf. Passing Judgment, ITLECHER MENTSH HOT ZICH ZAYN SHIGOYEN.

MISHUGGENER (m.), MISHUGGENE (f.)

A nut, a wack, a TSUDREYTE(R).

An old Yiddish conundrum asks, What is it that stands up on the roof and says "Cock-a-doodle-doo" but isn't a rooster? Answer: A MISHUGGENER.

See Chap. IIIA, "mishugge; mishuggene"; IIIB, "Michíganer" for "Michigander."

MIT IM IZ A YO YO UN A NEYN NEYN.

With him a yes is yes and a no, no. He's a man of decision.

MIT FUL GEFIL

Lit., with full feeling; from the heart.

MOYD

Dame.

ALTE MOYD   Old Maid.

See OYS KALEH! (VAYTER A MOYD!)

Cf. Family, MEYDEL.

MOYSHE KAPOYR

Moses Upside-Down.

This is the fellow for whom everything comes out wrong—like the one they tell of who spent a night at a hotel and left his own towel! The name derives from a comic character in a New York Yiddish paper during the 1920's.

See Exclam., PUNKT FARKERT!

MOYSHE PUPIK

Moses Belly-Button. (Sam the Sap)

See also CHAYIM SHMENDRIK, under SHMENDRIK.

MUTER-NAKET

Mother-naked; in one's "birthday suit."

MUZHIK

Peasant; a coarse person.

NEBBECHEL

Pathetic little soul.

See Chap. IIIA, "nebbish," *and* Exclam., NEBBECH!

NESHOME

Spirit, personality, soul.

A GUTTE NESHOME   A good soul.

A KALTE NESHOME   A cold personality.

See Endearment, MAYN NESHOME.

NUCHSHLEPPER

Lit., after-dragger. Hanger-on, tag-along.

NUDNIK

A bore, a pest.

A late official of the U. S. Employment Service in Pennsylvania told me that a certain Gentile woman in charge of a local office in his jurisdiction customarily identified herself on the phone with, "This is Mrs. Nudnik."

See Chap. IIIA, "nudnik," *and* Chap. IIIB, "Phudnik."

OPGEKUMENER

A once-rich man who has lost his wealth.

Cf. OYFGEKUMENER.

OPKUMEN MIT SHIHI-PIHI

To get along on a pittance; to get by on a shoe-string.

This may be related in structure to A SHIS PILVER (a shot of gunpowder), which also means a mere cipher as in 'SIZ DI VERT A SHIS PILVER (It's worth a shot of gunpowder). The initial letters of SHIHI-PIHI and SHIS PILVER are the same. (*See* Chap. I, Twin Forms, *re.* the deprecating "P.")

OYFGEKUMENER

Lit., one who has come up; *nouveau riche.*

OYSBAKEN DI BEYNER

Lit., to bake out one's bones. To sun.

OYSGESHPILT

Played out; worn out.

OYSGETSECHELT

Outstanding.

The Broadway show *The Zulu and the Zayda*[9] in 1966 had a song with this title.

OYS KALEH! (VAYTER A MOYD!)

No more bride! (A maid again!). The wedding's off! (of any plan that is scrapped after long preparation)

. *See also* Resig., NU, IZ NISHT GEFIDELT, under NU, IZ NISHT.

PASKUDNE

Bad, unpleasant, nasty, disgusting.

PASKUDNIK, PASKUDNYAK   A revolting cad. (*Cf.* Tribalism, LITVAK.)

PEMPIK

Short and stout man.

PETSHETSHE

Female pest (a kind of combined NUDNIK and KVETSH).

PISKEVATE

Talkative (from PISK, mouth).

PITSH, PATSH! VER VEMEN, VEYS ICH NIT.

Socko, whammo!—Who hit whom, I've no idea.

PLITSLING

Suddenly.

PORITS (m.), PRITSE (f.)

One of the Christian landed gentry.

A GANTSER PORITS   A whole man of leisure.

ZI ZITST VI A PRITSE. She sits like a rich landowner's wife. (of a woman who let herself be waited on, making no move to pitch in and help)

PROST

Coarse.

PROSTER (m.), PROSTE (f.)   A coarse person, one without learning or refinement.

PROSTAK   An ignorant boor.

See Chap. I, Taste, *and* Twin Forms, PROST UN PUSHET (under alliteration).

PUST

Hollow, empty, shallow.

PUST UN PAS   Insipid and idle.

PUSTOPASHNIK   Loafer, idler.

See Passing Judgment, PISTE MANSES!

REB NOTEH/HOT TOMID CHAROTEH.

Mr. Net/Has always regret. (of a person who customarily goes back on his word)

RICHTIKER (m.), RICHTIKE (f.) (ironic)

A real one, a pip.

See also ANTIK.

SHACHER-MACHER

A finagler, a sharp operator, a wheeler-dealer (from Heb. *socher*, merchant, and MACHER).

There is a somewhat similar ricochet word in English: "hokermoker," a variant of "hugger-mugger," from Middle English "mokeren," to conceal or hoard.

SHEYN

Fine, beautiful, lovely.

According to an old conundrum, the comparison is SHEYN, SHENER, m-mm-m!

See Chap. IIIA, "by" for "to" (*re*. BAY MIR BISTU SHEYN) *and* ZIS UN SHEYN below.

SHIKKER

A drunk.

The diminutive, SHIKKEREL, is a little more tolerant of the offender, *equiv.*, "a bit of a sot."

SHIKKER also means a sender or dispatcher, and a pun on this meaning appears in the joking description, ER IZ NIT KEYN SHIKKER; ER GEYT ALEYN. (He's no drunkard; he goes himself.)

See Chap. IIIB, "shikkered."

SHLATTENSHAMMES

A messenger boy; hence, a tale-bearer, a busybody.

Cf. Rel. and Cul., SHAMMES.

SHLEMIEL

A lummox, a blunderbuss.

There seems to be some confusion about the real meanings of this term and its companion, SHLIMAZEL, a pathetically luckless fellow. I know of an English class in a Pennsylvania college where the Gentile professor and one of his Jewish students disagreed on whether a certain character in a novel by Bernard Malamud was a shlemiel or a shlimazel. And many Jewish readers of *Games People Play* by psychiatrist Eric Berne have been bothered by the author's use of both terms, since he stretches them beyond their Yiddish meanings.

Actually, a shlemiel is an inept character, personifying a broad category that includes MOYSHE KAPOYR, MOYSHE PUPIK, a LEMEL, a SHMENDRIK, a NEBBECHEL, a SHMEGEGGI, et al. These are all shlemiels: saps, incompetents, bunglers who are "bright about doing dumb things." In analytic terms, says Theodor Reik, the shlemiel is a masochist with an unconscious need to fail.

Where does the word come from? One theory says it's a contraction of *sheluach min 'el* (sent away from God). Another traces it to the person named Shelumiel in a responsum of the Middle Ages who came home after a year's absence and found his wife with a newborn baby. After submitting the problem to the rabbi, he accepted the latter's decision that the child was his, much to the ridicule of his neighbors.

Still another theory traces the term to the Biblical Shelumiel, the son of Zurishaddai (Numbers 1:6), who was said to be always unsuccessful in battle. The Talmud identifies him with Zimri, the son of Salu (Numbers 25:8, 14), who had the bad luck to be killed as a public example by Phinehas after the Israelites had sinned with the Moabite women. (Accordingly, Heinrich Heine wittily suggested it was not Zimri who was struck by Phinehas' spear but a guiltless person named Schlemihl ben Zuri Schaday, "Schlemihl the First," from whom "we are descended.")

One might ask, therefore, whether at least one of these ancestral SHLEMIELS could not just as easily be defined as a SHLIMAZEL. Indeed, in Jewish folklore the terms have at times been used interchangeably. But there are certain shadings of difference. The SHLIMAZEL really seems to have been born under an unlucky star (the term is a combination of Hebrew *mazol*, constellation, and German *schlim*, unlucky), for no matter what he does, it turns out badly. He is an unfortunate soul, a poor devil—like the one who told the rich man that he just *had* to have some money. Why? Because if not, he would go into the hat business. And what is so terrible about that? Well, if he went into the hat business, you could be sure that henceforth all babies would be born without heads![10] Perhaps the best definition is to be found in two old Yiddish observations: A SHLIMAZEL FALT AFN RUKN UN TSUKLAPT ZICH DI NOZ (A shlimazel falls on his back and bangs up his nose) and VEN A SHLIMAZEL KOYLET A HON, GEYT ER;/DREYT ER ON A ZEYGER, SHTEYT ER (When a shlimazel kills a rooster, still it hops;/ When he winds a clock, right away it stops).

To emphasize the distinction, then, the shlemiel is hapless because of his own inadequacy; the shlimazel has the handicap of bad luck. Ex.: When a shlemiel tries to use a hammer, he drops it—on the shlimazel's toe.

See Passing Judgment, AZ ME SHPAYT DER ZOYNE . . . ; Destiny, TSUM SHLIMAZEL DARF MEN OYCH HOBN MAZEL; Chap. I, Twin Forms, *re.* SHLIM-SHLIMAZEL; *and* Chap. IIIA, "shlemiel" and "shemozzel."

Cf. LUFTMENTSH.

SHLEPPEN

To drag, to lug (what you have to do when you don't get pickup and delivery).

See Family, ARUMSHLEPPEN, *and* Chap. IIIA, "shlep."

SHLEPPER (pl. SHLEPPURIM)

Slob; bum.

See Chap. IIIA, "shlep."

SHLIMAZEL *See* SHLEMIEL.

SH'MA KOLEYNU

Lit., "Hear Our Voices"—a Yom Kippur hymn. By extension, an idiot (one who hears voices).

SHMATTE

Rag.

A 1969 sale catalog of the Ktav Publishing Company, New York book dealers, listed Philip Roth's licentious novel *Portnoy's Complaint* with the comment: "A shmatte."

The word can be a pointed pun in deprecating Father (TATTE-SHMATTE) or can provide a variety of bilingual puns: ZI IZ ZEYER A SHMATTE (She's a very smart one—ironic); SHMATTÉ (using the French ending, in ironic description of clothing material—i.e., a fancy rag),[11] etc.

See Family, MISHPOCHE, *re.* "Shmatsay."

SHMEGEGGE (*or* SHMEGEGGI)

A galoot, a bird-brain, a stupid character.

As picked up in American theatrical circles, this is sometimes used in the sense of "malarkey" or "bushwa."

The disdain involved prompts me to suggest that the term may be a combination of two other words for "fool": the vulgar SHMOK (*see* Chap. IIIA, "shmo") and YEKE or its German antecedent *Gecke* (*see* Tribalism, YEKE). Such a merged double noun would be rather similar to BEYTSEMER (*see* Chap. I, Twin Forms, end of discussion of synonyms in apposition).

SHMENDRIK

A sap, a clunk (from HENDRIK-SHMENDRIK—*see* Chap. I, beginning of Twin Forms).

CHAYIM SHMENDRIK Comic name for such a person.

A famous character of I. L. Peretz was FAYVEL SHMENDRIK, and Israel Zangwill created a SOSHE SHMENDRIK. The country home of actress Molly Picon is dubbed "Chez Shmendrik"—because her BOBBE,[12] on seeing it for the first time, commented that you have to be a little bit of a SHMENDRIK to put so much money into the ground!

In Peter Beagle's fanciful novel *The Lost Unicorn* (1968), a character is "Schmendrick the Magician." This is of course a pun on Mandrake the Magician of the comics with SHM-, i.e., Mandrake, Shmandrake.

See also SHMER'L *and* YUKEL.

SHMER'L

Undignified name for an inefficient or nondescript man (probably from a deprecation of the name BERYL).

SHMER'L NAR   Shmer'l the Fool (a classic character in Jewish folk humor).

SHNORRER

Beggar, panhandler; hence, also, bargainer, chiseler.

The shnorrer occupies a special place in Jewish folk culture. Since charity in Jewish tradition is an obligation, the wayfaring stranger could count on some kind of help. Sometimes this stranger was a bit arrogant about his just deserts. An old story tells of the SHNORRER who comes to a wealthy Jew for his yearly handout and is told that the contribution cannot be given this year, because the rich man's son has had financial reverses and the father must help out his son. The SHNORRER becomes indignant, noting that the son has no right to achieve help at his expense!

In the early days in America, most synagogues had a little hut on the premises to accommodate strangers overnight. Today, the SHNORRERS—usually spoken of as "transients"—absorb a steady portion of the budgets of local Jewish welfare funds. Most of these Jewish hoboes are uninterested in work; they like to get hotel, food, and transportation to the next appropriate town in which to continue their shnorring. In this way they see the United States many times over. One fellow, pleased at the treatment he received from the Jewish Community Center director in my community, told the latter, "It's a pleasure to do business with you!" Some are not above fabricating tear-jerking tales and impressive family connections. My husband once recognized a SHNORRER in Georgia by the spurious story he told, recalling he had heard it years earlier in Kentucky.

The term is often applied also to a certain species of representative of Jewish educational institutions, a MISHULACH (pl. MISHULOCHIM). These earlocked gentlemen with long black cloak and black hat descend in pairs at certain holiday seasons to solicit gifts to their institutions from leading citizens. They have been known to come to doctors' offices and retail establishments, belittling the prospective donor within earshot of patients and customers until they are given what they think is enough. This is a carry-over from the days before Jewish allied welfare appeals. It shouldn't happen any more, but some Orthodox organizations are dissatisfied with their official allocations and think they can do better with old-fashioned shnorring.

In Jewish women's organizations, a member being approached to work on a fund-raising project might say: "I'll do anything but shnor." That means, "I'm willing to work, but I won't go around asking for donations." A person who bothers all the manufacturers she knows to get things wholesale for her might be described as "a real shnorrer."

A famous story by Israel Zangwill (recently reissued) was titled *The King of Shnorrers.*

SHPOGEL-NAY

Brand-new (*lit.,* mirror-new).

SHPUREVDIK

Economical (what a good BALEBOSTE is).

ZI IZ ZEYER A SHPUREVDIKE. She's a wonderful manager.

SHTIK

Silly, sometimes objectionable, antics or "routine"; stuff; "line"; shenanigans. *Also* (*lit.*), piece.

ZAYNE SHTIK! His darned antics!

ICH VIL NIT KEYN SHTIK. I want no shenanigans.

The term has affected current slang. *See* Chap. IIIA.

Cf. Ann. and Arg., SHTIK! (under BIST A GROYSER FERD).

SHTIKEL

A little piece, a bit. *Also,* a bit of a, as in A SHTIKEL FILOSOF, a bit of a philosopher.

SHTUS

Inanity, utter nonsense.

'SIZ A GALEH GORNISHT.

It's nothing at all. "It doesn't amount to a row of pins."

See also 'SIZ BLOTTE.

'SIZ A GANTSER KOPDREYENISH.

It's a whole head-whirling thing. It's a complicated mess.

See also 'SIZ MIR A KOP VEYTIK.

'SIZ AZOY VI GEVINTSHEN.

Lit., It's like wished. I couldn't ask for anything better.
'SIZ BLOTTE.

Lit., It's mud. It's worthless; it's nothing worth talking about.
'SIZ FUN'M ERSHTN FESSEL. (ironic)

It's from the first barrel (*equiv.,* "top-drawer").

My father would thus express his disappointment when, in unpacking new merchandise, he found it of inferior quality. (Most of the time, he would seal up the carton and send it back; other times, he would sigh twice and continue to unpack.)
'SIZ MIR A KOP VEYTIK.

It's a headache to me.
'SIZ MIR AROP A SHTEYN FUN HARTSN.

Lit., A stone has come off my heart. A weight has been lifted from my spirits.

As an Israeli guide explains it, the reason there are so many rocks on the road from Lod airport to Jerusalem is that when Jews come to Israel, GEYT ZEY ALEMEN AROP A SHTEYN FUN HARTSN—A stone drops off every heart.
'SIZ TSU SHLECHT ARUNTERSHLINGEN UN TSU GUT AROYS TSU SHPAYEN.

It's too bad to swallow and too good to spit out. (expression of mixed feelings)
S'KRICHT IN HALZ.

Lit., It's climbing up the throat. It's nauseating. (A little more sedate than "I'm ready to puke.")

See also S'VAKST SHOYN FUN GORGL.
S'CHLYAPET.

It's pouring. (of rain)

How's that for onomatopoeia? (The verb is from Polish.)
SMARKATSH

Snot-nose.
S'VAKST SHOYN FUN GORGL.

It's already growing out of my throat.

A precious story about the late Dr. Jacob Z. Lauterbach of the Hebrew Union College (the same professor who interpreted the tennis-court sign as "Private? No! Visitors Allowed!") relates that this bachelor educator was very fond of cheese cake, and that before long all his dinner hostesses learned this. He was, as a result, constantly served the same dessert. It began to pall, and he finally expostulated in Yiddish: AZ EPPES VAKST FUN A BEYM, ZOGT MEN DI BROCHE, *Borey pri ho-eyts.* UN AZ

S'VAKST FUN DER ERD, ZOGT MEN, *Borey pri ho-adomo*. OBER AZ
S'VAKST SHOYN FUN GORGL, VOS FAR A BROCHE MACHT MEN?!
(Before eating something that grows from a tree, you say the
blessing, ". . . Creator of the fruit of the vine." And when it
grows out of the ground, you say, ". . . Creator of the fruit of
the earth." But when it's already growing out of your throat,
what kind of a blessing do you say then?!)[13]

TERETS

Excuse; alibi; answer to a difficult question.

TOCHES (Heb. *tachas*)

This has been defined by Prof. Chaim Gininger as "the part
of the body where the back ceases to bear an honorable name."

As noted in Chap. I, Vulgarity, the word has a variety of
uses, most of them playful, and has made certain inroads into
American slang, for which other details are given in Chap.
IIIA, under "tokus."

See also ER GEYT IM IN NOZ (*or* . . . IN TOCHES ARAYN);
ER HOT KADOCHES; Advice, MIT EYN TOCHES KEN MEN NIT
ZAYN AF TSVEY YARIDN; Rel. and Cul., beginning of YARMULKE.

TSITTERN

To tremble; to be nervous or anxious.

ER TSITTERT. He's afraid; he's quaking in his boots.

VOS TSITTERSTU? What are you so nervous about?

TSORE

Trouble (something the Jews have always had plenty of).

ER HOT TSORES. He's got troubles; he's got it rough.

'SIZ AN UMZISTIGE TSORE. It's an unnecessary (*or* undeserved)
trouble.

See Ann. and Arg., DU BIST TSU MAYNE TSORES; Family, end
of NACHES; Food and Drink, GEBAKINE TSORES; Chap. I,
Vulgarity, "TSORASS"; Chap. IIIA, "tsuris."

TSUDREYTER (m.), TSUDREYTE (f.)

A mixed-up person, a nut.

TSUSHPREYT

Spread out.

ER ZITST TSUSHPREYT. He sits spread out; i.e., He's lounging;
he's loafing; he's taking it easy.

TSUZEYT UN TSUSHPREYT[14] Scattered and dispersed; "spread
out all over the place." This was the name of a play by Sholem
Aleichem.

TSUTROGN

Anxious, beside oneself.

TSUTSHEPPENISH

Lit., something or someone that has gotten tacked on; a pest or pesty situation, a GEKLIPPENISH.

Sam Levenson defines this as "a trailer."

See Ann. and Arg., VOS TSHEPPEST DU TSU MIR?

Cf. Exclam., TSHEPPE NIT!

TSVEY SHTET KRIGN ZICH IBER A ROV.

Two cities are fighting over a rabbi. (Neither one wants him.)

According to the tale from which the line comes, Kovne argued that the gentleman should be rabbi for Vilna, and Vilna insisted he should be rabbi for Kovne. The description therefore applies to any situation in which the two parties are in polite dispute, each pressing on the other what he himself does not want.

TUMEL

Noisy activity; disturbance.

ZEY HOBN GEMACHT A GANTSEN TUMEL. They created a big commotion; they made an awful lot of noise.

In the comic strip *Joe Palooka* over a decade ago, Joe had a next-door neighbor named "Mr. Toomul," who was constantly quarreling with his wife and making a lot of noise.

See Chap. IIIA, "tumeler."

UNGEDUYET

Pouting, moody, blue.

VOS KUKSTU OYS AZOY UNGEDUYET? Why are you looking so unhappy? (*See also* FARKRIMT above.)

VALGEREN

To wander (what a single son away from home finds it necessary to do, NEBBECH).

ER VALGERT ZICH NOCH ARUM IN NEV YOK. He's still wandering around—i.e., is unmarried—in New York.

VAYBISHE REYD

Wives' talk, women's prattle.

This is what drives men into the other room for *their* conversation—which is of course more manly, consisting of governmental problems (dirty politics) and women (dirty jokes)!

VOS S'IZ AFN LUNG/IZ AFN TSUNG.

What's on the lung/Is on the tongue; i.e., Whatever he feels,/off his tongue he reels. (of the tactless person who doesn't know how to "hold his tongue")

VU DER KENIG MUZ GEYN TSU FUS

Where the king must go on foot.

This light-hearted reference to "going to the bathroom" takes the rich down to Everyman's level. (*See* the similar combination of humor and de-statusizing in Passing Judgment, OREM UN RAYCH,/IN BOD ZAYNEN ZEY BEYDE GLAYCH.)

YACHNE

A female loud-mouth, a slattern—a little stronger than YENTE. (Originally a girl's name.)

YARID

A fair; hence, hustle and bustle, commotion, "circus."

'SIZ DORTEN A GANTSER YARID. It's a real circus over there.

Sholem Aleichem's autobiography was entitled *FUN'M YARID*, usually translated as *From the Fair*.

Cf. Advice, MIT EYN TOCHES KEN MEN NIT ZAYN AF TSVEY YARIDN.

YENTE

Once a girl's name, this connotes a gossip, a hag, a nag, a "washerwoman." A popular character of B. Kovner was Yente Telebende. The character became so widely known, her name was used as a jocular synonym for YENTE.

The word has often since been fooled around with. Playwright S. J. Perelman, in *The Beauty Part,* burlesqued a California street intersection as "La Paloma and Alte Yente" (Old Hag). A current bilingual pun is the term "Oriente," defined as a Chinese gossip.

See Passing Judgment, ES IZ DI EYGENE YENTE, NOR ANDERSH GESHLEYERT; Chap. I, Taste, MAYN BOBBE YENTES TAM.

YESHIVE BOCHER

Seminary student; hence, often, an unworldly type.

The statement ER IZ A YESHIVE BOCHER can, depending on the intonation, mean either "He's a scholar" or "All he has is book learning."

See Food and Drink, ESSEN TEG (under ESSEN).

YOLD

A fool.

YUKEL

A yokel, a nincompoop.

YUKEL FAYVISH A derisively comic name, *equiv.,* "Joe Shmoe." (*See also* CHAYIM YANKEL *and* MOYSHE KAPOYR.)

YUNGATSH

A brute, a BULVAN.

ZAFTIG

Juicy—usually applied to a shapely woman.[15]

This term became part of Army slang in World War II, as in the line in Leo Rosten's novel *Captain Newman, M.D.:* "Now there was a lusty, zaftig piece of woman." It was used—spelled "ZOFTIK"—as the signature of a letter-writer to columnist "Dear Abby" in 1966.

See beginning of Chap. III.

ZEY FARDREYEN IM DI YOREN.

They're tangling up his years; i.e., They're getting him all tangled up.

This offers a bilingual, slightly off-color, description of a man who's being catheterized: "ZEY FARDREYEN IM DI urine." (*Cf.* Chap. I, Vulgarity, "TSORass.")

ZEY FAREDN IM DI TSEYNER.

They're talking his teeth out. *Equiv.,* "They're talking him deaf, dumb and blind."

ZEY HOBN ZICH BEYDE LIB—ER ZICH UN ZI ZICH.

They're both in love—he with himself and she with herself.

ZEY KRATSEN ZICH DORTEN.

Lit., They're scratching themselves over there. They're poking around; they're taking their time.

See Exclam., EYDER ME KRATST ZICH OYS.

ZEY SHUSHKEN ZICH DORTEN.

They're whispering over there. (They're probably up to something.)

ZEY VOYNEN VI CHAZERIM.

They live like pigs.

ZI HOT A BREYTE DEYE.

Lit., She has a broad opinion. She does all the talking.

ZI HOT ALEH MAYLES.

She has all the virtues; she's got everything.

Cf. Advice, ALEH MAYLES IN EYNEM/IZ NITO BAY KEYNEM.

ZI HOT A PISKEL. (ironic)

She has a little mouth. She can open her mouth (and let you have it).

ZI HOT GOLDENE HENT.

She has golden hands. (of one who knits and sews to perfection)

Also, ER HOT GOLDENE HENT. (of a skilled surgeon)

These are often heard in translation. A New York radio

account of the world's first heart transplant spoke of the performing surgeon as "the man with the golden hands."

ZI HOT GROYSE OYGN.

She has big eyes. She's a snoop. *Equiv.*, "Sees all and hears all."

In the play *Invitation to a March* by Arthur Laurents, Celeste Holm observed: "In a small town, people have big eyes. They can forgive what you do for love, but not what you do for money."

ZI KRICHT AF DI VENT (*or* AF TISH UN AF BENK).

She climbs on the walls (*or* on tables and chairs). She's a great housekeeper.

Cf. Passing Judgment, ME KRICHT AF DI GLAYCHE VENT.

ZI VEYNT UN BAKT BEYGEL. (ironic)

She cries and bakes bagels; i.e., She complains a lot but has it plenty good (*see* Food and Drink, BEYGEL).

Also, ZI VEYNT UN EST VERENIKES. She cries and eats VERENIKES (Food and Drink).

ZI VIL NIT TSURAYSN DEM SPODIK. (ironic)

Lit., She doesn't want to tear her cap. She doesn't want to strain herself.

Cf. Ann. and Arg., FARDREY NISHT KEYN SPODIK!

ZIS UN SHEYN

Sweet and lovely.

The old popular song "Sweet and Lovely" was written by Harry Tobias, who mentioned in a recent radio interview that he took the phrase from his mother's optimistic philosophy that everything would be ZIS UN SHEYN.

ZIS VI HONIK

Sweet as honey.

DEATH

AF GOT TOR MEN KEYN KASHE NIT FREGN. VOREM ER ZOGT, "AZ DU VILST VISN DEM TERETS, KUM TSU MIR."

You mustn't ask questions of God. For he says, "If you want to know the answer, come to me."

A FOYL'N IZ GUT TSU SHIKN NUCHN MALACH-HAMOVES.

A lazy man makes a good messenger to fetch the Angel of Death.

An old story illustrates the implication here, that no one is ever really ready to die: An elderly man who lived in the forest found himself becoming weaker and weaker. One winter's day his supply of firewood ran out, and he went outdoors to gather some. With much effort he put together a pile of sticks upon a rope which he had spread out on the snow. He managed to tie a knot, but when he tried to lift the bundle, he couldn't do it. Overcome with despair, he lifted his eyes to heaven and cried out, "My God, send me Death." Immediately the Angel of Death appeared and said, "You sent for me; what do you want?" And the old man, quickly changing his mind, replied, "I'm having trouble getting these sticks up onto my back; could you help me?"

A GEPEYGERTER (m.), GEPEYGERTE (f.)

A dead one; one who is done for, "a dead duck."

Also as verb and adjective, GEPEYGERT is a disdainful term, most often used with reference to animals, as in A GEPEYGERTE KATS (a dead cat). The word for "dead" referring to people is GESHTORBN (which *see*).

A LEVAYE

A funeral.

This has been punned on with (H)ALEVAY (Destiny), to wish a person a bad end.

AZ ICH ZOL DERLEBN SHTARBN, ZOL ICH HOBN AZA BAGRUBNS!

If I live to see myself die, may I have such a burial! (my father's report of a beautiful funeral service)

This is reminiscent of the story quoted under Destiny, DOS HEYST GELEBT!

AZ ME DERMONT ZICH ON DEM TOYT, IZ MEN NIT ZICHER MITN LEBN.

When you start thinking about death, you're a goner.

AZ 'SIZ BASHERT EYNEM DERTRUNKEN TSU VEREN, VERT ER DERTRUNKEN IN A LEFL VASSER.

If someone's fated to drown, he'll drown in a spoonful of water.

ER IZ NIFTER.

He's departed; he's gone; he's no more.

Jesting reply: NIFTER, PIFTER, ABI GEZUNT.[1]

ER IZ SHOYN AF YENER VELT.

He's already in the other world. He has passed on.

ER IZ SHOYN NISHT DO.

He's already gone. He died.

GESHTORBN

Died; dead.

There's a story about the stranger in town who gets taken home for a meal. His host discovers that the visitor is from his old home town and begins to ply him with questions about how certain residents of the community are getting along. The baker? GESHTORBN. The tailor? GESHTORBN. The synagogue beadle? GESHTORBN. And so on, for a long list of old acquaintances. The host is becoming terrified and asks in horror what happened to the place—was there a plague, or a pogrom, how could so many people have died already? The stranger stops eating long enough to explain, AZ ICH ESS, HOB ICH ALLEMEN IN D'RERD! (When I'm eating, everyone can go to hell!)

GILGUL (Heb. *gilgul hanefesh*)

Transmigration of souls; a transmigrated soul.

Though rejected by most Jewish philosophers, this doctrine was a part of the Zohar (*see* Rel. and Cul., KABOLE) and became a general belief in Hasidism.

A special form of the doctrine held that the individual's soul was at times overshadowed by other souls, and that if these latter were guilt-ridden from their previous existence, they could do harm in their host body and should be expelled. (*Cf.* Ann. and Arg., A DIBBUK!)

HESPED

Eulogy.

KADDISH

Prayer in praise of God which is recited in the name of the dead. (*See* Chap. I, end of Famil. with God.)

In Orthodox tradition, it is the male children who observe the Kaddish ritual. For this reason, an only son might be introduced with, DOS IZ MAYN KADDISH (This is the boy who will say Kaddish for me).

There's a story about a little boy who comes home from Hebrew school, and whose father asks him what he is learning. The boy says he is learning to read the Kaddish. Incensed, the father goes to school the next day and berates the teacher. "After all, look at me," he yells, "how soon do you think I'm going to die?" The teacher tells him, "You should live so long as it'll take your son to learn the Kaddish!"[2]

In the traditional prayerbook, the Kaddish appears not only

in connection with remembrance of the departed, but also in other portions of the service, serving as a divider of the different sections of the liturgy.

Leonard Bernstein has composed a "Kaddish Symphony."

ME ZOL ZICH KENEN OYSKOYFN FUN TOYT, VOLTN DI OREME LAYT SHEYN PARNOSSE GEHAT.

If people could hire others to do their dying, the poor could make a nice living.

OLEV 'A SHOLEM (Heb. *alav hashalom*); sometimes corrupted to OLEM B'SHOLEM

Lit., Upon him be peace. May he rest in peace.

OLEHA HA SHOLEM Peace to her memory; may she rest in peace.

Each is customarily spoken after the name of a deceased person. Today, these are most commonly put in translation: May . . . rest in peace.

See also ZECHER LIVROCHO.

SELIG

Blessed.

Spoken after the name of a deceased person, as in TATTE SELIG (Papa, may his memory be blessed).

See Chap. I, Superstition, for its use as a boy's name.

SHTARBT MEN IN DER YUGEND, IZ ES AF DER ELTER VI GEFINEN.

If you die in your youth, it's great for your old age.

SHTEYN

Stone, gravestone. *Also, fig.*, weight or worry, as in Char. and Des., 'SIZ MIR AROP A SHTEYN FUN HARTSN.

TACHRICHIM MACHT MEN ON KESHENES.

Shrouds are made without pockets. "You can't take it with you."

TSUM SHTARBN DARF MEN KEYN LUACH NIT HOBN.

For dying you don't need a calendar.

The LUACH has been an important part of Jewish life. Not only the numerous holidays and fast days had to be kept track of but also the anniversaries of deaths (*see* YORTSAYT). All of these fall on a different date each year, because the Hebrew calendar is based on movement of the moon around the earth rather than that of the earth around the sun, the basis of the civil calendar. In recent years, more and more printed civil calendars have been carrying indication of the major Jewish holidays, making things a little simpler for American Jews and

keeping other Americans informed of their fellow Americans'
YONTEYVEN.[3]

YORTSAYT

The anniversary of a death—which family members observe
by attendance at synagogue (*see* KADDISH) and by lighting of
the YORTSAYT LICHT (light) at home on the eve of the anniversary. These cheap wax-filled glasses are commonly sold in
supermarkets in big-city areas. They hold enough wax to burn
for twenty-four hours. More modern forms of the YORTSAYT
LICHT are the patina-finish brass bases from Israel which hold
either a replaceable candle or a specially designed electric bulb.
Another variety is the one supplied by funeral directors, a tall
glass holding a candle that burns for the seven days of mourning
(*see* ZITSEN SHIVE).

The keeping of "YORTSAYT lists" is a part of every synagogue's functions. The date of death of immediate family is
recorded for congregational members, and names are read at
services on the anniversary of that date. Some congregations
have two lists, one following the Hebrew calendar, one the
secular. Since families that follow the Hebrew calendar have a
different date to observe each year, some Jewish bookshops in
the big cities sell framed lists of ten-year-or-more dating for any
given YORTSAYT. Actually, anyone can figure out the dates himself by consulting a Jewish encyclopedia. The article on "calendar" usually contains a fifty-year-or-more projection of the first
day of each Hebrew calendar month as it relates to the secular
one. Occasionally, though, one can hit a snag because of the
irregular number of days in the Hebrew calendar months. The
definitive solution is a book one can buy giving daily YORTSAYT
projections for a hundred years.

ZECHER LIVROCHO (Heb.)

May his (*or* her) memory serve as a blessing. (usually added
after a written reference to the departed)
See Chap. IIIA, "of beloved memory."

ZITSEN SHIVE

To "sit SHIVE."

This is the custom of staying indoors for seven days of mourning after a death in the immediate family, receiving visitors
while sitting on low stools. The stools are rarely used today,
but the expression still holds.

"Are they going to sit?" means, "Are they going to sit

SHIVE?"—i.e., Will they be at home for condolence calls? Some insensitive souls even like the bantering "sit 'n shiver."

Traditionally, visitors bring something sweet to the bereaved.
ZOL ER ZAYN A GUTER BETER.

May he be a good pleader. (said in reference to a departed relative or friend)

It's been observed that this and other expressions, like ZOL ER DERLANGEN A ZCHUS (May he deliver a merit) gave the impression of the dead as being busily engaged in intercessions with God for their dear ones down below.

ZOL ICH AZOY LEBN VI ICH VIL SHTARBN! (ironic)

May I so live, as I want to die!

The irony here is that ZOL ICH AZOY LEBN is often used to intensify an idea (*see* Life and Health, ICH ZOL AZOY LANG LEBN!). But in this instance it negates the thought: although death is being asked for, death is actually being resisted. *See* the similar situation in the story under A FOYL'N IZ GUT TSU SHIKN . . . above.

Note the comparative form of wishing, which appears in several other expressions. *Cf.* Destiny, (H)ALEVAY VOLT ES AZOY YO GEVEN VI ES VET NIT ZAYN.

DESTINY

AF MAYNE ERGSTE SONIM VINTSH ICH ES NIT!

I don't wish it on my worst enemies![1]

AF MAYNE SONIM GEZUGTGEVOREN!

It should happen to my enemies! (of something unpleasant)

See also ZAYN MAZEL AF SHTEYNER GEZUGTGEVOREN!

AF MIR GEZUGTGEVOREN!

It should happen to me! (Often *abbrev.*, AF MIR GEZUGT!)

AF UNZ ALEH GEZUGTGEVOREN! It should happen to all of us!

AF ALEH YIDDEN GEZUGTGEVOREN! May it be wished on all Jews! This is often used ironically, as in response to a statement like "He doesn't earn very much." (No? We should all do as well!)

See Chap. IIIA, "should" and "shouldn't" for "may" and "may not."

A GEDILLE (HOT MIR GETROFN)! (sarcastic)

A great event (happened to me)! (I should celebrate, I suppose!)

A (GROYSE) GLIK GETROFN! (ironic)

Such a (big) stroke of luck! (I'm dancing from joy!)

AN UMGLIK!

A misfortune!

George Jessel once said on TV that he came from "Imglik, Ohio"—an obvious use of this term. ("IM-" is an alternative pronunciation.)

See Chap. I, Twin Forms, AN UMGLIK, A MALYERE!

A SHEYNE VELT, A LICHTIKE VELT, NOR VI FAR VEMEN?

A beautiful world, a glorious world, but oh, for whom?

AY, 'SIZ SHLECHT!

Oh, it's bad!

'SIZ MIR SHLECHT! I've got trouble!

AZ GOT VIL, SHIST A BEYZIM.

If God wills, even a broom can shoot (i.e., anything is possible).

AZ S'REGENT MIT GOLD, SHTEYT YEYDER MAN UNTER A DACH. (sardonic)

If it rains gold, every man is standing under a roof.

AZA YOR AF MIR!

Lit., Such a year for me! I wish I had it that good! (Ex.: ER HOT A VAYBEL—AZA YOR AF MIR! He's got a little wife— I wouldn't mind having someone like her wished on me!)

AZ S'GEYT, GEYT ES, UN AZ S'GEYT NIT . . .

When things go right, they sail along; and when they don't . . . (Reminiscent of "Trouble comes in bunches.")

AZ S'VERT NIT BESSER, VERT MIMEYLE ERGER.

If things don't get better, you can be sure they'll be worse.

CHASVECHOLILE! (*or* CHOLILE V'CHAS!)

May it be far from us! "Perish the thought!"

Often shortened to CHOLILE! and commonly heard as TOMIR —CHOLILE!—(Suppose—God forbid—). The latter is frequently ironic.

Also, CHASV'SHOLEM! *Lit.*, "Quiet and peace!" This is a more positive way of saying the same thing.

DANKEN GOT!

Thank God!

Sam Levenson defines this as "Diaper Service."

DER MENTSH TRACHT,/UN GOT LACHT.

Lit., Man thinks, and God laughs. "Man proposes; God disposes."

DI SHO ZOL NIT ZAYN. . . .

May the hour (*or* time) never come. . . .

Cf. IN A GUTER SHO.

DOS HEYST GELEBT!

That's what I call living! (approval or self-satisfaction at an enjoyable experience)

The expression was given an ironic twist in a story about a poor Jew who visits the impressive grave of Rothschild and exclaims, DOS HEYST GELEBT!

ES KEN NIT ZAYN!

It can't be!

EYN GOT, UN AZOY FIL SONIM!

One God, and so many enemies!

See also Rel. and Cul., PURIM, A SACH HOMENS UN EYN PURIM.

FUN ZAYN MOYL, IN GOTS OYER.

Lit., From his mouth into God's ear. May God hear what he has said (and fulfill it)!

GOT HOT LIB DEM OREMAN UN HELFT DEM NOGID.

God loves the poor and helps the rich.

GOT IN HIML!

God in heaven!

GOT SHIKT DI REFUE FAR DER MAKEH.

God sends the remedy before the affliction.

The Hebrew and Yiddish term for remedy (*refuah*, REFUE) inspired the naming of the drug "Refuin," used in treating cancer.

GOT ZITST OYVN UN PORET UNTN.

God sits on high and makes matches below.

GOT ZOL UPHITN!

May God protect us from it!

(H)ALEVAY!

This response to a statement about fate may be used with reference to the future, present, or past: May it be so!; Would it were so!; Would that it had been so!

See Death, A LEVAYE.

(H)ALEVAY VOLT ES AZOY YO GEVEN, VI ES VET NIT ZAYN.

Would that it might be, as surely as it won't. (For the form of wishing here, *see also* ZOL ICH AZOY VISN FUN MAYNE TSORES below.)

ICH ZOL HANDLEN MIT LICHT, VOLT DI ZUN NIT UNTERGE-GANGEN.

If I dealt in candles, the sun wouldn't set.

This comes from an epigram of the eleventh- and twelfth-century poet Ibn Ezra.

See similar story quoted under Char. and Des., SHLEMIEL.

IN A GUTER SHO

In a good hour. May what you say come true soon.

KEYN EYN HORE (ZOL NIT ZAYN).

No evil eye. May there be no evil eye.

Superstition about the evil eye goes all the way back to primitive Egypt. The fetish has been shared by many cultures and is still taken seriously by some. In Pennsylvania a number of months ago, an Italian-American man shot a neighbor because he believed the latter had put an evil eye on him and his family.

See Chap. I, Superstition *and* Rhyme, bilingual joke; Imprec., ER VARFT IM A BEYZ OYG; Food and Drink, FRESSER; Chap. IIIB, "canary" for KEYN EYN HORE.

ME DARF ZAYN SHTARK VI AYZEN!

You have to be as strong as iron! (How can an ordinary person stand it?)

MITN KOP KEGN DER VANT—MUZ MEN OBER HOBN A VANT! (ironic)

Knock your head against the wall—but you have to have a wall! (I haven't even got that!)

See Ann. and Arg., KLAP KOP IN VANT!

NIT DO GEDACHT!

May it not be thought of here! (comment on another's unhappy fate)

NIT FAR DIR (*or* AYCH) GEDACHT! May it not be thought of for you!

NIT FAR MIR (*or* UNZ *or* KEYNM *or* KEYN MENTSHEN *or* KEYN YIDN) GEDACHT! May it not be thought of for me (*or* us *or* anyone *or* any person *or* any Jew)!

Also, NISHT FAR MIR (*or* KEYNM, etc.) GEZUGT. May it not be wished on . . .

NOR MAYNE FRAYNT ZOLN ES VISN!

Only my friends should know it! (An exclamation at pleasure—something you obviously wouldn't want your enemies to experience! *Cf.* AF MAYNE SONIM GEZUGTGEVOREN!)

OY, A KLUG IZ AF MAYNE YOREN!

Woe, a plague is upon me!

See Imprec., A KLUG AF IM!

RIBOYNE-SHEL-OYLEM, HEYB MICH NIT UN VARF MICH NIT!

Ruler of the Universe, don't raise me up and don't throw me down! (How about just letting me be?)

RIBOYNE-SHEL-OYLEM: KUK AROP FUN'M HIML UN KUK DIR ON DAYN VELT!

Ruler of the Universe: look down from heaven and take yourself a look at your world!

'SIZ AZ ACH (*or* OCH) UN VEY.

Lit., It's like alas and alack. It's really pathetic.

See Chap. I, Psychol. Insight, AZ DER MELAMED KRIGT ZICH MITN VAYB, 'SIZ AZ ACH UN VEY TSU DI TALMIDIM.

'SIZ BASHERT.

It's destined. It's meant to be.

'SIZ MIR GUT! (ironic)

I've got it good, all right! Things are just great!

'SIZ MIR GUT, ICH BIN A YOSSEM! Hooray, I'm an orphan! The source of this ironic line is Sholem Aleichem's character Mottel the Cantor's Son, who naïvely delights in the freedom and attention he gets when his father dies. It can be used as an ironic commentary on any sorry situation.

'SIZ MIR ZEYER ZIS. (sometimes ironic)

Everything's very sweet. "Everything's rosy."

See Char. and Des., ZIS UN SHEYN.

TSUM SHLIMAZEL DARF MEN OYCH HOBN MAZEL.

Even for bad luck you need some luck.

This recognizes the gradations of misfortune and the possibility that "it could always be worse" (Chap. IIIA).

Cf. Chap. IIIB, "There's MAZEL in SHLIMAZEL."

VOS S'VET ZAYN MIT KOL YISROEL VET ZAYN MIT REB YISROEL.

Whatever happens to the people Israel will also happen to Mr. Israel. That is, the fate of the individual Jew is tied up with that of his people.

ZAYN MAZEL AF SHTEYNER GEZUGTGEVOREN!

Only stones should know his luck!

ZOL ICH AZOY VISN FUN MAYNE TSORES (VI ICH VEYS NIT). . . .

May I so know of my troubles (as I don't know). . . .

ZOL ICH AZOY VISN FUN BEYZ VI ICH FARSHTEY EPPES IN. . . . May I know as little of evil as I understand about. . . .

These comparative forms of wishing are similar to that under Death, ZOL ICH AZOY LEBN VI ICH VIL SHTARBN!

ZOL IR (*or* IM *or* ZEY) DER OYBERSHTER BAHALTEN.

May the One Above protect her (*or* him *or* them).

This is commonly heard on Yiddish programs of New York's WEVD as charitable contributions from listeners are acknowledged.

ZOLN MIR LEBN UN LACHEN!

May we live and laugh!

ZOLST NIT VISN FUN AZELCHE ZACHEN (*or* TSORES).

May you not know of such things (*or* troubles). I hope you never have to live through such things.

ZOLST FUN DOS NIT VISN. May you not know that. May you be spared that.

See Chap. IIIA, end of "know from" for "know."

ENDEARMENT

As you know by now, Yiddish is informal and intimate. Here's a sampling of common pet terms and diminutive suffixes, some of which were briefly discussed in Chap. I.

AN ARABEREL

A little Arab (affectionate description of my then young son by his paternal grandmother, a Palestinian, on finding he liked Middle Eastern foods).

AY-LI-LU-LI-LU

Lullabying sounds, *equiv.*, "La-la-la-la-la," which appear in various folk tunes sung to children.

BUBELE

Honey-child, sweetie-pie, puddin'.

This affectionate term has been heard often on TV (even in the clowning "Merci, BUBELE!") and turns up in other unexpected places, like the restaurant in Philadelphia where a Puerto Rican waitress was heard addressing her young son with the term. The announcer on my local radio station (not Jewish) has lately been signing off with, "Good-bye, BUBELE."

The bilingual "Buby" has also been taking on. I've noticed it frequently in the affectionate speech of a Connecticut relative married to a Catholic.

-EL

Dear, little, as in SHVESTEREL (little sister); DUVIDEL *or* "Davidel" (Dear David).

In some words, an extra consonant is added for euphony before the suffix, as in CHAZENDEL (fine CHAZEN—*see* Rel. and Cul.).

The Pennsylvania TV weather forecaster's "foggel" or "foggle" for light fog may reflect this influence from Yiddish as well as from German.

-ELE, -LE

Little, simple, as in SHTUBELE (little house), BUCHELE (little book); dear little, my own dear, as in AVRAMELE or "Abele," MAMMELE (dear little mother—often addressed to a baby girl), TATTELE (little father—to a male infant), NARELE (dear little fool).

An old story tells of a woman in a Jewish grocery store who fishes a pickle out of the barrel and asks the grocer the price. He answers, "A nickel." In those days, pickles were priced at a penny or two according to size, with only the large ones costing a nickel. The woman puts the pickle back and picks out a slightly smaller one, asking in a tender tone, "And how much is this PICKELE?" The grocer mimics in reply: "This PICKELE is just a NICKELE!"

Modern Hebrew has picked up this popular diminutive suffix, particularly in terms like *Abale* (Daddy) and *Imale* (Mommy).

-ENYU

Dear, sweet, as in GOTTENYU! (Dear sweet God!—exasperation at fate)[1]; TATTENYU (Father dear—also to God the Father)[1]; MAMMENYU (Mother dear; dear sweet Mother; Mother mine); SURENYU (dear sweet Sarah).

An old friend of mine, named Edna Mae, was always called by her mother EDNAMEYENYU. Even the Purim SUDEH (Rel. and Cul.) might be referred to as the SUDENYU (it appears so in an old Hasidic song), and a mother might say SHLOFENYU (Sleep, my sweet) to her child. In the 1930's, a comic Yiddish song of some New York left-wing intellectuals derided the simple-minded female radical with a Galitzianer[2] pronunciation: YACH VIL ZAYN A KOMUNIST A GITE, BOLSHEVIK A GETRAYE (I will be a good Communist, a loyal Bolshevik), the refrain being AY VAY, LENENYU (O my, dear sweet Lenin).

-ETSHKE, -ITSHKE

Little, tiny, darling, as in KAPETSHKE (tiny drop); BOB-BITSHKE (Darling Granny, Grannykins); AMERITSHKE (Darling America), a term that appeared in songs of the immigrant period.

-EVITSH

Dear little, as in USHEREVITSH (dear little Usher—a boy's name, sometimes rendered as Asher or Arthur); CHAZERE-VITSH (dear little hog—a doting term for a NASHER); MAM-ZEREVITSH (*lit.*, dear little bastard; darling devil).

EYTSEREL

Precious one.

-INKE

Dear little; tiny one, as in MAMMINKE (dear little mother—to a baby girl); ZISINKE (little sweet one, little sweetheart); PITSINKE (tiny one); PITSIMONINKE (darling mite; adorable little charmer).

-KE

Dear *or* little, as in MOTKE (dear *or* little Motte).

The ending is also used on various nouns, as in PISHERKE (Chap. I, Vulgarity) or the adoption "Presidentke," a good-natured reference to the head of a woman's organization.

-LACH, -LECH

A plural ending (as in KREPLACH, Food and Drink), this may also be tacked on endearingly to an existing plural, as in KINDERLACH (dear children).

-LEB

Short form for LEBN (life) attached to a name, as in SASH-ALEB (Sasha, my life).

See MAYN LEBN, below.

MAYN FESSEL HONIK

My barrel of honey.

My father used to tell a story about the man who wanted to take his wife along on a wagon trip but wanted to avoid paying toll charges for her. He therefore had her climb into the wagon with the merchandise he was carrying and covered over the top. When he was stopped at a toll point and asked what he had in his wagon, he gave a list of miscellaneous products, including the item of A FESSEL HONIK (a barrel of honey). The inspector wanted to see for himself and lifted up the cover, exposing the hidden woman. "And what do you call this?" he demanded. The driver of course replied, "That's my barrel of honey."

MAYN LEBN
  My darling (*lit.*, my life).
MAYN LIBE
  My love.
  LIBE, MAYNS   Love of mine.
MAYN NECHAME
  My comfort; my darling.[3]
MAYN NESHOME
  My soul.
  Entertainer Elly Stone relates that her mother exudes affection over Elly's young child with MAYN ZISE NESHOME! (My sweet soul!), and that Elly's husband, who knows very little Yiddish, one day attempted to emulate his mother-in-law's exuberance at his daughter and came out with: MAYN MISE NESHOME! (*Cf.* Imprec., A MISE MESHINNE AF DIR!)
MAYN TAYERE (sometimes ironic)
  My dear one.
  TAYERE may also mean expensive, just as "dear" has both meanings in English, and a husband confronted with bills for his wife's expensive clothes might sigh, "MAYN TAYERE VAYBL" (My dear little wife).
MIR ZOL ZAYN FAR DIR.
  May your hurt be mine. Let me suffer for you. (a mother offering sympathy to a child who has hurt himself)
  This readiness of the simple Jewish mother to suffer for her child has roots in ancient Hebrew feeling, as can be seen in the story of David and Absalom (II Samuel 18:33) : ". . . O my son Absalom! . . . Would God I had died for thee, O Absalom, my son, my son!"
OY, IZ DOS ZIS!
  Oh, is that sweet!
  Rabbi Samuel Silver of Stamford, Connecticut, well-known to radio and TV audiences, likes to use this Yiddish phrase. When his sons were little, he would grab one and put him on his lap while he was talking and then suddenly give him a bearhug and exclaim, "OY, IZ DOS ZIS!"
  See Chap. IIIA, "How sweet it is!"
OYFELE (pl. OYFELACH)
  Little child (*lit.*, birdy, chick—reminiscent of "my chickadee," "my little ducky-wucky").

-SHE

Dear, as in BOBBISHE (dear Grandma, Granny); MAMMISHE (Mommy).

SHLOF, MAYN KIND

Sleep, my child.

This was the title of a poem by Sholem Aleichem which became a famous lullaby, still sung to various melodies.

TOCHTEREL

Dear daughter, little daughter. (Sometimes ironic, as in NU, TOCHTEREL, VOS ZOGSTU? Well, dear daughter, what do you have to say for yourself?)

TSATSKELE

Little ornament, little toy.

This has been defined by Ruth and Bob Grossman as "what a Jewish child thinks is its first name."

Cf. Char. and Des., A GANTSE TSATSKE.

-TSHIK

This conveys a certain breeziness, like "fella" or "my boy" as in MEYORTSHIK for a boy named "Meyer." (The adopted term "boy" could at times become BOYTSHIK.)

-UTSH

My own name, Lillian, has been often rendered bilingually as "Lillutsh."

YINGELE MAYNS; MAYN YINGELE

Dear little boy of mine; my dear little boy.

"Mayn Yingele," a famous lullaby by Morris Rosenfeld, composed in 1887, portrays the hard-working sweatshop hand who leaves early in the morning before his son is up and returns at night after he is in bed. It wails: "O, strange is my own flesh to me"—foreshadowing a problem that has beset American fathers of later generations. They may be earning more, but they don't see much more of their children.

-ZHE

This familiar ending, which connotes "so" or "then," is joined to all kinds of words. Witness GIBZHE MIR (So give me) or the popular expressions which are also titles of old songs: ZAYZHE MIR GEZUNT (variant of ZAYT MIR GEZUNT—Chap. I, Concerns about Life and Health) or VO'ZHE VILSTU? (So what do you want?).

See also Exclam., NU, *re.* NUZHE.

ZUNELE (MAYNS)
Dear son (of mine).

Many of the above suffixes were combined, as in MOTKELE, "Lillutshkele," BALEGOLTSHIKEL (good-natured reference to a BALEGOLE, a coachman—who might first become a BALEGOLTSHIK), PITSINYUNKILE or PITSINYUNTSHIKEL (variants of PITSINKE). Such compounding of intimacy even appears in a term like SHAZHESHE (Hush, then, my little one), spoken by a mother in a poem by Jacob Glatstein.

In some cases, a regular suffix would be tacked on after the diminutive, as in A KLEYN KEPELDIKER (Char. and Des.). One could even combine the diminutive ending with one of derogation, as in A SHNAYDERUKEL (a mere little tailor).

Pet terms, too, were often multiplied, as in the lullaby: PATSHE, PATSHE, KICHELACH, EYTSEREL MAYN SHEYNER; PAPA'T KOYFN SHICHELACH, ZUNELE MAYN KLEYNER (Clap, clap, sugar buns, little treasure, my pretty one; Papa'll buy little shoes, dear young son, my little one).

The second generation used to poke fun at the whole endearing process by projecting incongruous pet names like the French-Yiddish "Raoulele" or English-Yiddish "Montmorencyel."

EXCLAMATIONS AND CATCH PHRASES

A CHIDDESH! (ironic)
A surprise! (What's so surprising about that?)
ADO LIGT DER HUNT BAGROBN!
Here's where the dog lies buried! *This* is the point!
ADO, OT ADO.
Here, right here.
AF A MAYSE FREGT MEN NIT KEYN KASHES.
You don't ask questions about a story. It's a story—let me tell it. (to the person who "gets technical" about the details of a joke)
Cf. BLAYBT A KASHE; Rel. and Cul., DI FIR KASHES.
A FARGENIGEN!
A supreme delight!
AF DER ELTER
In one's old age. (Often humorous, as in the English self-

mocking "in my old age": I've finally gotten around to it!)

AF TSALOCHES! (corruption of Ger.-Heb. *auf tsu l'haches*)

Lit., Just to make you angry! For spite!

See also DAVKE.

A GANTSE GEDILLE (GEMACHT)! (critical)

A whole celebration (made) over it! (It's not *that* important!)

See Destiny, A GEDILLE (HOT MIR GETROFN)!

A GEFERLECHE ZACH! (ironic)

A terrible thing! What a catastrophe! (OYCH MIR trouble!)[1]

Also, A GEFERLECHE MAYSE! A terrible tale! What a tragedy! (For that you want sympathy?)

A GROYSER YICHES! (ironic)

A big honor! (*See* Rel. and Cul., YICHES.)

AHIN UN AHER

Lit., there and here. Hither and yon; hither and thither.

I heard an Israeli guide some months ago quip that directions of north, south, east, and west are DU,[2] DORTEN, AHIN UN AHER —here, there, thither and hither.

Notice that we have two kinds of order here. DU, DORTEN goes from here to there, and AHIN UN AHER goes from there to here. English also says it both ways, in "to and fro" and "back and forth." My father always said the logical but unidiomatic "forth and back," obviously influenced by AHIN UN AHER.

NISHT AHIN UN NISHT AHER Neither here nor there; betwixt and between; neither one nor the other.

AKLAL, HOT GOT GEHOLFN . . . .

Finally, God helped . . . .

A LEBEDIKE VELT!

A lively world! (Things are hopping, all right!)

A MECHAYE!

What a delight! What a pleasure! (the taste of Mama's strudel, or the feel of "baking" on the beach—anything that pleases; from Heb. "life-restorer")

When my daughter was two years old and given a drink of juice, she used to put out her arm with the drink and exclaim, "A MEHAYIM!"—an amusing mixture of this exclamation and the toast L'CHAYIM![3]

AMERIKE GANEF!

America the sharpie! (Where but in America?)

This expresses the startled admiration of the immigrant at

what can happen in this unique land. The exclamation is still often used and may have inspired Harry Golden's phrase "Only in America."

See Char. and Des., GANEF.

Cf. Chap. IIIA, "It's their America."

A NECHTIKER TOG!

Lit., A yesterday's day! Ridiculous! Don't you believe it! (comment on an improbability or a lost cause)

ARAYNGECHAPT!

Squeezed in! (of something good worked into a busy schedule)

See Advice, CHAP ES ARAYN!

ARAYNGESHLOFN!

You slept it up! That's sleeping! (to a family member coming down to breakfast at noon)

A RETENESH!

A riddle! A quandary!

A SHANDE UN A CHARPE

A shame and a disgrace.

This is sometimes playfully put as "a shandie an' a harpie." (Who knows—it may yet become "a shanty an' a harpie"!)

A SHEYNE GELECHTER! (ironic)

A pretty laughter! A fine thing to laugh about!

This has been humorously defined as "hiccuping on Yom Kippur." (Traditional Jews neither eat nor drink on Yom Kippur. *See* Rel. and Cul.)

A SHEYNE MAYSE! (ironic)

A pretty tale! *Equiv.,* "A pretty kettle of fish!" or "A likely story!"

AY!

Ah! My! Oh dear! Oh my goodness!

This can express more than consternation. It may also show satisfaction, as in AY, GUT OPGEGREPST! (Ah, that was a good burp!).

Notice, there's a slight difference between AY! and OY! (which *see* below). With AY! there is an intake of breath, making it a bit more intense than OY!, which expels the breath moaningly.

The effect of AY! is multiplied in repetition:

1) AY-AY! My husband makes an adjective out of this by labeling as "AY-AY Jews" those who react exaggeratedly to every

instance of anti-Semitism, real or imaginary. (*Cf.* the story about the NUDNIK in introduction to Tribalism.)

2) AY-AY-AY! (Said with a shaking of the head.) I recall a Jewish women's organization meeting at which a vote was taken on a proposal involving a large sum of money. When it was clear that the "ayes" had it, one woman exclaimed in mock concern, "AY-AY-AY!"

This can also be used as an adjective, *equiv.,* "hotsy-totsy": NISHT AZOY AY-AY-AY (not so wonderful or impressive), or as a noun, as in ZEY MACHEN DERFIN A GANTSER AY-AY-AY (They're making a "federal case" out of it). As a noun it also lends itself to punning. My husband once spoke of the "AY-AY-AY of Jewish life" (i.e., causes of concern) as Ignorance, Indifference and Intermarriage.

An old quip distinguishes between AY-AY-AY and OY-OY-OY: "To have money is not so AY-AY-AY, but not to have it is OY-OY-OY."

3) AY-AY-AY-AY-AY! This repetitive form, spoken on one normal speech level, is also used by Pennsylvania Germans. But a characteristically Jewish usage puts emphasis on the third syllable, often in sarcasm: AY-AY-*AY*-AY-AY! (Tsk, tsk, *tsk,* tsk, tsk! You don't say!)

AZ HOR VET VAKSN DO . . .

When hair grows here . . . (said with index finger of one hand jabbing at the other palm).

This is a skeptical prediction of when something will get done, *equiv.* "when hell freezes over." In New Haven, Connecticut, a Negro retail salesman often uses it in translation. I'm told he picked it up from a Jewish co-worker.

AZOY?(!)

So?(!) Really?(!) Is that so?(!)

AZOY REDT ZICH! (ironic)

Lit., So it says itself! Nice theory! Theoretically, yes, but . . . !

Also, AZOY ZOGT MEN. So they say.

AZOY VI DU KUKST MIR UN

Just as you look me over; just like that. (of something that happened unexpectedly)

BAY MIR PEYLSTU!

You've got *me* convinced! It's all right with me!

BIM, BUHM

Hasidic tra-la-la-.

The sounds can be very expressive, and some old folk tunes have no words at all beyond the BIM, BUHM. A song in a well-known cantata, "The Seven Golden Buttons," starts with L'KOVED SHABBES BIM, L'KOVED SHABBES BUHM, L'KOVED DEM HEYLIGN SHABBES (In honor of the Sabbath BIM, in honor of the Sabbath BUHM, in honor of the Holy Sabbath) and ends with L'KOVED DEM HEYLIGN BIM BUHM (in honor of the Holy BIM BUHM).

Some big-city disc jockeys have at times slipped into a hybrid humming like "ya-da-BIM-BUHM-ba-ba-BIM-doy."

BLAYBT A KASHE.

It remains a question. We haven't solved it.

BOPKES! (deprecating)

Beans! (A little more sedate than "bull!")

See Char. and Des., ER VEYST FUN BOPKES.

BORCHASHEM (Heb. *Boruch ha-Sheym*)

Praised be the Lord.

See also GOT TSU DANKEN, Chap. I, Concerns about Life and Health.[4]

DAVKE

Precisely for that reason; for spite.

DER REBBE MEG; DER TALMID TOR NISHT! (usually shortened to DER REBBE MEG!)

The rabbi may; the student mustn't! It's okay for a person in authority to break the rules! (Reminiscent of "Do as I tell you, don't do as I do.")

DI RECHENUNG IZ DO, OBER DI GELT IZ NISHT DO.

The reckoning is here, but the money isn't. (wry comment after accounting for "where the money's gone")

DOS HALT MIR IN AMERIKE! (ironic)

This keeps me in America! This is what I call important!

Obviously the product of an immigrant generation (which might at least theoretically consider leaving), the comment is still heard in translation, "This holds me in America!"

DOS IZ . . .?! (ironic)

This is . . .?! This is what you call . . .?!

See Chap. IIIA, Declarative Form in Questions.

DOS IZ O'GEREDT.

Lit., That's talked out. That goes without saying.

DOVOR ACHER (Heb.)

Another thing, another explanation, another matter. (used euphemistically for "pig," "scoundrel")

DU ZOGST MIR! (ironic)

You're telling *me!*

EH!

This little exclamation can convey all kinds of meanings, depending on the intonation and facial expression. There's an old Yiddish story which demonstrates the point. Two men meet, and one asks the other how he is. "EH!" the second man replies lightly (*equiv.*, not bad), "how are you?" "EH!" the first one responds in kind, inquiring further, "How's your wife?" "EH!" (What can you expect?). "How's *your* wife?" "EH!" the first replies in similar tone, adding, "How are your children?" "EH!" (the same old problems); "how are *your* children?" "EH!" (similarly); "how's business?" "EH!" (in disgust); "how's *your* business?" "EH!" (with the effect of FEH! below). Then they both agree, "AY, it's so good to talk out your heart."

This story may have inspired Allan Sherman's comic rendition of the many ways to say "Oh boy."

EPPES

Here's a versatile little word. It's not only a noun, meaning "something," as in TU MIR EPPES (Ann. and Arg.) or EPPES ESSEN (Food and Drink, ESSEN), but it's an expressive particle as in EPPES A BEKANTE—something of an acquaintance—or KUKST OYS NISHT GUT, EPPES—You don't look right, somehow.

It was ironically used in the comic strip *Abbie an' Slats* by Raeburn Van Buren, for a movie producer's name: "Epis Epic."

See Chap. IIIA, "eppis."

ES DACHT ZICH MIR. . . .

It seems to me. . . .

ES KEN ZAYN.

It could be.

ES MACHT NIT OYS.

It doesn't matter.

ES TUT ZICH!

Such doings! Such goings-on!

One night my daughter was calling everyone "tootsie." I couldn't resist the pun, ES TUT ZICH DO! (Such goings-on here!)

VOS TUT ZICH DO (IN HOYZ *or* IN SHTIB)? What's going on here (in the house)?

ETVOS

Just a little.

EYDER (*or* BIZ) ME KRATST ZICH OYS

Before (*or* until) a person scratches himself out—i.e., gets started.

See Advice, NU, KRATS ZICH OYS; Char. and Des., ZEY KRAT-SEN ZICH DORTEN; Chap. IIIB, "KRATS around."

EYN KLEYNEKAYT! (ironic)

Lit., One littleness! A minor matter, indeed!

FAR (*or* IN) A NOVINE

For a change.

FARSHTEYST?

Do you understand?

FARSHTEYSTU MIR *Lit.*, you understand me—a phrase used in mid-sentence, like ". . . , understand," *or* ". . . , you understand, . . ." Dialect stories have often put this ". . . y'unersten' me . . ."

FEH!

Expression of disgust or contempt (probably a combination of EH! and PFUI!)

This has been used on TV.

FOLG MICH A GANG! (ironic)

Lit., Follow me a way! A nice little jaunt! (You won't catch *me* going!)

FREG NISHT!

Don't ask! (You just can't imagine! I can't tell you!)

This used to be rendered "Dunt esk" in dialect stories.

There's an old joke about two men who meet and walk along for several blocks in silence. One finally says, "Why don't you ask me how my family is, how my business is?" The other responds, "NU, so tell me, how is your family, and how is your business?" And the first man replies, "AY, FREG NISHT!"

FUN DER VAYTN

From a distance.

ICH HOB IM LIB FUN DER VAYTN. I love him from a distance, i.e., I prefer him at a distance.

FUN DOS MACHT ER A LEBN?

From that he makes a living?

This is the punch line of several stories. One that was popular during the lifetime of Albert Einstein tells of an elderly Jew who asks his grandson to explain what Einstein's theory of relativity is. The young man tells him that if a beautiful girl sits on your lap, an hour seems like a minute, whereas if you sit on a hot stove, a minute seems like an hour. The old man, dumfounded, strokes his beard and asks, UN FUN DOS MACHT ER A LEBN?[5]

GEFUTZIVET!

Played out! (comment in the card game Twenty-One, when a player's cards total more than twenty-one and he is forced out of the game)

GETROFN!

Right! You got it!

NISHT GETROFN! Wrong! You missed it! You got it wrong! (*See* Resig., NU, IZ NISHT GETROFN.)

PUNKT GETROFN! (often ironic) Exactly right! On the button!

GIB ZICH A RIR!

Bestir yourself! Get a move on!

GICH!

Fast! Hurry!

GICHER! Faster! Speed it up!

GLAT AZOY

Just so; for no special reason.

Also, GLAT IN DER VELT ARAYN *Lit.,* just into the world; "out of the blue."

GUT GEZOGT!

Well said! Well spoken! (often approval of skillful repartee, as in "You said it, boy! You told him!")

G'VALD!

Help! Heavens!

OY, G'VALD (GESHRIGN)! O, help (besought)! This has been adopted by entertainers and crops up in unexpected places. I heard a Gentile salesgirl in a Milford, Connecticut, specialty shop murmuring to herself as she was dressing a window, "Oy, gevawld; every time I carry that manikin, the head falls off."

A lively old song, "G'valdzhe Brider" asks, "Heavens, brothers, why are you sleeping? It's already time for prayers and study! Without them, what good are you in this world, or the next?" In a more solemn vein, the word has been used dramatically in a poem by H. Leivick, "G'vald, Yidden, Zayt Zich Nit Meyaesh" ("G'vald, Jews, You Must Not Despair"), based on the Warsaw ghetto uprising in 1943. There the word is interpreted as meaning Forever.[6]

See Char. and Des., ER SHRAYT G'VALD; Resig., GEY SHRAY G'VALD; Ann. and Arg., KLAP KOP IN VANT UN SHRAY G'VALD!

HENG UN BRENG

Lit., Hang and bring; get it if you have to hang for it; "by hook or by crook."

HOO-HA

Wow! Oh boy!

In the first generation, this conveyed either real or mock admiration, depending on the intonation. In the second generation, it is almost always humorous.

See Chap. IIIA.

ICH VEYS VI AYN UN VI OYS.

I know when to butt in and when to butt out. I know my place.

ICHEL-PICHEL

An exclamation of distaste, a bit lighter in tone than "Ugh!" and containing a certain humorous note. Presumably from ICHEL, a possible variant of IKKEL or EKKEL (nausea)—*see* Chap. IIIA, "ickle." Perhaps also influenced by ICH'L (I will), being a light taking-down-a-peg of a person who is enumerating all he is going to do (*see* Chap. I, beginning of Twin Forms *re.* the deprecating "P").

ICH VIL NIT VISN FUN KEYN CHOCHMES.

I don't want to hear any words of wisdom; i.e., Cut the philosophy, let's have some action; Quit stalling.

IN AMOLIKE TSAYTN

In the olden days.

IN MITN (*or* MITSKE) D'RINEN

In the middle of everything; without so much as a how-do-you-do.

IPSI-PIPSI! (ironic)

Very fancy!

Like the bilingual "fancy-shmancy" (Chap. IIIB), this may have been the poor man's way of criticizing luxury he couldn't afford himself. But it carried the implication that the taste is not the best, and that the lushness is unnecessary. Today it's always used with a smile.

The first half of the term may have developed from HIPSHE. (*See* Char. and Des., A HIPSHE MEYDEL, *and* Chap. I, beginning of Twin Forms, *re.* the deprecating "P.")

KUK NOR UN!

Just take a look at that, will you!

My husband, who came to the United States at the age of five, is reported to have exclaimed at his first sight of snow in Ohio: KUK NOR UN DI VAYSE BLOTTE! (Just look at the white mud!)

See also Chap. IIIA, "Give a look."

KUM AHER!

Come here!

KUM HAYNT, KUM MORGN

Come today, come tomorrow. (of a chronic procrastinator)

L'HAVDIL (Heb.)

If such a comparison were possible; i.e., to distinguish the sacred and profane, "to go from the sublime to the ridiculous."

A well-known Latin equivalent is: *Si parva licet componere magnis* (If one may compare small things with great).

Leo Rosten, in *The Joys of Yiddish* (1968), attributes the term to the end-of-the-Sabbath ceremony, but that is of course HAVDOLE (Rel. and Cul.).

LO'MIR GEYN.

Let's go.

LO'MIR MACHEN NACHT.

Lit., Let's make night. "Let's call it a day."

LO'MIR REDN FUN FREYLICHER ZACHEN.

Let's talk about more cheerful things.

See Chap. IIIA, "So what else is new?"

LO'MIR REDN TACHLIS.

Lit., Let's talk purpose. "Let's get down to cases."

Often heard as, "Let's talk TACHLIS."

See Family, 'SIZ NITO KEYN TACHLIS DORTEN.

MACH SHABBES DERMIT! (sarcastic)

Celebrate the Sabbath with it!

This is said of something you consider inadequate for your purpose. *Equiv.*, "What do you expect me to do with *that*? How far could I get with *that*?" It reflects the special attention given to the Sabbath meal and the Old World Jew's frequent need to "make SHABBES" with limited provender. (*See* Rel. and Cul., SHABBES.)

MAZEL TOV! (Heb. *mazol tōv*, good constellation)

Congratulations! Cause for celebration!

A sign reportedly seen in a Bronx synagogue read: "Mazel

Tov, God is alive and well, visiting hours—every day." (This was apparently in rejoinder to the popular talk about the Christian "God is dead" theology.)

See Chap. IIIA.

ME DARF IM GEBN A KNIPL IN BEKL!

He deserves a fond pinch in his dear cheek! (of someone who merits approval)

ME DARF IM OYSKISHEN BEYDE BAKN (*or* DI BEYNER)!

We should kiss up both his cheeks (*or* his bones)! (delighted approval of a performance)

See also Chap. I, Concerns about Life and Health, A GEZUNT IN DI BEYNER!

ME KEN CHALESHEN!

You can faint (from it)!

ME KEN DERHARGET VEREN!

You can get killed! (No football—understand? You're going to get your diploma in one piece!)

Today the expression is almost always humorous and seems to have inspired the 1966 movie title *A Man Could Get Killed* as well as the novel by Weldon Hill, *A Man Could Get Killed That Way.*

ME LEBT A TOG!

One lives a day! Some fun! (comment on one's own or someone else's enjoyment)

Also, ME LEBT A CHAZERISHEN TOG! One lives a swinish (i.e., carousing) day!

MIDEYE (Heb. *Mi yōdeya*)

Who knows? God knows how.

MISHUGGE!

Crazy! Nuts!

ME KEN MISHUGGE VEREN! You can go out of your mind! It can drive you batty!

See Char. and Des., MISHUGGENER.

NA DIR! (sometimes exasperatedly)

Here you are! Here it is! Take it!

See Chap. I, Special Names.

NEBBECH! (sometimes ironic)

What a pity! 'tis a pity!

See Char. and Des., NEBBECHEL.

NISHKOSHE

Fairly well; not bad.

NISHT GESHTOYGEN, NISHT GEFLOYGEN (*or* NIT GESHTIGEN, NIT GEFLIGEN)

Lit., neither risen nor flown; "without rhyme or reason."

NOCH (ironic)

Yet—as in "NOCH 'pretty' VIL ER!" (Yet "pretty," he wants! —It isn't enough she comes from a good family and has money?)

See Chap. IIIA, "Yet" as Ironic Intensive.

NOCH A BISSEL(E)

A little (bit) more.

NOCH A MOL

Once again.

See Ann. and Arg., NOCH A MOL . . . , UN VIDER A MOL . . . !

NOCH VI!

Lit., Yet how! You bet your life! (probably related to German *und wie*—each having been suggested as a source of the old "And how!")

NU?

Well?

This famous exclamatory question reflects the gregarious character of Jewish existence: someone is always waiting for someone else! Growing impatience makes for NU-NU? and NU-NU-NU? If these don't work, there is NUZHE? (Well, then? Really, now!)

NU is also used before a host of other questions, like NU, VOS ZOGSTU? (Well, what do you say?) and practical statements like NU, IZ NISHT (Resig.).

It may sometimes appear at the end of a statement or question, as in LO'MIR GEYN—NU? (Let's go—huh?) or VI LANG DARF ES NEMEN—NU? (How long does it have to take—anyway?). *Cf.* Chap. IIIA, ". . . no?"

OTADER

This one here.

OY!

Oh my! Alas! etc.

This is the chief ingredient of the YIDDISHE KRECHTS (*see* Tribalism). Alone, or repeated (OY, OY!; OY-OY-OY!; OY-OY-OY-OY-OY! and its variant OY-OY-*OY*-OY-OY!), or combined with other terms (OY G'VALD!; OY GOT!; OY VEY'Z MIR!), it can express all human frustrations and agonies.

It can also have the ironic lightness of "Boy!" or "Oh boy!" as in the story about the poor immigrant Jew who answers the

phone and is asked, "Is this the residence of John D. Rocke-
feller?" He exclaims, "OY, have *you* got the wrong number!"
(This line, by the way, came through in a 1966 movie title,
Boy, Did I Get a Wrong Number.)

Similarly, OY-OY-OY can have the force of the old intensive
"I'll say!" or "and how!" Someone once asked me whether I
(a rabbi's wife) was Jewish. My reply: "OY-OY-OY Jewish!"

OY is apparently used by non-Jewish Russians, for I noticed a
recently translated story by Yevgeni Yevtushenko had the line,
"Oy, comrades! I've found a chicken-god!"

Both OY-OY and OY-OY-OY are used by Gentiles in eastern
Pennsylvania, probably reflecting influence from German as well
as Jewish speech.

See OY VEY IZ MIR!

OY, DAYN SOK HOT MIR BAGROBN!

Oh, my, your fruit jelly has buried me!—i.e., is killing me!

This jokingly places the blame for some problem on a minor
matter which both parties know is not the real cause. The line
is from an old story about a man who sits down to dinner stating
that he is not very hungry but who accepts every item his wife
offers him and even asks for seconds. At the conclusion of the
overeating, his wife brings him a glass of tea and asks whether
he would like in it a teaspoon of SOK (home-made fruit preserves). He debates the question and then decides, okay, he'll
have the SOK. During the night, he wakes up with a belly-ache
and exclaims, OY, BECKY, DAYN SOK HOT MIR BAGROBN!

I'm reminded of this story whenever I see someone packing
away a heavy meal replete with fancy dessert and then asking
for a sugar substitute for the coffee or tea—as though that
extra bit of sugar would matter very much!

OY VEY IZ MIR!

O woe is me!

This is usually contracted to OY VEY'Z MIR!—with emphasis
on either VEY'Z or MIR! It may also be shortened to OY VEY!
or VEY'Z MIR! The term has been heard on TV in various
forms. One pointed use occurred several years ago on *McHale's
Navy,* when a Japanese character expressed dismay with "OY
VEY" and was answered by an American with "Sayonara!" In
the comic strips, *Li'l Abner* once had a character who was a
famous New York artist, ironically named "Troy Vay."

A column in the *Las Vegas Israelite* is named "Oy Veygas."
See also VEY, VEY.

PFUI! (Ger.)

FEH!

This expression of distaste is believed to be the source of "phooey."

See Chap. I, Superstition.

P-S-S-SH!

Tremendous!

Sholem Aleichem, in his "Superlatives in Yiddish," offered the comparison: "Much, more, p-s-s-sh!"

PUNKT FARKERT!

Exactly the opposite! (a genteel form of "ass backwards")

TOMIR FARKERT. Could be just the opposite.

See Char. and Des., MOYSHE KAPOYR.

SHA!

Quiet!

ZOL ZAYN SHA! Let's have it quiet!

SHA, SHA. . . . Quiet, now. . . . (in softer and coaxing tone, as in the effort to quiet a crying baby) or SHA! SHA! Quiet, please! The term was used in a Yiddish Tin Pan Alley offering in the 1920's: "Sha, Sha, di Rébbitzen" (Quiet, Here Comes the Rabbi's Wife).

An older folk song dealing with the way the czar lives tells how he sleeps at night: They fill his bedroom with feathers and throw him into them, and three divisions of soldiers stand outside and yell, "Sha! Sha! Sha!"

My husband designates as "SHA-SHA Jews" those who are supersensitive about their identity and who feel Jews should stay in the background and not be too conspicuous. (*Cf.* "AY-AY Jews" under AY!)

SHA, SHTIL! Be quiet, be still! This too is the title of an old folk song, one which announces that the Hasidic REBBE will be dancing soon.

SHTIP UN SHA! Stuff and hush!—i.e., Eat away and be quiet! (to a talkative child at table)

SHLEP MICH, ICH GEY GEREN!

Pull me, I go willingly! Reminiscent of "He chased her till she caught him."

SHLOF GICHER, ME DARF DI KISHEN!

Sleep faster, we need the pillows! Hence, speed it up—others are waiting!

SH'MA YISROEL! (Heb. *Sh'ma Yisroeyl*) (ironic distress)

Help! (*Lit.*, Hear, O Israel!—from the prayer that begins thus. *See* Rel. and Cul., SH'MA.)

S'HOT ZICH MIR FARGLIST. . . .

I got a hankering for. . . .

'SIZ KEYN MELOCHE NIT.

It's no craft. "There's nothing to it."

'SIZ SHOYN TSAYT!

Lit., It's already time! The time has come! It's about time!

'STAYTSH! (corruption of Ger. *wie heist's auf Deutsch*—How's that in German?)

Really! Imagine that! You don't mean it!

TAKEH

Really, indeed, after all.

This can be either a question or exclamation, or even a simple adverb as in TAKEH GUT—indeed good, good after all. It is often heard in the bilingual "TAKEH fine."

TAP NISHT!

Don't touch!

This well-known warning from Mama stopped the kids from snitching goodies intended for company. When the girls grew up, they found it could good-naturedly stop many a "wolf" who knew Yiddish.

TSHEPPE NIT!

Don't disturb things! Don't monkey with it!

Cf. Char. and Des., TSUTSHEPPENISH.

TU VOS, TUT GOT

Lit., do what, does God; i.e., so God helped even matters up. Hence, to get even.

An old story plays on the literal meaning of the expression by telling of a Jew who complains to a friend about the outrageous rates of a certain hotel and ends with the ironic line, TU VOS, TUT GOT, GANVE ICH A ZILBERNE LEFL (. . . I stole a silver spoon).

UN AN EK . . .

And finally . . .

UN FARTIK!

And finished! *Equiv.*, "And bingo! . . ." as in "He was

stringing her along for years—he couldn't get married because of his sick mother, he had to send his kid brother through school —UN FARTIK! Last week he eloped with his new secretary."

See Chap. IIIA, ". . . and finished!" for ". . . and zoom!"

V'AZOY NEMT MEN DI KATS IBER 'EM YAM?

How do you get the cat over the ocean? (of a situation in which you want to bring together two widely separated things or people, such as a woman in Texas and an eligible man in Canada)

VEY, VEY

My, my!

VI A MUL

It all depends.

VO'DEN? (contraction of VOS and DEN)

What then? What else?

VOS IZ DER YONTEF?

Lit., What's the holiday? What's the occasion? (Why all the fuss?)

VOS-RUFT-MEN-ES

What-do-you-call-it.

VOS TUT MEN?

What to do?

YAVNE VI YASNE!

Verily, forsooth! (ironic comment on the veracity of a statement)

From the Prayerbook Hebrew meaning "True and enduring is Thy word."

YOSHER? (reprimand)

Do you think that's right? (Can you justify it?)

This was asked in a recent letter to the *New York Times* criticizing author Irving Howe for having used, in a *Times* review, text from a book he had co-authored years earlier, without crediting either the source or the other author.

ZOLST MIR ANTSHULDIKEN!

You should excuse me!

This is usually jesting—reminiscent of "beggin' yer pardon" —and has become quite common in translation, developing a number of new forms. *See* Chap. IIIA, "You should excuse me . . ."

Also, ANTSHULDIK MIR! Excuse me!

FAMILY

AGUNE (Heb. *agunah*)

A woman whose husband has disappeared.

The Talmud has detailed discussions of the problems presented for such a woman if she wishes to marry again. (Orthodox divorce requires the husband's consent.) To maintain the stability of marriage, Jewish law asked for *corpus delicti,* or proof of death. James Michener's *The Source* touches on the human difficulties in such a situation, which was the focus of an earlier novel by Michael Blankfort, *The Strong Hand.* Actually, however, the Talmud had its advocates of leniency, and the letter of the law was sometimes relaxed for the sake of the *agunah.*

The mass emigrations to the United States in the early part of this century, when many men went alone with the plan of working and saving enough to send steerage tickets for wife and children, made it easy for some men to shuck off families in the Old Country by never sending what they had promised. Some poignant folk songs of the period portray such behavior.

ALMONE (Heb. *almanah*)

Widow.

One of the most famous of Yiddish lullabies, "Rozhinkes mit Mandlen" (Raisins and Almonds), tells of an ALMONE who must watch over her infant child and whose TSIGILE (little goat) goes out to trade for the family, to sell raisins and almonds. (*See* Food and Drink, MANDLEN.)

ARUMSHLEPPEN

To drag around with, as in going with a fellow with no prospects of marriage: VI LANG VESTU MIT IM ARUMSHLEPPEN? (How long are you going to drag around with him?)

Cf. Chapter IIIA, "shlep."

A SHLECHT VAYB IZ NOCH TOMID GERECHT.

A bad wife is always right, to boot.

See also Passing Judgment, end of introduction, *re.* relationship of man and wife.

A TSULOSTER KIND

A spoiled child; a brat.

A VILDE CHAYE

A wild animal (an undisciplined child):

AZ DER TATTE SHEYNKT DEM ZUN, LACHEN BEYDE—AZ DER
ZUN SHEYNKT DEM TATTEN, VEYNEN BEYDE.

When the father supports the son, both laugh—when the
son supports the father, both cry.

Parental pride about not asking help of children was very
strong. Witness *also:*

ME ZOL NIT DARFN ONKUMEN TSU KINDER (May we not have
to ask help of children) *and*

BESSER AF DI VELT NIT TSU LEBN EYDER ONKUMEN TSU A
KIND (Better not to live than to become dependent on a child).
This was actually a popular Yiddish song.

AZ DI MUTER SHRAYT AFN KIND "MAMZER!" MEG MEN IR
GLOYBN.

When a mother yells "bastard!" at her child, you can believe
her.

Cf. Chap. I, end of Twin Forms, A MAMZER, A GANEF;
Chap. IIIB, "A.M."

BOBBE, BUHBE

Grandma.

See Chap. IIIB, "Bubby" for BOBBE . . .

Grandma was somehow used for a number of ironic or deprecating expressions. *See* Chap. I, Taste, MAYN BOBBE YENTES
TAM; Ann. and Arg., VEN DI BOBBE VOLT GEHAT A BORD . . . ;
Char. and Des., BOBBE MAYSE. Of course BOBBE was also a
mother-in-law, a family member commonly subject to derogation (*see* SHVIGER). The further fact that three generations
often shared the same household—particularly in the first few
years of marriage (*see* KEST)—may have accentuated the situation.

BRUDER

Brother.

See Greetings and Partings, GUTER-BRUDER.

CHASINEH

Wedding.

See SHVER, AZ ME HOT CHASINEH MITN . . . ; Ann. and
Arg., A NAYE CHASINEH!; Char. and Des., GEFOREN TSU DER
CHASINEH UN FARGESN DEM CHOSSEN; Passing Judgment, 'SIZ
NUCH DI CHASINEH.

CHOSSEN

Bridegroom.

ZOL ER ZAYN YUDEL, ZOL ER ZAYN NOSSEN,/ABI A CHOSSEN. Let's have Yudel or Nate, I don't care whom,/As long as he can be a groom!

That may have been how Papa felt, but his MEYDEL-in-waiting had her own bit of rhyme:

ICH VIL NISHT NEMEN/ABI VEMEN. I don't want to take/ Just any old Jake.

On SIMCHES TOYRE (Rel. and Cul.), the man honored by being called up to the Torah to read the concluding portion of Deuteronomy was the CHOSSEN-TOYRE (Bridegroom of the Torah) and the one chosen to read the first portion of Genesis was the CHOSSEN B'REYSHIS (Bridegroom of "In the beginning . . . .").

See Char. and Des., GEFOREN TSU DER CHASINEH UN FARGESN DEM CHOSSEN.

CHOSSEN-KALEH

Bridal couple.

CHOSSEN-KALEH HOBN GLEZERNE OYGN. Bride and groom have glass eyes. ("Love is blind.")

CHOSSENS TSAD UN KALEHS TSAD, MAZEL TOV! Groom's side and bride's side, congratulations!

This was an exuberant point at old-time weddings, at which all the relatives were expected to join in the dance. A large circle of dancers was formed, and those who got the urge would go into the center one or two at a time to do a Russian *kazatske* or a Rumanian and Hungarian *tshardash*. Periodically the outer circle would stop and clap hands in time with the energetic inner-circle performance.

CHUPEH

Wedding canopy.

This is generally used in Orthodox and Conservative wedding ceremonies. A portable cloth covering attached to four poles, it is symbolic of the room in the home of the groom to which, in pre-Talmudic times, the bride was escorted for consummation of the marriage. A modern adaptation is an arch created with tall potted plants aslant on stands.

Sholem Aleichem's comment on a CHUPEH: "You enter it living and you come out a corpse."

Often heard today as "Hupy."

DER KLEYNER (m.), DI KLEYNE (f.)

The little one. The baby.

DI EYER ZAYNEN KLIGER FAR DI HINER. (sarcastic)

The eggs are smarter than the hens. (of children who think they know more than the parents)

ELTERN

Old folks; parents.

Cf. Exclam., AF DER ELTER.

ER HOT A SHTIMME! (*or* A KELLICHEL!)

He's got a voice! (of a child who really lets himself be heard)

ER KVELT.

He's glowing with pride. (what a man does when he has NACHES, which *see*)

ER TIPPET MIT DI FIS.

He's stamping his feet. He's having a tantrum.

EYDIM

Son-in-law.

EYGENER (m.), EYGENE (f. and pl.)

One's own; relative; fellow Jew.

EYGENE, AZ ZEY VEYNEN NIT, FARKRIMEN ZEY ZICH CHOT-SHBE. If your own don't cry with you, at least they screw up their faces. (There are times when it's good to have family.)

EYN KIND IZ AZOY VI EYN OYG.

One child is like one eye.

EYNIKEL (pl. EYNIKLACH)

Grandchild.

See NACHES.

FARZESENEH

A spinster (*lit.,* one who is left sitting).

FETER

Uncle.

FUN DER MUTERS KLOP[1]/VERT DEM KIND NIT KEYN LOCH IN KOP.

A mother's swat when she sees red/Won't give a child a hole in the head (i.e., isn't serious).

GEBENTSHT MIT KINDER

Blessed with children.

GET

Divorce.

The story is told of a couple celebrating their golden wedding anniversary who are asked by a friend, "Tell me, in fifty years of marriage, didn't you ever think of a GET?" The man replies, "MORD (Murder)? Yes! GET? No!"

BAY TOG TSUM GET;/BAY NACHT TSUM BET. By day they're ready for divorce;/By night they're back in bed, of course (the "happy scrappers"). *See* VI TSVEY SHLOFN AF EYN KISHEN, . . .

KALEH (Heb. *kallah*)

Bride.

VEYN ZICH OYS, VESTU VEREN A KALEH. Cry yourself out; you'll become a bride. (to a weeping girl)

This is related to the fact that brides were expected to cry before a wedding—presumably to get rid of past sadness and prepare themselves for the new life ahead. An old custom in Eastern Europe was to play a KALEH BAZETSEN (A Melody for the Bride) before the wedding ceremony, to move her to tears. And the wedding jester aimed at bringing tears as well as laughter to all in attendance. It's been suggested that these tears were symbolic of the Jews' mourning for the ancient temple in Jerusalem.

As noted in Chap. I, the Torah was spoken of as the bride of Israel, and the Sabbath as the SHABBES KALEH, the Sabbath bride. It is intriguing that in the Babylonian exile Jewish communities observed *kallah* months in the spring and late summer, when people stopped work and gathered to be taught by leading rabbis. In line with this tradition is the modern use of the term to designate a study session, often attached to the conferences of American Jewish religious organizations.

See also MEYDEL, KALEH MEYDEL; Ann. and Arg., A CHESOREN, DI KALEH IZ TSU SHEYN!; Char. and Des., OYS KALEH!; Passing Judgment, ALEH KALEHS ZAYNEN SHEYN . . . .

KEST

The period of "keep" (usually at least a year) that a bride's parents gave a bridal couple, who moved right in with her family.

Current parental subsidy of married college students seems like only a modern variation on KEST. (And isn't the young bride working while her husband studies providing a new form of dowry? *See* NADN.)

KESUBE (Heb. *ketubah*)

Marriage contract.

Orthodox and Conservative wedding ceremonies still include this document, which stipulates a certain sum to be paid the woman in case of divorce or the death of her husband. Dating from at least the fifth pre-Christian century, it was intended to protect the woman's rights and was theoretically no longer needed after the eleventh century, when Jewish divorce was forbidden without the wife's consent. But the certificate became an *objet d'art*, appearing in varied shapes and with striking decorations, down to the late nineteenth century. It now usually has mere sentimental value.

A sixteenth-century writer, Israel Nadjara, parodied the KESUBE in a marriage contract between God and Israel.

It's ironic that a supermodern female, Ruth Dickson, author of *Married Men Make the Best Lovers*, advocates a trial marriage of seven years, "with a contract, with options."

KIMPETORN

A woman in labor or newly delivered of a child; hence, one requiring solicitous attention.

English has no counterpart for this word, which conveys a great deal about traditional Jewish family life. One sometimes hears it today in such remarks as "I feel like a KIMPETORN, with everybody fussing over me" or "What's the matter, are you a KIMPETORN or something?"

See Ann. and Arg., DAYN TSUNG IZ EFSHER IN KIMPET?

KISHEN KVETSHER

A cushion squeezer: a suitor who comes and spends the time sitting at home. A "lounge lizard."

Cf. Char. and Des., KVETSH.

KLEYNE KINDER, KLEYNE FREYDN; GROYSE KINDER, GROYSE ZORGN.

Little children, little joys; big children, big worries. Psychoanalyst Theodor Reik noted that a sudden remembrance of his father voicing this proverb about his behavior helped him to live through a certain trying episode as a parent himself!

KLEYNE KINDER TROGT MEN AF DI HENT; GROYSE KINDER AFN KOP. Little children are borne in our arms; big children are weights on our heads.

KLEYNE KINDER LOZN NIT SHLOFN, GROYSE KINDER LOZN NIT LEBN. Little children don't let you sleep; big children don't let you live. (*See* Ann. and Arg., ME LOZT NIT LEBN!)

MAMME

Mother.

Two sentimental songs of the immigrant generation which

can still jerk tears from Yiddish-speaking audiences are "A Brivele der Mammen" (A Letter to Mother) and "Mayn Yiddishe Mamme" (My Jewish Mother).

See Tribalism, YIDDISHE MAMME; Endearment, -ELE, MAMMELE; TATTE-MAMME below.

MAN UN VAYB ZAYNEN EYN LAYB.

Husband and wife are one flesh.

This presumably derives from Genesis 2:24: "They shall be one flesh."

MAYNE KINDER ZAYNEN GOTS VUNDER.

My young ones are God's wonder.

MECHUTEN (m.), MECHUTENESTE (f.), MECHUTONIM (pl.)

Relative by marriage—specifically, parent of son-in-law or daughter-in-law.

English has no parallels for these terms, which reflect the familial character of traditional Jewish life. I think it was Sam Levenson who dubbed these relatives "the Loyal Opposition." In the United States, the word MECHUTONIM is sometimes loosely used for "in-laws," and the breezy MECHUTS or MECHUTZ may be a short form for it or for the singular forms, as in "My MECHUTS are (*or* "My MECHUTZ is) coming tomorrow."

MEYDEL

Girl.

KALEH MEYDEL Marriageable young lady.

VU KUMT ER TSU AZA MEYDEL? *Lit.*, Where does he come to such a girl?—i.e., How does he rate such a girl? (The idiom sometimes comes through in American Jewish speech: "How does he come to her?")

Cf. Char. and Des., MOYD.

MISHPOCHE

Relatives, family, clan.

A small group of Jewish students at Arizona Western College reportedly calls itself "The Mishpoche Club." To counter advertising of New York's Chase Manhattan Bank, which announces "You have a friend at Chase-Manhattan," a teller at the Israel Discount Bank several years ago began saying, "At the Israel Bank you're MISHPOCHE." Now the same bank has advertised itself in *Commentary* (March 1969) as "the bank you feel related to."

Sid Caesar once played on the term in a TV spoof of a Japanese film, dubbing a twelfth-century warrior "Gantse Mishpuchah." (The warrior's betrothed was "Shmatsay." *See* Char. and Des., SHMATTE.)

MIZINKE

Youngest daughter ("little finger").

The marriage of the MIZINKE occasioned great joy, expressed in the gay folk song "Di Mizinke Oysgegebn" ("The Youngest Daughter Married Off"). This represented a lightening of parental worries, since daughters were customarily married off chronologically (as the Biblical Jacob discovered the hard way!). An old folk-observation is that when a mother has married off all her daughters, she may sit with her arms folded: i.e., her chief job has been accomplished.

The youngest son is a MIZINIK.

NACHES

Joyous satisfaction and pleasure, usually derived from family.

KLOYBN NACHES To gather joy.

SHEPN NACHES To draw pleasure.

NACHES FUN KINDER Joyous satisfaction from children.

A New York Reform rabbi has established a "NACHES Fund" to supply camp scholarships, for which he encourages contributions to honor any NACHES-producing events such as the birth of a grandchild. (*See also* SIMCHA.) On New York's Yiddish radio station, common acknowledgments of a listener's contribution are: IR ZOLT HOBN NACHES FUN AYERE KINDER UN AYERE EYNIKLACH (May you have pleasure from your children and your grandchildren) and ZOLT IR LEBN BIZ AYER UR-EYNIKELS BAR MITZVE (May you live till your great-grandchild's Bar Mitzvah).

A reverse twist was reported recently in the *London Jewish Chronicle*: a Bar Mitzvah boy responding to a toast at the festivities stated, "I don't know much Yiddish, but I know two words, TSORES[2] and NACHES. TSORES is what you get from parents—NACHES is what you get from grandparents."

NADN (Heb. *nadan*)

Dowry.

Sam Levenson calls this "matri-money."

See PERINEH.

NOR A SHTEYN/ZOL ZAYN ALEYN.

Only a stone/Should be alone. Everyone needs a family.

PERINEH.

Featherbed, customarily part of the NADN.

My parents' PERINEH was two large pillows. These were so well stuffed, they were later converted into a half-dozen normal size pillows, which are still being used by children and grandchildren.

PLEMENIK

Nephew.

PLEMENITSE   Niece.

SHADCHEN (pl. SHADCHONIM)

Matchmaker, marriage broker.

According to Sholem Aleichem, this gentleman was "a dealer in livestock." There are many old tales about how he plied his trade. In one such story, the SHADCHEN approaches a young man to tell him he has a beautiful girl for him, and the young man says he isn't interested. "Well," the SHADCHEN continues, "if you're not interested in looks, I can give you a girl with money." "Don't bother me" is the reply. Undaunted, the SHADCHEN says, "Look, I can give you a girl with a dowry of twenty thousand rubles." The prospect replies, "I don't care about money." "NU, if you don't care about looks or money, you must want a girl with YICHES. I can give you one who's descended from generations of rabbis." Exasperated, the young man explodes, "Look. When I marry, it's going to be for love and nothing else." "Oh," says the SHADCHEN, "why didn't you say so? If it's love you want, I've got that kind too!"

The SHADCHEN was once an institution in Jewish life, and the effectiveness of his talents is reflected in the old folk-saying, A GUTER SHADCHEN KEN TSUNOYF-BRENGEN A VANT MIT A VANT. (A good matchmaker can bring two walls together.) Today, he has been largely replaced by co-ed campuses, student tours and causes, discotheques and computers—to say nothing of resort hotels and cruises for older eligibles.

More common today is the SHADCHENTE, any female with an amateur instinct for bringing unattached (not to say "loose") people together. When she has the knack, such a female may be indulgently dubbed by her husband, "My SHADCHENTE." In New York, in recent years, one such single female went into the business and snagged the first catch (a dentist) for herself.

According to an old Yiddish song, Moses was the SHADCHEN for the match between the Torah and the poor little Jew (*see* Chap. I, Famil. with God).

SHADCHEN is sometimes punned on with "shot-gun." It's

been in Webster's dictionary for years, spelled "Schatchen." (The Third Edition now also gives "Shadchan.")

SHIDDUCH (pl. SHIDDUCHIM)

A match, a betrothal.

A SHEYNE SHIDDUCH   A beautiful match.

FUN KRUME SHIDDUCHIM KUMEN AROYS GLAYCHE KINDER. *Lit.*, From crooked matches come out straight children. Bad matches beget good children. This seems contrary to modern belief that a happy relationship between parents produces the best children. Yet perhaps our modern theories don't take cognizance of the fact that a good relationship between the parents does not necessarily mean good handling of children. Some husbands and wives make good lovers, providers and housekeepers, but poor parents; whereas some who are not as well attuned to each other or to their work do a conscientious job of parenthood. Since Jewish life emphasized the home and family, perhaps the effort expended on the children was even greater in those cases where the parents were less than well matched. (But what, after all, is a "bad match"? People often choose— and presumably enjoy—life partners whose appeal outsiders don't appreciate: "What did he ever see in her?")

However, we might interpret the statement somewhat differently. KRUME here may mean "dissimilar," suggesting that the resulting variety in the home contributes to the children's growth. Indeed, the proverb may lend support to the notion that "opposites attract," implying that even though the backgrounds and personalities may not be similar there can be a strong bond in the family and a successful rearing of children.

SHNUR

Daughter-in-law.

As Maurice Samuel is fond of pointing out, the intonation of this term might depend greatly on the character of the daughter-in-law. DEM REBBENS SHNUR (the rabbi's daughter-in-law) could convey all of the respect and admiration associated with the REBBE himself, or else a gentle mocking of the young woman who might take her status a bit too seriously.[3]

DI TOCHTER SHTROFT MEN, DI SHNUR MEYNT MEN. You rebuke the daughter but mean the daughter-in-law. (used with reference to any situation of indirect criticism or "displaced aggression")

SHVEGERIN

Sister-in-law.

SHVER

Father-in-law.

Is it so SHVER (hard) to be a SHVER? In Yiddish the two words are alike.

AZ ME HOT CHASINEH MITN SHVER,/SHLOFT MEN MITN BER. If your father-in-law you wed,/A bear shares your bed. This reflects the prohibition against marriage between a father and his son's widow which appears in Leviticus, among other proscribed unions.

SHVESTER

Sister.

SHVESTERKIND

Cousin.

SHVIGER

Mother-in-law.

The poor mother-in-law has been the butt of ironic jokes in Yiddish as much as in English. An old conundrum asks why Adam, the first man, lived as long as he did, and the answer is: Because he didn't have a SHVIGER. Sholem Aleichem noted that for that reason Adam was "the only happy man."

Sam Levenson calls a SHVIGER "John's Other Wife." She's also been defined as "another mouth to heed." The old-time daughter-in-law put *her* gripes in rhyme: GEY ICH GICH, RAYS ICH DI SHICH;/GEY ICH PAMELECH, ZOGT ZI ICH KRICH (If I go fast, my shoes won't last;/If I slow my pace, she says I'll never win a race).

SHVITSER

Perspirer (humorous term for a suitor).

DI SHVITSERS ZAYNEN DO (The perspirers are here) was my father's announcement that my sisters' boyfriends had arrived! *See* Char. and Des., FARSHVITST.

SIMCHA

Celebration.

Some Jewish women's organizations have a "SIMCHA Fund," to which donations are made to commemorate happy occasions like birthdays, weddings, anniversaries, etc. The funds are used for worthy social causes.

The term has been used a good deal in advertising in American Jewish periodicals, as by the Yuban company, which calls its product the "Simcha Coffee," or the Black and White Scotch makers, who ask: "So why wait for a Simcha?"

See Passing Judgment, VOS KLENER DER OYLEM, ALTS GRESSER DI SIMCHA.

'SIZ NIT MIT VEMEN TSU GEYN TSUM TISH.

It isn't a person you would want to sit down to dinner with, or whom you can converse with; there's no breeding there. (of a prospective suitor)

'SIZ NITO KEYN TACHLIS DORTEN.

Lit., There's no basis for negotiation there. There's nothing worth considering. (mother judging a marital prospect for her daughter, or man appraising a business proposition)

Often heard today as: "There's no TACHLIS there."

See Exclam., LO'MIR REDN TACHLIS.

TATTE

Father, papa, dad.

See Endearment, -ELE, *re.* TATTELE; -ENYU *re.* TATTENYU; Char. and Des., SHMATTE; TATTE-MAMME below.

TATTE-MAMME

Parents.

Though Yiddish has formal terms for father and mother, FOTER and MUTER, these are bypassed in favor of the more intimate TATTE-MAMME for parents.

TOCHTER

Daughter.

See Endearment, TOCHTEREL.

TSVILLING

Twin.

VAKST A MENTSH!

You're becoming a person! (approval of a child who exhibits gratifying signs of growing up right)

VI TSVEY SHLOFN AF EYN KISHEN,/DARF DER DRITTER NIT MISHEN.

When two who argue share a bed,/Don't butt into what is said. (Marital squabbles are unpredictable—as already observed.)

YINGEL

Boy

See Endearment, YINGELE MAYNS . . . ; Chap. IV., *re.* displacement by "boy."[4]

ZEYDE

Grandpa, grandfather, or—as one comic defines it—"grand-child's press agent."

See Passing Judgment, VER IZ GEVEN ZAYN ZEYDE?; Chap. I, Twin Forms, DER ZEYDE, SAVA.[5]

ZUN

Son.

See Endearment, ZUNELE (MAYNS).

FOOD AND DRINK

Jewish food has a certain pull. As Herman Wouk amusingly demonstrated in *Marjorie Morningstar*, there are Jews who are completely divorced from Jewish religious or community life but who cannot live without their kosher corned beef and pickles. (These are the type that American rabbis have been berating for years as "gastronomic Jews.") It is intriguing that two of the warmest literary evocations of Jewish cooking were written in German by converts to Christianity—Moritz G. Saphir and Heinrich Heine.

Indeed, Heine, in discussing the merits of *schalet*, or TSHOLNT, expressed regret that "the Christian Church, which borrowed so much that was good from ancient Judaism, should have failed to adopt *schalet* as its own." If the Church does this, he suggested, ". . . the Jews, at the very least, will adopt Christianity out of conviction . . . because, as I clearly see it, it is *schalet* alone which holds them together in their old faith." But he ironically added the comment of a Jewish friend, that "no sooner will the renegades who go over to the new faith get a whiff of *schalet* than they'll begin to feel homesick again for the synagogue"!

Saphir drooled over this same dish, spelling it *scholet*—and noting that Heine's spelling of *schalet* was perhaps due to the latter's having exclaimed on eating it, "Ah!" whereas he himself called out "Oh!" Neither one of these men, however, could match the earthy compliment on a soup offered by the Dutch Jewish writer Hermann Heijermans: "It's just as if a little angel had pissed on your tongue!"

In the United States, comedians like Eddie Cantor, Sam Levenson and Buddy Hackett have poked nostalgic fun at the Jewish road to heartburn (Cantor once said he wished Jewish food could give you "instant" heartburn instead of at two o'clock in the morning), and they have actually followed in the tradition of Jewish literary humor. Sholem Aleichem offered the comparison of "fat, fatter, KUGEL," and Saphir referred to KUGEL as a cannonball (the latter term having since been ascribed to a matzo ball).

Some so-called Jewish dishes were of course originally Russian or German, Hungarian or what-have-you. Wherever they lived, the Jews picked up culinary ideas, and they spread around their own versions of the adopted foods every time they moved. If there is any real "melting pot" in the United States, it is the pot on the stove of a Jewish housewife! She was raised on a pot-pourri of dishes originating in many countries and retains that cosmopolitan taste.[1]

The variety of VERTLECH and VITSN—aphorisms and witticisms—dealing with food, both here and under other categories,[2] reflects the importance of food in the life of the average Jew. This may be partly due to some "oral" fixation, as some have suggested. But it would seem to be, more practically, a sign of the uncertain economic conditions under which Eastern European Jewry lived, in which the presence or absence of food was a constant concern.

It should be remembered too that food plays an important part in Jewish religious culture. The whole system of kashruth (Rel. and Cul., KASHRES) called for awareness of how meat or poultry was slaughtered and of whether a fish had scales and fins or an animal had cloven hoofs besides chewing the cud (only such could be eaten). The separation of milk and meat foods involved a great consciousness about what was being eaten and when: one had to wait six hours after eating meat before partaking of dairy products. And different dishes, pots and utensils were used for milk and meat dishes, with completely different ones for milk and meat during Passover. In addition, there was an impetus from the nature of family Sabbaths and holidays, on which special foods would be prepared, or—on fast days—when all food would be withheld.

The doting Jewish mother who plied her offspring with food has been the butt of Jewish jokes for years, from Milt Gross's caricature of over a generation ago, "Nize Baby, Eat Anodder Piece Baldvin Hepple," to the modern pun on the famous line ESS, ESS, MAYN KIND (Eat, Eat, My Child) which appears in the name of an imaginary new Israeli vessel, "s.s. MAYN KIND."

The average Jew does like to eat and considers himself a MEYVEN[3] of good food and of various matters connected with it. Peruse the following and see whether he doesn't have good reason!

AF YENEMS SIMCHA HOT MEN TOMID A GUTN APETIT.

At someone else's party you always eat with gusto.

A HUN IZ GUT TSUM ESSEN ZALBENAND: ICH UN DOS HUN.

A chicken makes good eating for two: me and the chicken.

Cf. Passing Judgment, AZ AN OREMAN EST A HUN. . . .

A KRANKN FREGT MEN; A GEZUNTN GIT MEN.

A sick man, you ask; a healthy one, you serve. (reply to someone who asks whether to bring out the food)

This is less officious than it sounds, being usually said with a smile by the husband of the inquiring hostess. It's so well-known, the second half is often left unspoken.

ALEH GUTTE ZACHEN!

All good things! (of an attractively spread table)

AYNGEMACHTS

A general term for all kinds of home-made jams and relishes. Two popular Passover varieties used minced beets or radishes boiled with honey and sugar.

Miss Esther Sakolski of Riegelsville, Pennsylvania, sister of the late economist-author Aaron M. Sakolski and descendant of the famous Rabbi Yom Tov Lipman Heller, sixteenth- and seventeenth-century commentator on the Mishnah, is known to her great- and great-great-nieces and -nephews as "Auntie AYNGEMACHTS" because she remembers them yearly at Passover with jars of this home-made treat! (Her recipe calls for beets and crushed pineapple.)

AZ ME LEYGT ARAYN, NEMT MEN AROYS.

Lit., When you put in, you take out; i.e., If the ingredients are good, how can the results be bad?

This reminds me, in a reverse way, of a story my father liked to tell: A poor man heard about a wonderful dessert, torte, that the rich enjoyed, and asked his wife to make him some. "But for torte I need eggs," said his wife, "and I have none." "NU, so make it without eggs." "But for torte I also need nuts, and I have none." "So make it without nuts," he countered. "Use whatever you have, but please make me some torte." His wife dutifully did what she could with the limited ingredients she had available. When she served the result to her husband, he took a bite and looked very puzzled. "You know," he said, "I think the rich don't know what good eating is. How can they make such a fuss about torte?"

BEBLECH

Beans. (a smaller variety than BOPKES—*see* Exclam., BOPKES!)

BEKERAY

Bakery; baked goods.

See Char. and Des., "-AY."

BEYGEL

A very hard, doughnut-shaped roll, for which the dough is first boiled and then baked. No wonder it's been described as a "concrete doughnut" or "a doughnut dipped in cement"! It can of course be softened by warming in the oven and is fine that way or sliced and toasted, though it's often eaten just as it comes. It's classically served with lox (smoked salmon) and cream cheese—making a combination that Kraft's Philadelphia Cream Cheese heralds as "Pure LOXury."

The Yiddish word, by the way, is the same in the plural as in the singular. This explains why the concoction is often spoken of as "lox and bagel" rather than "lox and bagels." The force of the phrase was strikingly demonstrated a couple of years ago by a two-and-a-half-year-old Philadelphia girl. Her mother had been introducing her to the traditional children's stories and got her two goldfish, which they named "Goldie" and "Locks" in honor of the heroine of "The Three Bears." When her grandfather arrived and asked the little girl the names of her fish, she unexpectedly replied, "Lox and Bagel"! She may have been partly influenced by TV children's cartoons. I heard one cartoon villain say, "I'll go disguised as Sir Lox and Bagel."

Time was when only Jewish groceries sold bagels. Today they're seen in supermarkets across the country, and many a Gentile has succumbed to their appeal, sometimes even at church suppers. To meet their widening popularity, at least two household aids have been marketed: a bagel and lox platter (which I saw in a suburban Massachusetts home), containing two wooden spires for holding the bagels and marked sections for lox, cream cheese and tomatoes; and a "Safety Bagel Holder," which a New York department store offered with pertinent advice: "Don't cut the Hand that Feeds You." A "Biography of a Bagel," addressed to neophytes, appears on the plastic bags of various brands, suggesting a variety of intercultural recipes: "Pizza Bagel," "Grilled Cheese and Tomato on Bagel," "Toasted Garlic Bagels," etc. And in Venice, California, in recent years, a beatnik hangout called itself "The Existentialist Bagel Shop." (As a Newark, New Jersey, reporter commented, "What zen?")

This acceptance by non-Jews is the basis of a current "inside" quip: a Gentile woman remarks to a Jewish friend: "I just love bagel and lox. But tell me, which is the bagel and which is the lox?"

The vogue of the bagel has other intriguing aspects. Many a young mother has discovered that a bagel makes a fine teething ring, and in the field of jewelry a tiny gold bagel has appeared for charm bracelets. In Connecticut, the famous Lender's Bagel Bakery (and its snack shop, the "Bagel Board") not only offers a year-round variety of flavors like onion, pumpernickel, sesame, etc., as well as a tiny cocktail size, but once a year it comes out with green bagels for St. Patrick's Day. As though this were not enough, out in Illinois painted bagels have been used as decorations for Christmas trees!

In Jewish folklore, the question was asked, "How do you make a bagel?" and the logical reply was, "You take a hole, and put some dough around it." But this wasn't easy for the man who made bagels for a living. One such couldn't sleep at night, moaning to his wife that costs were going up and it took a lot of dough to go around the bagel's hole. "Well," his spouse replied, "then why not make the hole bigger?" "Oy!" he countered. "If you make the hole bigger, it takes even more dough to go around it!"

Another old question, which may have occurred to you, too: "Why is it called a bagel?" Reply: "Because it has a hole in the middle." "But why does it have a hole in the middle?" "Because without the hole it wouldn't be a bagel."[4]

But where did the bagel come from? This query has been dealt with by a number of light-hearted "scholars" both here and abroad. The first mock dissertation I know of, by E. I. Ginsberg, appeared in a South African quarterly and was reprinted here in the *Jewish Digest* in 1963. According to Ginsberg, a Jewish baker in the time of good King Sobieski of

Poland (seventeenth century)[5] devised the bagel for the billiards-loving Count Baigel, as a handy food that could be kept on a cue stick and bitten at while he was pursuing his favorite sport. (This is reminiscent of the popular history of the sandwich. See MOROR.)

Israel's El Al Airlines meanwhile got out a humorous booklet, "El Al Looks into the Bagel" (with a cover picture of a pilot holding a bagel lorgnette).[6] This too suggested the time of King Sobieski, noting that when that monarch entered Vienna after liberating the city from the Turks, the grateful citizens clung to his stirrups, and that "bagel" is a corruption of the German word for stirrups, *Boegel!* After Horace Sutton's travel column in the *Saturday Review* quoted from this booklet in 1964, a number of SR readers were inspired to offer their own pseudo-academic histories.

Wherever it came from, the bagel is clearly going places. Not only is it flown regularly to the new Lindy's East restaurant in Hong Kong, but before the Pope left for home on his American visit in 1965, he was sent a gift of bagels and lox by a New York delicatessen. Although *Esquire* magazine chose to nominate this deli proprietor for a CHUTZPA award, I assume that the Pope— and numerous readers—had a greater appreciation, both spiritual and gustatory, of this complimentary gesture. And many, I am sure, would take to their bosom the good-humored Yiddish description of a down-and-outer, ER BAKT BEYGEL (He's baking bagels—a process once carried on in cellars).[7]

As a matter of fact, the bagel may even be reaching other planets. I'm told that a Martian recently landed his flying saucer on earth, with a flat tire. He saw a Jewish delicatessen with bagels in the window and decided they were just the right size so he went into the store and asked for "a few of those tires." The proprietor told him to try eating one. He took a bite, smiled and said, "You know, they're good; they ought to be delicious with lox!"[8]

See LAKS; Char. and Des., ER IZ IM SHULDIK DI LOCH FUN A BEYGEL; Chap. IIIA, "bagel."

BLETL (pl. BLETLACH)

Thin leaf of dough used in making BLINTZES.

The batter is poured on a hot, lightly buttered frying pan and immediately poured off. The remaining thin coating is fried slightly and then knocked out of the pan onto a clean towel, there being allowed to cool and later being filled with cheese and fried.

A food column in my local newspaper in 1966 featured blintzes and noted that the leaves are easier to make on tefloncoated pans. I haven't tested the advice, but in the picture the BLETLACH looked thicker than the authentic product should be. As any BLINTZES-MEYVEN can tell you, the lightness of the BLETL has a lot to do with the relative degree of delectableness achieved.

As with English "leaf," the word has other meanings: a tree leaf, or a page of writing as in Peretz's *Yontef Bletlach* (*Holiday Leaves*).

BLINTZES (sometimes half-affectionately, MLINTZES)

A classic dish, made by putting a spoonful of cottage cheese (mixed with egg yolk and seasoning—some use salt, some sugar) onto the fried side of a BLETL, tucking in the sides of the dough, and rolling. These finished rolls are fried quickly in butter or margarine and served with sour cream and/or jelly. They're especially good with blueberry preserves. According to Harry Golden, the reason that Nelson Rockefeller won over Averill Harriman in the New York governor's race in 1958 is that Rockefeller showed a better appreciation of blintzes and sour cream during Lower East Side campaigning! (A recent analysis of New York voting habits, however, notes that such ethnic appeals no longer carry weight among Jews.)

A number of Reform rabbis have fond memories of a Negro waiter at their seminary dormitory in Cincinnati who used to ask, "You-all want some more blisters at this table?"

BLINTZES are associated with the Shevuoth holiday (*see* Rel. and Cul., SHVUES), but are popular at any time, particularly in warm weather, often after BORSHT. They're available in supermarket freezer cabinets, but the frozen product is a far cry from the real thing, despite enthusiastic advertising (*see* Chap. IIIA, end of "nosh").

BOB

A large dark bean, cooked and served cold as a snack. Like NAHIT, traditionally served at a PIDYENABEN (Rel. and Cul.). BOB was a NASH of Lithuanian Jews; NAHIT, of Russian Jews.

BOKSER

These hard brown fruits known as "St. John's bread" are

customarily served on CHAMISHO OSER B'SHVAT (Rel. and Cul.), along with other typical Holy Land fruits like figs, dates, etc.

BORSHT

A cold soup, usually of grated red beets, flavored sweet and sour, and FARVAYST (whitened) with egg yolk. Served with sour cream and boiled potatoes, often also with diced cucumbers and/or onion and chunks of hard-boiled egg. (I think it was comedian Eddie Cantor who once gave this description of his favorite dream: the Atlantic Ocean was a sea of borsht and planes were flying over it, dropping down hunks of boiled potato!)

Other varieties are spinach borsht, known as STSHAV, and hot cabbage borsht, made with meat, cabbage, tomatoes and other vegetables.

The dish derives from the Russian *borshch*, cow parsnip, having originally been made from that vegetable. This may help account for the occasionally used spellings of "bortsch" or "borshch." But the commonly seen "borscht" seems to reflect a German influence and was a pet peeve of the famous A. A. Roback, who felt that anyone who recognized Yiddish as a full-fledged language should feel no need to insert the German "c" in the "sh" sound.

It is said that there was once a Russian czar who drank so much soup he nearly BORSHT.

See Char. and Des., BILLIG VI BORSHT; Passing Judgment, MIT EYN EY KEN MEN A GANTSE SHISL BORSHT FARVAYSEN; Chap. IIIB, "not to know from BORSHT."

Cf. ROSSEL.

BROMFN

Brandy.

GOT IZ GOT, UN BROMFN IZ BROMFN. God is God, and brandy is brandy.

See also Chap. I, Learning, *"Odom yessodo mey'ofor vey'sofo ley'ofor"*—BEYNE-LE-BEYNE IZ GUT A TRUNK BROMFN.

In spite of such earthy defenses of drink, Jews had relatively little alcoholism. They were accustomed from childhood to the drinking of wine for the Sabbath KIDDUSH and the Passover SEYDER (Rel. and Cul.), and the men would often have a SHNAPS at SHUL on cold winter mornings. (The small places of worship of course had limited heating, and it was difficult to warm them up in time for early-morning services.) Today, when Bar Mitzvah celebrations are held in the social halls of synagogue buildings after the religious service, liquor is frequently served. This may seem shocking to some Christians, but it bespeaks the informality that Jews have always shown in SHUL—even at worship. In Judaism, there are no theological intermediaries between the individual and God as there are in Christianity—no parallel figures for Jesus or Mary; and the fact that most men could read Hebrew for themselves meant that they were not dependent on the pulpit leader either. (*See* Rel. and Cul., MINYEN.)

The fact too that the synagogue was more than a place of worship—being used regularly for study and for a place of meeting—contributed to the informality. Above all, if a people felt enough at home with God to argue with Him, they would also feel at home in His sanctuary and its environs!

This may even help to explain a phenomenon that bothers some American Jews: the tendency of Jewish comedians to joke about Jewish religious holidays and customs. This kind of thing is really "in-group" humor, but the practitioners of the craft are bringing their Catskill Mountain routines into "all-American" living rooms, with nary a thought for the preparedness of their listeners and what the material may mean to them.

BULBE

Potato.

An old folk song attests to the ever-present BULBE in the poor Jew's diet: BROYT MIT BULBE, FLEYSH MIT BULBE . . . HAYNT UN MORGN BULBE . . . OBER SHABBES NUCHN TSHOLNT A BULBE KUGELE, ZUNTIK VAYTER BULBE (Bread with potato, meat with potato . . . today and tomorrow potato . . . but on the Sabbath after the TSHOLNT, a little potato KUGEL, Sunday potato again).

BULKE

Roll.

BUREKES

Beets.

CHALLE

Sabbath and holiday bread.

The Sabbath loaf is oval-shaped, with a braided top. The CHALLE used for the New Year is round. It is not braided but has a border of dough which circles inward and upward to the top center.

These breads used to be baked at home. Some women still make their own—the general press carried a recipe for Rosh Hashono CHALLE in the fall of 1966—but in many areas it is available (in varying quality) in supermarkets. Big-city Jewish bake shops of course have an excellent version. It's usually spelled "Challa" or "Halla," from which has come the mongrel "Holly." (*See* Chap. IIIB, "Holly" for CHALLE.)

CHAREYSHIS (Heb. *charōshes*)

One of the symbolic foods of the Passover seder: a mixture of chopped nuts and apple, seasoned with sugar, grated lemon rind and wine.

This commemorates the mortar worked into bricks by the Israelites when they were slaves in ancient Egypt.

See MOROR.

CHAZER (pl. CHAZERIM)

Pig, hog, swine.

The chief forbidden food, this gave rise to a variety of figurative uses. *See* Chap. I, Realism, AZ ME EST CHAZER . . . ; Advice, ES PAST VI A CHAZER (under ES PAST SHOYN GORNIT); ZAY NIT KEYN CHAZER *and* VILST ZAYN RAYCH? ZAY ZIBN YOR A CHAZER; Ann. and Arg., FARMACH DAYN (CHAZERISHEN) PISK!; Char. and Des., ER HOT AZOY FIL GELT, VI A YID CHAZERIM; ER HOT ZEY FAYNT, VI A YID HOT FAYNT CHAZER; ES FIT IR, VI A CHAZER A ZOTL; CHAZERAY (under -AY); CHAZERISH; *and* ZEY VOYNEN VI CHAZERIM; Endearment, CHAZEREVITSH (under -EVITSH); Exclam., ME LEBT A CHAZERISHEN TOG! (under ME LEBT A TOG!); Passing Judgment, DI KRO FLIT HEYACH UN ZETST ZICH AF A CHAZER; FUN A CHAZERS EK, KEN MEN KEYN SHTRAYMEL NIT MACHEN; *and* CHAZER KOSHER FISSEL.

See also Exclam., DOVOR ACHER.

CHOMETS (adj. CHOMETSDIK)

Food containing leaven, which is not PEYSACHDIK (which *see*).

A current quip terms the end of Passover, when one gets back to eating bread and other CHOMETS, "home free."

CHREMZLACH

Fried pancakes or baked squares, made of eggs, water, matzo meal and seasoning—sometimes served with meat and gravy, sometimes with jelly or powdered sugar.

See also LATKES.

CHREYN

Grated horseradish, flavored with beet liquid. Served with GEFILTE FISH or FLANKEN.

The Buitoni Company has been advertising "Italian Chrain," which is its canned Marinara Sauce, and which we are told makes a dip for gefilte fish which "never makes your eyes water." Obviously, such a pale substitute is not what comedian Buddy Hackett was referring to on TV when he described the procedure of making "huhreyn," which he indicated "clears out your nose, clears out your ears, clears out your navel."[9] The making of CHREYN is a procedure associated with the old-time Passover. Not only was the fresh horseradish grated by hand, but the beet flavoring came from a crock of beets that had been put up before Passover for making BORSHT. Today, of course, it's easier to buy CHREYN ready-made in a jar, with the kosher-for-Passover sticker on it if you wish, and BORSHT, as already noted, comes in jars as well. (What memories the third and fourth generations have missed!)

COMPOT

Compote—a stew of mixed dried fruits.

This is a traditional dessert for holiday meals, especially during Passover. (It's actually a very realistic corrective for the binding effect of matzo.)

Also, fig., life's portion. *See* Chap. I, Famil. with God, OY, GOT, FARZICH MAYN COMPÔT. . . .

COTLETN (from French *côtelettes,* source also of "cutlet")

Meat patties. Kosher hamburgers.

DRELYES *See* P'TSHA.

ES *DARF* ZAYN GUT! EYB 'SIZ NIT GUT, VEL ICH DIR LOZN VISN.

It's *supposed* to be good! If it isn't good, I'll let you know. (Papa's explanation of why he didn't compliment his wife's or daughters' cooking)

Cf. comment under ZUP.

ESSEN

To eat; eating; food.

EPPES ESSEN Something to eat. (I know of at least two delicatessen restaurants with this name: one in Florida, one in Indiana.)

ES LOZT ZICH ESSEN! *Lit.,* It lets itself be eaten! It's so tasty!

ESSEN TEG Eating days. The Old World seminary student's system of being fed by different families various days of the week. Most such students were destitute, and the families pro-

viding them with meals considered it an honor to do so—
though they often had hardly enough for themselves. A touching
story with this title by Lamed Shapiro depicts the human elements in such situations. (*Cf.* Char. and Des., YESHIVE
BOCHER.)

GOYISHE ESSEN Gentile food; food that is unappealing to
the Jewish palate. Ex.: pig's feet, scrapple, chipped beef, etc.

GROBE ESSEN Coarse food; peasant fare.

'SIZ GUTTE ESSEN! It's good eating!

VAYBISHE ESSEN Women's food; "tea-room stuff" (my husband's opinion of Schrafft's, or of a fruit-salad-and-cottage-
cheese platter, or anything creamed on toast!)

Cf. FRESSER.

ESSIK FLEYSH

Lit., acid or vinegar meat. A sweet-and-sour pot roast.

A popular Jewish cookbook calls for lemon juice, brown
sugar and crushed gingersnaps, but these ingredients are probably a little different from those my BOBBE used!

ES TSUGEYT IN MOYL!

It melts in your mouth!

EYDER FAR ZIBITSIK YOR SHTARBN, IZ BESSER ESSEN . . . .

Rather than die before seventy, it's better to eat . . . (whatever is being served).

This is an ironic compliment on food, offered with a smile.

See also: EYDER TSU SHTARBN FUN HUNGER . . . .

EYDER TSU SHTARBN FUN HUNGER, IZ SHOYN BESSER TSU ESSEN
GEBROTNS.

Rather than die of hunger, it's much better to eat a roast.

EYELE (pl. EYELACH)

Little egg—the undeveloped egg found in the chicken when
Mama pulled out the internal organs.

This little egg yolk was usually cooked in the chicken soup,
and the children would vie for the award.

FARBAYSEN

Lit., after-biting. Dessert.

FARFEL

Bits of rice-like noodle, served as a vegetable.

MATZO FARFEL Bits of matzo, sprinkled into soup.

FARKLOPT

Heavy (what KNEYDLACH should *not* be; the opposite of
LAYCHT VI A FIDDER—light as a feather).

FLAKE-ITA

Corruption of *facaluite,* a Rumanian dish of mashed kidney beans, which Maurice Samuel describes in his autobiography as "covered with a dark sauce and burnt onions." It "had the consistency of plaster of Paris just before it sets; one could count on it to be on the stomach pleasantly until the next day."

FLANKEN

Meat from the cow's flank. A popular soup meat, served with CHREYN.

H. L. Mencken (who was a Gentile) once said of this dish: "Jewish boiled beef with real horseradish is the dish of the gods." Harry Golden has also lyricized kosher boiled beef and horseradish.

FLEYSHIK, FLEYSHEDIK

Relating to meat, as opposed to milk (*see* MILCHIK).

FLIGL

Wing of poultry—the part that the younger kids usually got.

The term has been fooled around with on TV and in the comics, as in Sid Caesar's hangout named "La Fligl" and the *Li'l Abner* character "Eagle Eye Fleegle."

FLOMEN

Prunes.

There's an old story about a woman whose mouth is very large and who goes to the doctor to see if he can help her. He tells her to practice saying "prunes" and to come back in a month. When she returns, she complains that her mouth is even larger than it was. The doctor says, "Why? Didn't you practice saying 'prunes'?" "Yes," she answers; "I went around saying it all day." "Let me hear you," says the doctor. And lo, there is his patient saying FLOWMEN, with her mouth stretched wide. (This pokes fun at some of the Yiddish dialects.)

FLOMEN YUCH Prune juice. As a descriptive term, this is ironically derogatory, as in AN ANTIK FUN FLOMEN YUCH (*see* Char. and Des., ANTIK).

FORSHPAYS

Appetizer.

Most common examples of this, now found on many restaurant and hotel menus: chopped liver, pickled herring, gefilte fish.

FRESSER

One who overeats: a glutton (a stronger term than NASHER, under NASH).

Often used endearingly: MAYN FRESSER—my food-gobbler; or ER IZ A FRESSER, KEYN EYN HORE—He's a tremendous eater, no evil eye (*see* Destiny, KEYN EYN HORE).

In his memoirs, I. L. Peretz recalled that the Jews of his Polish home town, Zamoscz, were known to the Jews of She-breshin as DI ZAMOSCZER FRESSERS (the Zamoscz Gluttons), presumably because most of them were better off financially than their Shebreshin brethren and could eat better. (In his home, Peretz said, they had KASHE soup every day.)

See also Char. and Des., ER EST AZOY VI NUCH A KRENK.

GANEF

This was a kind of cross between KUGEL and TSHOLNT. It had a dough base, the center of which was filled with goose meat, rice, beans and other ingredients. Like TSHOLNT, it was baked slowly overnight, and during this time the fat, juices and flavors were mutually absorbed and "stolen" (*see* Char. and Des., GANEF).

"In order to be able to eat and digest a GANEF," in the words of Moritz G. Saphir, "one has to have the stomach of a Jew who grew up in Russia, and then, as a grown man, traded with oil of roses in Turkey, and finally spent six weeks as an invited guest in Berlin. Such a man, and such a man only, is competent to eat a GANEF on the Sabbath Day."

GANZ

Goose.

This lends itself to punning, as in GANZ GUT! (for GANTS GUT!—very good!). The joke can refer literally to a well-prepared goose, or can play bilingually on two American slang uses: gloating when some devil has gotten what was coming to him and "had his goose cooked" or expressing satisfaction at getting away with a certain lewd hand motion that many males can't resist at a closely passing female.

Cf. Chapter IIIA, "gunsel."

GEBAKINE TSORES (ironic)

Baked troubles. (what many a poor Jewish housewife had to serve for the Sabbath—often used in reply to the question, "What do you have to eat?")

See Char. and Des., TSORE.

See also GEHAKTE TSORES *and* "GEHAKTE labor," both under GEHAKTE LEBER.

GEDEMPTE FLEYSH

Potted meat, pot roast.

GEFILTE FISH

Lit., stuffed fish.

Made from several varieties of fresh fish (usually white fish, carp and pike), ground with onion and then chopped very fine and mixed with egg, seasoning, water and crumbs, fashioned into pieces and cooked in a stock of carrots, onions, fish head, skin and bones. Served cold on lettuce with CHREYN, and sometimes with YUCH.

If you're lazy, of course, you can get it in jars. But not every brand of "ready-made" comes close to the real thing. As with borsht, different families prefer different brands.

Is gefilte fish brain food? A delicatessen proprietor in West Haven, Connecticut, apparently thinks so. A sign on the wall proclaims, "I have the thinking man's gefilte."

GEHAKTE LEBER

Chopped liver.

Next to herring, this is *the* Jewish FORSHPAYS. It's what the French call *paté.* Theirs uses goose livers; the Jewish version is usually of beef or chicken livers or both. It's made by chopping or grinding cooked liver with sautéed and/or fresh onions, celery and hard-boiled egg, and mixing with salt, pepper and chicken fat. Calorie-conscious moderns and those who find chicken fat a nuisance to make or obtain now substitute corn oil or (if not concerned about kashruth) melted margarine plus mayonnaise.

The term has led to other expressions. If you're working at something that's a pain in the neck, just smile and call it "GEHAKTE labor." If you've had a hectic day of tending sick children and arguing with the cleaning man about torn drapes he won't make good, and your husband walks in and asks "What's for supper?" then answer pointedly, GEHAKTE TSORES! (Chopped troubles!).

GRIVEN, GRIVENES, GREBENES

Bits of fried onion and chicken skin left over from the rendering of chicken fat. Sometimes added to mashed potatoes or munched on as a snack.

HAK-FLEYSH

Chopmeat.

HALISHKES *See* PRAKES.

HELZEL

Lit., little neck. Roasted neck of fowl, stuffed with a mixture of seasoned flour and goose or chicken fat.

Moritz G. Saphir opined that for the two weeks Lord Byron took to compose his famous "Hebrew Melodies" he ate this tasty MAYCHEL. "That was because while eating Gefüllt Hälsel[10] he could hear the whispering of the cypresses of Babylon, could make out the lament of the waves on the Jordan, could discern the wail of the harps of the grieving Exiles with the yoke around their necks while their own groat-stuffed Gefüllt Hälsel still bore the wounds of the slaughterer's knife."

Cf. KISHKE.

HERRING

Herring.

MARINIRTE (pickled) HERRING is the most famous variety, made from uncooked salt herring. Others are MATJES and SHMALTZ herring. GEHAKTE (chopped) herring is made from raw salt herring, onion, apple, bread and vinegar.

Herring was a staple of the poor Jew's diet and was usually purchased whole from a grocer's bucket. In Europe, it would even be bought in open-air markets and eaten on the run, much as Gentiles consumed oysters and clams while standing. Note this colorful description by Der Tunkeler:

"All of a sudden I noticed a lusty woman in a SHAYTEL[11] wearing an oilcloth apron. She was selling MATJES herring from a pail. Around her had gathered a crowd of customers. For each customer the woman pulled a herring from the pail, skinned it first on the right side then on the left in almost the same way that one skins a banana. And when the herring remained bare and glistening with fat, she picked it up by the tail and dunked it in a bowl of sliced onions so that when she pulled it out again it was covered with pieces of onion, like flypaper with flies on a hot summer day. The customer delicately lifted the herring by the tail, threw his head back and, holding the herring above his mouth like a bunch of grapes, devoured it with a few well-timed bites."

Today, of course, herring has become more DELIKATNE, more delicate or dignified. It comes in cool jars and is offered whole, in chunks or fillets, plain pickled, in sour cream or in wine sauce. (The wine version was even marketed for a predictably short time with a red cherry to carry out the punning title of "Cherry Herring"—playing on the name of the Scandinavian liqueur Cherry Heering!)

See Chap. IIIA, "maven."

HOMENTASH (pl. HOMENTASHEN)

Lit., Haman's pocket—sometimes rendered "Haman's hat" —a triangular little cake with poppyseed or fruit (commonly prune) filling, eaten on PURIM (Rel. and Cul.). Also known as HOMENOYREN (Haman's Ears).

These cakes are believed to be of relatively recent origin. While the filling of poppyseed (MON) is thought to be associated with the tyrant Haman's name, the shape has sometimes been related to George Washington's hat, sometimes to that of Napoleon, both interpreted as symbols of liberation. In the case of the name HOMENOYREN, the shape may have been a pointed reference to Haman's stupidity.

Recipes for HOMENTASHEN have been appearing in general food columns of newspapers and magazines, and the product seems to be entering the all-year food market for both the Jewish and Gentile trade. I've seen them in supermarket bakery departments in Pennsylvania and Connecticut completely out of season.

HONIK

Honey.

In the Old Country, when three-to-five-year-old boys started their Hebrew lessons, a drop of honey was placed on their tongues, to symbolize the sweetness of learning. On Rosh Hashona, the New Year, it is traditional to serve honey in some form—slices of apple to be dipped in honey, LEKACH or TEYGLACH—to symbolize the hope that the forthcoming year will be sweet.

See Endearment, MAYN FESSEL HONIK; Char. and Des., ER VET SHOYN KEYN HONIK NIT LEKN.

ICH SHTARB AVEK!

I'm dying away! (of hunger)

ICH SHTARB A TEYTE. *Lit.,* I'm dying a dead one. I'm starving dead away.

IGERKE

Cucumber.

This lends itself to the bilingual pun, "Eagerke" for an eager female.

KAKEPITSI

An unappetizing concoction—what Ruth and Bob Grossman describe as "everything but the kitchen stove, which is optional."

KARPES

Greens—one of the symbols used at the Passover SEYDER (Rel. and Cul.), representing spring. Parsley or celery is usually used, dipped in salt water as a reminder of the tears of the ancient Jews when they were slaves in Egypt.

KARTOFEL

Potato.

See also BULBE.

KASHE

Buckwheat groats.

Served as a side dish with meat, topped with gravy. Sometimes mixed with noodles, making KASHE MIT LOKSHEN or KASHE VARNITSHKES—available frozen as "Kasha Bowties," containing noodles of that shape. Also used in soup with lima beans and meat (*cf.* FRESSER).

See Advice, MISH NIT OYS KEYN KASHE MIT BORSHT; Char. and Des., ER HOT GEMACHT DERFIN A KASHE.

The word also means "question"; *see* Exclam., AF A MAYSE FREGT MEN NIT KEYN KASHES.

KATSHKE

Duck. *Also*, loosely, chicken.

Fig., young woman, as in ZI IZ NIT KEYN KATSHKE (She's no spring chicken).

I have childhood memories of the phonograph record "Marching through Georgia," with which we used to sing along; at a certain point, we changed the line to: "Hoo-ray, hoo-ray,/ DI KATSHKE HOT GELEYGT AN EY (the duck has laid an egg). This was of course on the same level as the American schoolboy's words for the *Carmen* Toreador Song: "Toreador, don't spit on the floor;/Here's the cuspidor, waddaya think it's for."

KATSHKEVAL

A strong Greek cheese, which evokes heady memories in those who were exposed to it.

KAVE

Coffee.

Borden now has an instant-coffee product named "Kava."

KICHEL (pl. KICHELACH)

A mild egg-puff type of biscuit. *Also*, a cinnamon bun.

PATSHE, PATSHE, KICHELACH (Clap, Clap, Sugar Buns) is

the title of an old lullaby—referred to at end of Endearment. In both languages, little children inspire the association of a sweet bun.

KIFFEL

Hungarian finger-shaped pastries filled with lekvar.

KISHKE

Stuffed intestine.

This is what a Jewish cookbook calls "beef casing" and what Sam Levenson calls "sections of fire hose"! It is similar to HELZEL except for the casing, which can be eaten, and except for the fact that the stuffing is somewhat moister.

KISHKE is often called "derma," and the road to the Catskill Mountains, where the many Jewish hotels serve this Old World dish, has been dubbed "The Derma Road."

"Derma" presumably comes from the Latin word for skin, and it would seem more logical to use it for HELZEL, which is made of the skin of a fowl's neck. The Grossinger cookbook does this, calling the item "Helzel or Derma"; but other Jewish cookbooks use "derma" for KISHKE, and the well-traveled New Yorkers I have queried in the matter insist that the popular conception of derma is KISHKE.

One of the top forty popular discs in 1963 was "Who Stole the Kishke." As the *Jewish Digest* observed, non-Jewish teen-agers were buying the platter like mad but were also going slightly mad because they couldn't figure out what Kishke was!

See Char. and Des., ME TSURAYST IM DI KISHKE.

KNEYDLACH

Matzo balls, served in chicken soup during Passover.

Though these are available in jars, there is nothing quite like the feeling of satisfaction at making your own when they turn out light and fluffy. I try a different recipe almost every year! One that has been especially successful calls for beating egg yolks and whites separately; another calls for seltzer in place of water.

The usual ingredients are eggs, matzo meal, water and seasoning. Some people use soaked crumbled matzo instead of the meal and add fried onions. Some cook the balls right in the soup; others do it separately in boiling water.

KNISHES

Puffs of flaky dough filled lightly with chopped liver or mashed potatoes or sometimes with cheese, and baked. Served hot. (In large size, they may be served with the main course; in tiny form, they make delicious appetizers.)

These used to be available only through one's own efforts or those of a kosher caterer. Today in small communities, where Gentile-operated hotel catering services handle Bar Mitzvahs and Jewish wedding parties, Gentile chefs are beginning to make KNISHES, even as they have learned to make chopped liver. But those of this type which I've bitten into so far are, sad to report, FARKLOPT.

See Chap. IIIA, "nosh," *re.* "nish nosh."

KNOBL

Garlic.

A modern quip notes that four nickels will put you on a New York subway, and KNOBL will get you a seat. If you don't enjoy having others shy away from you, remember the advice given earlier: AZ ME EST NIT KEYN KNOBL, SHTINKT MEN NIT!

But let's be fair. Garlic does have its merits. Not only is it thought to have medicinal value (the Talmud says it will increase seminal flow; Eleanor Roosevelt's doctor prescribed it in pill form to help her memory), but its taste and aroma are by no means anathema to all. Moritz G. Saphir extolled its praises in German on more than one occasion, suggesting that King David would eat garlic before sitting down to play his harp and that the prophetess Deborah ate garlic before chanting her inspired songs. Indeed, according to him the poet Homer always packed a supply of garlic before embarking on a journey and it was the magic of garlic that Solomon used to attract the Queen of Sheba!

KOSHER

Conforming to Jewish dietary laws (*see* Rel. and Cul., KASHRES). Hence, acceptable, trustworthy, particularly in the negative: NISHT AZOY KOSHER (not so kosher).

Both positive and negative forms have been picked up in American slang, and some new uses have been developing. *See* Chap. IIIA.

Cf. TREYF.

KREPLACH

Small puffs of noodle dough filled with chopped liver (making what Sam Levenson has called "meat balls with sport jackets") or sometimes with cheese, and boiled.

The similarity to Italian ravioli has been capitalized on by Chef Boy-ar-dee, which advertises its Cheese Ravioli in Jewish publications as a variety of "Cheese Kreplach."

An old psychiatrist story deals with the mother whose son has a strange fear of KREPLACH. The doctor advises her to have the boy watch as she makes them, so that he can see what goes into them and be convinced there is nothing to fear. She goes home and shows the boy first how she makes the filling, saying "There's nothing to be afraid of there, is there?" "No, Mama." Then she shows him how she rolls and cuts out the dough and asks, "There's nothing to be afraid of there, is there?" "No, Mama." Then she spoons the filling onto the cut-out pieces and says, "There's nothing to be afraid of there, is there?" Again, "No, Mama." Then she says, "Now we cover the filling like this"—and the boy shrieks, "Yahhhhh KREPLACH!" Sargent Shriver, former director of the Office of Economic Opportunity (OEO) was reported in the *National Observer* as telling this story in connection with the problems of that agency: "You can collect all the ingredients we have here at OEO and examine them one at a time, and everyone shrugs without interest. But you put them all together and call it the 'War on Poverty' and people will look at it and scream 'Yahhhhh KREPLACH!' "

KRUPNIK

A thick soup of potatoes and grits, which was almost the exclusive food of poor Jews in Old Russia. When they could afford it, they added meat, or a bit of butter.

KUGEL

There are two chief varieties of kugel: potato or noodle. In either case, the basic ingredient is mixed—the noodles having been parboiled or the potatoes having been grated raw and drained—with beaten eggs, melted goose or chicken fat and seasonings and—in the case of the potato variety—flour, and baked until crisp.

Some modern variations of noodle kugel use butter or margarine and seedless raisins and/or cottage cheese, but they then become a MILCHIKE dish, whereas the kugel of Jewish folklore and literature is associated with FLEYSHIKE meals. Sholem Aleichem's and Moritz G. Saphir's definitions of kugel, which are quoted in the introductory note to this section, were based largely on the ingredient of poultry fat.

See Chap. I, Psychol. Insight, MIT A YIDN IZ GUT KUGEL TSU ESSEN. . . .[12]

KVATS

Mush.

MACH NIT KEYN KVATS (Don't make a mush), a mother might say to a child who is beginning to mash up his food.

Cf. Char. and Des., ER HOT GEMACHT DERFIN A KASHE.

LAKS (from German *lachs*, salmon)

Smoked salmon, popularly known as "lox."

This is the famous breakfast companion of cream cheese and bagels, often eaten for lunch, supper or an evening snack. Sometimes fried with eggs (after brief soaking in water to remove some of the salt, unless the lox is the Nova Scotia variety, which is practically unsalted) and served with tomatoes, mashed potatoes, cottage cheese, and sour cream.

Though lox with cream cheese is common in Scandinavian countries, where other sea foods are also popular, the teaming up with bagels is a Jewish contribution. (*See* BEYGEL.)

A number of Jewish high-school seniors were among the outstanding "Presidential scholars" invited to lunch at the White House on June 7, 1966. Some noticed the delicate pinwheel hors d'oeuvres made of rolled lox and cream cheese. These presumably reflected Scandinavian rather than Jewish influence —though conceivably those in charge may have had possible kosher Jewish students in mind, for another variety of hors d'oeuvres on the table was a pinwheel of ham and cream cheese.

As whodunit fans well know, the exploits of "Loxfinger" have parodied those of the famous "Goldfinger" (with Secret Agent "Oy Oy 7" in place of "007").

One quip has it that lox is "herring with high blood pressure." Another dubs it "the rich relation of a herring." A more recent one asks if you've heard of the Jewish man who left home lox, stocks and bagel. It's said too that when Israeli troops reached the Suez Canal in June of 1967, they grabbed the lox.

LATKES

Pancakes.

This usually means potato pancakes, made from grated raw potatoes and traditionally served on Chanuka. (Recipes for such LATKES have appeared in food columns of many general newspapers in recent years.) It may also refer to Passover pancakes (*see* CHREMZLACH).

LEKACH

Honey cake.

See HONIK.

LOKSHEN
Noodles.
As a jokester has advised, LOKSHEN should not be cooked too long—not over three feet. A Pennsylvania Jewish Community Center recently dubbed its series of sports contests "The LOKSHEN Bowl."

H. L. Mencken cited this word (spelled "lukschen")[13] when he should have given A LANGER LOKSH (Char. and Des.).

See KASHE *and* KUGEL; Advice, CHAP NIT DI LOKSHEN FAR DI FISH, under CHAP NISHT!

Cf. Tribalism, LOKSH.

MACHEN SHABBES
Lit., to make Sabbath. To observe the Sabbath in customary fashion: to light the Sabbath candles and serve the Sabbath meal.

See Rel. and Cul., SHABBES; Exclam., MACH SHABBES DERMIT!

See also 'PRAVEN SHABBES.

MAMMELIGE
Rumanian corn porridge, served with sour cream.
The term was also used disparagingly for a Rumanian Jew, since this was the chief food eaten by poor Rumanians. (*Cf.* Tribalism, LOKSH.)

MANDELBROYT　*See* MANDLEN.

MANDLEN
Almonds.
These were often served as a snack with raisins, and a famous old song by Abraham Goldfaden is entitled "Rozhinkes mit Mandlen." (*See* Family, ALMONE.)

The term also refers to featherweight dumplings for soup. The Manischewitz firm appropriately calls its product "Soup Nuts."

MANDELBROYT　Almond bread. A crisp cake, baked in slices.

MASLINES
Olives.
This term usually refers to the black wrinkled ones in olive oil.

MATZO
The unleavened bread used during Passover to commemorate the flight from Egypt under Moses, when bread dough had to be packed up before it could rise.

One way of eating matzo that is fondly remembered calls for rubbing the piece of matzo with onion and then spreading it with home-made chicken fat and sprinkling with salt. Of this MAYCHEL, Sam Levenson has commented, "I've never sampled marijuana, but I can't imagine that it would produce a more glowing sensation than golden chicken fat on hemstitched boards."

MATZO BRAY Matzo broken up into shards, soaked in seasoned egg and water and fried, served plain or with sour cream and/or jelly. This was known among Russian Jews as PRĂZHINITSE.

See Chap. IIIA, "matzo."

MAYCHEL
Culinary offering; concoction; delicacy.

ME SHIT ARAYN A BISSEL. . . .
You throw in a little. . . .

This was the form of the personal recipe—before the days of measuring spoons and cookbooks. It helps explain why, every so often, something was NISHT GERUTN (turned out badly), and why the American daughters of old-time Jewish cooks had to work extra hard to duplicate their mothers' offerings.

The second generation is always just a bit self-conscious about this phrase, because of the taboo English term the verb suggests.[14]

MEYER
Carrot.

MEYER TSIMMES *See* TSIMMES.

MEYER is also a boy's name. *See* story under Char. and Des., ER DREYT A KOP.

MILCHIK, MILCHEDIK
Relating to milk, as opposed to meat.

A recent "Kosher Birthday Card" billing itself "for Someone who has everything," provides two gold-color toothpicks, one MILCHIK and the other FLEYSHIK.

Rabbi Arthur A. Chiel has noted that in Winnipeg, Canada, a little synagogue established by Sholem Aleichem's favorite uncle was known as Di Milchike Shul (The Dairy Synagogue), because its members were the lowly Jews in town, as against the more affluent ones who had money for meat. Years earlier, when Sholem Aleichem named his famous fictional milkman Tevye Der Milchiker, he was giving the term this same jocular meaning.[15]

See Chap. I, Punning, for joke explaining why MILCHIKS is

eaten on Shevuoth; Chap. IIIA, "dairy" for "dairy products."
MOROR (Heb.)

Lit., bitter herb. Sliced or grated horseradish—symbolic food
of the Passover seder representing the bitter experience of the
Jews in ancient Egypt.

At one point in the service, MOROR is eaten together with
CHAREYSHIS. The two are often combined between two bits of
matzo, making a "Hillel Sandwich"—so named because the
ancient Rabbi Hillel is said to have eaten the symbols this way.
(The fourth Earl of Sandwich, who could not take time to
leave the gaming tables to eat and had meat brought to him
between bread slices, may have inspired the English name for
it, but he did not *originate* the sandwich!)

See Rel. and Cul., SEYDER.

NAHIT

Cooked chick peas, seasoned and served cold as a snack.

Cf. BOB.

NASH

A snack.

NASHER   A nibbler; a person with a sweet tooth. *See also*
Endearment, -EVITSH, CHAZEREVITSH.

NASHERAY   Goodies for nibbling between meals.

Various forms have appeared in American usage. *See* Chap.
IIIA, "nosh."

NEM FAR DI. KINDER.

Take for the children.

This was the old-time hostess's generous offering of goodies
to take home with you. Today it's always quoted with a smile.

OPPRAVEN SHABBES   *See* 'PRAVEN SHABBES.

PAREV

Neither FLEYSHIK nor MILCHIK, hence capable of being used
with either meat or dairy foods.

PEYSACHDIK

Kosher for Passover, as distinguished from CHOMETSDIK.

On Passover, according to tradition, one eats only unleavened
bread (*see* MATZO) and other foods which have not come into
contact with leaven or which by their process of growth do not
suggest leaven. (The strictness of such observance varies greatly
today.)

A relative of mine likes to convert this into the playful
"Paskedicky."

See Rel. and Cul., PEYSACH.

PILSE *See* P'TSHA.

PINENEH

Banana.

PIRISHKES

Baked half-moons of sweet dough, filled with chopped fruit.

PIROGN

Baked half-moons of dough filled with cooked meat and served as a side dish with soup (or sometimes filled with mushrooms, fish, potato or cheese).

PRAKES

Rolled cabbage leaves stuffed with chopmeat (often with added rice) and cooked in tomato sauce, seasoned sour or sweet-and-sour.

Rumanian and Hungarian Jews call them HALISHKES.

Also a favored dish of non-Jewish Ukrainian Americans, these are available in varying quality in jars and cans, as "stuffed cabbage."

'PRAVEN SHABBES

To prepare a Sabbath meal.

'PRAVEN A SEYDER To prepare a meal for the Passover seder.

PRĂZHINITSE *See* MATZO.

P'TSHA (also known as DRELYES in Galicia and as PILSE in Rumania)

Boiled calves' feet or shin—a dish that was sometimes prepared for the Sabbath in place of TSHOLNT.

One method of preparation was to boil the meat until it came off the bones, allowing it to set. The following day it was reheated and when soft again poured over a beaten egg yolk, with a touch of garlic and vinegar added. Another method called for cutting up the meat and boiling it, then using the juice, to which was added hard-boiled egg and garlic. The mixture was allowed to jell and then cut in wedges.

This offering would be rated by many as GROBE ESSEN (*see* ESSEN). Its contribution to digestive distress is a common ploy of entertainers.

PULKE

Thigh of a fowl; drumstick.

PUPIK (pl. PUPIKLACH)

Fowl gizzard. *Also*, belly-button.

As food, the organ is used in soup or fricassee. As a light-hearted term, it has a variety of popular uses. *See* Ann. and Arg., ES GEYT MIR IN PUPIK ARAYN!; Char. and Des., BIZ 'EM PUPIK; ER KLERT, TSI A FLOY HOT A PUPIK; *and* MOYSHE PUPIK; Chap. IIIB, "That doesn't hurt *my* PUPIK!"

ROSSEL

This term means different things to different Jews. Maurice Samuel has described it as a Rumanian version of stew, noting that it is "nearer to an Irish stew than to goulash." But a house-wife of Austrian-Jewish extraction tells me it is a pot roast; while several others insist it is a kind of beet soup, one saying it includes meat, another not, one noting it is a pickled-beet essence that is added in the making of Passover borsht. Other informants say it is the brine of pickles or sauerkraut.

These latter descriptions would appear to explain the imagery in the old vulgar characterization, ER DREYT ZICH VI A FORTS IN ROSSEL (He's moving around like a f-rt in brine: i.e., He's going through a lot of motions, but they don't mean a thing).

SHMALTZ

Chicken or goose fat.

See Chap. IIIA.

SHNAPS

Whiskey.

MACHEN A SHNAPS　To have a drink.

SHNIPSEL　A little SHNAPS; a snifter.

SHTRUDEL

A rolled pastry with fruit and nut filling.

In its authentic form, this is a heavenly concoction, the supreme Jewish baked offering. Most second-generation American Jews have sentimental memories of the dough being rolled and rolled until it was almost thin enough to be seen through. A Pennsylvania chemist I know fondly recalls his mother's requirement that the thinness allow for reading the newspaper through the dough! This is an unusual attainment, not likely to be equaled today. Although recipes for strudel appear in several popular cookbooks, most women are content to buy the finished product if they can (it's available in decent quality only in big cities) or to simplify the baking by using frozen strudel dough (also available only in big cities), or just to leave strudel as one of the delicacies they eat outside the home, when they're attending catered affairs or staying at Jewish resort hotels. This is a pity, for home-made strudel is a real family treat. Children can help make it—just as they can help make HOMENTASHEN—and they and their father can delight in its mastication as in no other BEKERAY.

SILOTEH

Pickled lettuce.

SMETENEH

Sour cream.

This is used in cold borsht, on cottage cheese or blintzes, on chunks of tomato, cucumber and radish, etc.

Cf. Char. and Des., ME KEN IM GETROYEN VI A KATS SMETENEH.

SOK

Home-made fruit preserves.

A teaspoon added to a glass of tea made a very tasty drink— a trick being suggested these days for blackberry julep by radio nutritionist Carleton Fredericks.

See Exclam., OY, DAYN SOK HOT MIR BAGROBN!

STSHAV *See* BORSHT.

TAM

Taste; flavor.

The term is being used in much advertising in American Jewish periodicals, reaching some incongruous levels of "cultural syncretism." Notice the cheese which is heralded as "Ta'am[16] of Switzerland" (how many Jews have ever lived there?!)[17] or the Italian spaghetti sauce with "Grandissimo Ta'am!" "Ba-Tampte" is a brand name of refrigerated pickles—which, as the jar cover indicates, "means tasty."

See Chap. I, Taste, *re*. MAMMELES TAM, etc.

TEY

Tea.

A GLEZELE TEY   A little glass of tea. The custom of drinking tea in a glass has lately been ribbed with, "Would you like a cup of tea in a glass or a glass of tea in a cup?" More than twenty-five years ago, when my father asked in a cafeteria for tea in a glass, the man behind the counter asked if he wanted iced tea. No, my father explained, he wanted hot tea, but in a glass. Thereupon the man called out down the line, "Hot tea, in a glass!" and his cry was picked up and repeated at the other end, "Hot tea, in a glass!" Needless to say, my father stood red-faced until the tea was delivered and then felt everyone in the place watching him as he carried his odd drink to a table.

On cold winter nights, when he would come home after closing the store, my father would sit down to a glass of tea and warm up his hands around the glass while waiting for it to cool enough to be sipped over the cube of sugar placed under his tongue. (The sugar lasted him much longer than it did me when I tried this. There was a certain easy detachment about it, like the "light rein" recommended for raising children. My sucking was too direct and serious, and the sugar got used up much too fast.)

TEYGLACH

Chunks of dough boiled in honey, to which nuts are sometimes added. Customarily served on Rosh Hashona.

See HONIK.

TREYF

Not kosher.

TREYFNYAK   One who eats TREYFE food.

See Rel. and Cul., KASHRES, *and* Chap. I, end of Realism, AZ ME FREGT, IZ TREYF.

TRUNK

A drink.

TSHOLNT

Sabbath roast.

This is the tasty roast of meat and vegetables (usually potato, rice and beans) that was put in the oven before sundown on Friday and roasted slowly overnight and into the morning, to be eaten when the family returned from synagogue on the Sabbath. The motivation was to avoid cooking on the Sabbath, but it is interesting that slow roasting of meat is being advocated today by nutritionist Adelle Davis.

See Heine's rhapsody on TSHOLNT (for which he uses the German-French spelling *schalet*) in the introduction to this section.

TSIBILE

Onion.

See Chap. I, Imprec., ZOLST VAKSN VI A TSIBILE . . . .

TSIMBROYT

"With-bread"; something to go with bread to make a poor Jew's meal.

As Maurice Samuel recalls his Rumanian childhood, TSIMBROYT could be garlic, rubbed into rye-bread crust, or halvah, eaten with white bread.

TSIMMES

Stewed vegetable and/or fruit, occasionally including meat. Most commonly, a sweet concoction of carrots and potatoes, sometimes called MEYER (or MEYREN) TSIMMES (carrot stew). FLOMEN TSIMMES uses potatoes, prunes and sometimes raisins.

The presence of TSIMMES on resort-hotel menus is affecting many a Gentile's vocabulary and palate. Several seasons ago, a woman whose church was planning to conduct a Passover SEYDER (Rel. and Cul.) asked me whether TSIMMES would be an appropriate vegetable to serve. I said yes, it would be most appropriate, but how did she know about it? Her husband, she replied, had been to a business convention at a Catskill Mountains hotel, where TSIMMES was served, and he liked it very much.

Last fall my local newspaper carried a recipe for "carrot pudding," which it identified as a "traditional item on the menu for Rosh Hashona." This was of course TSIMMES, though not so labeled.

The word has a figurative meaning of "fuss." *See* Chap. IIIB, "such a TSIMMES."

VARNITSHKES *See* KASHE.

VASSER MIT MILCH

Water with milk (a hot drink, sipped from a glass, over a cube of sugar held under the tongue—considered good for a cold or sore throat).

VAYN

Wine.

VAYNIK Richly flavorsome. This has been punned on with VEYNIK, too little.

VEN HUNGERT A NOGID? VEN DER DOKTER HEYST IM.

When does a rich man go hungry? When it's doctor's orders. (The poor man obviously does it on his own!)

VERENIKES

Half-moons of dough filled with red cherries or blackberries that have been boiled with sugar, lemon juice, cornstarch and water; the whole boiled in salt water and served with sour cream.

See Char. and Des., ZI VEYNT UN EST VERENIKES, under ZI VEYNT UN BAKT BEYGEL.

VISHNIK

Fruit cordial, liqueur.

YUCH

Broth. *Also*, gelatinous liquid from cooking of gefilte fish.

(Some people heat this till it liquefies and spoon it over the fish.)

Sam Levenson has defined YUCH as "liquid lead."

ZAROZE

Gravy.

See Passing Judgment, GIB A BEHEYME A ZAROZE.

ZUP

Soup.

My mother's vegetable soup, which had a split-pea base and included a half-dozen other vegetables with meat, would evoke my father's jesting approval after he had broken crackers or bread into it: "Good for plastering a wall with!" This kind of inverted compliment was obviously related to the old idioms EYDER FAR ZIBITSIK YOR SHTARBN . . . *and* EYDER TSU SHTARBN FUN HUNGER . . . .

TSORES MIT ZUP IZ GRINGER TSU FARTROGN VI TSORES ON ZUP. Troubles are easier to take with soup than without.

GREETINGS AND PARTINGS

A GAST IN SHTUB!

A guest in the house! (to someone who hasn't been around for a long time)

A GUTE NACHT!

Good night!

A GUTN TOG! (*or* A GUTN!)

Good day! Good-bye!

A GUT VOCH!

A good week! (parting on the Sabbath)

(A) GUT YOR!

A good year! (reply to other greetings or partings; thus GUT YONTEF!, GUT YOR!; A GUTE NACHT!, A GUT YOR!; etc.)

A LANTSMAN!

A countryman! (discovery that someone comes from the same part of the world that you do)

Though originally this referred to the Old World, second- and third-generation American Jews use it good-humoredly. Two New Yorkers meeting in Paris, for instance, might chucklingly use the exclamation.[1]

CHAVER (m.), CHAVERTE (f.) (pl. CHAVERIM, CHAVERTES)

Comrade, pal.

Cf. Chap. I, 2d par. of note to Acronyms; Chap. IIIA, "cobber."

GUTER-BRUDER

Lit., Good brother. Chum, my friend. (Often ironic as in NU, GUTER-BRUDER—Well, chum—implying, "What do you have to say for yourself?")

GUT MORGN!

Good morning!

GUT SHABBES!

Good Sabbath!

Now often heard at the synagogue as "Good SHABBES!"

A GUT SHABBES ZOL IN AYCH ARAYN. May a good Sabbath enter into you; i.e., May the spirit of the Sabbath suffuse you. A brother of mine recently said this to one of the elderly gentlemen in his synagogue and found the old man's eyes lighted up with wonder and delight at hearing this from an American-born Jew!

GUT YONTEF!

Good holiday!

See (A) GUT YOR above; Chap. I, Rhyme, "GUT YONTIFF, Pontiff."

HOB ZICH A GUTN ZAYT-ZICH. (light-hearted parting)

Lit., Have yourself a good be-yourself. *Equiv.,* Have fun; take care.

L'SHONE TEYVE (Heb. *l'shono tōvo tikoseyv*—pl. *tikoseyvu*)

May you be inscribed for a good year. (greeting for ROSHE-SHONE—Rel. and Cul.)

This refers to the "Book of Life," in which worthy souls are inscribed for the year ahead. (*Cf.* Passing Judgment, VER ES HALT DI PEN, DER SHRAYBT ZICH ON A GUT YOR.)

NOR AF SIMCHAS.

Only on celebrations; i.e., May we meet only at happy times. (parting after a funeral or other sad event)

This has led to various forms like "I hope we'll meet on happier occasions."

NU, VOS HERT ZICH?

So what's new? "So what do you hear from the boys?"

See also VOS HERT MEN IN YAM? *and* VOS IZ NAYES?

Cf. IIIA, "So what else is new?"

RABOYSAY!

Gentlemen!

SHOLEM ALEYCHEM!

Lit., Peace be unto you! Hello!

Customary reply: ALEYCHEM SHOLEM!

Lewis Browne, the famous rabbi-turned-author of the 1930's, used to tell of the time he was on a visit to Tahiti and went out for an early morning stroll on the beach. Obeying a wild impulse, he called out to the elements, "SHOLEM ALEYCHEM!" and was startled to hear the reply, "ALEYCHEM SHOLEM!" He looked around and discovered another man some yards away, who turned out to be an American Jew too![2]

"Sholom Aleychem" is the title of two well-known Hebrew songs, one of them a traditional hymn for the Sabbath. In Israel, the Hebrew word *shalom* is used for both greeting and parting. (Note three different spellings here for the first word: SHOLEM, *sholom, shalom*—Yiddish, Ashkenazic or Biblical Hebrew, and Sephardic or modern Hebrew.)

V'AZOY (*or* VI) GEYT ES?

How's it going? How are things?

Usual replies:

ME DREYT ZICH. One maneuvers; one manages. (*Cf.* Char. and Des., ER DREYT ZICH UN FREYT ZICH.)

ME LEBT. One lives.

ME MUTSHET ZICH. *Lit.,* One tortures oneself. One suffers. (This and the preceding are sometimes combined: ME LEBT UN ME MUTSHET ZICH.)

V'AZOY ZOL ES GEYN? How should it go? EH! (*See* Exclam., EH! *and* Chap. IIIA, Answering a Question with a Question.)

VOS HERT MEN IN YAM?

What's new at sea?

Reply: ME CHAPT FISH. They're catching fish.

VOS IZ NAYES?

What's the news?

See Chap. I, Rhyme, "VOS IZ NAYES, Pius?"

VOS MACHT A YID?

How's a Jew doing?

This has a certain good-natured heartiness and warmth. I asked it of a brother at a recent family gathering, where a number of the third generation were present with non-Jewish spouses. It brought more than the usual chuckle.

VOS MACHT DOS KIND?

How's the child? How's His Nibs?

VOS MACHT ER?

How is he doing?

Common reply: FREG NISHT! (*See* Exclam.)

VOS MACHT IR? (*or* VOS MACHSTU?)

How are you?

Usual reply: V'AZOY ZOL ICH MACHEN? EH! How should I be doing? Struggling along. (*See* last reply under V'AZOY GEYT ES? above *and* Chap. I, Superstition.)

ZAY GEZUNT; ZAYT MIR DERVAYL GEZUNT; etc. *See* Chap. I, Concerns about Life and Health.

ZAY NIT KEYN FREMDER.

Don't be a stranger.

This parting word from a host means: "Keep in touch; let's hear from you." It's still used in translation by the first generation and—usually spoofingly—by the second generation.

ZETST ZICH AVEK!

Sit down! Make yourself comfortable!

IMPRECATION

The colorful cursing to be found here is at once captivating and chilling—since much of it was flung at children by their mothers. But we have been told that neither hurler nor hurled-at took the language at its face value. One author suggests that the extravagance of speech provided such emotional release for the parent that it actually discouraged physical punishment, and that the procedure might well be copied. A cuss, in other words, may do less harm than a swat!

To young Sholem Aleichem such verbiage was fascinating, providing inspiration for his first literary effort, a compilation of his stepmother's billingsgate! But there must have been many youngsters who had no creative means of transmuting the experience and who never learned to let it roll off their backs. Certainly there were some who, after emigrating to America, identified the world of the SHTETL with this coarse manner of speech and turned their backs on Yiddish language and literature.

In any case, there would seem to be a dramatic difference in the generations with regard to the use of such expressions. Life in the European SHTETL was difficult at best, and the offspring were often innocent targets of their mothers' grievances against society. The later strains and adjustments involved in settling in a new country with a strange language could not help fostering the use of all the Old Country expostulations. But these were gradually tempered. Even in the SHTETL there was the negative form of curse, mentioned in Chap. I. On these shores, an American-born grandmother I know recalls being warned at the beach with the relatively restrained, if illogical, exclamation: GEY NIT IN YAM, VEST CHAPN A KALT, VEL ICH DIR HARGENEN! (Don't go into the ocean, you'll catch a cold, and I'll kill you!). Today the invective Yiddish used with some American Jewish children seems largely confined to three threats—so mild that they are listed not here but under Annoyance and Argument: ICH'L DIR BALD GEBN! (I'm gonna give it to you!), which is often spoken good-naturedly; the more forceful ICH'L DIR BALD DERLANGEN! (In a minute I'll let you have it!); and the common hybrid, "Do you want a PATSH (slap)?" Apparently parent-child relations have not changed much since Talmudic times, when one rabbi cautioned that parents should never threaten a child but should either punish him promptly or say nothing!

There must be some connection between Jewish word-consciousness (discussed in Chap. I) and the verbal inventiveness that shows up in Yiddish argument as well as imprecation. It is probably no accident that, as Dr. Karl Menninger has observed, "The Irish throw bricks, the Italians throw knives; quarreling Jews throw words."

A DUNER ZOL IM TREFN!
　　A thunder should happen to him!
　　This reflects the mistaken notion that danger came from thunder rather than lightning.
A FINSTER LEBN (*or* TOG *or* SOF) AF IM!
　　A dark life (*or* day *or* end) to him!
　　FINSTER ZOL DIR VEREN! May it get dark for you!
　　See Char. and Des., FINSTER; Rel. and Cul., ALEH YIDDEN KENEN ZAYN CHAZONIM . . . (under CHAZEN).
　　See also A SHVARTZ YOR AF IM!
A KLUG AF IM!
　　A plague upon him!

A KLUG TSU COLUMBUSN! A plague to Columbus! (Because of him, we were fooled into coming to America!) The difference between the immigrant's dream and sweatshop reality was poignantly expressed in the old song, "A Grine Cuzine"—A Greenhorn Cousin—in which the initial exclamation of LEBN ZOL DI GOLDENE MEDINE!—Long live the Golden Land!—shifts to BRENEN ZOL COLUMBUSES MEDINE!—To blazes with Columbus's land! This same disillusionment was expressed in a parody of the Passover Haggadah by A. M. Sharkansky (*see* Rel. and Cul., HAGODE). Accordingly, it's been suggested that Columbus's first name was not Christopher, but "Klugtsu"!
ALEH CHALOYMES ZOLN OYSGEYN TSU *ZAYN* KOP!

May all dreams (i.e., nightmares) go out to *his* head!

See also BEYZE CHALOYMES AF DIR!
A MAKEH IM!

Lit., a boil (or sore) upon him! May a calamity befall him!

If someone suggests you ought to give something to a third person against whom you have a grievance, your reply might be: GEBN? A MAKEH VEL ICH IM GEBN! (Give? A curse I'll give him!)

Maurice Samuel recalls that his Uncle Leon, when he came home wet and weary from operating open-air merchandise stalls on rainy market nights in England, would complain that he went out not on markets, but on MAKEHS.

See Chap. IIIA, "mockie."

Cf. Chap. I, Vulgarity, *re.* ER HOT A MAKEH.[1]
A MISE MESHINNE AF DIR!

A violent (or unnatural) death to you!

NEM ARAYN A MISE MESHINNE! Take in an unnatural death! There's an old story about a German officer who was boasting to a Jew about all the foreign cities that had been taken by the German army. The Jew asked whether they had yet taken A MISE MESHINNE, and the bragging German said not yet, but he was sure that they would soon be taking that like all the others!

The comic strip *Joe Palooka* by Ham Fisher—Tom DePetra used the same kind of private joke when an American Indian girl told Jerry Leemy: ". . . you have done so much for our tribe that you are one of us! And my father is a descendant of Chief Miesa Meshinna!"

See story under Endearment, MAYN NESHOME, *and* Chap. IIIA, "sheeny."

AN UMGLIK AF IM!

A misfortune upon him! Damn him!

A SHLAK ZOL IM TREFN!

May he have a stroke!

See negative form for this in Chap. I, Superstition[2]; *and* Chap. IIIA, "shlock."

A SHVARTZ YOR AF IM!

A black year (i.e., a year of hardship) on him!

An old conundrum asks what the difference is between a six-year-old Negro child and a seven-year-old Negro child. Answer: A year? No! A black year! (This recognizes the difficulties of Negro existence.)

Also, ZOL ER FARSHVARTZT VEREN. May he become blackened by fate.

Cf. Char. and Des., A SHVARTZ YOR; Tribalism, SHVARTZER.

BEYZE CHALOYMES AF DIR!

Bad dreams upon you!

DI BEYNER ZOLN IM OYSRINEN!

May his bones be drained of marrow!

See also ER ZOL NOR ANLOYFN!

DI ERD ZOL IM AYNSHLINGEN LEBIDIKERHEYD!

May the earth swallow him up alive!

ER VARFT IM A BEYZ OYG.

He's throwing him a bad eye. He's hexing him. He's trying to spoil things for him.

See Destiny, KEYN EYN HORE. . . .

ER ZOL NOR ANLOYFN!

He should only shrivel up!

GESHVOLN ZOLSTU VEREN!

May you swell up!

Cf. Passing Judgment, DER GVIR BLOZT ZICH, UN DER OREMAN VERT GESHVOLN.

GEZETST ZOLSTU VEREN!

May you explode! May you split a gut!

GEY IN D'RERD!

Go into the ground! Go to hell!

GEY MITN KOP IN D'RERD ARAYN! *Lit.*, Go with your head into the ground! Take your head and go to hell! *See* Chap. I, Imprec., IN D'RERD ARAYN! *and* ZOLST VAKSN VI A TSIBILE. . . .

See also ZOLST FOYLN IN D'RERD! below.

GEY TSUM RICH!

Go to the devil!

A RICH IN DAYN TATTEN ARAYN! A devil into your father!

A RICH IN DAYN TATTENS TATTEN! A devil into your father's father! (This multiplying of a curse is somewhat similar to the multiplying of punch lines in humor, discussed in Chap. I. Similar English form is the eighteenth-century "A mottled pox on you!")

Cf. Resig., CHAPT ES DER RICH!

TSUBRECH DAYN KOP (*or* DAYN FUS)!

Break your head (*or* your leg)!

See also ZOLST TSUBRECHEN BEYDE FIS!

TSU *ZAYN* KOP ZOL ES OYSGEYN!

Lit., May it go out to *his* head! May *he* be the one afflicted with this!

Cf. ALEH CHALOYMES ZOLN OYSGEYN TSU *ZAYN* KOP!

VER TSUHARGET!

Get murdered! Get shot!

DERHARGET ZOLSTU VEREN! Killed, you should get!

Y'MACHSH'MŌ (V'ZICHRŌ)! (Heb.)

May his name (and his memory) be blotted out!

This was used with the mention of any anti-Semitic tyrant. In modern times it has been heard with reference to Haman (Rel. and Cul., HOMEN) and Hitler.

ZOL ER KRIGN DEM TOYT.

May he be stricken with death.

See Chap. IIIA, "Drop dead."

ZOL ER OYSGETRIKNT VEREN!

May he dry up!

This is more sinister than the English slang "Dry up!" which meant to stop talking. It's another way of saying DI BEYNER ZOLN IM OYSRINEN! *or* ER ZOL NOR ANLOYFN!

ZOLST BRENEN (VI A FAYER *or* VI A LICHT)!

May you burn (like a fire *or* like a candle)!

ZOLST FARLIREN ALEH TSEYNER ACHITZ EYNM, UN DOS ZOL DIR VEY TON!

You should lose all your teeth except one and that should ache!

ZOLST FOYLN IN D'RERD!

May you rot in the ground!

ZOLST TSUBRECHEN BEYDE FIS!

You should break both your legs!

LIFE AND HEALTH

ABI GEZUNT

As long as you're healthy.

If we had to choose one Yiddish expression that best epitomizes Jewish experience and attitude, this might be it. Regardless of what we have suffered and endured, it says, if we have our health we're still kicking! It was used years ago in a song with words by Molly Picon: "Abi Gezunt, Kenen Mir Gliklach Zayn" (As Long as We're Healthy, We Can Be Happy).

But there was also some good-natured, almost gruesome irony on the subject, as in:

ABI GEZUNT—DOS LEBN KEN MEN ZICH ALEYN NEMEN! (As long as you're healthy—you can always take your own life!) This is on a par with the expressions noted in Chap. I: NIFTER, PIFTER, ABI GEZUNT! and "Cancer, shmancer, ABI GEZUNT."

The expression has been a favored ploy of advertising copywriters the past few years—so much so that it's been used inappropriately. Ex.: A Sunsweet Prunes ad in a national American Jewish weekly showed an attractive female opening a box of prunes, with the heading: "ABI GEZUNT"; and others have carried the streamer: "ABI GEZUNT with Sunsweet Prunes." As the writer should know, ABI GEZUNT is not called for in either instance; what he should have said was TSU GEZUNT (to health) or FAR'N GEZUNT (for health).

Again, around the High Holy Days, a full-page ad of a liquor company in a leading literary magazine carried the text:
"5726?
1966?
ABI GEZUNT."

This was trying too hard, and seemed in poor taste for the most solemn days of the Jewish calendar.

A LEBN AF DAYN KEPPELE!

A life on your dear little head!

A story often told in the wintertime concerns a young boy who goes to see Santa Claus in a department store. Santa puts him up on his knee and asks what he wants for Christmas. The little boy replies, "I don't want anything for Christmas. I'm Jewish, and I would like a bicycle for Chanuka." Whereupon Santa pats him on the head and exclaims, "AY, A LEBN AF DAYN KEPPELE!"[1]

Also, A GEZUNT AF DAYN KEPPELE! Health on your dear little head! There's a recent story about the Jewish astronaut who says good-bye to his mother. She asks where he is going, and he says, "Into orbit." She replies, "A GEZUNT AF DAYN Capsuleh!"

See Chap. IIIB, "keppy."

A LEBN IN DI BEYNER!

A life in your bones! (enthusiastic approval of a child)

A MENTSH ZOL LEBN SHOYN NOR FUN NAYGERIKAYT VEGN.

A person should live if only for curiosity's sake.

AZ ME LEBT, DERLEBT MEN ALLES.

If you live, you see everything.

Also, AZ ME LEBT, EST MEN. If you live, you eat; i.e., you taste all kinds of experience and have to stomach a good deal.

AZ ME VIL NIT ALT VEREN, ZOL MEN ZICH YUNGERHEYD OYF-HENGEN.

If you don't want to get old, you should hang yourself while you're young.

This may seem morbid, but it is a sardonic reproach to those who cannot accept the difficulties of adulthood, including the inevitable old age.

GEZUNT UN PARNOSSEH!

Health and livelihood!—a common toast, similar to L'CHAY-IM! (Chap. I, Life and Health).

GEZUNT VI GEZUNT—VU NEMT MEN OBER BULBE?

Never mind my health—where do I get some grub (*lit.,* potato)?

GEZUNT ZOLSTU ZAYN!

May you be healthy! (hearty approval of something done or said)

ICH ZOL AZOY LANG LEBN!

I should live so long! (of something that is certain)

Also, ICH ZOL AZOY LEBN UN ZAYN GEZUNT! I should be that sure of life and health!; *and* ZOLSTU AZOY LANG LEBN! May you be as sure of long life! These are *equiv.,* "Honest!"; "I swear it!"; "You can depend on it!"

See Chap. IIIA, "should" and "shouldn't". . . .

Cf. Death, ZOL ICH AZOY LEBN VI ICH VIL SHTARBN!

LANG LEBN ZOLSTU!

Long may you live! (approval of action)

My father's enthusiastic approval of Campbell's tomato soup

was LANG LEBN ZOL CAMPBELLN! (May Campbell live long!)[2]
ME KEN MACHEN DEM CHOLEM GRESSER VI DI NACHT.
You can blow up the dream to be bigger than the night.
See also VOS DER MENTSH KEN ALTS IBERTRACHTEN, ...
VOS DER MENTSH KEN ALTS IBERTRACHTEN, KEN DER ERGSTER
SOYNE IM NIT VINTSHEN.
What a person can think up for himself his worst enemy
can't wish on him.
Cf. Destiny, AF MAYNE ERGSTE SONIM. . . .
VOS TOYG DER GUTER KOP, AZ DI FIS KENEN IM NIT TROGN?
What use is a good head if the feet can't carry it?
Again, the importance of health.

PASSING JUDGMENT

As is evident in almost any category of expression, the Jews
have been adept at observing life. They've been crystallizing
their perceptions into aphorisms and wise sayings ever since
their forebears did it in Hebrew, chiefly in what is known as
the Book of Proverbs in the Bible. They did it in Aramaic, the
language of the Talmud and Midrash, the language that Jesus
spoke. They did it in Ladino—or what some scholars prefer to
call Judezmo or Sephardi—the combination of Spanish, Greek
and other Mediterranean tongues spoken by Sephardic Jews.
They did it in German; and they did it in Yiddish. In Yiddish,
especially, the perceptions have been clothed in colorful phrases
and ironic twists and are very much alive in popular speech
today.

Many Yiddish observations have counterparts in other languages. For example, DORTEN IZ GUT VI MIR ZAYNEN NITO
(The place where we aren't, always seems good) is reminiscent
of "The grass is always greener on the other side of the fence."
This testifies to the universality of human experience. In the
literature of proverbs, many judgments are paralleled even
more closely in a variety of languages, and it is not always
possible to tell where they started. In Chapter I, Psychological
Insight, we saw the Yiddish admonition, VER ES HOT A GEHAN-
GENEM IN DER MISHPOCHE, FAR DEM TOR MEN KEYN SHTRIK
NIT DERMONEN (Don't speak of a rope to someone who's had
a hanging in the family). I recently heard a Pennsylvania radio

announcer quote an Irish saying that was almost identical: "Mention not a rope in the house of someone who's been hanged." In this instance, perhaps the Yiddish came first, since there is an earlier and even keener statement in the Midrash: "He who has been bitten by a snake would be terrified thereafter by a rope."

Consider FIL M'LOCHES,/VEYNIK BROCHES. This is literally, Full of talents, few blessings—equivalent to "Jack of all trades, master of none." It may indeed have been borrowed; yet it shows a characteristically Jewish stamp—the use of the religious concept of BROCHES and the ever popular use of rhyme.

Since the Jews lived in many countries, they must have passed on some of their own folk sayings and also picked up others from the languages around them. But, as A. A. Roback observed, "Only those are selected that are in accordance with the genius of the people borrowing them. . . . It is inconceivable that they [the Jews] should ever borrow, without giving up their identity, the following two Russian sayings: 'Love your wife like your soul and beat her like your fur coat' and 'A dog is wiser than a woman; it does not bark at its own master.' " Though Jewish women did not have equal rank with men in the performance of religious rituals in the synagogue, they were accorded a central place in the home and were never thought of in such brute terms. More typical is the ironic Yiddish proverb, ALEH VAYBER HOBN YERUSHE FUN ZEYER MUTER CHAVE (All wives take after their mother Eve). The Jewish male could thus dispose of female nagging and get back to his work or studies![1]

Thousands of Yiddish proverbs have been recorded, and many more are being collected and await collection. The merest sampling is included here along with judgments of various kinds. (A number of course appear in other categories and in other chapters as well.) You will notice that irony, rhyme and psychological insight seem especially characteristic.

A BARG MIT A BARG BAGEGN ZICH NISHT, OBER A MENTSH MIT A MENTSH KENEN ZICH BAGEGN.

A mountain doesn't meet another mountain, but a person *can* meet another person. (It's always possible for human paths to cross.)

This is sometimes quoted at parting from someone who lives

in another part of the world and whom you are unlikely to see again, in the sense of "It *is* possible; let's hope we do meet again."

A CHAM MIT BILDING IZ NIT MER VI A GEBILDITE CHAM.

A dope with education is just an educated dope.

See also A NAR KEN MEN HAKN UN BROTN, . . . under A NAR BLAYBT A NAR.

AF A FREMDER BORD IZ GUT TSU LERNEN SHEREN. (ironic)

Someone else's beard is good to learn barbering on.

A FREMDER BLAYBT FAR A VAYL/UN ZET A MAYL.

A stranger stays for a while/And sees a mile. That is, A newcomer can see (and appreciate) much that we take for granted.

Sometimes heard as A GAST AF A VAYL/ZET AF A MAYL. A guest for a while/Sees for a mile.

AF TSVEYEN IZ SHTARKER.

With two, it's stronger. "Two heads are better than one."

AF YENEMS HINTN IZ GUT TSU SHMAYSEN. (ironic)

Someone else's behind is good to whip. (It's easy for you to talk.)

A GANTSER NAR IZ A HALBER NOVI.

A whole fool is half a prophet; i.e., What seems very foolish is sometimes wise. Often *abbrev.*, A NAR IZ A NOVI.

Cf. DOS HARTS IZ A HALBER NOVI.

A GAST IZ VI A REGN: AZ ER DOYERT TSU LANG, VERT ER A LAST.

A guest is like rain: if he stays too long, he becomes a pest.

Also, AN OFTER GAST/FALT TSU LAST. A frequent guest/ Becomes a pest.

A GEVORENER/IZ ERGER VI A GEBORENER.

A convert to religion sworn/Is worse than one that's to it born.

Why "worse" and not "better"? This reflects the sad experience with apostates: Jews who converted to Christianity were often more zealous about their new faith—and hence worse in their attitude toward Jews—than born Christians. Part of the reason for this is that into the nineteenth century (and even into our own time, in branches of the Greek Orthodox Church) converted Jews were required in the baptism ritual to renounce and curse all their Jewish relatives, including spouses.

Cf. Rel. and Cul., MESHUMED, A MESHUMED IZ NIT KEYN YID UN NIT KEYN GOY.

A GROYSER OYLEM, UN NITO KEYN MENTSH!

A crowd of people, and not a real person among them!

A HALBER EMES IZ A GANTSER LIGN.

A half-truth is a whole lie.

Also, DER EMES IZ DER BESTER LIGN. The truth is the best lie.

But, FAR DEM EMES SHLOGT MEN. For the truth you get beaten up.

Cf. EMES IZ NOR BAY GOT UN BAY MIR A BISSEL.

A KABTSEN BLAYBT A KABTSEN.

A pauper remains a pauper.

A KATS KEN OYCH KALYE MACHEN.

A cat can spoil things, too; i.e., Plans can be wrecked in ways we least expect. (Even one insignificant person can cause trouble if he shows up at the wrong time.)

ALEH KALEHS ZAYNEN SHEYN; ALEH MEYSIM ZAYNEN FRUM. (ironic)

All brides are beautiful; all the dead are pious.

ALEH YEVONIM/HOBN EYN PONIM.

All military men/Have one mien. All soldiers (*or* barbarians) look alike.

The Hebrew *yevanim* meant "Greeks." The ancient Greeks, with their polytheistic religion and loose standards of morality, were considered heathens and barbarians. The later Yiddish term was applied to Russian troopers and often connoted a brute or a vandal.

See Char. and Des., ER HOT ARAYNGEFALEN VI A YOVEN IN SUKEH.

A MENTSH IZ NOR A MENTSH.

Lit., A person is only a person. We're only human.

A NAR BLAYBT A NAR.

A fool remains a fool.

Also, A NAR KEN MEN HAKN UN BROTN, UN ER BLAYBT A NAR. You can chop and broil a fool, and he'll remain a fool.

A NAR IZ AN EYBIKER TSAR. A fool is an eternal misfortune[2] (hence, nuisance).

A NAR TOR MEN NIT VAYZN KEYN 'ALBE ARBET. A fool should never be shown a half-done job. (He won't be able to visualize the finished product, and he'll only discourage the effort.)

A NAR VAKST ON REGN. A fool grows without rain.

GOT HOT GEGEBN DEM NAR HENT UN FIS UN IM GELOZT LOYFN. God gave the fool hands and feet and let him run.

YEYDER NAR IZ KLIG FAR ZICH. Every fool is smart for himself.

Cf. A GANTSER NAR IZ A HALBER NOVI.

See also BIZ ZIBETSIK YOR . . . *and* ZEY ZAYNEN UNZERE CHACHOMIM . . . below; Char. and Des., SHMER'L NAR (under SHMER'L); Endearment, -ELE, NARELE; *and* Chap. I, beginning of Learning.

A NISHT-VELENDIKER IZ ERGER VI A NISHT-KENENDIKER.

Being unwilling to learn is worse than ignorance.

A NIT-FARDINER/IZ A NIT-FARGINER.

A non-earner is a begrudger. He who isn't earning/Is enjoyment-spurning.

AN OYLEM/IZ NIT KEYN GOYLEM.

Lit., The crowd is no dummy. As Isidore Goldstick has aptly put it, "The masses/Are no asses."

See Ann. and Arg., A GOYLEM!

ARBET MACHT DOS LEBN ZIS.

Work makes life sweet.

A SHEYN PONIM COST GELT.

A pretty face costs money.

A TOYBER HOT GEHERT, VI A SHTUMER HOT DERTSEYLT, AZ A BLINDER HOT GEZEN, VI A KRUMER IZ GELOFN.

A deaf man heard a mute tell how a blind man saw a cripple run. (neat way of discounting gossip)

AZ AN OREMAN EST A HUN, IZ ODER ER KRANK ODER DI HUN.

When a poor man gets to eat a chicken, either he or the chicken is sick.

Cf. Food and Drink, A HUN IZ GUT TSUM ESSEN ZALBENAND . . . .

AZ DER VOREM ZITST IN CHREYN, MEYNT ER AZ 'SIZ KEYN ZISERES NISHT FARAN.

A worm sitting in horseradish thinks nothing sweeter exists. (a spicier form of "Ignorance is bliss")

This is the obvious source of the chapter heading "Sweet Horseradish" in Sam Levenson's autobiography, *Everything but Money.*

AZ DOS MEYDEL KEN NIT TANTSEN, ZOGT ZI DI KLEZMER KENEN NIT SHPILEN.

When the girl can't dance, she says the band can't play. (Alibi Anne)

AZ ICH VEL ZAYN VI ER, VER VET ZAYN VI ICH?

If I'm to be like him, who will be like me?

This is a marvelous defense of individualism, of the importance of each person's expressing his own God-given uniqueness. A similar idea appears in a precious Hasidic story about the beloved Rabbi Zusya, who remarked before his death that in the coming world he would not be asked "Why were you not Moses?" but rather "Why were you not Zusya?"—i.e., "Why did you not develop all of your own potentialities?"

AZ ME GEYT TSVISHN LAYT, VEYST MEN VOS S'TUT ZICH IN DER HEYM.

When you get out among people, you know what's going on in your own home.

AZ ME SHMIRT DI REDER, GEYT DER VOGN.

If you grease the wheels, the wagon rides. (Money talks.)

See Advice, ME DARF IM SHMIREN.

AZ ME SHPAYT DER ZOYNE IN PONIM, ZOGT ZI AZ S'REGNT.

If you spit in a whore's face, she'll say it's raining.

This has also been said of the SHLEMIEL.

AZ ME ZITST BAY'M TEPL, EST MEN.

If you sit beside the pot, you eat; hence, He who's close to the till gets his fingers into it. (of a treasurer of an organization, for instance)

AZ M'IZ TSU KLIG, LIGT MEN GOR IN D'RERD.

When you're too smart, you're really done for.

See also VOS DER MENTSH FARSHTEYT VEYNIKER, IZ ALTS FAR IM BESER.

AZ S'KUMT TSUM LEBN, SHTARBT MEN.

Just when it comes time to live, we die.

BIZ ZIBETSIK YOR LERNT MEN SEYCHL, UN ME SHTARBT A NAR.

Until we're seventy we keep getting smart, and we die fools.

CHAZER KOSHER FISSEL.

The pig shows his little kosher foot. (of a crook trying to pass himself off as honest)

The pig has a cloven hoof, one of the requirements of kosher animals, but does *not* chew his cud and is therefore TREYF (*see* introduction to Food and Drink). I assume the expression derives from an observation in the Midrash: "The pig spreads out its paws as though to say: 'See! I am clean.'"

CHUTZPA GILT!

Cheek helps! A little nerve goes a long way!

See Char. and Des., CHUTZPA.

DER BESTER SHUSTER FUN ALEH SHNAYDERS IZ YANKEL DER BEKER.

The best cobbler of all the tailors is Jake the Baker.

DER GVIR BLOZT ZICH, UN DER OREMAN VERT GESHVOLN.

The rich man boasts (*lit.*, blows himself), and the pauper gets swollen.

This puns on BLOZT ZICH and VERT GESHVOLN. (*See* Imprec., GESHVOLN ZOLSTU VEREN!)

DI KRO FLIT HEYACH UN ZETST ZICH AF A CHAZER.

The crow flies high and lights onto a pig.

Cf. the similar thought in M'IZ KLIG UN KLIG, UN AZ S'KUMT TSU EPPES, BAMACHT MEN ZICH (Chap. I, note to beginning of Vulgarity).

DOS HARTS IZ A HALBER NOVI.

The heart is half a prophet. (We should trust our feelings.)

DOS LEBN IZ NIT MER VI A CHOLEM—OBER VEK MICH NIT OYF!

Life is just a dream—but don't wake me up!

EMES IZ NOR BAY GOT UN BAY MIR A BISSEL.

Truth rests only with God and with me a little.

EYB ME HOT GORNIT IN KOP, DARF MEN HOBN EPPES IN FIS.

If you have nothing in the head, you have to have something in the feet; i.e., If you aren't a brain, you have to "shake a leg" to get somewhere.

EYN VELT, UN ALEH CHAYES.

One world, and all animals. "It takes all kinds to make a world."

EYNEM DACHT ZICH/AZ BAY YENEM LACHT ZICH.

Each tends to assume/The other's free of gloom (*lit.*, laughing).

See also YEYDER HOT ZICH ZAYN PEKL.

FAR DER VELT MUZ MEN MER YOYTSE ZAYN VI FAR GOT ALEYN.

For the world you have to be more faultless than for God Himself. (People are hypercritical.)

FAR GELT BAKUMT MEN ALLES, NOR KEYN SEYCHEL NIT.

With money you can get everything except sense.

FUN A CHAZERS EK KEN MEN KEYN SHTRAYMEL NIT MACHEN.

You can't make a fur mitre out of a pig's tail.

This is reminiscent of the English "You can't make a silk purse out of a sow's ear." However, A. A. Roback observed that the contrast in the Yiddish expression is much sharper, for to the Old World Jew the pig was vile and the rabbi's fur hat was a symbol of spirituality.

GESHMAK IZ DI FISH/AF YENEMS TISH.

Tasty is the fish/On another's dish (*lit.*, table).

See also introduction above, DORTEN IZ GUT VI MIR ZAYNEN NITO, *and* EYNEM DACHT ZICH . . . above.

GIB A BEHEYME A ZAROZE. (ironic)

Give a cow a gravy. (Would a cow appreciate a gravy? That's how this valuable thing is appreciated by that boor.) *Equiv.*, "casting pearls before swine."

GISTU, BISTU.

Lit., If you give, you are. "If ya gives, ya gits"—i.e., If you have something others want, they'll take an interest in you.

This has been applied sardonically to the Great Powers' interest in the Arab nations and the oil they have to offer.

GURNIT MIT GURNIT IZ ALTS GURNIT.

Nothing plus nothing is still nothing.

ITLECHER MENTSH HOT ZICH ZAYN SHIGOYEN.

Every man has his own peculiar quirk.

ITLECHER YID HOT ZAYN SHULCHEN-ORUCH (UN ZAYN SHIGOYEN). Every Jew has his own code of laws[3] (and his own kind of lunacy). This reflects the fact that each Jew, in studying religious law, didn't hesitate to interpret it according to his own understanding. (*See* introduction to Tribalism.)

See also Chap. IIIB, "Everyone has his own MISHUGAS."

ITLECHER SHTOT HOT IR MISHUGGENEM.

Every town has its nut.

KEYN B'REYRE IZ OYCH A B'REYRE.

No choice is also a choice.

See Chap. I, Realism, A B'REYRE HOT MEN? *and* Advice, HOB NIT KEYN MEYRE/AZ DU HOST NIT KEYN ANDER B'REYRE.

KEYN SHTROM KEN MEN MIT A SHPENDEL NISHT FARHALTEN.

You can't stop a stream with a sliver.

ME HERT KLINGEN UN ME VEYST NIT VI.

One hears ringing and doesn't know where. That is, It rang a bell, but he doesn't know which one. (comment on an explanation that's partly right but essentially wrong)

ME KRICHT AF DI GLAYCHE VENT.

They're climbing on the straight walls. They're trying to do the impossible.

Cf. Char. and Des., ZI KRICHT AF DI VENT.

ME TANST AF ALEH CHASINEHS.

They dance at all the weddings. "They have their fingers in every pie."

This has been applied good-naturedly to the national Jewish organization B'nai B'rith, which has a wide variety of programs.

ME VERT ALT VI A KU/UN ME LERNT ZICH ALTS TSU.

You get old as a cow/And still learn how. We keep on learning all through life.

But *cf.* BIZ ZIBBETSIK YOR. . . .

MIT EYN EY KEN MEN A GANTSE SHISL BORSHT FARVAYSEN.

With one egg you can whiten a whole pan of borsht; i.e., One good thing, though it be little, can be put to use for a large purpose.

See Food and Drink, BORSHT.

NIT GENUG VOS DER NOGID IZ A NOGID, GILT NOCH ZAYN KVITL OYCH!

Not enough that a rich man is rich, his checks are good, yet, too!

ODER ME DARF NISHT, ODER ES HELFT NISHT.

Either it isn't necessary, or it won't help.

This fits an amazing number of human situations. Next to ABI GEZUNT, it may be the most widely usable key to Yiddish ironic philosophy. A specific application of the same idea appears in:

A GUTER YID DARF NIT KEYN BRIV, A SHLECHTN YIDN HELFT NIT KEYN BRIV. A letter of recommendation isn't needed by a good Jew, and it won't help a bad one.

"*Olom ke'minhogo noheg*"—DERIBER ZET TAKEH DI VELT AZOY OYS!

"The world goes on its ancient way"—that's just why it looks the way it does!

OREM UN RAYCH/—IN BOD ZAYNEN ZEY BEYDE GLAYCH.

Poor and rich/—In the bath they're equal, without a stitch.

PISTE MANSES! (*or* PUSTE MAYSES!)

Idle tales! Empty talk!

SHLOFN SHPET BRENGT OREMKAYT.

Sleeping late brings poverty. Reminiscent of the opposite and broader "Early to bed, early to rise, makes a man healthy, wealthy and wise."

SHPILST ZICH MIT *IM!* (ironic)

Lit., You're playing with *him!* Look whom you're fooling around with! Some guy to get involved with!

'SIZ AROYSGEVORFINE GELT.

It's money thrown out. It's money down the drain.

'SIZ DI EYGENE YENTE, NOR ANDERSH GESHLEYERT.

It's the same old hag, just differently veiled (i.e., with a different cover-up). Reminiscent of "No matter how you slice it, it's still baloney."

See Char. and Des., YENTE.

'SIZ NUCH DI CHASINEH (*or* NUCH'N YONTEF).

It's after the wedding (*or* after the holiday). It's an anticlimax. "The party's over."

'SIZ NUCH DI CHASINEH UN FAR'N BRIS (It's after the wedding and before the circumcision) was my comment on the drop in attendance at services on a Sabbath after the High Holy Days and before SUKOS.

'SIZ ODER GOR ODER GORNISHT.

It's either all or nothing. It's either one extreme or the other.

'SIZ SHOYN NISHT FRI! (ironic)

It's already not early! (of a situation that's pretty far gone)

Re. the negative irony here, *see* Char. and Des., ER VET SHOYN KEYN HONIK NIT LEKN.

'SVET GORNISHT HELFEN!

It won't help a bit! (putting a damper on a proposed solution)

This is often used good-naturedly.

'SVET HELFEN VI A TEYTEN BANKES.

It'll help like cupping a corpse. It's no use.

Cupping was a medical procedure for bringing down a high fever. It made use of small glass cups, whose rims were moistened and then applied with pressure on arms, chest and back. Molly Picon recalls that though the cups were removed after ten or fifteen minutes, she had white circles on her body for weeks afterward.

A recent comic definition of this expression is "Hair Tonic."

TSU FIL IZ UMGEZUNT.

Too much is unhealthy.

ME KEN TRACHTEN TSU FIL OYCH. You can think too much, too. (*See* Chap. I, Psychol. Insight.)

TSU FIL KOVED IZ HALB A SHANDE. Too much honor is half a shame.

VOS 'SIZ TSU IZ UMGEZUNT. Anything in excess is unhealthy.

An old story has two men in conversation, during which one quotes VOS 'SIZ TSU IZ UMGEZUNT. His companion counters that sometimes a TSU can be desirable, as when a bad wife dies: VEN DI ERD DEKT IR TSU (when the earth covers her over). A bit morbid, perhaps, but characteristic of the ready pun in Yiddish speech.

See also AZ M'IZ TSU KLIG, ...

TSVEY GOYLIM GEYEN TANTSEN.

Two dummies are going to dance. (of two incompetents who become partners)

VEN ALEH MENTSHEN ZOLN TSIEN AF EYN ZAYT, VOLT ZICH DI VELT IBERGEKERT.

If everyone pulled in one direction, the world would keel over.

Variety and difference make for balance! This is a worthy defense of the characteristically Jewish difference of opinion. An ironic jest often quoted by rabbis is that the only thing two Jews can agree on is how much a third Jew should give to charity. An old story has it that three Jews were stranded on an island, and that when they were picked up several years later the island had three synagogues. Another version has one Jew stranded. When he is picked up, the rescuers see two synagogues. Asked why he needed two, he replies that one is the SHUL he stays away from. (*See also* stories quoted in introduction to Tribalism.)

VER ES HALT DI PEN, DER SHRAYBT ZICH ON A GUT YOR.

He who holds the pen inscribes for himself a good year.

This is an ironic reference to the ROSHESHONE hope of being inscribed in the Book of Life for the coming year. (*See* Greetings and Partings, L'SHONE TEYVE.) It is reminiscent of "God helps those who help themselves."

VER IZ GEVEN ZAYN ZEYDE? (ironic)

Who was his grandfather (that he should be so proud)? That is, Who does he think he is? What's *his* pedigree?

See Family, ZEYDE.

VOS DER MENTSH FARSHTEYT VEYNIKER, IZ ALTS FAR IM BESER.

The less a person understands, the better off he is. (sardonic comment on the difficulties that intelligence and sensitivity involve)

VOS KLENER DER OYLEM, ALTS GRESER DI SIMCHA.

The smaller the crowd, the better the party.

See Family, SIMCHA.

VOS ME HOT VIL MEN NIT, UN VOS ME VIL HOT MEN NIT.

What we have we don't want, and what we want we don't have.

VOS MER GEVART,/MER GENART.

The longer you wait,/The more cheated your fate. (When you're too fussy, you get fooled in the end.)

YEYDER HOT ZICH ZAYN PEKL.

Everyone has his own bundle of trouble. "Everybody's got something."

YEYDER HOT ZICH ZAYNS. Everyone has his.

YEYDER TEPL HOT ZAYN DEKL.

Every pot has its cover. There's someone for everyone in this world (even for the likes of him!).

Cf. Chap. I, Rhyme, YEYDER VOREM/HOT ZAYN DOREM.

ZEY ZAYNEN UNZERE CHACHOMIM VAYL MIR ZAYNEN ZEYERE NARONIM.

They're our sages because we're their fools.

This bitter irony about the wisdom of supposed authorities expresses aptly the resentments that are so often felt toward "experts" in government and diplomacy.

ZINGN KEN ICH NIT, OBER A MEYVEN BIN ICH!

I can't sing, but a connoisseur I am!

See Chap. IIIA, "maven."

Cf. Rel. and Cul., CHAZEN.

RELIGION AND CULTURE

It is intriguing how many popular Yiddish terms come under this heading. Religion and group experience played an important part in the life of the Jew. Not only was his folk culture a cycle of Sabbaths, holidays and fast days, but it included prayers and rituals for daily living, for every stage of life.

Notice how religious concepts colored terms of everyday social use. A cooperative free-loan association was a G'MILUS CHESED, which means "bestowal of lovingkindness" in Hebrew. The word for "charity," TSEDOKE, is from the Hebrew word for "justice": i.e., it is only just to help those in need. And an organization for helping the poor was an OYZER DALIM (comforter of the poor).

In the proverb TOYRE IZ DI BESTE S'CHOYRE (Torah is the best merchandise), we see—as Yudel Mark has observed—not only the sociological fact that Jews were often tradesmen, but the additional fact that they placed the study of Torah above their means of livelihood. This proverb has been preserved in several old lullabies, in which the line rhymes with YANKELE (or YUDELE) VET LERNEN TOYRE (Little Jacob—or little Yudel —will study Torah).

At the same time, the ironic wit which served as an armor against fate and a weapon for jousting with God made capital of familiar religious terminology as well.

Give a look:

AFIKEYMEN (Heb. *Afikŏmen*)

Piece of matzo which is hidden before the SEYDER on Passover. At a certain point in the service, the children are given a chance to hunt for it, the finder getting a prize.

My husband speaks of this search for the Afikomen as "the seventh-inning stretch," noting the wisdom of our ancestors in providing this break in the ritual so that the youngsters' attention is not lost. (Similar insight is evident in the Purim holiday. *See* GRAGER.)

AGODE (Heb. *Aggadah*)

Story and legendary material of the Talmud.

Cf. HAGODE.

ALIEH (Heb. *aliyah:* ascent)

Honor of being called to the pulpit to read from the Torah or to recite a blessing before or after the Torah reading (*see* BROCHE) or to open and close the Ark, etc.

A more colloquial term is OYFRUF—calling up. (*See* Chap. IIIB, "woof-woof" for OYF-RUF.)

A recent joke in the Yiddish *Day-Journal* tells of a man arrested for robbery who indicates to the judge that he once gave a Torah scroll to the synagogue. "In that case," replies the judge, "I will give you an ALIEH: *aliyah shishi*—six years." This plays on the sixth ALIEH of the Sabbath service.

AMIDE (Heb. *Amidah*)

Adoration—prayer recited before the open Ark.

An eight-year-old girl in London was reported to have been overheard by her mother as she discoursed to her younger sister on "Sir Francis Drake and the Spanish *Amidah.*"

ANI MAYMIN (Heb. *Ani ma'amin*)

Lit., I believe. Credo—referring to the Thirteen Articles of Faith of Maimonides.

A famous song with that title was sung by the doomed Jews who entered the Hitler crematories in the 1940's.

APIKORES (pl. APIKORSIM—from the name of the Greek philosopher Epicurus, by way of Heb. *epikuros,* free thinker)

Heretic.

ARI

Lion—nickname for sixteenth-century mystic Rabbi Yitschok Luria.

This rabbi was the teacher of Joseph Karo, who compiled the SHULCHEN ORUCH. He was thought by some to be the Messiah. One fascinating fact about his career is that the cooperative colony he established had to disband because the wives of his followers could not get along!

The term is short for Hebrew *Haari,* "the Lion"—itself an acrostic of *ha'elohi rav Yitschak,* "the divine rabbi Isaac" (or, as some prefer, of the Hebrew-Yiddish *Adoneynu* REBBE YITSCHOK—"Our Master REBBE YITSCHOK").

Cf. Chap. I, Acronyms.

BAL SHEM TOV (familiarly, DER BAL SHEM *or* DER BESHT—*see* Chap. I, Acronyms)

Title given to the pious Jew who founded the Hasidic movement in the eighteenth century, the watchword of whose life was: "Remember this always: wherever you are, God is with you. Why, then, ever be afraid?"

BAR MITSVE (often pronounced BAL MITSVE)

A Jewish boy of thirteen who, having completed a prescribed course of study, participates in a special Sabbath Service and is inducted into the adult religious community.

Usually translated as "Son of the Commandment." Actually means "Eligibility for doing good." (BAR is Aramaic, from Hebrew *Ben,* literally "son," but connoting "inheriting" or "eligibility." MITSVE, from Hebrew *Mitzvah,* is literally "commandment" but connotes "commandment to do good.")

The term is also used to refer to the religious service involved and, loosely, to the party that usually follows. TV viewers have heard the leader of an instrumental group say, "Let's make it good, boys; we may get a Bar Mitzvah." This means, of course, "Someone may hire us to play at a Bar Mitzvah party."

In recent years, the party has often taken on the dimensions of a wedding, and the planning of a Bar Mitzvah has become a great social undertaking. I recall one mother in the throes of

preparation who jokingly said, "I wish he'd run off and elope!"
A recent little book attempts to help the mother in her plans so
she won't have to feel that disturbed.

Many rabbis have been deploring the fact that there is often
too much "bar" and not enough *mitzvah* in the occasion. In
some circles, the religious ceremony itself (usually on Saturday
morning) may be attended by only a small family group, with
a large crowd of guests at the Saturday night party. Sometimes
there is a special table at the party for the boy and his contemporaries; other times there is an extra celebration for the youngsters the following day. So important has the partying aspect
become, that in one Long Island community a boy who had not
studied for Bar Mitzvah at all was nevertheless given a big
shindig for his thirteenth birthday, so he would not feel "left
out"!

Jews have been poking their own fun at these trends. According to my husband, "A Bar Mitzvah is a party preceded by a
religious service." Concerning said party, a couple of Pennsylvania vocalist-comediennes have a number which speaks of
"champagne flowing like a river,/with a model of my boy in
chopped liver." A recent joke popular among rabbis tells of the
Bar Mitzvah at which the caterer wheels in a large cake of ice,
out of which steps the Bar Mitzvah boy! But truth is sometimes
wilder than humor. At a Bar Mitzvah celebration in New York
several years ago, the caterers brought out a tremendous cake
with tall lighted tapers—so tall and so numerous that they set
off the sprinkler system! As the French puts it, *Plus ça change,
plus c'est la même chose.* In sixteenth-century Poland, the Bar
Mitzvah SUDEH, or feast, became so elaborate, Jewish leaders
imposed a communal tax to discourage extravagance!

Still, some families exercise their own restraint. I recall being
told by a relative in New Jersey that she had attended a Bar
Mitzvah that was "extremely simple," with the explanation:
"They're *very* wealthy people." There are others, of course,
than the very wealthy who allow themselves to be simple—
particularly in small communities, where in Reform congregations the Bar Mitzvah is often part of the Friday evening
service. And the religious ceremony is indeed an impressive one,
in which you sense the continuity of generations when the father
and grandfathers are called up to the Torah to join the young
man and offer the traditional blessings. This, plus the fact that

Judaism seems to "demand things of its young people" is the impression that Christians often admiringly express.[1] (The Hebrew and other instruction usually takes a number of months in addition to the usual religious-school curriculum.)

Reform Judaism in the late 1880's abolished Bar Mitzvah and introduced instead a Confirmation service at Shevuoth for boys and girls in the tenth year of religious school—most of them fifteen or sixteen. (*See* SHVUES.) Around the 1920's Bar Mitzvah began "coming back," and it is more usual today for a Reform Jewish boy to observe the ceremony than not. Confirmation has been retained, though some boys "drop out" after Bar Mitzvah. Some Conservative congregations have also instituted Confirmation.

The term is often heard as an English verb: "He's the rabbi who Bar Mitzvah'd me" or "I was Bar Mitzvah'd in the old temple."

See Family, NACHES; Food and Drink, BROMFN.

BAS MITSVE

The equivalent, for girls, of BAR MITSVE. Introduced by the Conservative movement, and adopted by some Reform congregations.

BENTSHEN

To bless.

BENTSHEN LICHT To recite the blessing over the candles on Sabbath and holiday eves.

Cf. Family, GEBENTSHT MIT KINDER.

BEYS 'AMIGDESH (Heb. *Beys Hamikdosh*)

The Holy Temple of ancient Jerusalem.

BEYS MEDRESH *See* MEDRESH.

BIKUR CHOYLIM

Sick visit. *Also,* an organization devoted to helping the indigent sick.

The custom of visiting the sick goes back to Biblical times and was considered a duty in the Talmud, which noted that the Gentile sick should be visited too. In the Middle Ages, Jews would visit the sick after leaving the synagogue on Sabbath morning. Many congregations today have a "sick committee," which visits patients at the hospital either in place of or in addition to the rabbi.

BIME (Heb. *bimah*)

The pulpit.

BINTEL BRIV

Letter-bundle; letter-box—name of column conducted by *DI FORVERTS (Jewish Daily Forward)* in the early 1900's and the subject of some recent reminiscing.

B'REYSHIS (Heb.)

This is the opening phrase of Genesis, customarily translated as "In the beginning." Sometimes used figuratively.

See Family, CHOSSEN.

BRIS (from Heb. *b'rith milah*)

Circumcision.

Traditionally performed on the eighth day of life of a Jewish male infant. The occasion is one of rejoicing and is followed by refreshments for family and friends.

The physical merits vs. drawbacks of circumcision are discussed periodically in various quarters, sometimes quite emotionally by non-Jews. There is apparently no indisputable evidence that it is advisable medically, even though it is becoming quite common among American Gentiles as a presumed aid against infection. (In other parts of the world, of course, many peoples other than the Jews follow the practice, usually at later ages.) Rabbinical leadership prefers that it be viewed as a religious rite exclusively, even though its original meaning among the ancient Hebrews is uncertain—despite the many references to it in the Bible and Talmud. The practice has a strong hold on modern Jews, whether or not it is accompanied by a religious ritual.

See MOYEL.

BROCHE

Blessing, benediction.

"Does he know the BROCHES?" might be asked about someone who has unexpectedly been called up to the Torah. (Separate blessings are recited before and after the reading from the Torah scroll.)

A recent joke tells of the Jewish woman who wants to have a Christmas tree but needs to salve her conscience about it. She calls up an Orthodox rabbi and asks if he can say a BROCHE over the tree to make it acceptable. He vehemently turns her down. She calls a Conservative rabbi, and he too tells her no, by no means could he sanction her use of a Christmas tree. She finally calls a Reform rabbi and asks if *he* would approve her tree and say a BROCHE over it. He assures her it is all right to have the tree if she wishes it. "But tell me," he asks, "what is a BROCHE?" This mirrors the derision in which many Orthodox Jews hold Reform rabbis, whom they consider to be little different from GOYIM, implying that the Reform rabbis know nothing about Hebrew law and learning. In point of fact, of course, most Reform rabbis are highly educated, in Jewish as well as general studies. Most are endowed too with a good sense of humor and even enjoy telling such jokes on themselves.

See Char. and Des., S'VAKST SHOYN FUN GORGL and introduction to Passing Judgment *re.* FIL M'LOCHES,/VEYNIK BROCHES.

CHABAD

A branch of the Hasidic movement (*see* CHOSID) which emphasizes the role of the intellect, the term being an acronym of three Hebrew words: *chochmah, binah* and *deyah* (wisdom, understanding and knowledge).

The term is the accepted designation of the LUBAVITSHER Hasidim (*see* end of REBBE).

CHAMISHO OSER B'SHVAT

The "New Year of the Trees," a holiday coming six weeks after CHANUKA and marking the time when planting begins in the Holy Land.

Many synagogue religious schools distribute plants to the children in observance of the day.

See Food and Drink, BOKSER; Chap. I, Famil. with God, note *re.* alternate name, TU B'SHVAT.

CHANUKA

The winter holiday which commemorates the victory of the Maccabees over the Syrians in the second pre-Christian century, generally considered to be the first recorded battle for religious freedom.

According to tradition, when the temple had been cleansed of the Syrians' defilement of it, the Eternal Light (*see* NER TOMID) of the sanctuary was lighted, with enough oil that would normally last for a day, but it miraculously burned for eight days. For this reason, Chanuka is celebrated for eight days, the lights of the menorah being lighted on the eve of each day. (*See* MENOYRE.)

As rabbis have often noted, Chanuka could well be celebrated by Christians also, for if Judaism had not survived that encounter with the Syrians, Jesus (who was born over a hundred years afterward) would not have been a Jew with his background of monotheistic Scripture, and Christianity might never have arisen. Actually, centuries ago the Church Fathers gave recognition to the event by including the First and Second Maccabees in their version of the Old Testament (these are not included in the Hebrew Bible), and up until the fifth century the Church observed a day in memory of Hannah and her seven sons, whose martyrdom is described in II Maccabees. In line with current ecumenism, during the past few years Chanuka programs have been held in some Catholic institutions, though the candle-lighting ceremony has been adapted in Christian terms.

Increasingly, Chanuka is being observed in public schools, in joint Christmas-Chanuka celebrations. But Jews are not always happy about this. For one thing, the dates of the two holidays do not always fall close to each other and the idea may seem forced. For another, many such programs are almost totally Christian in character, representing Chanuka by a Hebrew song or two which may have no relation at all to the occasion. Most importantly, in view of the problem of separation of church and state, many Jews feel it would be preferable not to introduce Chanuka into the schools, that neither it nor Christmas belongs there. However, in the realistic here-and-now, there is probably some psychological boost for the Jewish child when *his* holiday too is recognized as existing and he is not completely the outsider.

Although a minor holiday in the Jewish calendar, Chanuka has been taking on new importance because of the impact of Christmas. Chanuka gift-wraps and home decorations are being widely used in families with young children, some of whom are putting lighted menorahs in the window, as is done by many Christians at Christmas. (This practice was customary for Jews centuries ago, but it became dangerous as an identification of the Jewish home in a season when anti-Semitic outrages were common. *See* DI BLINDE NACHT below.)

Indeed, to many American Jews Christmas is a perennial problem. Should a Jew celebrate Christmas? To what extent? If he omits the religious aspect of the holiday (as so many Gentile Americans do anyway) and merely adopts the secular trappings like gifts and cards and Santa Claus and a tree, will it help or confuse his children? And how will his truly Christian neighbor look at it all? Should a Jewish physician have a

Christmas tree in his office? (One such—an active member of a Conservative congregation—explained to me, "They expect it." But I have known Gentile doctors and dentists who did not have trees.) Jews may laughingly call their tree a "Chanuka bush," but s'VET GORNISHT HELFEN.[2] Besides, what happens when the dates of the two holidays are far apart?

As in so many other areas, Jews vary greatly in their practice, and the bi-cultural experience is not new. I recall that Anne Frank's diary noted the observance of "St. Nick's Day" as well as Chanuka when her family and their fellow refugees were hiding from the Nazis in Holland. And I remember that the late saintly American rabbi Abraham Cronbach once reported having had a tiny Christmas tree on the mantle next to the Chanuka menorah for the benefit of his young daughter. (It apparently did not dilute her Judaism. She married a rabbi.)

There are many spellings: Chanuka, Chanukah, Hanuka, Hannuka, Hanukka, Hanuko, etc. Cartoonist Fr. Mac dramatized the difficulty of making the choice in a picture of his little priest "Brother Juniper" painting a sign on the church's outdoor bulletin board:

"HAPPY
~~HANUKA~~
~~HANNUKKA~~
~~CHANNUKA~~
~~CHANNUKKA~~
FEAST OF LIGHTS
RABBI GOLDBERG."

CHANUKA GELT   Chanuka money—traditional gift for the holiday. Children used to receive coins, but today they often get paper money, along with other gifts (frequently a different gift on each night of the holiday).

See DREYDEL; stories under BROCHE *and* Life and Health, A LEBN AF DAYN KEPPELE!

CHASID *See* CHOSID.

CHAZEN (pl. CHAZONIM)

A cantor—synagogue functionary who chants parts of the religious service.

Reform Judaism in the late nineteenth century dropped the use of a cantor and introduced the mixed choir instead. In the past generation, however, the Reform movement has established several schools for the training of cantors, and many

Reform temples have both a choir and a cantor. (At the same time, many Conservative congregations have added female choirs while retaining the cantor.)

There are a number of ironic stories about CHAZONIM. One tells of the famous CHAZEN who is approached by a poor itinerant colleague asking for the privilege of performing in his SHUL. The great cantor is certain that the fellow has no voice, but gives in to his pleading and takes him to the synagogue. There the guest CHAZEN attempts to sing but does very poorly. He afterward apologizes to his host for having lost his voice. The latter says it is a pity (A RACHMONES). The itinerant tells him not to be distressed, he is sure his voice will come back. And his host replies ironically, "That's the pity—that it *will* come back!"

ALEH YIDDEN KENEN ZAYN CHAZONIM, OBER MEYSTNS ZAYNEN ZEY HEYZERIK. All Jews can be cantors, but usually they're hoarse. This reflects the ready criticism of the cantor's performance, every man thinking he could do as well. An old record by Ludwig Satz, "Gey Zay a Shammes" (Go Be a Shammes), presented a SHAMMES's burlesque of the CHAZEN's performance: "SHA-BOS, BO-SHA, SHA-BOS, BO-SHA" and then in faster tempo: "SHA-BOS, BO-SHA, SHA-BOS, BO-SHA—AY, A FINSTER LEBN AF IM!" (Sab-bath, bath-Sab, Sab-bath, bath-Sab—O, a black life upon him!)

On the other hand, when a man did well, he was appreciated warmly. I remember one of my father's favorite records, "A Chazendel af Shabbes" (A Fine Cantor for the Sabbath), which had the famous Mordecai Hershman singing OY, OY, OY, OY, OY, OY, OY, HOT ER GEDAVENT! (Oh, My, My, Did He Chant the Prayers!).

The inspired chanting of a CHAZEN is supposed to have once saved three thousand Jews from slaughter. The remarkable incident took place in the Ukraine in 1648 (a year, by the way, that the Kabalists had predicted the Messiah would come). The infamous Chmielnitzky had been directing his Cossacks, aided by Tatars, in a wild outbreak of Crusading violence, and at sunset the few thousand remaining Jews in the region assembled in a Jewish cemetery for a last-ditch resistance. As a band of Tatars approached, a certain Cantor Hirsch among the Jews asked permission of the Tatar officer to recite a prayer for the dead and began chanting *Eyl moley rachamim.* . . .[3] The fervent plea to God was so spell-binding, that the Tatar leader commanded his men to retreat.[4] (A ransom was later extracted, but the Jewish lives had been spared, at least for a time.)

See Tribalism, YIDDISHE KRECHTS; Passing Judgment, ZINGN KEN ICH NIT OBER A MEYVEN BIN ICH; Endearment, -EL; Chap. I, Psychol. Insight, AZ M'IZ BAROYGES AFN CHAZEN. . . .

CHEVRE-KADDISHE

Lit., holy society; burial society.

This institution of Jewish life in earlier centuries has become outmoded. Whatever such groups still exist usually take care of Jewish paupers' burials.

A fascinating remnant of the tradition is the annual "Chevre-Kaddishe Dinner" held by many Conservative and Orthodox congregations. The feast is free, and guests come prepared to make donations, usually in someone's memory. The cantor sings the *Eyl moley rachamim* in memory of those departed since the last dinner, and a master of ceremonies introduces humor into the occasion, calling on various members to "say a few words." They vie with one another in telling stories, but—as one participant has put it—"they all know what they're there for."

CHEYDER

Hebrew school.

Memories of CHEYDER in the United States have provided material for Jewish comedians as well as for middle-aged alienated intellectuals who deplore the personality and pedagogy of the MELAMED in whose charge they were put in ill-kept quarters. For Hebrew lessons today the buildings and instructors may be modern, bright and clean, but the teachers still have trouble keeping order. Where the MELAMED used the ruler and threatened with his strap, the modern Hebrew teacher takes all he can and then sends the kid to the office. But at bottom, the problem is youth itself. It just doesn't want to be cooped up for study in the late afternoon, after a day at regular school.

There are today a number of Jewish parochial schools in which Hebrew is taught as a regular part of the curriculum. Presumably these have solved some of the human problems of the CHEYDER and of its modern synagogue counterpart, the three-afternoons-a-week Hebrew school.

CHEYREM

Excommunication—a procedure now obsolete.

A famous Jew to receive CHEYREM was the seventeenth-century Dutch philosopher Baruch Spinoza, who was ahead of his time. (Though critical of both Judaism and Christianity on grounds of reason, he never questioned the existence of God; it was his conception of the nature of God that troubled his contemporaries. Today we of course know the phenomenon of Jewish thinkers—including even a few rabbis—who believe that God is dead or that He never existed at all.)

CHILUL HASHEM   *See* HASHEM.

CHOSID (pl. CHASIDIM)

Member of a Hasidic sect.

The Hasidic movement emerged in the eighteenth century, appealing to the unlettered Jew as a relief from the stiff intellectualism of the rabbis. It emphasized joy rather than duty in the individual's relationship to God and gave rise to many pious tales, songs and dances. A number of the tales, collected by the philosopher Martin Buber and also by the American rabbi Louis I. Newman, are available in English (the latter in paperback). In the past decade or so they have had some impact on American Jewish intellectuals. Novelist Norman Mailer even attempted his own commentaries on certain Hasidic sayings.

See REBBE.

CHUMESH

Study text of the Pentateuch, the first five books of the Bible, the so-called Five Books of Moses (Genesis, Exodus, Leviticus, Numbers and Deuteronomy), comprising the text of the Torah scroll which is kept in the Holy Ark.

CHURBN (Heb. *churban*)

Destruction.

For centuries this was applied to the destruction of the Temple in Jerusalem. In the present generation, it denotes the Nazi holocaust of 1938-1945. Books dealing with the holocaust are often referred to as "Churban literature."

DAVENEN

To chant the Hebrew prayers; to pray.

ER KEN GUT DAVENEN. He can chant the Hebrew prayers very well.

An ironic little story by Peretz tells of a poor tailor whose son, a doctor, comes to visit. The father asks his son to accompany him to SHUL, but the son presents various arguments against praying: God does not need to be told of our troubles; He knows them. Why then pray? To tell Him how great He is? He knows that too. And He must find it embarrassing to be constantly praised. The father thinks and then says, "What you say is true. But tell me, you still have to pray, no?" (*See* similar story *re.* DAVENEN MINCHE in Chap. I, Famil. with God.)[5]

One theory traces DAVENEN to Hebrew *daf*, leaf or page; another to Middle Low German *daven* or *doven*, to be noisy, as in the chirping of birds. (*See* introduction to Tribalism *re.* a Sholem Aleichem story.)[6]

See SHOKLEN.

DAYEN

Judge of the rabbinical court.

DERECH ERETZ

Lit., the way of the land. Propriety; good manners.

See ERETZ YISROEL.

DER OYBERSHTER

The Most High; The One Above (reminiscent of, though more reverent than, "The Man Upstairs").

See Destiny, ZOL IR DER OYBERSHTER BAHALTEN.

DI BLINDE NACHT

The blind night. Christmas Eve.

In the Old World it was unsafe for Jews to be out on Christmas Eve. On that night they therefore stayed away from the synagogue and could not study the holy books; hence the night was "blind."

DI FIR KASHES

The Four Questions—part of the Passover SEYDER ritual—beginning with *Ma nishtano halaylo hazeh mikol haleylōs?* (Why is this night different from all other nights?).

See HAGODE; Char. and Des., CHOCHEM, A CHOCHEM FUN DER MA NISHTANO; Chap. III;[7] Exclam., AF A MAYSE FREGT MEN NIT. . . .

DIN

A ruling; a rabbinic judgment of a dispute.

DIN TOYRE   A legal suit tried before a rabbinical court.

DOS PINTELE YID

Lit., the dot (i.e., the basic ingredient) of a Jew; the fundamental spark of Jewish identity.

See also YIDDISHKAYT.

DREYDEL

Little top used on Chanuka for a game of put-and-take.

On each of the four sides of the top, there is a Hebrew letter which stands for one of the four words associated with the holi-

day: *Neys godol hayo shom* (A great miracle happened there).
For the purposes of the game, these four Hebrew letters were
made to stand for the four Yiddish words NIT or NISHT (Not),
GANTS (Whole), HALB (Half) and SHTEL (Put). Though
most of today's children are raised with English rather than
Yiddish as their mother tongue, the values of the letters are
learned without reference to their Yiddish origin. Thus, when
I asked a third-generation American Jewish twelve-year-old
what the letters meant, I was told: "Nothing; Take All; Take
Half; Put (either one or half, whatever is decided on)."

During the last few decades, a leading New York candy-
maker (a refugee from Hitler Germany) has popularized not
only chocolates in the shape of DREYDELS—with the Hebrew
letters in color on gold wrappers—but colorful plastic DREYDELS
containing assorted candies and tiny gifts. These are distributed
to children in many synagogue religious schools, and have often
been presented to Gentile playmates by Jewish children. I remember one year when the parents of a Jewish girl presented
such DREYDELS to all members of their daughter's Girl Scout
troop, which contained just a handful of Jewish girls, and all
the members of the troop were delightedly learning to "play
DREYDEL." (Where but in America?)

A recent version of the plastic DREYDEL, by the way, contains
a built-in pencil sharpener in the head. (AMERIKE GANEF!)

DROSHE (Heb. *drash*)

Interpretive material; hence, sermon, lecture.

Cf. P'SHAT.

ERETZ YISROEL (Heb. *Eretz Yisroeyl*)

Land of Israel.

EREV

Eve; just before.

EREV SHABBES   Before the Sabbath (which begins Friday
evening).

EREV YOM KIPPUR   Before Yom Kippur.

American Jews sometimes jokingly speak of Christmas Eve
as "EREV Christmas." In fact, a New York school teacher has
published a volume of light-hearted poems in Yiddish, including
one with this title, which is of course a Yiddish version of "The
Night Before Christmas." The organization of Irish-born Jews
in New York, the Loyal League of Yiddish Sons of Erin, holds
an annual "EREV St. Patrick's Day Banquet"!

ESRIG *See* SUKOS.

FREYLACHS

Lit., cheerfulness. A lively musical number, for spirited dancing—without which no family celebration was complete. (*See* Family, CHOSSEN-KALEH.)

GABAY

Treasurer of a synagogue.

GEMORE

Portion of the Talmud which comments on and interprets the material in the MISHNE (*see* TALMUD).

The GEMORE was written in Aramaic, the language the Jews brought to Palestine when they returned from the Babylonian exile and which completely supplanted Hebrew in their everyday speech by the third pre-Christian century.

GENEM (contraction of GEHENEM)

Hell.

GER

Convert to Judaism.

An old story tells of the GER who came to town and asked for financial help. Since it was considered a MITSVE to aid a GER, he was enthusiastically assisted wherever he went. But soon word got out that he was not a GER at all, but an ordinary Jew. The next time he asked for help, he was turned down and berated for his action. "Why?" he objected. "You're complaining because my father was a Jew. Would it be better if he had been a Gentile?" (*Cf.* joke quoted under Tribalism, VOS MER GOY, ALTS MER MAZEL.)

A well-known modern GER is Negro entertainer Sammy Davis, Jr. Comedian Joey Bishop is reported to have taken credit for Sammy's conversion, quipping: "Now Sammy wants me to turn colored."

GLIKEL

A seventeenth-century Yiddish author, Glikel of Hameln was the mother of twelve children, twice widowed, who sold jewelry on credit and started writing her famous memoirs at the age of forty-six (to teach her children how to live moral lives) and completed them at seventy-four! Like so many ancestral Jewish mothers, Glikel had no conflicts about home and career. She combined them matter-of-factly, of necessity. (*Cf.* Tribalism, YIDDISHE MAMME.)

Her name of course meant "a little stroke of luck." (*Cf.*

Chap. I, end of Concerns about . . . Destiny, Superstition *and* Special Names; Destiny, A (GROYSE) GLIK GETROFN! *and* AN UMGLIK!)

G'MILUS CHESED

Lit., bestowal of lovingkindness. A free-loan association.

This was an important part of Jewish community organization and was transported to these shores. It is usually operated by officers of local synagogues. American credit unions have built on the principle of cooperative ownership of a pool of money to allow for lower interest rates than those charged by banks, but the G'MILUS CHESED charges no interest at all. It is a cooperative effort at self-help for those most in need of it.

GOD'L (pl. G'DOYLIM)

A person in high office; a VIP.

See Chap. I, Learning, GOD'L B'TOYRE.

GOEN (Heb. *gaon*)

A genius; a scholar of great erudition.

The title has been accorded to occasional great scholars from the sixth to the eighteenth centuries. One of the most famous was Saadia Gaon, born in Egypt in the ninth century, who was the father of scientific Biblical criticism.

A foreign professor at the Hebrew Union College a generation ago amused his rabbinical students one day by declaiming the great mind of a certain authority: "And Hai Gaon was a real son of a Gaon! He was the son of Sherira Gaon."

GRAGER

Purim noisemaker used by children whenever the name of wicked Haman is heard in the synagogue reading of the Book of Esther (a wonderful way of making sure that the children listen to the long story).

ER HERT IM VI HOMEN HERT DEM GRAGER. He hears him the way Homen hears the GRAGER; i.e., He's completely oblivious. (*See* HOMEN.)

HAGODE (Heb. *Haggadah*)

Ritual service of the Passover SEYDER.

The text presents—in narrative, symbol, song, and even game (*see* AFIKEYMEN)—an account of the ancient Hebrews' liberation from Egyptian bondage. It is essentially an instrument of education, to remind every generation of what "the Holy One, blessed be He," performed "with a strong hand and an outstretched arm" when their forefathers were slaves in

Egypt. It is a humble identification with one's ancestors[8] and a joyful celebration of their deliverance.

More than two thousand editions of the Haggadah have been published over the centuries, in twelve languages, in almost sixty cities of the world. They have taken many forms, from the highly decorated versions with illuminated script displayed at the Jewish Museum in New York, to simple booklets issued free by charitable and commercial sponsors (including food and wine companies as well as banks).

The late Arthur Szyk, specialist in illuminated script, produced an unusual edition of the Haggadah in the 1940's, and this London publication was recently reissued in Israel. Several American versions of the Haggadah have been illustrated by well-known modern artists, the most recent one by the late mural painter Ben Shahn. Some Conservative rabbis have prepared their own versions of the Haggadah text. At least one of these has been distributed free in supermarkets the past few years. The Reform movement has its own version of the Haggadah, and the Reconstructionist movement (which embraces Jews of various persuasions) also has its own, containing new material dealing with the CHURBN victims. A prayer for the Jews of the Soviet Union is now commonly added.

The style of the Haggadah has been used for parody on various subjects: the disillusionment of early immigrants to the United States, the distaste at Tammany Hall corruption, the indignation at the British administration of Palestine in the Mandatory period. Even observance of the Purim holiday was subject to irreverent mocking in a Haggadic parody.

See Chap. I, Acronyms, *yaknehaz.*

HAKOFE *See* SIMCHES TOYRE.

HALOCHE

Legal material of the Talmud.

HAMEYTSI (Heb. *hamōtsi*)

The Hebrew grace before meals: *Boruch Ato Adōnoy, Elōheynu Melech ho-ōlom, Hamōtsi lechem min ho-orets* (Praised art Thou, O Lord our God, King of the universe, Who bringest forth bread from the earth).

This is recited, and sometimes sung, in unison. I noticed a recent guest pronounced the last two words (*min ho-orets*) as "Minnie Orets." I couldn't be sure whether she had been badly instructed in Hebrew or was making an irreverent joke. Predictably, I've since heard this blessing referred to as "Minnie Horwitz"!

HASHEM

The Name. The Holy One.

See Chap. I, Famil. with God, *re.* avoidance of God's name; Exclam., BORCHASHEM.

CHILUL HASHEM   Profanation of the Name; blasphemy.

HASHONO RABO

The seventh day of SUKOS.

HASKOLE (Heb. *Haskalah*)

The Enlightenment.

This was an eighteenth-century movement aimed at keeping Jews abreast of cultural and philosophical developments in the world around them. It was in essence a renaissance, which de-ghettoized the Jewish mind and inevitably contributed to the process of secularization which was intensified in the nineteenth and twentieth centuries.

HAVDOLE (Heb. *Havdalah*)

The ceremony for ushering out of the Sabbath.

A special braided candle is lighted, and blessings and prayers are recited over the candle, a wine cup and box of spices.

Although this is chiefly Orthodox custom, in the past two decades many camps and week-end youth conclaves, including those sponsored by Reform Jewish agencies, have instituted the Havdalah service. It is especially moving in the outdoors.

HEKSHER

Kosher certification—assurance by an Orthodox rabbi that the products or premises are in compliance with the dietary laws.

HERSHELE OSTROPOLYER

Little Hershel from Ostropol, a famous droll character who lived in the Ukraine in the late eighteenth century, attached to the "court" of a Hasidic REBBE.

Many well-known jokes in Jewish folklore—particularly those about the people of Chelm[9]—have been attributed to Hershele, and numerous anecdotes have been told about him.

Cf. MOTKE CHABAD.

HILLEL

A wise and gentle rabbi of the first pre-Christian century.

One of Hillel's widely quoted aphorisms—"What is hateful unto you, do not to your fellow men"—was part of his reply to a heathen who had offered to take on the Jewish faith if the

entire Torah could be explained while he stood on one foot.[10]
To this summary Hillel added: "That is the whole of the Law.
The rest is commentary; go and learn."

Hillel's negative advice was earlier put in the positive, in
Leviticus 19:18 (". . . thou shalt love thy neighbor as thyself
. . . .") and also later by the founders of Christianity, e.g.,
"As ye would that men should do to you, do ye also to them
likewise"—Luke 6:31). It is interesting that the second portion
of his advice to the heathen also came through in part in a similar summary of the requirements of Christianity: "Therefore
all things whatsoever ye would that men should do to you, do
ye even so to them: for this is the law and the prophets" (Matthew 7:12).

HOMEN

Haman, the evil counselor of King Ahasueres in ancient Per-
sia, as told in the Biblical story of Esther.

As Dick Schaap has quipped, Ahasueres was "the old Persian
king who married a nice Jewish girl." The Bible story tells us
that Haman plotted against the Jews but was stopped when
Queen Esther interceded with her husband the king after her
cousin Mordecai had informed her of Haman's plans. Haman
was tricked by his own evil, being killed by hanging, the fate
he had advocated for Mordecai.

See MEGILLE; Food and Drink, HOMENTASH.

HOREH

The *hora*, a group folk dance of the Palestinian pioneers,
known and danced by Jews the world over.

An orchestra leader at a recent wedding on Long Island introduced it as "an ancient tribal rite." His dating was wrong, but
the spirit was right!

KABOLE (Heb. *Kabalah*)

The mystical movement which devoted itself to speculations
about God, the universe and the awaited Messiah, discovering
hidden meanings in Scripture by complicated formulas of analysis.

The letters of the alphabet had numerical equivalents, and
the Kabalists would substitute these for the letters of certain
passages, or they would assign to each letter of a word the
initial or abbreviation of some other word; or they would substitute for a letter the one which precedes or follows it in the
alphabet. The Shield or Star of David (MOGEN DOVID) was

interpreted to represent the seven days of the week, the Sabbath being the hexagon in the center and the six outer triangles the six week days. It was also divided into four rhomboids, indicating the directions of north, south, east and west. It was further considered to represent, as a Messianic symbol, the zodiacal sign of Pisces[11] (Feb. 21 to March 20), the time of year when the Messiah was expected to appear.

The fundamental Kabalistic work, the Zohar, influenced many Christian philosophers and theologians.

See last paragraph under CHAZEN; Chap. I, note to Acronyms.

KAPORES

Atonement sacrifice.

This old Orthodox custom has provided colorful material for comedian Buddy Hackett as well as the memoirs of S. N. Behrman (*The Worcester Account*).

SHLOGN KAPORES, *lit.*, to beat a sacrifice or to drive out sins, involved the holding of a chicken by the legs and swinging it over one's head while reciting certain prayers. The fowl was then slaughtered, and either it or a contribution of its value was given to the poor.

Performed on the day preceding the Day of Atonement, the ritual was a throwback to the ancient custom of offering sacrifices to God for one's sins. Actually, the procedure was discarded before the Middle Ages, but it somehow kept coming back, despite the fact that many scholars derided it. One of the earliest Jewish parodists and satirists, Judah Alharizi, in the thirteenth century, challenged the practice through the character of a rooster who flies to the top of the synagogue and pleads for his life, using language of the prophets!

More alive than the custom today are the ironic expressions it led to: AF KAPORES DARFST ES HOBN! (Advice); A SHEYNE, REYNE KAPORE! (Resig.); ES TOYG AF KAPORES (Char. and Des.); DER YID IZ A KAPORE HON (Tribalism).

ZAYN DI KAPORE FAR (to be the sacrifice for) lightly denotes "to be in love with," *equiv.* "to be crazy about."

KASHRES

The system of kashruth observance, or "keeping kosher."

The detailed regulations for such observance (see introduction to Food and Drink) were developed by the rabbis on the basis of two charges contained in Leviticus 11:3-12: "Whatsoever parteth the hoof, and is cloven-footed, and cheweth the cud, among the beasts, that may ye eat" and "These may ye eat of all that are in the waters: whatsoever hath fins and scales . . ." plus the negative commandment that appears twice in Exodus and once in Deuteronomy: "Thou shalt not seethe a kid in his mother's milk."

Though the Reform movement originally rejected the binding force of kashruth, some Reform Jews today "keep kosher" (there are even kosher kitchens in some Reform temples), and many who don't do so still avoid pork. Some tend to be more observant than usual during Passover.

In general, the modern process of "keeping kosher" varies greatly. One might suppose, from the increased sales of "kosher" canned and frozen foods, that American Jews have become more observant with respect to kashruth. But the answer is not so simple. For one thing, many Gentiles have been discovering kosher foods as part of the cosmopolitan trend in food merchandising, encouraged by self-service shelving and freezer cabinets. For another, many American Jews buy such foods without being similarly strict about other aspects of their food purchase and handling. You may often see in the same market basket a jar of kosher beet borsht and a package of frozen crabmeat, or a can of Heinz vegetarian beans (which carries the "U" label signifying endorsement by the Union of Orthodox Rabbis), along with a ham.

Even among those women who buy meat from a kosher butcher, the pattern varies. Some do not bother at all with the soaking and salting process that is required before cooking (to ensure the removal of all blood). Some limit their kosher meat-buying to liver and chicken—which they believe are somehow never as fresh when TREYF. Some may be strict about buying kosher meat and keeping two sets of dishes, yet be willing to eat shellfish or other forbidden foods outside their own homes. (New York's late mayor Jimmy Walker is supposed to have commented once concerning his attendance at many Jewish public dinners: "Unlike my Jewish friends, I eat TREYF at home and kosher on the outside.") Some will even serve shrimp, but only down in the game room.

I recall the remark of a graduate student at a large Midwestern university, a fellow who came from a Conservative family and who was faithful about attending Friday night services: "Ham is no good. But bacon I like." What this young man forgot is that whether or not he liked it was not supposed to determine his practice in the matter. There's an old story about a man who weepingly tells a friend that he has eaten ham, and the friend says, "Well, don't cry about it. Just don't do it again." "But you don't understand," he says. "I'm crying because I liked it!"

See Food and Drink, KOSHER, CHAZER, FLEYSHIK, MILCHIK, PAREV.

KEYLE

A learned man (*lit.* a vessel, a container; hence, one who contains great knowledge).

KEYVER AVOS

Customary visit to graves of departed family prior to the High Holy Days.

KIDDUSH

Blessing over the Sabbath wine.

KOL NIDRE

"All Vows"—prayer sung at the beginning of the Yom Kippur Eve service.

This prayer has a strong emotional impact, solely because of its stirring melody and its opening position in the ritual for the solemn Holy Day. Its meaning is unclear, for it asks for release from all vows. It is sometimes explained as reflecting the status of the Jew in the Middle Ages, when forced conversions were common, and when the Jew was attempting to absolve himself of guilt in taking such Christian vows under duress. But the prayer is older than that. The original wording asked for release from personal vows of the preceding year which had not been carried out. That form was criticized by Jewish religious scholars as early as the ninth century. In later periods the prayer was interpreted as referring to personal vows that might be made in the future. In any case, rabbinic law emphasizes that the Kol Nidre prayer may not be used to annul obligations to others.

The popular score for the prayer has been linked in form to Catholic church music. Dr. Johanna Spector has traced it to the cantillation used in eighth-century Babylonia for the opening portion of Genesis as it was then customarily chanted on the afternoon of Yom Kippur. The melody forms the basis of concert pieces by Max Bruch and Arnold Schoenberg, and fragments have been spotted in two Beethoven works (C Sharp

Minor Quartet, Opus 131, and Trio Opus 9, No. 3). Rabbi
Isaac Mayer Wise, founder of Reform Judaism, is said to have
played the Kol Nidre on the violin at his own services!

KOVED

Honor, respect, glory.

See Passing Judgment, TSU FIL KOVED IZ A HALBER SHANDE,
under TSU FIL IZ UMGEZUNT.

L'KOVED   In honor of, as in L'KOVED SHABBES, in honor of
the Sabbath (*see* Exclam., BIM, BUHM).

See also YICHES.

KOYEN (pl. KOYNIM)

Descendant of the Aaronite priesthood.

Many families named "Cohen" are true KOYNIM (Heb.
kohanim), but some are not. It is interesting that many such
descendants know of their ancestry, the fact having been passed
on orally from generation to generation.

In Orthodox and Conservative synagogues, certain ritual
privileges are still reserved for the KOYEN. In the reading of
the Torah, for instance, the KOYEN is called to the pulpit before
the LEYVI.

See PIDYENABEN.

KRISHME   *See* SH'MA.

LAMEDVOVNIK

A thirty-six-nik—i.e., one of the thirty-six "hidden saints"
who were supposed to exist in every generation, usually unrec-
ognized as such by their fellows.

This belief (which grew out of a statement in the Talmud)
led to many folk legends. The modern novel *The Last of the
Just* by André Schwarz-Bart built on this tradition.

The term is from two letters of the Hebrew and Yiddish
alphabet, *lamed* and *vov*, whose numerical values are thirty and
six respectively. (*Cf.* KABOLE.)

LERNER

A learner—a man who spends all his time in study of Torah
and Talmud.

There are still such men in the Orthodox quarter of Jerusalem and even in New York. Certain priestly orders of the
Catholic Church probably are related to this age-old pattern of
lifetime study of Holy Writ.

LEYVI (pl. LEVIIM)

A Levite—descendant of the tribe of Levi, who were functionaries in the ancient temple; hence recognized for special participation in Orthodox ritual. *Also*, a man's name.

LOSHEN KOYDESH

Holy Tongue; the Hebrew language.

Because Hebrew was the language of Scripture, it was contrasted with the language of everyday use, MAMME LOSHEN (which *see*). In recent years, the contrast has been narrowing. In Israel Hebrew has become the daily language, and—as noted earlier—Yiddish is enjoying a new appreciation as the language of the martyrs.

LULEV *See* SUKOS.

MACHZER

Holiday prayerbook.

See Chap. I, Acronyms, *yaknehaz*.

MAGID (pl. MAGIDIM)

Itinerant preacher; orator.

Sholem Aleichem's definition: "A man who can't sleep because he's bothered by a Biblical quotation."

MAMME LOSHEN

This is usually translated "mother tongue," referring to the Yiddish language; but it's been observed that the phrase really connotes "mother's tongue," reflecting the fact that Yiddish literature was popular among the women, in contrast to Hebrew literature, which occupied the more learned men.

As noted in Chap. I, Rhyme, the current interest in Yiddish has been dubbed "a mad rushin'/to MAMME LUSHEN."

MAŌZ TSUR (Heb.)

Rock of Ages—hymn sung at Chanuka:

Rock of Ages, let our song praise Thy saving power;
Thou amidst the raging foe wast our shelt'ring tower.
Furious they assailed us, but Thine arm availed us,
And Thy Word broke their sword when our own strength
    failed us.

MASKIL (pl. MASKILIM)

Lit., an enlightened one. A member of the Haskalah (*see* HASKOLE).

MEDRESH (pl. MEDROSHIM)

The Midrash, a collection of many detailed interpretations —often allegorical—of the Bible text over a period of roughly one thousand years, up to about the thirteenth century. *Also*, a midrash, a single such interpretation.

According to Rabbi William G. Braude of Providence, his published work on the Midrash has been dubbed "The Rabbi's Mish Mash."[12]

BEYS MEDRESH   Place of study; academy, synagogue.

MEGILLE

A scroll—especially the scroll of Esther, which is read aloud in the synagogue on PURIM.

As noted earlier, the story takes a long time to read; hence the popular description of a long story: A MEGILLE *or* A GANTSE MEGILLE (*see* Chap. IIIB, "a whole MEGILLE"). Sam Levenson describes this as "the Income Tax Long Form."

If the story is long and complicated, it can become A FARSH-LEPTE KRENK (Char. and Des.).

MELAMED

Hebrew teacher.

See CHEYDER.

MELAMEDKE   Wife of a MELAMED.

MENOYRE (Heb. *menorah*)

Sabbath or festival candelabrum.

The Sabbath menorah has seven holders, to accommodate a candle for each day of the week. The Chanuka menorah has nine holders, to hold a candle for each of the eight nights of the holiday plus the SHAMMES candle, with which the others are lighted. (The first night, one candle is lit, the second two, and so on until the last night, when all the candles are lighted.) Special blessings are recited for both Sabbath and Chanuka candle-lighting. At Chanuka, these are followed by the singing of MAOZ-TSUR (which *see*).

Most candelabra seen in Christian homes at Christmastime have seven holders. But on a recent visit to the home of a Presbyterian minister and his wife during the Christmas season, my husband and I were shown a newly acquired menorah, which had nine holders. When I commented that it was a Chanuka menorah, they happily noted their awareness in the matter.

MESHIACH

The Messiah.

A story about the foolish city of CHELM tells of the Jew who was given the job of sitting at the village gate to await the arrival of the Messiah. When he complained that his pay was too low, he was told: "Sure it's low. But consider: the work is steady."

See also story in Chap. I, Famil. with God; Advice, VET MESHIACH GEBOREN VEREN MIT A TOG SHPETER.

MESHUMED

Lit., a destroyed one; i.e., one who has destroyed his identity. A baptized Jew; an apostate.

A MESHUMED IZ NIT KEYN YID UN NIT KEYN GOY. A Jewish convert to Christianity is neither a Jew nor a Gentile. This is an ironic observation that such a person is usually not fully accepted as a Christian, nor is he any longer accepted as a Jew —with perhaps a touch of the feeling that the monotheistic Jew can never fully accept Christian religious doctrine. A similar idea is expressed in a German witticism: "A baptized Jew is an empty leaf between the Old and New Testaments."

Interestingly enough, a Jew who became a Catholic priest was assigned to Israel in the Assumption Order and was recently sent to the United States by the Israel Tourist Ministry, to promote tourism by Christians.

See also POSHE.

MEZUZE

A mezuzah, the small object mounted on the doorway of a Jewish home, containing two sections of Deuteronomy (6:4-9; 11:13-21).

The first section contains the SH'MA and the V'OHAVTO (which *see*); the second envisions the good things that will come to pass if God's instructions in the former section are carried out. Both end with, "And thou shalt write them upon the doorposts of thy house and upon thy gates."

In the Reform movement several generations ago, the mezuzah was considered to be a superstitious object, involved with the primitive belief that God would protect any home so marked (as He was supposed to have done before the exodus from Egypt, when the Hebrews marked their doorways with blood from the paschal lamb). But in recent years, with the reacceptance of other rituals, many Reform Jews have been using mezuzahs.

A practical problem has arisen in some apartment-house buildings, both here and in Israel, where the framing around the apartment door is metal rather than wood. In such cases the mezuzah can presumably be cemented on, but a midwestern company was reported about a year ago to be working on a possible magnetic case for mounting. The story is told that one

Israeli landlord informed his tenants that they could "plug in" to a central mezuzah on the roof!

MIKVE

A specially constructed pool, fed by a natural water source, for ritual immersion.

Orthodox tradition prescribes MIKVE immersion for women seven days after the end of menstruation, before cohabitation. Among Hasidim, some men practice immersion before the Sabbath and holidays and at other times for purification. (A Hasidic SOYFER in Israel recently told an American visitor that his father, also a scribe, had stopped his transcription of the Torah every time he came to the word "God" in order to go to the MIKVE and purify himself.)

MIKVE immersion is also part of Orthodox conversion ritual, as was detailed in Noah Gordon's novel *The Rabbi*. It is of course the forerunner of Protestant baptismal immersion.

Though the use of the MIKVE declined greatly in the New World, the past fifteen years have seen a limited revival of the practice among young Orthodox families. A number of modern tiled installations (called "ritualaria") have been built, mostly in suburban communities. However, the average American Jewish couple would be surprised to learn that they might be expected to abstain from sexual union for the menstrual period plus a full week afterward and that the wife should then visit the MIKVE before union. I heard a well-known Jewish physician who lectures widely on sex and marriage tell an audience at a Jewish Community Center that intercourse during menstruation is perfectly all right—without even mentioning the fact that Orthodox tradition forbids it, to say nothing of other factors that might affect non-Jews as well.[13] Perhaps this Jewish physician wasn't even aware of the Orthodox tradition. Ordinarily neither Reform nor Conservative rabbis discuss these regulations with the people they join in marriage, and even among members of Orthodox congregations, knowledge and observance of the rules are far from universal.

Yet modern Orthodox opinion stresses the importance of the MIKVE, noting that in addition to the obligation of carrying out Talmudic law, there may be unknown health benefits from the spring-fed waters and from the presumed thoroughness of cleansing due to the recommended crouching position and muscle contractions. Medical studies have noted a lower incidence of cervical cancer in Jewish women than in Gentile women, and some Orthodox spokesmen credit the MIKVE, also pointing out that among Jewish women this cancer rate is lower for the poor, who are more likely to use the MIKVE than their more affluent sisters. (There may of course be other factors involved—in the first instance, Jewish male circumcision; in the other, the presumable tendency of the well-to-do to ignore not only the MIKVE but all or part of the abstention period.)

Among Jewish comedians, joking references to the MIKVE are fairly common—so much so that many Gentiles are familiar with the term. I recall a Lee Leonard radio program on which the guest was Brian Kelly, of the TV *Flipper* series. A listener called in to ask Kelly whether they were adding any new swimmers to the program, noting that if so, he would be useful: he used to be a lifeguard at a MIKVE. Leonard commented to Kelly, "He's putting you on," and the latter replied, "I know." Jokes of this kind have always seemed in rather bad taste to me—though perhaps they are just one stage beyond the flippancy about religious practice that was discussed earlier (*see* Food and Drink, BROMFN). Actually, among the Hasidim there are instances in which male observers are called for, and this fact may be the basis for such MIKVE jokes. (In practice in those cases, the woman may cover herself with a sheet, or the man may be in a separate room.)

MINCHE

Twilight devotions in the daily liturgy.

See story quoted in Chap. I, end of Famil. with God.

A recent joke has an interesting twist. A scholar is presenting an afternoon lecture on "The Nature of Prayer in the Talmudic Period, with Particular Reference to the Character of Prayer in Our Own Time." He talks on and on, and notices that one by one his listeners are departing. Finally, the last man gets up to leave, and the speaker stops and asks whether he can't wait till he has concluded. "Sorry," the man answers. "I'm already late for MINCHE. I have to join the others at SHUL." This pokes fun at the scholars who may know a lot about the history of Judaism but don't really practice it: the laymen know when to stop talking about it and go to pray! (*See also* last item under MINYEN.)

MINYEN

Ten men, the minimum number required for conducting an Orthodox or Conservative service.

Men observing YORTSAYT often have to round up a man or two to "make a MINYEN" for the daily early morning service. The requirement presumably derives from Abraham's dialogue with God in Genesis 18:23-32, where God agrees that if there are ten righteous men to be found in Sodom he will not destroy the city.

NAYN RABONIM KENEN KEYN MINYEN NIT MACHEN, OBER TSEN SHUSTERS YO. Nine rabbis can't make a MINYEN, but ten cobblers can. (assertion of the importance of the little man)

See Chap. IIIB, "filet MINYEN."

MISHNAYES

Books of the MISHNE.

MISHNE

Basic portion of the Talmud. Contains oral law and teachings concerning the legal material in the Torah. (*See* TALMUD.)

The MISHNE has been parodied as a scholar's joke for PURIM. During the time of Prohibition in the United States, it was also parodied in a presentation of the evils attendant to non-observance of the law.

MISHNE TOYRE   The *Mishna Torah*, a work by Maimonides which summarizes the spiritual and ethical content of the Talmud.

MISNAGID (pl. MISNAGDIM)

Opponent of the Hasidim. An educated Jew who supported the tradition of learning and duty as against the Hasidic preachment of simple faith (*see* CHOSID).

MITSVE

A religiously worthy act. A commandment; a good deed.

Tradition has it that there are 613 *mitzvoth* in the Hebrew Bible, including both positive and negative commandments or precepts. Though various compilers over the centuries have differed sharply on how these precepts should be classified, they seem to have agreed on the number 613, first totalled in the third century.

In the folk mind, the doing of MITSVES would help insure one's place in the hereafter.

See BAR MITSVE.

MOGEN DOVID

Star of David.

This six-pointed star has long been known as a Jewish symbol, though its origins are obscure and it has at times been used as a decorative or good-luck symbol by non-Jews. The house next door to the one I and my family live in has a small Star of David on one of the gables—set in red tiles on a gray slate roof. The building is over fifty years old and was built by a Gentile and has always been lived in by Gentiles. Similarly, in a bureau drawer of a rented summer cottage in New England several years ago, I discovered a sticker trademark in the form of a Mogen David, the three corners of one triangle being used for the company initials, "F & H," and the sides of the other triangle carrying the name of the furniture line and the two cities in which the company had outlets.

The Mogen David appears on the flag of the modern State of Israel, and to Jews behind the Iron Curtain it can have great emotional meaning. A few years ago in Russia, for instance, during the brief nongovernmental cultural exchange with Israel, the Israeli singer Geula Gill performed, and a poster about the program used one of the Russian letters in the form of a Mogen David—the only Jewish symbol on the poster. A Jewish taxi driver in Moscow explained to an American journalist for the *Jewish Daily Forward* that there were only four such posters in all of Moscow, with a population of 650,000 Jews. Why? "Because of the MOGEN DOVID," he said. "They begrudge us that bit of joy."

According to the *Jewish Digest*, Ruben Amaro, a Yankee infielder, wears both a Star of David and a Christopher Medal on the same neck chain. (His wife is Jewish.) But he could simplify. As the *Catholic Reporter* put it, "the spirit of ecumenism has reached the marketplace": an ad in the *National Observer* offered a combination St. Christopher Medal and Star of David on "a good luck charm for all." ("How Can You Lose—with Both Sides Going for You?") Since then, a more inclusive "brotherhood necklace" has been seen in New York—containing both these items plus a cross. I'm reminded of the symbol that a California congregation of "Jewish Christians" invented some years ago: a cross inside a Star of David. A less friendly symbol is that used by an underground group in Egypt which is anti-Nasser and anti-Jewish: a Mogen David pierced by the sword of Islam.

MONTEFIORE

This name crops up in folk humor, as in the interchange between two men discussing a possible SHIDDUCH of their children, one correcting his original demands of dowry with: "So a relative of Moses Montefiore I'm not, either. . . ." It refers to Sir Moses Montefiore, member of an Italian-English family, many of whose members distinguished themselves in public life and letters. Sir Moses, who lived to the ripe age of a hundred (1784-1885) was loved by Jews the world over, as he intervened with many governments in Europe and Asia to help stay persecutions. A successful industrialist and sheriff of London, he was a pious Jew who gave away a large portion of his income in personal and institutional charities, both Jewish and general.

MORE NEBUCHIM

Guide for the Perplexed, a Hebrew book by Maimonides which was a philosophical defense of Judaism.

The late Ben Hecht's book of the 1940's, *Guide for the Bedeviled*, dealing with anti-Semitism, was presumably a conscious building on that phrase.

MOSHEL

Example; parable; comparison.

Mashalim were common in the Bible and Talmud, and also in the words of Jesus.

L'MOSHEL   For example. (*See* Chap. IIIA, "a for instance.")

MOTKE CHABAD

A famous nineteenth-century jester of Vilna, Poland, to whom many folk-sayings have been attributed.

Re. his surname, *see* CHABAD.

MOYEL

A mohel—a religious functionary who performs circumcisions. The modern mohel receives both religious and technical training. Although circumcisions are frequently performed by surgeons (sometimes with a Reform rabbi conducting the religious ritual), many Jews prefer to use a mohel, not only because of his religious background but also because of his wider experience and presumably greater skill. However, since the introduction of "the clamp"—a device for gently crushing together the outer and the thin inner layer of skin to be removed —there is little room for ineptness. Nevertheless, Orthodox opinion—including that of Orthodox medical spokesmen—advocates that only a mohel perform the act, to emphasize its religious rather than medical character.

The MOYEL has been defined as "a surgeon who performs only at parties" (*see* BRIS). On a TV *Tonight* show, actor Ed Ames went much further in presenting Johnny Carson with a tomahawk as the "official symbol of the Cherokee MOYEL"— alluding to an earlier session in which a thrown tomahawk had hit a man in the groin, creating what was dubbed a "frontier BRIS." This is pretty risqué "in-group" stuff. (*Cf.* Chap. IIIB, comment under "A.K.")

MOYSHE RABBEYNU

Customary form of reference to the Biblical Moses, meaning "Moses our Teacher."

A letter addressed to "Moyshe Rabbeynu of the World's Fair" is said to have been delivered in 1965 to Robert Moses, head of the New York World's Fair.

See Chap. IIIB, "Moishian."

MOYSHEV ZKEYNEM

Old folks' home.

A wry tale by Sholem Aleichem tells of Reb Yozefel's effort to convince a visiting contractor in Kasrilevke that he should donate an old folks' home to the town. The rich man finally is persuaded and the building is erected—but unfortunately it is never occupied since there are no funds with which to operate it. "This has ever been the fate," says the author, "of the little folk of Kasrilevke: when they dream of good things to eat—they haven't a spoon; when they have a spoon—they don't dream of good things to eat."

MUSAF

Prayer added to morning worship on the Sabbath and holidays.

NEDOVE

Charitable contribution.

GIT A NEDOVE—Give a donation—is the request I remember being made of my father by the assorted SHNORRERS (Char. and Des.) who came around at various seasons.

NER TOMID

Eternal Light.

This is a fixture in every synagogue, hanging before the OREN KOYDESH. (Some churches also use it.)

When my daughter was about five, I overheard her debating with several children as to whose father had the most dangerous job. Her rabbi father, she argued, had a *very* dangerous job, because during every service he had to stand under the Eternal Light, and if that ever fell on him, he could get killed! (*See* Exclam., ME KEN DERHARGET VEREN!)

NILE

The fifth and concluding service of the Day of Atonement.

OREN KOYDESH

The Holy Ark, where the Torah scrolls are kept.

OYLEM HABE (Heb. *Ōlom Habo*)

The World-to-Come.

See Death, ZOL ER ZAYN A GUTER BETER.

PARIK *See* SHAYTEL.

PASKENEN A SHAYLE

To decide a question of religious law.

ER HOT GEPASKET A SHAYLE. He gave a judgment on a question of religious law.

"That's a real SHAYLE" is equivalent to "That's the $64,000 question."

See Chap. IIIB, "Charlie" for SHAYLE.

PEYES

Earlocks—seen on bearded Orthodox males who follow strictly the prohibition against shaving (Leviticus 19:27; 21:5).

In his memoirs, Peretz recalled that his grandfather's PEYES were so long, he often unconsciously chewed on them when he was studying. I'm reminded of the man my father knew whose eyebrows were so bushy that he had to lift them up with his hands before he started to read!

In parts of Pennsylvania and Ohio one sometimes sees Amish men with beard and earlocks attired in the long black coat and black hat associated with certain Orthodox Jews, and it is sometimes difficult to tell whether they are Amish or Jewish. When my children were young I once took them horseback riding in Ohio, and we were all fascinated by the young red-haired earlocked blacksmith who fixed a loose horseshoe for us.

Boys with PEYES are occasionally seen playing ball in Brooklyn—in an area which, as noted earlier, has been spoken of as "rue de la PEYES." (*See* the colorful motorcycle incident noted under PURIM.)

PEYREK

Section or chapter, often with reference to PIRKEY AVOS, a special portion of the Talmud.

PEYRESH (pl. PEYRUSHIM)
Commentary.

PEYSACH
Passover, the spring festival which commemorates the exodus from Egypt under the leadership of Moses. Orthodox and Conservative Jews observe eight days, Reform Jews seven.
See SEYDER.

PIDYENABEN (Heb. *pidyōn ha-ben*)
Redeeming the son.
This is a home ceremony held a month after the birth of a first-born male. It is based on the ancient practice of claiming the first-born male for service in the Temple. The father gives a token sum of money to a KOYEN to redeem the child from such service. Family and friends then partake of refreshments (*see* Food and Drink, BOB *and* NAHIT). Though the ritual was dropped by Reform Judaism, sometimes members of Reform congregations observe it for the sake of Orthodox grandparents.
The event has been jokingly referred to as "pig-in-the-pen." *See* Chap. IIIB.

PIKUACH NEFESH
Saving of life. An emergency in which religious laws may be suspended.
Jewish religious regulations were always made subject to special circumstances. The rule regarding fasting on Yom Kippur, for instance, was not to be followed by pregnant women, young children, the ill or elderly.

PILPEL
The process of making extremely fine distinctions in Talmudic discussion, *equiv.*, legalism, hair-splitting.
A well-known New York lawyer and agency executive has this surname. We may surmise that he was genetically well-equipped for his profession!

PIRKEY AVOS
"Sayings of the Fathers," a section of the Talmud containing quotable reflections of the famous rabbis.

POSHE
Sinner.
POSHE YISROEL *Lit.*, a sinner against Israel. A heretic. (*See* Passing Judgment, A GEVORENER/IZ ERGER VI A GEBORENER.)

POSSIK
Bible verse.

P'SHAT

Literal meaning—one of the types of discourse on the Torah to be found in the Talmud, other types being DROSHE (which *see*), REMEZ (hint, suggestion) and SOD (secret meanings, the basis for speculation in the Zohar—*see* KABOLE).

PURIM

The Feast of Lots. Spring holiday based on the Biblical story of Esther.

See GRAGER; MISHNE; last paragraph under HAGODE.

A SACH HOMENS UN EYN PURIM. A lot of Hamans and one Purim (i.e., So many anti-Semitic tyrants, and only one holiday celebrating a victory over one of them). *Cf.* Destiny, EYN GOT UN AZOY FIL SONIM!

PURIM SHALACHMONES Purim gift. Though not widely practiced today, an exchange of presents used to be associated with the holiday. Sholem Aleichem wrote a delightful story about two servant girls who meet on Purim, each carrying a basket of home-baked HOMENTASHEN and other goodies which she is supposed to deliver to the other's employer. They sit down on the grass to talk and get curious about what is in each other's baskets. The inevitable happens: they taste just a little, and a little again. By the time their baskets are delivered, there is so little left that each receiving family feels insulted by the other.

Times have changed. Could Sholem Aleichem have predicted a "SHALACHMONES Delivery Service"? That's what was set up one year in a Williamsburg, Brooklyn, Hasidic community. A couple of enterprising boys rented Vespas and, according to a newspaper columnist, "zoomed through the streets of Williamsburg, black hats tied to the head, sideburns flying . . . ." Not only that. The giving of SHALACHMONES to Orthodox neighborhood children was recently automated by an engineer who installed a coin ejector outside his door. When his bell rang, a quarter slid out, with a note saying "Happy Purim!"

PURIM SUDEH Purim Feast. Part of the traditional celebration at the SUDEH was the PURIM SHPIEL, a dramatic spoof of the Book of Esther or other portions of the Bible. (A recent Yiddish-English show on Broadway was such a presentation, though not billed as such and offered completely out of season.) Many religious schools and Jewish community centers sponsor Purim masquerades for young children, with crowning of Queen Esther, etc. The practice goes back to the door-to-door entertaining by Purim masqueraders in the Middle Ages. (*See* Endearment, -ENYU, *re.* SUDENYU.)

PUSHKE

Charity box.

Aside from any at SHUL, a PUSHKE was almost universal in Jewish homes of the first American generation. Today it's usually spoken of as the "Blue Box" by members of Hadassah, who distribute it and handle collections from it for the "J.N.F.," the Jewish National Fund (which acquires land and improves it for settlement through irrigation, afforestation, etc.). Some forty lesser organizations still distribute PUSHKES. In many households, it is customary to place charity in the PUSHKE on Friday evenings, when lighting the Sabbath candles.

REB

Mr. (sometimes humorous, as in REB YANKEL—*see* Char. and Des., CHAYIM YANKEL)

REBBE

Title of Hasidic rabbi—a more intimate term than that used for the traditional rabbi, ROV (which *see*).

REBBENYU Dear REBBE.

The individual REBBE had his own personal following, most of them simple folk who put great trust in his wisdom and powers and followed him around in his public appearances, when he would "hold court" and they would feast—foreshadowing the practice of the "Father Divine" movement among American Negroes. Many old songs and stories attest to this childlike faith, and some indicate the loyalties aroused when adherents of one REBBE argue with followers of another REBBE concerning the relative miracle-working powers of their spiritual leader.

One famous REBBE was Nachman of Bratzlav, known as Der Brátzlaver, who was a great story-teller and improvised orally many of the mystical tales that have come down to us through his disciples. Another great REBBE was Leyvi-Yitschok Fun Berditshev (*see* Chap. I, conclusion of Famil. with God).

Hasidic REBBES were a kind of dynasty, passing on their position to their sons. This is one factor that led to the deterioration of the original spiritual impulse of the movement (*see* CHOSID), since some of the inheritors lacked true piety.

There are still some conscientious REBBES practicing today, more or less as described in Chaim Potok's novel *The Chosen*. One such REBBE, recently deceased, led his Hasidic sect in Brooklyn to establish a settlement in the New York countryside (reminiscent of some of the cooperative Christian settlements in this country in earlier times) ; another encouraged his adherents to move to the Holy Land. A famous LUBAVITSHER REBBE periodically travels and lectures in the U.S., and there are even a few circles of LUBAVITSH-minded students on college campuses (*see* CHABAD).

Peretz, who had a great influence on nineteenth-century Yiddish writers, has been described as their "literary REBBE."

See TSADIK; ARI; BAL SHEM TOV.

REBBINER

In the Old World, a rabbi or educated Jew commissioned by the Government to act as an official representative of the Jewish community.

Such an official was usually not much respected by the Jews whom he was supposed to represent. Yiddish writer David Bergelson's story "In a Backwoods Town" presents an all-too-human picture of a REBBINER in an obscure post, where life is not very uplifting and he is unable to rise above the situation himself, much less help others to do so.

Interestingly enough, Sholem Aleichem was for a time a REBBINER—appointed at the age of twenty-one, in the Province of Poltava.

REBBITZEN[14]

Rabbi's wife.

Sam Levenson has defined the REBBITZEN as "a rabbi's brain trust." My husband describes her as "a girl who's foolish enough to marry a rabbi, but smart enough to know what to do about it." There's a joke about the man who tells his friend that his son has decided to be a rabbi, and the friend comments, "What kind of job is that for a nice Jewish boy?" The same reaction is often encountered when a young lady decides to marry a rabbi: What kind of life is that for a nice Jewish girl?

True, there are hazards to being a REBBITZEN—as there are to being a Protestant minister's wife. But there are also untold rewards. And the term itself is a delightful one. It combines the loving feeling for the old-time REBBE with a certain touch of light humor. I recall a time when I wanted to put in a word at a student bull-session and was held up with the parrying, "Shall we let the REBBITZEN talk?"

The minister's wife has nothing like this. The nearest she

can come to it is in the rare term which H. L. Mencken once recorded, "ministress," but that does not have the suggestion of humor and of affectionate disrespect that is found in REB-BITZEN. Occasionally you may find a rabbi's wife who takes offense at the term. But such a lady, I suspect, takes herself a little too seriously!

Reform rabbis, in annual conferences, have often discussed the possibility of ordination of women. One popular objection is: What could you call a female rabbi's husband?! (My astute brother Alvin A. Mermin suggests REBBESMAN. This should help clear the way!)

ROSHESHONE

Rosh Hashono, the New Year, which comes in the autumn and ushers in the Days of Awe, or Ten Days of Penitence, which culminate in Yom Kippur.

See SLICHES; Greetings, L'SHONE TEYVE; Passing Judgment, 'SIZ NUCH DI CHASINEH UN FAR'N BRIS, under 'SIZ NUCH DI CHASINEH.

ROV

Rabbi.

A leading American rabbi reports that a youngster who was asked to distinguish between a rabbi and cantor replied: "The cantor sings, and the rabbi tells you what page."

In Europe, worshippers found their own page! There the ROV was a formal personality who pored over Scripture and adjudicated disputes on the basis of the moral law and had few of the administrative and civic responsibilities of the modern American rabbi. (Though many American rabbis are also scholars, the pursuit of learning for its own sake is not as highly appreciated in them as it was in their European colleagues. One Reform rabbi notes that he had his secretary take telephone calls and explain that "the rabbi is busy thinking," but that his congregants resented this. When he had her drop the word "thinking," his preoccupation was acceptable!)

See Char. and Des., TSVEY SHTET KRIGN ZICH IBER A ROV.

Cf. REBBE and REBBINER; Chap. IV, *re.* RABAY.

SEDREH

Weekly portion of the Torah read at Sabbath services, or portion assigned for study by children in the Hebrew School.

SEYDER

The ritual meal on the eve of the first day of Passover.

Orthodox and Conservative Jews also have a second SEYDER on the eve of the second day. In labor-Zionist circles, a "third seder" is held at the end of the week, at which the proceedings are given historical and literary emphasis, rather than a religious one, with readings from Jewish literature taking the place of the HAGODE text.

The seder is traditionally a home ceremony, but many congregations hold community seders for those unable to have them at home.

The "Last Supper" of Jesus was of course a seder, and the ceremony is sometimes observed by modern churches (*see* Food and Drink, TSIMMES).

My husband and I were amused one Passover when a photographer from the local paper who had been assigned to get a picture of the event came into the temple and asked him, "Are you Mr. Seder?"

See HAGODE; Food and Drink, CHAREYSHIS, CHOMETS, KARPES, 'PRAVEN A SEYDER (under 'PRAVEN SHABBES).

SEYFER (pl. SFORIM)

Important book (Talmudic or rabbinical); *also,* a Torah scroll.

SEYFER TOYRE   A Torah scroll.

SHABBES

The Sabbath—the seventh day, on which " . . . God finished the work which He had been doing and rested . . . " (Genesis 2:2).

Because of this, and because "God blessed the seventh day and declared it holy . . ." the Jew similarly rested from all work and gave the day a special aura of reverence. In eras when people were used to working long days and nights, without the daily entertainment that modern man takes for granted, the weekly day of rest and thankfulness to God was life-restoring. It was the high point of the week, the goal that challenged every struggling OREMAN to scrape together enough to have a decent meal for the Sabbath, though he might have to starve the rest of the week.

See MENOYRE, PUSHKE *and* SHALESHUDES; Food and Drink, MACHEN SHABBES; Greetings, GUT SHABBES.

SHABBES GOY   A Gentile who performed certain tasks which a Jew was forbidden on the Sabbath—such as the lighting of a lamp at SHUL on a winter's Friday evening. (This was interpreted as the making of a fire, which represented physical work, forbidden for the day of rest.)

A modern anecdote from West Germany tells of a Jewish deputy in the West German Parliament, named Altmaier, who had been invited by the then president of the Federal Republic of Germany, Theodor Heuss, to report on a trip to Israel. Altmaier came to see the president on a Friday afternoon, and they talked for some time. Heuss offered Altmaier a cigar, but noticed the latter's hesitancy. Realizing that the sun had set, and that the Jewish Sabbath had already begun, Heuss is supposed to have said, "If I were you, dear Altmaier, I would jump at the chance to have the President of Germany act as my SHABBES GOY and light my cigar!"

SHACHERIS

Morning service.

SHALACHMONES   *See* PURIM, PURIM SHALACHMONES.

SHALESHUDES

Music and refreshments on the afternoon of the Sabbath.

In ancient times, only two meals were eaten on weekdays, and the Sabbath was distinguished by a festive third meal, accompanied by song. That festive Sabbath observance developed into SHALESHUDES. In the early 1920's in Palestine, it took a further turn when Bialik originated the *Oneg Shabbat* (Joy of the Sabbath), at which cultural programs of discussion and music were combined with refreshments and sociality. The term *Oneg Shabbat* is commonly used today to refer to the social hour after synagogue services on Friday nights, at which forum discussions sometimes take place.

See Chap. I, Famil. with God, MLAVEH MALKE.

SHAMMAY

Shammai, famous rabbi of the first pre-Christian century, who is quoted in the Talmud. He and Rabbi Hillel represented major differing schools of thought.

SHAMMES (pl. SHAMMOSIM)

A sexton, a beadle.

This was the synagogue handyman, bottom rung of the functionary ladder, which also included ROV, CHAZEN, and SHOYCHET. These functions often coalesced in the CHAZEN-SHOYCHET (cantor-shochet) or SHAMMES-SHOYCHET or even in the ROV-CHAZEN (rabbi-cantor) or (best for the congregation, if they could find him!) the rabbi-cantor-shochet.

Where there were three men in the positions of rabbi, cantor and SHAMMES, there was a certain conscious "pecking order" —beautifully spoofed in the joke about the Sabbath service in which the rabbi gets up and beats his breast, exclaiming, "O Lord, I am nothing!" Impressed by this action of the rabbi, the cantor also rises, beats his breast and declaims, "O Lord, I am nothing!" The SHAMMES is naturally inspired by the other two and he also rises, beats his breast and tells God, "O Lord, I am nothing!" Whereupon the rabbi looks at the cantor and whispers: "Look who thinks he's nothing!"

The SHAMMES was usually a Jake-of-all-trades. He knew Hebrew, of course, and could read from the Torah or otherwise DAVEN if needed, and was a real MEYVEN of the talents of rabbi or cantor (*see* story under CHAZEN). Today, of course, the American middle-class synagogue has no SHAMMES, but a building custodian, who is more often than not a Gentile.

See Chap. IIIA, "shamus,"; IIIB, "NU, DARF MEN GEYN IN college?"

Cf. MENOYRE *re.* "SHAMMES candle"; Char. and Des., SHLATTENSHAMMES.

SHATNES

A mixture—specifically, of linen and wool—prohibited by the Bible (Leviticus 19:19 and Deuteronomy 22:9-11).

Strictly Orthodox men will not buy a suit without a "non-SHATNES" label.

The rabbi in Harry Kemelman's *Saturday the Rabbi Went Hungry* used the principle of SHATNES to solve a dilemma for a member of his congregation: by reasoning that a mixture of architectural styles is SHATNES, he vetoed a proposed addition to the temple which had displeased the man who was committed to pay for it, freeing the man to donate a separate building on another site.

SHAYTEL

Wig worn by strictly Orthodox women. Also known as a PARIK.

The principle involved was that a married woman should cover her head in the presence of strange men, to avoid arousing their erotic interest through the hair. Apparently the rabbis took no account of the fact that the wife was thereby being made less attractive to her husband too—or were they counting on this, to control the man's passion and give him more time for study? At any rate, women being what they have always been, things changed a bit in practice. Simple coverings gave way to wigs. Even when the practice of shaving the head became the rule (beginning in the Middle Ages), the women first used various types of silk headdress, known as a KUPKE, and then went about adorning them with embroidery and even with diamonds. So what did the men really accomplish?!

In recent years, with the modish wig in general fashion, Jews have been jokingly referring to it as a SHAYTEL, a fancy one being accorded a French accent: SHAYTÈL!

SHEHECHEYONU

Hebrew prayer of Thanksgiving, recited on eve of major holidays and at important milestones or special achievements.

The words are: *Boruch Ato, Adōnoy, Elōheynu, melech hoōlom, shehecheyonu, v'kimonu, v'higiyonu, laz'man hazeh* (Praised art Thou, O Lord, Our God, King of the universe, Who hast sustained us and preserved us and brought us to this joyous day).

ME DARF ZOGN A SHEHECHEYONU. We should say a prayer of thanksgiving.

SHECHINE

God's presence or radiance.

SHLEYME HAMELECH (comb. of Yiddish and Heb.)

Lit., Shlomo the King. King Solomon.

A famous musical composition by Ernest Bloch is "Schelomo."

SH'MA

Judaism's declaration of faith, which is recited twice daily by Orthodox Jews and several times in every Jewish Sabbath and festival service: *Sh'ma, Yisroeyl, Adōnoy Eloheynu, Adonoy Echod,* and is followed by the V'OHAVTO (which *see*).

As a bedtime prayer, the SH'MA is known as KRISHME (from Heb. *Kriath Sh'ma*).

See Exclam., SH'MA YISROEL!; Char. and Des., SH'MA KOLEYNU.

SH'MIN-ESRE

The series of benedictions forming the heart of daily prayers.

SH'MINI ATZERES

The Eighth Day of Assembly, or the Feast of Conclusion; the first of the last two days of SUKOS.

See SIMCHES TOYRE.

SHOKLEN

To move the upper part of the body back and forth while in prayer.

This movement is characteristic of the Orthodox male as he "davens." It goes back at least to Talmudic times. The Hasidim are especially vigorous at it.

The basis for the practice is sometimes found in Psalm 35 :10: "All my bones shall say: Lord, who is like unto Thee . . . ?"

SHOYCHET

Kosher slaughterer; a shochet.

See SHAMMES.

SHOYFER

Ram's horn, or shofar, blown at High Holy Day services, interpreted as the Call to Conscience.

According to the *Jewish Digest*, a student at Northwestern University in 1967 was playing his shofar with the college band, helping to exhort the school's football heroes to action!

SHTETL

Jewish town in Eastern Europe—a culture whose destruction began with the Bolshevik Revolution and ended with the Nazi holocaust.

See Char. and Des., FUN A SHTETL VERT A DERFL.

SHTRAYMEL (from Polish *stroj*, gala attire)

Velvet hat trimmed with fur, worn by Old World rabbis and Hasidim on the Sabbath and holidays.

The term is sometimes used humorously for any odd hat.

See Passing Judgment, FUN A CHAZERS EK KEN MEN KEYN SHTRAYMEL NIT MACHEN.

SHUL (*or* SHIL)

Synagogue.

The term derives from German *schule*, school. (The synagogue was traditionally a place of study as well as worship. Before the twentieth century, Jews were barred from most schools and had to create their own means of education.)

See Chap. I, Famil. with God, ICH VEL DOS NIT FARDINEN IN SHIL. . . .

SHULCHEN-ORUCH

Lit., Prepared Table. List of religious laws from the Bible, compiled by Joseph Karo, sixteenth-century Kabalist.

SHVUES

The spring festival known as the Feast of Weeks, or Shevuoth, which comes seven weeks after the first day of Passover. Pentecost.

Originally an agricultural festival, the holiday became associated with the revelation of the Ten Commandments to Moses at Mount Sinai. In Reform temples, SHVUES services include the Confirmation ceremony for young people completing the tenth grade in the religious school. (This is a different ceremony from that of BAR MITSVE or BAS MITSVE, which *see*.)

The traditional food for SHVUES is BLINTZES (Food and Drink) ; *see* Chap. I, beginning of Punning, for joke explaining why.

SIDDUR

Prayerbook.

SIMCHES TOYRE

Rejoicing over the Law—the final day of SUKOS, when the concluding portion of the last book of the Torah (Deuteronomy) is read in the synagogue, followed by the opening portion of the first book (Genesis), symbolizing the constant rereading and study of Torah.

A colorful part of the traditional service is the HAKOFE, a processional with the Torah scrolls, exalting and exulting in God's word.

See Family, CHOSSEN.

SLICHES

Penitential prayers recited during the Ten Days of Penitence between ROSHESHONE and YOM KIPPUR.

SMICHE

Ordination.

SOYFER

A scribe who writes the text of the Torah scroll (in ink on parchment).

A famous SOYFER was the Biblical Ezra, of the fifth pre-Christian century, who played a significant role in the perpetuation of Judaism. He is credited with collecting lost scrolls and restoring the Torah in Palestine after the Babylonian exile, reading the text aloud from a wooden pulpit to the people of Jerusalem.

See second paragraph under MIKVE.

SUKOS

The Feast of Booths, which commemorates the wanderings

of the ancient Hebrews through the desert after they left Egypt, until they reached the Promised Land in Canaan.

The holiday incorporates gratitude to God for the bounty of the fall harvest and is supposed to have inspired the Pilgrims, who were Bible readers, in their establishment of the American holiday of Thanksgiving.

It used to be customary for each family to build its own SUKEH, or simple hut, outdoors and to take its meals there during the week of SUKOS, symbolizing the experience of eating in frail booths during the desert period. In Brooklyn, Hasidic REBBES often had evening visitations from their flock, many of whom would arrive at ten o'clock and sing and dance through the night. Indeed, one incident in the 1930's has become a joke. A Gentile man who lived near a Hasidic REBBE became disturbed at the sounds of celebration coming from his neighbor's SUKEH, and on the third day he took the REBBE into court, citing the SUKEH as a public nuisance. The defense lawyer explained to the judge that it took time to build the hut, and it would also require time to take it down. "Well," said the judge, "I'll give you a week to get it down." Since this was already the third day of SUKOS, it meant the REBBE could finish celebrating the holiday and then take down the SUKEH!

It is possible now to buy pre-built, collapsible SUKEHs, and some families have taken to using them. Others prefer to build their own. For many it is a religious and social event to visit the SUKEH of relatives and friends. For the most part, however, the SUKEH is erected at one's synagogue, and the women of the congregation decorate it with fruits and vegetables. These are distributed to the children after the service. (In some quarters, as in the best-selling novel *Remember Me to God,* the SUKEH may be called a "sukie.")

Two symbols from the Holy Land identified with the SUKOS service are the ESRIG (citron) and LULEV (palm branch). These are combined with myrtle twigs and willow branches and waved at certain points in the service. One of many interpretations is that these represent the glorification of God and His great powers.

TALIS (pl. TALEYSIM)

Prayer shawl worn by most Orthodox and Conservative males thirteen years old or older. It was discarded by Reform Judaism in the nineteenth century, but has been "coming back" to some extent, chiefly in the apparel of the rabbi and cantor and among the men called up to the pulpit (*cf.* ALIEH).

A recent "inside" quip defines a mink stole as a "Hadassah TALIS."

TALIS KOTN

A small TALIS worn as an undergarment by strictly Orthodox males.

TALMUD

The Talmud, a collection of rabbinical commentaries on the laws of the Hebrew Bible, compiled during the first five centuries of the Christian era. Included are the MISHNE, which comments on the Torah, and the GEMORE, which comments on the MISHNE. Most editions of the Talmud also contain the comments of Rashi,[15] page by page. A new edition which is being issued gradually in pamphlet form contains all of this plus the English translation.

See Chap. I, Punning, ALLES SHTEYT IN TALMUD[16]; Char. and Des., TALMID CHOCHEM, under CHOCHEM.

TALMU'TOYRE

Talmud-Torah. A place where one studies Torah and Talmud. Hebrew School.

TAYTSH

Meaning.

The meanings of words, including their origins, were closely scrutinized by men trained in Talmud. One of my strongest childhood memories of my father is of his asking, on encountering some new expression, VOS IZ DER TAYTSH? (What does it mean? How would you translate it?)

Cf. Exclam., 'STAYTSH!

TEYKU

Lit., "Let it stand." An unanswerable intellectual question.

This comes from Talmudic Hebrew. It was a convenient last resort for any Scriptural disputant who was pushed into a philosophical corner. Maurice Samuel suggests the English spelling TECCOU, as an acrostic for "Till Elijah, Coming, Clarifies Our Understanding."

T'FILIN

Phylacteries—used by some Orthodox and Conservative men in weekday morning prayers.

These consist of two leather straps, each of which is attached to two small boxes containing different sections of Deuteronomy and Exodus. One strap is wound around the left arm and hand, the other around the forehead. The practice is a literal application of Deuteronomy 6:8, "And thou shalt bind them for a sign upon thy hand, and they shall be for frontlets between thine eyes."

LEYGN T'FILIN To lay phylacteries.

T'FILIN ZEKL Bag (usually embroidered silk) in which phylacteries are kept.

In Orthodox and Conservative synagogues, it is customary for boys to receive T'FILIN and a TALIS on their Bar Mitzvah. Some synagogues have a "Talis and T'filin Club," made up of boys who have attained Bar Mitzvah and are studying further.

TILIM

Psalms.

TISHEBOV

The ninth of Av (eleventh month of the Hebrew calendar), on which pious Orthodox Jews fast, to mourn the two destructions of the ancient temple: by Nebuchadnezzar in 586 B.C.E. and by Titus in the year 70.

TOYRE

Torah. Specifically, the first five books of the Hebrew Bible (*see* CHUMESH). Generally, moral law, all Jewish sacred literature; hence, knowledge.

DI TOYRE HOT KEYN GRUND NIT. Scripture is bottomless.

VU TOYRE, DORT IZ CHOCHME. Where there's knowledge (of Scripture), there's wisdom.

See TALMU'TOYRE *and* introduction above *re.* TOYRE IZ DI BESTE S'CHOYRE.

TROP

Written accent signs for indicating the cantillation of Scripture and prayer.

This term was borrowed from the medieval church's "troparion" (a short hymn) and represents the mechanical designation of NIGUN, melody (*see* Chap. I, Intonation).

TSADIK (pl. TSADIKIM)

A great and wonder-working Hasidic rabbi. A saint.

TSEDOKE

Charity (*see* introduction above).

Cf. Chap. I, Acronyms, ER IZ A GUTER B'TSEDEK.

TSENE-RENE

A Yiddish book popular among women, which was basically a paraphrase of the Torah, with related interpretations and stories from the Talmud and other ethical and prayer material.

The book—written by Jacob ben Isaac Ashkenazi—has been read for several hundred years. Ironically enough, it was published in a German translation in 1934, just before Hitler's genocide program. The name comes from Hebrew *tsenah urenah* in Song of Songs 3:11 ("Go forth, O ye daughters of Zion, and behold!").

V'OHAVTO

The prayer which comes from Deuteronomy 6:4-9: "Thou shalt love the Lord thy God with all thy heart, with all thy soul, and with all thy might . . ." and which follows the first line of the SH'MA.

YARMULKE

Skullcap—worn at prayer by both Orthodox and Conservative males and at all times by some of the Orthodox.

A grandmother of my acquaintance recalls that her pious grandfather used to ask her bare-headed brother, "FARVOS IZ DAYN TOCHES BESSER VI DAYN KOP?" ("Why is your rear end better than your head?"), answering his own question with: "FAR DAYN TOCHES IZ FARDEKT UN DAYN KOP IZ NISHT FARDEKT" ("Because your rear end is covered and your head is not covered"). (*See* Chap. I, Vulgarity.)

Reform Judaism, in the nineteenth century, eliminated the wearing of the YARMULKE. As the eminent Reconstructionist Rabbi Mordecai M. Kaplan has quipped, "Many a Conservative Jew becomes a Reform Jew at the drop of a hat." Today, however, even in Reform congregations, one sometimes sees it worn—but feeling on the subject can run high, and congregations have been known to split on the issue, despite the fact that both covering and uncovering of the head have precedent in earlier periods of Jewish history.

An old conundrum asks, How do we know that Abraham wore a YARMULKE? And the reply is, SHOYNZHE IZ ER GEGANGEN *ON* A YARMULKE? (So tell me, could he have gone *without* a YARMULKE?)

The simple YARMULKE is a solid color—usually black, navy, or white—but fancier versions abound. Those at the Chief Rabbinate chapel in Jerusalem are purple with yellow embroidery. Some Orthodox Jews use a tiny knitted one, often multi-

colored, which looks like a doily. I understand that straw YAR-
MULKES from Japan are available in New York.

Some twenty years ago, my husband was asked by a Protestant
professor's wife at the University of Connecticut to get a YAR-
MULKE for her elderly father-in-law, who was partly bald, to
keep his head protected as he sat on the porch. In 1965, the
YARMULKE became the so-called "freedom cap" worn by the
freedom marchers in Selma, Alabama. Because the Reform
rabbis who were in the march decided they ought to be identified
in some way as Jews, they sent for some YARMULKES. When the
Negro marchers saw them they wanted to wear them too, so a
thousand YARMULKES were obtained by air express from a
Brooklyn manufacturer. (This "freedom cap" was later changed
to a hat. *See* Chap. IIIA, "entitled" without the "to.")

But traffic has worked both ways. Some months ago a cantor
who had been invited to present a program of "Songs of the
Bible" at St. Olaf College in Minnesota discovered that he had
no YARMULKE with him. None of the three local Jewish families
had one, but he was helped out by the Episcopal minister, who
lent him his skullcap for the occasion!

It is said that the Israeli Finance Minister, preparing to
write a check, put on a YARMULKE. A bystander asked, "Why
do you have to cover your head to write a check?" His reply:
"That's the only coverage I've got!" It may have been an
association with "coverage" that prompted one race-horse owner
to name his nag "Yarmulke." According to the *Jewish Digest,*
such a horse was running in 1967!

YEHŌASH

Pseudonym of Solomon Bloomgarden, nineteenth- and twen-
tieth-century poet famous for his Yiddish translation of the
Bible and of Arabic, French and English classics (including
Longfellow's *Hiawatha*).

YESHIVE

Seminary.

See Food and Drink, ESSEN TEG, under ESSEN.

YICHES

Status, prestige.

In the Old Country, this was something you got by birth if
your family was very learned or very wealthy. Such a family
had a coveted "seat by the eastern wall" in the synagogue.
A PROSTER (a coarse man) could sometimes buy YICHES by

marrying into a respected family, if he was wealthy enough that his lack of learning could be overlooked in the arranging of a SHIDDUCH.

The term is often used humorously today. A writer who has published in a prestigious magazine without pay might say, "For that I got just YICHES."

An old ironic joke tells of the man who comes to town to see the president of the synagogue and inquires about him of a leading citizen. "That good-for-nothing?" his informant responds—"I wouldn't wish him onto you!" Another townsperson of whom he inquires also upbraids the president: "That GANEF? May his bones rot in the ground!" After similar reactions from others, the visitor finally is able to locate the man, and when he sees him, he asks, "Tell me—it must be an awful job being president of the synagogue; why do you do it?" The reply: "For the YICHES!"

See Exclam., A GROYSER YICHES!; Char. and Des., A GROYSER M'YICHES.

YIDDISHKAYT

Jewishness; the fine qualities of an authentic Jew.

YOM KIPPUR

The Day of Atonement, the most solemn day of the Jewish calendar, culmination of the Ten Days of Penitence following ROSHESHONE and associated with fasting and confession.

A fascinating incident in the Korean War, originally reported by the late Billy Rose, involved a Marine corporal from New York who on the day scheduled for an attack on Seoul, got up as usual well before dawn to say his morning prayers but refused any food or drink, because it was Yom Kippur. He put in an active day of fighting, heroically stopping an enemy sniper from shooting at the commanding officer, but in the process got shot three times himself. The surgeon who performed the difficult operation said it owed its success to the fact that there was almost no food in the patient's stomach.

Despite the solemn character of this Holy Day, a number of jokes have been made about it. (*See*, for instance, the definition under Exclam., A SHEYNE GELECHTER!) A recent one tells about the office boy who informs a caller: "Mr. Cohen isn't in. This is Yom Kippur." The caller replies, "Well, Mr. Kippur, please tell Mr. Cohen I called."

Yom Kippur is also associated with the story of how the

famous presidential adviser Bernard Baruch made his first million. It seems he was sitting at his desk one autumn, deliberating about selling his copper stocks. A call from his mother reminded him that the following day was Yom Kippur. "You mean Yom Copper," he joked. "I have plans for tomorrow in copper." But his mother pleaded with him to observe the Holy Day and prevailed on him not to go into the office in the morning. The day after Yom Kippur, Baruch discovered that his copper stocks had taken an unexpected rise, making him a rich man.

See KOL NIDRE above; Chap. I, Realism *and* Rhyme, "GUT YONTIFF, Pontiff"; Char. and Des., SH'MA KOLEYNU.

Cf. PIKUACH NEFESH.

YONTEF (pl. YONTEYVEN)

Holiday.

See Char. and Des., ME MACHT A GANTSEN YONTEF; Greetings, GUT YONTEF!

ZMIRES

Devotional songs sung at table on the Sabbath and Holy Days.

ZOGACHTS

Lit., expression. The musical improvisation of a CHAZEN.

RESIGNATION

ABI VAYTER

As long as we can go on.

This consolation in mere existence was a popular ghetto phrase during the Nazi period.

ABI VI

As long as somehow—i.e., no matter how, when or where, as long as it's done.

A SHEYNE, REYNE KAPORE

A pretty, clean sacrifice; i.e., no harm done, it'll be an atonement (said at breaking or losing something).

This connotes the meticulous scrutiny that the ancient priests gave to sacrificial offerings, to ensure that they were free of blemishes. (*See* Rel. and Cul., KAPORES.)

Also, AF KAPORES ZOL ES ZAYN! Let it be for sacrifice! (A more exalted form of "Good riddance to bad rubbish.")

AZOY GEYT ES!

That's the way it goes! Such is life!

CHAPT ES DER RICH!

The devil take it!

Cf. Advice, DER RICH'L IM NIT NEMEN.

GAM ZU LETEYVE. (Heb. *gam zu letōvo*)

This, too, is for the best.

GEY SHRAY G'VALD. (ironic)

Go holler protest. Go fight City Hall.

See Exclam., G'VALD! *and* Chap. IIIA, "Go" as an ironic substitute for "Try and". . . .

GEY VEYS. (ironic)

Go know. Who could have known. Who would have guessed it.

See Chap. IIIA, "Go" as an ironic substitute. . . .

ICH VEYS?!

Lit., I know?! You think I know?

This has a distinctive intonation:

ICH　　　　VEY-　　　　EYS?!

Also, VEYS ICH VOS. What do I know. Darned if I know.

VEYS　　　　ICH　　　　VOS.

ME GEVEYNT ZICH (*or* ME VERT ZICH TSUGEVEYNT) TSU DI TSORES.

You get used to your troubles. Reminiscent of "You can get used to anything."

MEYLE, ...

Well, what can you do. . . .

MIT DER PUTER AROP

With the buttered side down.

This is the way, we are told, that the slice of bread always falls! EYB NISHT, 'SIZ GEFALEN AF DER LINKER ZAYT: If not, it's fallen on the wrong side![1]

My daughter, who had often heard the above expressions, once remarked as she retrieved a piece of bread from the floor, "This bread isn't Jewish." I knew what she meant: it had fallen on the right side for a change, with the butter up!

NU, IZ NISHT.

So, it didn't pan out.

NU, IZ NISHT GEFIDELT. So, there won't be any fiddling—i.e., So the wedding is off. (*See* Chap. IIIA, "Ish kabibble." *See also* Char. and Des., OYS KALEH!)

NU, IZ NISHT GETROFN. Oh well, so we guessed wrong.

NU, IZ FARFALEN. Well, so we lost a chance.

'SIZ MAYN DAYGE. (Often shortened to MAYN DAYGE.) (ironic)

Lit., It's my worry. I should worry. I'm not going to let it bother me.

See Advice, A DAYGE HOSTU.

'SIZ SHVER (UN BITTER) TSU ZAYN A YID.

It's hard (and bitter) to be a Jew.

This contains both sighing resignation and realistic facing of hard facts.

SHVER TSU ZAYN A YID was a play by Sholem Aleichem, in which the famous actor Paul Muni, then Muni Weisenfreund, first came to the attention of the theatrical world. This was a dramatization of the author's story "Der Blutiker Shpas" ("The Bloody Hoax"), which was based on the false ritual-murder charge of the Russian government against Mendel Beilis in 1913. Maurice Samuel's book on the Beilis case, *Blood Accusation*, was inspired by Sholem Aleichem's work on the subject, as was also, presumably, Bernard Malamud's novel *The Fixer*.

See Food and Drink, note to ME SHIT ARAYN. . . .

VER VEYST?!

Who knows?!

VOS IZ GEVEN IZ GEVEN, IZ NISHTO.

What has been has been, is no more.

This acceptance of fate was more than simple resignation. It was a recognition of the need to concentrate on the present and future, and was buttressed by the somewhat similar VOS 'SIZ NECHTN GEVEN VET SHOYN MORGN NIT ZAYN (What existed yesterday will not be here tomorrow). Both of these were subjects of old popular Yiddish songs, which can still evoke memories of the generation which schooled itself not to look backward to the Old Country but to find its way in the New World. (*See* Chap. I, Realism.)

TRIBALISM

The expressions in this section mirror, in a variety of ways, the insecure status that has been the historical lot of the Jews. All too often the victims of unprovoked assault, they naturally identified themselves as Jews in their thinking. It is not surprising that a number of expressions are directed against those from whom the shabby treatment came. Defensive-aggressive uses of terms like GOY and SHEYGETS, BEYTSEMER[1] and LOKSH helped the average Jew to get rid of some of his hostilities and bolster his self-esteem. Recent bilingual jokes about Christmas, like "Santa KLUHTZ," "Merry KRATZ MICH (Scratch Me)" and "Deck the halls with boughs of CHALLE" are—if not in the best of taste—somewhat similar reactions of the outsider, who finds compensation in favorable judgments of his own group, like YIDDISH HARTS, YIDDISHER KOP, YIDDISHER TAM. (On a somewhat higher level is the English jingle: "Roses are reddish,/Violets are bluish,/If it weren't for Christmas,/We'd all be Jewish.")

The fact that Jews had a tradition and culture about which they were knowledgeable and in which they could take pride did not, however, give them a superiority complex. Even the tradition of being the "Chosen People" could not do that— for as one of the complaints in Chap. I put it, What in the world were they chosen for, suffering and yet more suffering?

The various terms used to identify another Jew—not only the Yiddish FUN UNZERE and YEHUDI, but the English "one of us" and "M.O.T." (Member of the Tribe)—indicate a consciousness of minority status, which is also seen in the sensitivity to Gentile opinion, as in A SHANDE FAR DI GOYIM. It would seem that the "clannishness" of which Jews have sometimes been accused was in essence a retreat from the hostile outer world.

Yet, as happens in any situation where people are in close quarters, the family members got on one another's nerves. In the first place, they reflected geographical prejudices, as will be seen under GALITZIANER and LITVAK. (Today in Israel, where there are Jews from all over the world, such pecking-order distinctions are very much alive.) Indeed, there were petty prejudices between the Jews of one community and another—as suggested under Food and Drink, FRESSER. Sholem Aleichem gave a delightful account of the differences in prayer sequence from one town to another and of how dramatically they showed up when a visitor from one SHTETL attended a synagogue service in another: the resulting lack of coordination among the worshippers could be so disturbing that it led to blows!

In the second place, being both highly individualistic[2] and demanding in their standards, the Jews were critical of one another as human beings. It has been recalled that a generation ago, there was speculation that the Nobel Prize might go to Bialik for his Hebrew poetry, and that when it did not, the perceptive poet remarked that it was just as well: this way Jews were asking, "Why didn't they give Bailik the prize?" If it *had* been given him, he said, they would be asking, "Why *him*?" This story is reminiscent of the one told by Asher Lee, wartime adviser to Winston Churchill, concerning the time Churchill asked him after dinner: "Tell me, Lee, if there were three of your co-religionists together would we have two Prime Ministers and one Leader of the Opposition or two Leaders of the Opposition and one Prime Minister?" Lee replied, "I think, sir, we'd have three Leaders of the Opposition." (Churchill, he said, took a puff on his cigar, raised his brandy glass and drank a silent toast.)[3]

It is not really surprising, then, that irritations at individuals might even at times break out in family terms: YIDDISHE BIZNES! (Jewish business!—annoyance at someone's having failed to keep an agreement or having caused unnecessary complications about some arrangement) or GOYIM ZOLN HOBN TSU TON MIT YIDDEN! (Gentiles should have to do with Jews!). Though these showed the absorption to some extent of the outer world's tendency to ascribe to the entire group the characteristics of some unpleasant individuals, such exclamations are just momentary outbursts and are not true self-hatred. It was rather more in the style of the exasperated complaints offered to God which were followed by reaffirmation of faith, that the Jew would (and still does) expostulate at his brother and then clasp him to his bosom.

Remember, too, that all such uncomplimentary terms represent in-group sentiments. Let no outsider use them. Every Yom Kippur Jewish worshippers castigate themselves for being "stiff-necked," but they don't want to hear a Gentile express the same idea. This is true of any cultural or national group. We Americans have certainly criticized ourselves freely in print, but we resent hearing the same criticism from outsiders, for we feel they haven't earned the right to say such things. Similarly, in good-natured fashion, the Negroes will use "nigger," and the Jews YIDDEL, among their own, but they will heartily resent the use of these terms by others.

Self-mockery has often shown up in in-group jokes, like the ironic definition of an anti-Semite as "a person who dislikes Jews more than is strictly necessary." And over-sensitivity is joshed about in various ways, as in the story about the NUDNIK who kept asking a busy railroad information director what time the next train was due in from Chicago, and who, when the trainman finally exploded at him, muttered, "ANTISEMIT!"

A current story tells of a Jewish woman in a train who looks at the young man sitting opposite her and asks the common question, "Are you Jewish?" He says, "No." "Really?" she asks. "Really," he replies. "Oh, my," she goes on, "I thought you were." A minute later, she asks "Are you sure you're not Jewish?" "Yes, I'm sure," he answers. The woman simply will not accept his denial and keeps expressing herself on the subject. At last, in desperation, the young man decides to shut her up and says, "Yes, yes, I'm Jewish. I am." Whereupon she says, "Really?" and he replies, "Really; I am a Jew." "Oh, my," she exclaims, "I just can't believe it." This new protest continues, and finally she leans over and says, "You know something? You don't *look* Jewish!"

A niece of mine, who worked in an Israeli kibbutz for part of her undergraduate program at Antioch College, wrote home about the two black-skinned Ethiopian Jews who had joined the kibbutz and who were such a novelty that kibbutzniks from other places had been coming to meet them. She had difficulty, she said, repressing the urge to say, "Funny—you don't *look* Jewish!" The same idea appeared some months ago in a cartoon showing a large square of matzo and a round cracker, with the caption, "Really? You don't look it."[4]

The Jews also realized they were not physically as agile as

the GOYIM, as we saw in the self-mocking Scriptural joke quoted in Chap. I (latter part of Learning). It is said of the Hasidic rabbi Zusya that whenever he met a Jewish boy, he would bless him with the words, "Be healthy and strong as a GOY." Yet there is the precious castigation of both Gentile physicality and Jewish mentality: GOT ZOL UNZ UPHITN FUN YIDDISHEN MOYACH UN GOYISHEN KOYACH![5] (God protect us from Jewish brain and Gentile brawn!) In Israel today, of course, the two have been combined. (See the recent story quoted in Chap. I, latter part of Learning.)

A SHANDE FAR DI GOYIM

A shame before the Gentiles. (Just think what "they" will say about us.)

This is an extension of the concern about appearances seen earlier: MENTSHEN VELN DEYNKEN (Advice) and VOS FAR A PONIM VET ES HOBN? (Chap. I, Taste).

See GOY.

ASHKENAZI (Heb.—pl. ASHKENAZIM)

A Jew of Central European stock (which the majority of Jews are today).

Cf. SEFARDI.

A YIDDISHER COMPLIMENT (ironic)

A Jewish compliment. Ex.: "You look so thin, dollink! You're maybe not feeling well?"

The approach came through in a recent ad that Northeast Airlines ran in American Jewish periodicals: "You look like you need a vacation."

British slang has a somewhat similar "Yorkshire compliment," meaning a gift that is useless to the giver and not wanted by the receiver.

A YIDDISH VORT

A Yiddish word.

This conveys the sense of good talk in congenial company—the "HEYMISHness" of herd warmth. A lone Jew in the Arkansas countryside might "hunger for a Yiddish word" with fellow Jews. Indeed, Susie Michael and Maurice Friedman, who for years gave performances of Yiddish folk songs around the country, told me once of the touching emotional responses they had seen on the part of Jews in the hinterland at hearing, for the first time in many years, A YIDDISH VORT.

The expression has been used in the title of a recent collection of poems by Jacob Glatstein, DI FREYD FUN YIDDISHEN VORT *(The Joy of the Yiddish Word)*.

BIST A YID?

Are you a Jew?

Somewhat like the "smelling out" that strange dogs give each other is this question which always occurred (and often still does) to Jews on first meeting. There is a precious Yiddish story my father used to tell about a Russian Jew who gets on a train and gingerly sits down next to a dignified and handsomely dressed gentleman, not daring to cover more than the edge of the seat. But he looks out of the corner of his eye at the newspaper the stranger is reading and sees that it is a Yiddish one. "AZOY!" he exclaims. "BIST A YID? NU, GIB SHOYN A RIK!" (So! You're a Jew? In that case, shove over!)

See also ICH BIN A YID.

DAYTSH (m.), DAYTSHE (f.)

A German (either Jew or Gentile).

See Char. and Des., A KRANKER DAYTSH.

Cf. YEHUDI.

DER GOY IZ TSUM GOLES NIT GEVEYNT.

The Gentile isn't used to Exile. Gentiles don't know Jewish troubles.

Cf. Char. and Des., LANG VI DOS YIDDISHE GOLES.

DER YID IZ A KAPORE HON.

The Jew is a scapegoat (*lit.*, a rooster for the atonement sacrifice—*see* Rel. and Cul., KAPORES).

ER IZ FUN UNZERE.

Lit., He's from ours. He's one of us, a Jew.

ER IZ FUN UNZERE YIDDEN. He's our kind of Jew.

GALITZIANER (familiarly, GALITZ)

A Jew from Galicia—the region of the northern slopes of the Carpathian Mountains, which was variously part of Poland and of the Austrian empire. (Today it is split up between Poland and Russia.)

The GALITZ was looked down upon by Russian and Lithuanian Jews[6]—who were returned the same contempt—in the manner that Austrian Jews were looked down upon by German Jews (who, being generally more highly educated and assimilated, also thought themselves superior to most other Jews). Intriguingly, however, Galician Jewry produced many outstanding scholars and writers, among them two famous men who eventually settled in modern Israel: Martin Buber (who though known as a German-Jewish philosopher,[7] was born in Vienna and raised in Lwow, Galicia) and S. Y. Agnon, the literary Nobel Prize winner.

GOY (m.—pl. GOYIM); GOYE (f.—pl. GOYES)

A Gentile. *Also,* an unlearned or nonobservant Jew.

A recent satirical piece by William M. Kramer about the quickness of Jews to claim great people as their own (through the "Center of Creative Jewish Ethnocentricity and its Division of Pure Invention") dealt with the findings of "Professor I. M. Nogoy."

The term GOYIM has been defined by Bob and Ruth Grossman as "what some of our best friends are," in ironic reversal of the statement associated with genteel anti-Semitism, "Some of my best friends are Jews." (A new twist has been provided by the Quaker leader commenting on the number of Jews in his church: "Some of my best Jews are Friends.")

See GOYISHER KOP; GOYISHE MAZEL; introduction above, GOYIM ZOLN HOBN TSU TON MIT YIDDEN; Rel. and Cul., SHABBES, SHABBES GOY; Chap. IIIA, "guy" *and* "yock."

GOYISHE MAZEL

Gentile luck. Good fortune that isn't really deserved.

English has a similar phrase, "Irish luck."

See VOS MER GOY, ALTS MER MAZEL.

GOYISHER KOP

Gentile head (as contrasted with YIDDISHER KOP, which *see*).

ICH BIN A YID.

I am a Jew.

In 1965 the American specialist in international law, William A. Hyman (since deceased) told me that he had met twelve colleagues at an international meeting and had stated in five languages, including the above Yiddish, that he was a Jew. All, he said, were amazed to discover that each one of them was also a Jew![8]

AZOY VI ICH BIN A YID. As sure as I'm a Jew.

LITVAK (m.), LITVISHE (f. and pl.)

A Jew from Lithuania—according to whom, the quip has it, there are only two kinds of Jews: LITVAKS and PASKUDNYAKS.[9] (*See* RUSESHER.)

To the Polish Jews, the LITVAK was A TSEYLIM KOP (a crucifix head), considered to be more prone to conversion than other Jews.

LOKSH (derisive)

An Italian.

The word means "noodle," which is of course the staple of Italian diet. In English, "macaroni" has had the same derogatory use.

Cf. Food and Drink, MAMMELIGE *and* LOKSHEN.

MARRAN (pl. MARRANEN)

A marrano, a Spanish Jew of the Middle Ages who was forced to convert to Catholicism but who secretly maintained the traditions of Judaism; *or* a descendant of such a family.

The marranos were not fully accepted by the Christian population, and their descendants—though usually no longer practicing Judaism—may still be a somewhat separate group of Christians. Such a group was reported in South America a few years ago.

The term "inverted marranos" has been applied to those Jews who instead of being outwardly Christian and inwardly Jewish are outwardly Jewish but without inner attachment to their faith, i. e., Jews in name only.

OPTON AF TERKISH

Lit., to "do in" in the Turkish manner. To play a trick on, to steal a march on.

The expression is believed to date from the Russo-Turkish War. An earlier English phrase was "Turkish treatment," meaning "barbarous usage." Turkish slurs have appeared in several other languages.

PEYLISHER (m.), PEYLISHE (f. and pl.)

Polish.

A PEYLISHE DRIPKE (derisive) A Polish slattern. This was a derogatory term for a Polish-Jewish housewife, used by Russian and Lithuanian Jewish women.

POLYAK (uncomplimentary—pl. POLYAKEN) A Pole.
English has the similar slur, "Polack."

RUSESHER (m.), RUSESHE (f. and pl.)

Russian.

In the opinion of some old-time LITVAKS, a Russian Jew was a RUSESHER CHAZER (Russian pig), and to some Russian Jews these name-calling brethren were, in turn, CHAZER'SHE LITVAKS (Swinish Litvaks).

SEFARDI (Heb.—pl. SEFARDIM)

A Jew of Spanish descent.

Cf. MARRAN.

SHEYGETS (pl. SHKUTSIM)

A Gentile male.

Also, derogatory: SHKUTS

The term is from Hebrew *shekets* (disgusting—because un-circumcised).

By extension, A GROYSER SHEYGETS—a very disrespectful fellow, a brat, a lout.

Today, the emotional connotations are less strong.

Cf. SHIKSE.

SHIKSE (familiarly, SHIKSEL *or* SHIKSELE)

Gentile female.

This does not have quite the same uncomplimentary associations which attached to SHEYGETS, though it is thought to be the source of several low slang terms in England (*see* Chap. IIIA, "shickser").

In the United States today, many a SHIKSE is active in a temple sisterhood and Hadassah chapter, knowing and doing more about her husband's faith than he, who is the real GOY in the family. An amusing account of such a phenomenon, "Marvin Marries a Shikse," appeared in the *Reconstructionist* some years ago. Harry Golden has also noted such a situation in North Carolina, where the super-kosher SHIKSE won't let her casual YIDDISHER husband use butter on his chicken sandwiches. His mother is supposed to have told him once, "See, why couldn't you have married a nice Jewish girl?"!

Cf. VOS DARFSTU A GOYISHE SHIKSE . . . ?

SHVARTZER (m.), SHVARTZE (f.)

Colored person; Negro; black.

From Yiddish SHVARTZ (black), this has always been considered less complimentary than the formal NEGER (Negro). Yet it seems more dignified than English "darky" or "blacky," and from the viewpoint of those who reject the term "Negro" it may after all be a right and proper word.

An old story—which has recently been told with a Catholic reference—is the one about a black man who is asked if he is Jewish and who replies, "Lord, no; I have enough trouble being a SHVARTZER."[10]

I would wager this is the same cant word that Eric Partridge, in his *Dictionary of Slang and Unconventional English,* lists as "schfatzer," and for which he innocently offers the meaning of "fellow, chap."

Cf. Imprec., A SHVARTZ YOR AF IM!

'SIZ GUT FAR DI YIDDEN?

Is it good for the Jews?

This personalized reaction to public events grew out of precarious position; yet the Jews kidded themselves about such self-centeredness. Not only is the expression itself used in jest, but there are various jokes on the same theme, like the famous one about the English, German, French and Jewish students assigned to write a paper on the elephant. The Englishman does a dissertation on "Hunting the Wild Elephant"; the German on the anatomical structure of the left knee-cap of the elephant; the Frenchman on the sex life of the elephant; the Jew on "The Elephant and the Jewish Problem."

In 1966 *Commentary* carried an article on baseball's Sandy Koufax, "Koufax the Incomparable," which discussed various ways in which Koufax's Jewish identity may have influenced his career, both in his own actions and in those of Gentiles. A dissenting reader ironically retitled the piece "Curve Balls: Are They Good or Bad for the Jews?" Another issue of the same magazine headed a book review: "Is It Good for Literature?"

TOTER

Lit., a Tatar (a Turk). An odd character; an outlandish fellow.

VOS DARFSTU A GOYISHE SHIKSE (*or* GOYISHEN GOY) AZ DU KENST KRIGN A YIDDISHE SHIKSE (*or* YIDDISHEN GOY)?

What do you need a Gentile heathen for, if you can get a Jewish heathen? (father to a son or daughter who is dating a Gentile)

Considering that this was the first generation talking to the second, it is remarkably good-natured in its caution against intermarriage. Though it may not be expressed in Yiddish any more, the general feeling against intermarriage still runs strong —sometimes much less casually than that Yiddish put it. Perhaps it is part of the delayed reaction to the Nazi experience. It may also reflect the guilt which some parents feel about their child's threatened "defection," the feeling that it is somehow their fault because they have not been better Jews. It may indeed symbolize a Jewishly unlearned generation with little but pure tribalism to hold onto. When some years ago a well-known American Jewish writer married a Gentile, his father was greatly disturbed, but according to *Time,* "Grandfather understood." Intermarriage has of course been a fact of life throughout Jewish history, even Moses having married a Midianite. Today, more often than heretofore, intermarriage does not mean "losing" the Jewish partner. The children are frequently raised as Jews, with the other partner sometimes being converted.

VOS MER GOY, ALTS MER MAZEL.

The more non-Jewish, the more luck.

A similarly sardonic conundrum asked, FARVOS GEYT ES A MESHUMED SHTENDIK GUT, UN A GER SHTENDIK SHLECHT? (Why do things go well for a baptized Jew and badly for a Gentile converted to Judaism?) Reply: VAYL A MESHUMED HOT A YIDDISHEN KOP MIT A GOYISHEN MAZEL, UN A GER HOT A GOYISHEN KOP MIT A YIDDISHEN MAZEL. (Because a baptized Jew has a Jewish head with Gentile luck, while a convert to Judaism has a Gentile head with Jewish luck. *See* GOYISHER KOP.)

See also story under Rel. and Cul., GER.

YEHUDI (Heb.—pl. YEHUDIM)

A Jew.

This has been used as a masculine name, as in that of the famous violinist Yehudi Menuhin. Over a generation ago, the question "Where's Yehudi?" was a popular line in a radio comedian's routine.

A great Hasidic rabbi of Pzhysha was known as DER YEHUDI (The Jew).

The plural YEHUDIM was a partly ironic, sometimes jeering term used by the poor immigrants from Eastern Europe, to refer to the earlier and more aristocratic Jewish settlers in the United States, the German Jews (DAYTSHESHE YEHUDIM) and other relatively assimilated and affluent Jews. The contrast between YEHUDIM and YIDDEN (*see* YID) is like the one that used to exist between "Israelite" and "Jew."

YEKE (disparaging)

A German Jew; a fool; an undesirable Jew.

This Yiddish and modern Hebrew slur appears to be related —as Professor Dov Sadan has suggested—to German *Geck* or *Gecke,* a vain or foolish person. (In Low German, "g" is often pronounced as "y.") It may also have been influenced by

German *Jäck*, a Rhineland term for Jacob that can be derogatory, and by the similar Yiddish YEKEL, a diminutive of YA(N)-KEV, from Hebrew *Yaakov*.

It may be pertinent that in Hebrew Jacob originally meant "heel-grabber," referring to Jacob's grabbing of Esau's heel in an effort to keep him from emerging first from their mother's womb. (Genesis 25:26.)

Indeed, in a sense YEKEL is an equivalent of YIDDEL: in Genesis 35:10-12, after Jacob had built an altar to God at Beth-el, God told him his name would thenceforth be Israel and that the land would belong to him and his seed. A deprecation of his name therefore could connote a deprecation of the people Israel. Similarly, there is the in-group exclamation of disdain (UNZERE YIDDELACH! (Our little Jews!), which thrusts upon the entire group the disapproval provoked by actions of one or more individuals. (But note the acceptance involved too. *See* the introduction to this section. Notice too that just as YIDDEL may be used affectionately, there is the affectionate diminutive of the name Jacob, YEKELE. A famous Hasidic rabbi was thus known.)

The name Jacob is also derided more tolerantly—*see* Char. and Des., CHAYIM YANKEL.

YEKE was further used by Lithuanian Jews to refer to certain of their own. It is reminiscent of the derisive English "kike" (Chap. IIIA).

Cf. Char. and Des., SHMEGEGGE.

YEKEL   *See* YEKE.

YID (pl. YIDDEN)
A Jew.

YIDDEL (pl. YIDDELACH—familiar; sometimes derogatory: *see* YEKE)   A little Jew. The term "little Jew" is a common description in general literature.[11] But this should not be surprising. "Like all Jews, I was undersized and sickly," wrote Isaak Babel in one of his stories, "and I suffered from headaches from studying too hard." In the Russian school to which Babel was finally admitted (after once being bypassed in favor of a Jewish boy with lower marks whose father could afford to bribe the corrupt school examiners) the quota was two Jews to a class of forty. Babel graphically described his successful second try, for which he had memorized three entire books, the oral examination calling forth streams of quotations on his part, including poems by Pushkin! One of his examiners, he said, exclaimed to the other: "What a people these little Jews of yours are! There's a devil in them!"

Even before going to the Russian school, though, Jewish boys of Eastern Europe, as we have noted earlier, were routinized for Hebrew study at a tender age and showed the physical signs of lack of sunshine and play.

The term YIDDEL, then, among the Jews themselves, expresses a combination of affection and recognition of their less than full status, as in the popular rhyme YIDDEL MIT DEM FIDDEL, the little Jew with his fiddle. The figure of the Old World Jew playing the fiddle has been made famous by the painter Marc Chagall—one of whose canvases was the presumable inspiration for the title of the Broadway musical production *Fiddler on the Roof,* which was based on Sholem Aleichem's stories about Tevye's daughters. A recent greeting-card advises, "On your vacation, take the sun the Yiddish way, Yiddel by Yiddel."

See Chap. IIIB, "Yiddified."

YIDDISHE KRECHTS

Jewish sigh or groan—one which embodies the woes and joys of the ages; hence, real feeling.

Of a fine cantor, one might say, ER HOT DEM YIDDISHEN KRECHTS (He has the real Jewish feeling). A recent bestselling novel referred to this feeling as YIDDISHE KVETSH, which is not completely synonymous. KVETSH may also mean "squeeze," as in KISHEN KVETSHER (Family). Both terms may mean "whine" or "complain," as in KVETSH (Char. and Des.) or NOR ME KRECHTST! (Ann. and Arg.)

See also Chap. IIIB, "KRECHTSing; . . . ."

YIDDISHE MAMME

Jewish mother. Hence, the epitome of motherhood.

Is this latter meaning chauvinistic? A decade ago, a Conservative rabbi in a small Eastern community greatly disturbed members of his congregation by exalting the Jewish mother above all others in a graveside eulogy with many Christians present.

The Jewish mother—as his congregants felt—is not superior to all others. But she may in fact be unique. True, the characteristics made familiar in best-selling spoofs are not really too different from those of many Gentile American mothers. The "momism" that Philip Wylie castigated some quarter-century ago was certainly an American phenomenon and contained some traits which are at times attributed to the Jewish mother.

But the satirized Jewish mother is obviously more than a product of American society. She reflects the vestiges of the last few generations of European Jewish experience, in which the mother was often both homemaker and breadwinner and tended to dominate the household. Some men devoted most of their time to study. The others were greatly hampered in their efforts to earn a livelihood by the many governmental restrictions placed upon the work and movements of Eastern European Jews ever since the Middle Ages. As a consequence, the mother, and often the children, had to pitch in most of the time to help scratch together a living.

In the New World, the difficulties of immigrant existence again forced many a Jewish mother into a hyperactive role in the family. In addition, she was fired with the desire to take advantage of the education available to her children—education which in Europe had been subject to restrictive quotas and which only the rare Jewish child could achieve (see story under YID, YIDDEL). This passion for education, encouraged by the Jewish emphasis on religious learning, drove the kids to school. And in a city like New York, with thousands grasping at free colleges, they had to study to beat the competition.

By osmosis, some of the next generation of daughters absorbed their mothers' attitudes, providing us with current types for affectionate debunking, as in the recent stage play in which the mother's parting line to the audience is: "Stay healthy, eat well, and be careful driving home."[12]

Apparently, though, Mama's pushing and protection didn't do much harm. One study of "overprotected" children shows that they managed to cut the apron strings later with no ill effects, that meanwhile they were better than average in physical development, in freedom from accidents and serious illness, in school adjustment and ability, and in social development; and that almost all outgrew whatever childhood behavior problems they had had. Indeed, other studies suggest the value of the warm, strong and goal-setting mother in producing eventual true independence of her children. It seems that early independence from maternal control merely shifts the child's dependency to the standards of the social group outside the home, making for the conforming, "other-directed" personality. Most important, perhaps, as a vindication of the "Jewish mother" is the finding of another study that mental illness is lower among Jews than in the general population, particularly in working-class families, which in the general population have the highest rate of serious mental illness.[13]

This doesn't need to imply, of course, that Jewish mothers are all domineering and possessive. Such traits are not in keeping with Jewish tradition, and don't really represent the kind of Jewish mother that the Conservative rabbi was eulogizing. The wives of the patriarchs and the rabbis, and of many a YID FUN A GANTS YOR[14] through the centuries (including my own mother) represented Jewish mothers whose strength was subtle and who exhibited the womanly traits of patience and forbearance. (*Cf.* Rel. and Cul., GLIKEL.) I assume it was this type of Jewish mother who inspired the old Yiddish sentimental tunes. (*See* Family, MAMME.)

The rabbis of the Talmud, by the way, discussed the nagging and domineering female in relation to her husband and concluded with an insight that seems as modern as the field of marriage counseling: the man must comport himself in such a way as to earn his wife's respect. In other words, a bossy female cannot be what she is unless she has a weak or passive husband who lets her get away with her roost-ruling. And there are a number of folk tales that demonstrate the change that comes about in such a wife when her husband suddenly asserts himself. (*Cf.* Passing Judgment, end of introduction.)

YIDDISHE ODER

Jewish vein. Deep-rooted feeling.

A person who has no YIDDISHE ODER has no YIDDISH HARTS.

YIDDISHER KOP

Jewish head. Resourcefulness and common sense.

See introduction above and conundrum under VOS MER GOY. . . .

YIDDISH HARTS

Jewish heart. Feeling of mercy.

A person with a YIDDISH HARTS shows RACHMONES, compassion, for others.

III. *How English Is Affected*

In 1945, on entering a New York publishing office in a new
dress, I was greeted by a co-worker with, "Mm-m-m . . . zaftig."
An out-of-towner, I was surprised to hear this Yiddish word
rolled so authentically on an Irish-American tongue. But of
course this was New York, home of half the Jews in America,
where Yiddish had for years been adding TAM to the American
language. Here, I reminded myself, many Gentiles understood
and even used a variety of Yiddish expressions, like MAZEL
TOV, SHIKSE, SHLEMIEL, etc.

What was true in New York in 1945 is becoming more and
more so across the country. The process, to be sure, is uneven.
Many a Gentile reader has to come running to Jewish friends
for explanations of the Yiddish terms strewn around the pages
of recent novels, and many a young Jewish reader comes to
older relatives for the same purpose. Others without such handy
interpreters are apt to feel frustrated and annoyed, wondering
why the terms are not translated, or why the book has no
glossary. It is the rare publisher today who bothers to provide
such explanations.

Indeed, Jews who know Yiddish are constantly surprised at
the extent of this diffusion of their in-group lingo. At the University of Chicago, an annual mock symposium on "The Latke
and the Homentash," which was dreamed up over two decades
ago by the late Rabbi Maurice Pekarsky as a light-hearted
holiday program for Jews on campus, today attracts overflow
crowds in the largest auditorium of the University. Several
years ago a social scientist attending a conference on public-
opinion research was struck by the Yiddish flavor in the pro-

gramming, when perhaps eighty per cent of those in attendance were not Jews. A skit dealing with Stephen Potter's ploys described one as "Ploy-nu"—meaning "Where are we now?" The project was titled "Get-gelt" and the improvement "Getmoregelt."[1] True, "gelt" is also a German word, which the attending Ph.D.'s might have been familiar with, but the fact that "nu" was also used leaves little room for question that Yiddish was at work.

How account for such "outside" appeal of Yiddish? First, let me say that in attempting to define certain terms in Chapter II, I was struck by the strong parallels in American English. Sometimes the spirit and the level of expression are identical in both languages. Sometimes the equivalent in American English is a little more crude; other times more crudity appears in the Yiddish form. But there is an earthy descriptiveness that characterizes both, and one can easily see why so many popular Yiddish expressions have been adopted by American slang.

By itself, this affinity of the two colloquial tongues (both having partial roots in German) could not account for the widespread absorption of Yiddish terminology. Many other factors are involved. To begin with, there is the temper of the times. Anxiety and frustration become a bit easier to take after an ironic quip, which is at the heart of Yiddish adoptions. After all, worries about war and inflation and racial strife we don't need. Who asked for them?!

Just as important is the force of economics: with a voracious need for novelty, any successful gambit is where you find it. Witness the "nebbish" gift items, the "Shmo" game, and the "BUPKIS Family" of zany dolls.[2] (Witness even the striking Hebraisms: "Why Is This Dishwasher Different from All Other Dishwashers?" and "Wherefore Is This Magazine Different from All Other Magazines?" Those ads of RCA and *Commentary* could only have been inspired by the first of the Passover seder's famous FIR KASHES. Indeed, an ad of El Al airlines asking "Why is this airline different from all other airlines?" actually provided four answers in the style of the Haggadah, each beginning "On all other airlines. . . .")

Then, too, other aspects of economics have stimulated the occurrence of Yiddish terms. Take the marketing of "kosher" foods, which has brought about a casual use of that word, often in unexpected places. A mass promotional letter from the Acme

Markets recently enclosed a booklet which entitled the bearer to trading stamps with the purchases of various grocery items, including "Ideal Kosher Spears." And a smaller food chain featured "Kosher Spears" in its newspaper advertising. Both of these instances occurred in an area where the Jews represent perhaps five per cent of the population.

The increasingly cosmopolitan taste of the American public may even be helping to make "kosher" a mark of epicurean quality. At least one packer of kosher meat products has encouraged this trend, conducting a successful advertising campaign, according to *Printer's Ink*, to make its line "go national."

Merchandising has also carried gefilte fish, borsht, matzo, bagels, blintzes, to small-town grocery shelves and freezer cabinets, bringing them to the attention of many Gentiles. "Tam Tam" and "Nosh o' Rye" crackers are further funneling Yiddish into general speech and diet.

In other byways of commerce, a company like General Foods finds that "appreciation for the other fellow's background helps to build good will and make more friends" and therefore supplies its salesmen with a booklet on "Familiar Jewish Words and Expressions" as an aid in approaching Jewish merchants. As a consequence, many Gentile salesmen have become familiar with such religious terms as MINYEN, CHAZEN, BRIS, BAR MITSVE, and with expressive words like NACHES and CHUTZPA, to say nothing of PASKUDNIK or MOYD. (As Shimon Wincelberg noted in *Commentary* in 1954, the approach of such material leaves something to be desired. The source is the Joseph Jacobs Organization, which recently issued a new illustrated version of the booklet, this apparently being supplied to liquor, soap and other industries as well.)

Besides the forces of the marketplace, the prevalence of Yiddish reflects, more fundamentally, the American Jew's changing status. The new sense of identity produced by events of the last quarter-century has been strengthened by the American trend toward religious affiliation and the emerging pattern of three dominant faiths. The common practice of having rabbi, priest and minister offer their respective blessings at public events, the sale of Star of David lockets alongside crosses in jewelry stores, the listing of Jewish holidays on civil calendars, the wide availability of Jewish New Year and other greeting cards—all these attest to a new kind of acceptance. Etiquette counselor Amy Vanderbilt, be it noted, points out the possible kosher eating habits of Jewish guests and the possible impropriety of sending a Christmas card to a Jew.[3]

With a surer place in society, then, the American Jew has been rediscovering himself and has been savoring, along with other aspects of his history, religion and culture, the first or second language of his parents or grandparents. Witness Yiddish terms as a humorous gimmick in kosher cookbooks, in imprinted paper napkins ("Have a Nash"), in recipe holders ("Baleboste Recipes"), to say nothing of the names given to bowling teams (the "Oy Veys" of B'nai B'rith in Detroit or the "Nudniks" of the Jewish Community Center in Easton, Pennsylvania). Unselfconscious sharing of this linguistic love has inevitably carried Yiddish into general speech and writing—where translations and derivatives are affecting popular syntax and intonation.

Beyond the pull of commercialism and the pleasure of acceptance, other factors serve to disseminate Yiddish. The increased mobility of Americans may allow one person to help circulate a Yiddishism from Maryland to Texas (as has been reported for the SHM- formula).[4] And a special form of that mobility, the move to the suburbs, has carried many Yiddish-inspired expressions into the ken of non-Jews. A further partial result of mobility is the increasing number of conventions being held at Jewish resort hotels, where Gentiles are learning to enjoy and pronounce such typical dishes as KISHKE and TSIMMES.[5]

Above all, we must remember two major influences: the growth of the various media of communication and the unparalleled development of entertainment in a time of expanding leisure. New York, whose speech is affected by about two million Jews, is the center of communications and entertainment, in both of which fields Jews are prominently involved. (Yiddish has even appeared in science fiction,[6] which Leslie A. Fiedler has suggested is essentially a Jewish genre.)

In itself, of course, the process is not new. English is full of borrowings from other languages, including many from Hebrew, and its adoptions from Yiddish go back more than two hundred and fifty years. Several pejorative terms for "Jew" from eighteenth-century England are based on common Yiddish words or phrases—e.g., "smous(e)"—as are certain underworld expressions like "ganef" (which dates to at least 1839 in England

and 1845 in the United States). By the latter part of the nineteenth century—over two hundred years after the Jews were welcomed back to England, having been banished from 1290 to 1657—a number of other Yiddish words were infiltrating the language in both England and the United States. In Britain, there were such terms as SHOFEL, SHNORRER and SHIKSE (with variations like "shickster" and "shakester"). Here in America, certain words which had previously been picked up by German—such as KOSHER in its figurative sense, MISHUGGE, MEZUMEN ("mazuma"), TOCHES ("tokus," "dokus")—were being used by Gentile Germans as far apart as Maryland and Kansas.

In the 1920's and 1930's, by which time Jews had become numerous in some New York occupations like furniture and shoe retailing, jewelry auctioneering and garment manufacturing, Yiddishisms like SHLEP, SHNUK ("shnook"), METSIEH, SHLAK ("shlock") were recorded as trade lingo in the pages of *American Speech*. By that time, too, GOY, SHADCHEN, BLINTZES, SHIKKER, SHMUS (shmoose) and other Yiddish terms were becoming known to big-city Gentiles.

Although some were duly recorded in the regular dictionaries, such expressions were not greatly diffused. True, they were used by some Jewish writers, by vaudeville and immigrant-life theatre, and by night-club performers, and were to some extent spread around in World War I. But it was not until the growth of radio and films that Yiddishisms like KIBITZER, "I should worry" and "If you'll excuse the expression" began to achieve wider circulation.

It is only in the past twenty-five years or so that the process has accelerated. Service slang of World War II made use of terms like ZAFTIG, "Joe Shmoe," etc. Both a burgeoning television and an expanded publishing industry have brought to the general populace some of the earlier trade loans like SHLEP and SHNUK, those of the underworld like GANEF or SHAMMES, and borrowings of the entertainment world like MEGILLE and MISH MASH, as well as the deprecating SHM- and the many translations like "Get lost," "I need it like a hole in the head" and "It shouldn't happen to a dog."

Over a quarter-century ago, Professor Roback observed in *Better English* that Yiddish had as yet influenced only the lower levels of the language, because Yiddish-speaking Jews rarely circulated in higher society and those who did found no need to make use of it. Although most of the Yiddish borrowings are still on the "lower levels," such cant, slang and colloquial terms are being more and more diffused to higher levels through television, journalism and current books, and more Jews are traveling in "higher society" (most notably, perhaps, on the faculties of colleges and universities), where their speech may be expected to convey certain Yiddish influences, possibly on a somewhat higher level. For whether or not they truly speak Yiddish, many second- and third-generation American Jews do make use of it—not only in terms picked up from the Americana of TV, but often in unconsciously absorbed syntax, as in "He was then first (ERSHT) establishing himself in the field" or in classic metaphors like: "It's the kind of job that just can't be done 'on one foot' (AF EYN FUS—Chap. II, Char. and Des.).

The essential element here is the element of acceptance, already alluded to, of Jewishness itself. And the resulting naturalness probably also explains the untranslated Yiddish terms in recent novels. In actuality the authors of such works have been unwittingly fulfilling a wish that Alter Brody expressed in the *American Mercury* back in 1926—a wish that Yiddish terms in Jewish fiction might yet appear unaccompanied by the relentless parenthetical translations, which in his view made the Yiddish itself pointless.

Though the explanation may not help the person who still needs a glossary (and that person may be Jewish), it does bear out the prediction of Dr. Roback in his *Curiosities of Yiddish Literature* (1933) that if American Jews were to give up Yiddish, English would be flooded by Yiddishisms. In other words, by the time that adjustment to the American environment would discourage use of the ghetto tongue, the new "at-home-ness" would stimulate a rediscovery of that tongue's unique warmth and color. The extent to which Yiddish has been "given up" may perhaps still be argued, and the crest of the flood may not yet be measurable. But the waters are clearly upon us.

IIIA. The Yiddish Is Showing

A general rule about the following listings: expressions discussed in earlier chapters, even though they may have had an impact on English, are not treated here unless there is something more to be said about them. For a few of the better-known terms not dealt with here, a reference is given to their earlier locations. A more complete selection of Yiddish influences would of course include additional items from chapters I and II as well as from IIIB.

a for instance (*or* a forinstance); give me a for instance

Two popular Yiddish expressions are involved here: GIB MIR A MOSHEL (Give me an example) and L'MOSHEL (for example). In translating the former into English, the first generation was influenced by the frequency of "for instance" in English and also by its Yiddish counterpart, L'MOSHEL. (The latter derives from Hebrew *l'mashal*, which is quite common in rabbinic literature. *See* Chap. II, Rel. and Cul., MOSHEL.)

The second generation quoted "a for instance" in good-natured jest. Now it's being adopted generally. Notice a sample from a syndicated book review by John Barkham: "A forinstance is the case of a Ring Lardner story he included in an anthology of humorous talks"; and from a news conference by former Secretary of State Dean Rusk: "Will you specify and give me a for instance." It's even been put in the plural, as in a Pennsylvania radio commercial: "We'll give you a couple of for instances here" and in a TV line introducing gift ideas: "Here are a few for instances. . . ."

The process is reminiscent of the spread of the form "irregardless." Starting as an error (presumably influenced by the word "irrespective"), this was humorously quoted by those who knew better. It began to appear in print, with the irony not always understood, and found its way into the latest edition of *Webster's New International Dictionary* (as a "nonstandard" form).

again with the . . .!

This annoyance at a person who has repeated some irritating statement or behavior has a Yiddish flavor. It can be followed by almost any part of speech, repeating whatever the annoyance has been. Ex.: the novel *The Conversion of Chaplain Cohen* by Herbert Tarr had a line in which the objection is to the use of the adjective "brave": "Again with the brave, David groaned."

For the next stage of exasperation, *see* Chap. II, Ann. and Arg., NOCH A MUL . . . UN VIDDER A MUL. . . .

"a little nothing" for "almost nothing"

From A KLEYN GURNIT, this is common in American Jewish speech, in such a sentence as "He picked it up for a little nothing."

The phrase presumably inspired the naming of the "little nothing" black dress which was featured in the early 1960's and which was followed by the " 'little nothing' bras" of Saks Fifth Avenue and the " 'Petit Rien' bikini panty girdle." Even hosiery got on the bandwagon, with the TV ad: "The Cantrice stocking in the black box is the little nothing by Cameo. . . ."

". . . already" for ". . . now"

The use of "already" at the end of a sentence is a direct translation of the Yiddish SHOYN, as in KUM, SHOYN! (Come, already!) or GENUG, SHOYN! (Enough, already!). English would normally use the mild "now" as in "Come, now" or the stronger "Come on, now!" But "Enough, already!" and "Let's go, already!" have been widely used on TV and seem to be making inroads into general speech.

Pennsylvania German also has a final "already," but it is somewhat different: "He has lost his respect for her long already."

". . . and finished!" for ". . . and zoom!"

This translation of UN FARTIK! (Chap. II, Exclam.) may take the place of "to make a long story short" or "before I knew it," as in the account a mother gave me of the time she was settling into a new home and left her young son alone for a few minutes: ". . . and finished! The kid had everything in a mess."

I've heard the expression in the English speech of both Jewish and Gentile Germans, and assume it must occur in German as well as Yiddish.

And how! *See* Chap. II, Exclam., NOCH VI.

Answering a Question With a Question

This common feature of Jewish speech is associated with intonation and probably grew out of Talmudic discussion. As noted in Chap. II, Greetings, the question V'AZOY GEYT ES? (How is it going?) may be replied to with the shrugging irony: V'AZOY ZOL ES GEYN? (How should it go?). Or notice the joke about the three U.S. Army chaplains who were playing cards while sitting in a tent and idly discussing the question of honesty. Both the priest and minister express the idea that lying is sometimes necessary; the rabbi holds that under any circumstances lying is sinful. Suddenly the commanding officer comes into the tent and asks, "Father Murphy, have you been playing cards? You know my rules on the subject." The priest says, "No, sir, I haven't." The CO asks the minister, and he too says, "No, sir." The CO then asks the rabbi whether *he* had been playing cards, and he replies: "With whom, sir?"

On hearing this story, my daughter asked, "What would have happened if the Jewish chaplain had been asked first? Oh! I know! He would have answered: 'Who, *me*, sir?' "

According to an old quip, a Jew was asked why he always answered a question with another question, and he replied, "Why not?" We must agree this is in tune with tradition, considering that many centuries earlier Cain answered an inquiry about Abel with: "Am I my brother's keeper?" (As one writer has pointed out, Cain wasn't Jewish, but the chronicler was!) Answering a question with a question is a favorite habit of psychiatrists and social workers. Perhaps this was an unconscious contribution of

Freud's Jewish background! Interestingly enough, a newspaper
financial column by William Doyle recently attributed this tendency to the Irish. I would venture to guess that if it *is* a characteristic of the Irish, they must have picked it up from the Jews
—in Ireland and the United States.[1] An old Yiddish conundrum
pokes fun at the whole process by asking why a kugel tin is wide
on the top and narrow on the bottom. The answer: "Why isn't
it narrow on the bottom and wide on the top?" (The double
incongruity here is that only the order of the question has been
reversed, not its facts.)

bagel
  American English spelling of BEYGEL (Chap. II, Food and
Drink).
  In TV production lingo, a bagel is a show with a hole in it,
lacking something.
  The word has also been used as a synonym for "Jew" or
"Jewish." In Brooklyn's Crown Heights, the Jewish anti-crime
patrol has been dubbed "The Bagel Lancers," and this phrase
has appeared in the title of a book on Jewish humor. In the
summer of 1966, columnist Earl Wilson noted that the ordinary
New Yorker's escape from the heat was a delicatessen at "Bagel
Beach, 54th St. and 7th Ave." A generation ago, this might
have been a slur. I remember the term as an in-group deprecation for a certain Connecticut beach frequented by lower-class
Jews. And I recall in my early childhood being taunted by Gentile children with the epithet "Jew-bagel." Perhaps symbolic of
the changing times is the fact that several years ago, when a
Gentile track star named Begel (pronounced like the food) on
Yale's team started off, the good wishes called out to him were:
"Lox of luck, Begel." Too, Jack Altshul of *Newsday* has re-
ported a rock 'n roll group called "The Bagels." He explains:
"You've heard of hard rock; they claim they're hard roll." But
Lender's Bagel Bakery hastens to advertise on the radio: "Con-
trary to popular opinion, the frozen bagel is not a new rock band.
You will find Lender's frozen bagels in freezers in supermarkets
across the country."
  In London, reportedly, the term has been heard pronounced
"bygel" and even "bageel"!
  As noted in Chap. II, in Yiddish the plural is the same form

as the singular. I have seen a similar usage in English on the labels of a bread supplier to the A & P: "Jewish Rye; Pumpernickle (sic); Bagel."

See "It can't hurt" *and* IIIB, "bialys."

"Better . . . should" for ". . . might better" or ". . . would have done better to"

This seems to derive from Yiddish BESSER ZOL ICH . . . (Better I should . . .) but may also reflect German, and Pennsylvania German, influence.

I've heard it in radio announcer's lingo ("Better we should stop the clock") and seen it in Inez Robb's syndicated newspaper column ("Better the boys should save their breath to cool their porridge") as well as in Howard Nemerov's poetry (" 'There's nothing in this for me,' he said aloud;/'Better the snow should be my lonely shroud.' ")

See also "should" and "shouldn't" for "may" and "may not. . . ."

Be well; Stay well; Go well (and come back well)

These translations of ZAY GEZUNT and GEY GEZUNT (UN KUM GEZUNT) occasionally appear in unexpected places. I recall the Kurt Weill musical *Lost in the Stars* (lyricist Maxwell Anderson), in which a departing father's line to his daughter is "Stay well, my child" and her reply is, "Go well, my father." Recently I heard Mimi Benzel signing off her WNBC radio program with the line: "Mother, stay well." And Joe Franklin on WOR likes to say: "Stay well and stay tuned." As indicated in Chap. I, such references to health on parting are common among Jews but often puzzling to Gentiles. Apparently, though, they're spreading out.

See also "Wear it in good health."

"bit" for "routine" or "stuff" *See* "shtik."

borax

In furniture, architectural and decorating lingo, this means cheap furniture of poor taste—the kind so often bought by poor immigrants on the installment plan. It's believed to derive from Yiddish and German BORGEN, to borrow. My guess is that it was a rendition of the colloquial noun BORGS, something on loan.

The term is sometimes used as an adjective for anything gaudy and even as an exclamation. "Borax-house" is a firm selling such merchandise. (*Cf.* "shofel.")

boss
Though derived from the Dutch word *baas* (master), this English term may also have been reinforced to some extent by the Yiddish BALEBOS (proprietor), from Hebrew *baal ha-bayis* (master of the house).
Cf. IIIB, "What are you BALESBOSTEVin' about?"

bubele   *See* Chap. II, Endearment.

"by" for "at"
In Yiddish, the similar-sounding BAY is the equivalent of French *chez* (at the home of). It is natural, then, that the first generation would say "He's by Alfred" instead of "He's at Alfred's." A similar sentence appears in a book by Nelson Algren: "I'll buy you a drink by Antek." But the usage hasn't spread too far as yet.

"by" for "to"
The Yiddish BAY, mentioned above, can also mean "to." *Ex.:* BAY MIR BISTU SHEYN (To Me You Are Beautiful). This was the title of a song which became very popular in bilingual form in the late 1930's. The words BAY MIR BISTU SHEYN were not translated literally in this popular version, which noted that the expression "means that you're grand."
In August 1969, a financial newscaster on WNEW radio noted that stocks were off a little but had rallied, and the regular announcer commented ironically: "That's by you a rally—it's off .44!" (*Cf.* "by" for "with.")

"by" for "with"
Again, the influence of the versatile Yiddish BAY, as in BAY MIR PEYLSTU (Chap. II, Exclam.). It shows up in "It's O.K. by me" or "It's all right by me" and in " . . . fine by . . . " as in chatty prose like the following in the *New York Times:* "He is regarded as a youngish-type people's critic, rather than middle-aged people's or dodderers', and this is fine by Mr. Fiedler."
The popular Jewish American greeting "How's by you?"

and its good-natured reply "By me is fine" have this same origin and have been picked up to some extent by other Americans. The inverted order is reminiscent of the Pennsylvania German "Throw me from the train a kiss," which graced the popular-song list some years ago. (*See* "Inverted Sentence Order.")

called up (to the Torah)
This refers to the honor of being called from a worshipping congregation to participate at the pulpit. (*See* Chap. II, Rel. and Cul., ALIEH.) One may hear, "He was called up at temple last night, and was he thrilled!"

chutzpa, chutzpah, chutspa, chutspeh, chuzpa, hutzpa, etc.
This Yiddish term for nerviness (Chap. II, Char. and Des.) has been heard on TV and seen in much current journalistic writing. It is listed in several dictionaries, including the Funk and Wagnalls' *Standard College Dictionary,* which in 1967 and 1968 advertised itself in the *New York Times* as "the only college dictionary with 'chutzpah.'" According to the *Jewish Post and Opinion,* a new real estate holding company in Philadelphia is "Chutzpa, Inc."!
See Chap. II, Food and Drink, end of BEYGEL.
The adjective CHUTZPADIK is common among Jews and sometimes crops up in odd places. The late American rabbi Stephen S. Wise was once in conversation with the late Dr. Edouard Benes, president of Czechoslovakia, when a student barged in to remind Dr. Wise that he was late for his (the student's) wedding, at which he had promised to officiate. Benes is reported to have asked whether the intruder was a student, and Wise to have replied, "A CHUTZPADIK student."

cluck, kluck
This term for an oaf, often in the redundant "dumb cluck," was popular a generation ago and seems to have come from Yiddish KLUHTZ.[2] In recent years the authentic "klutz" and "clutz" have been appearing (I have heard "dumb klutz" on TV), with the companion adjective "klutzy." *Time* has even made a verb of it: "Choreographer Kenneth MacMillan has attempted a compromise between dancing and acting that too often leaves Nureyev and Ballerina Margot Fonteyn with nothing to

do but klutz around the stage like actors who have forgotten their lines."

cobber

Reportedly an Australian term for "pal," "chum," this is believed to come from Yiddish (and Hebrew) CHAVER (Chap. II, Greetings).

compote

This French word for stewed fruit, which appears in both Yiddish and English, has been given an impetus in English through its use by American Jews. As noted in Chap. II, Food and Drink, the dish is a traditional holiday dessert. It is interesting that while most packers of mixed dried fruit call their products just that, a major brand-name stocked by independent grocers (including the average Jewish neighborhood store) calls it "compote."

"dairy" for "dairy products"

Ex.: "We're having dairy for supper." Refers to MILCHIKS, milk type of food, as differentiated from FLEYSHIKS, meat type of food. (*See* Rel. and Cul., KASHRES.)

This is so common a usage that French's mustard ran an ad in a Jewish monthly in 1963 advocating that its product be used for "any meat sandwich," adding: "Great with dairy, too!" A 1966 full-page ad in *Commentary* heralded a new Mazola margarine that is "100% dairy-free." This is a way of saying that the margarine is now PAREV (Chap. II, Food and Drink).

The abbreviation is similar to that in "Danish" for "Danish pastry" below.

"Danish" for "Danish pastry"

This short-form is common among lunch-counter personnel and at least partly reflects the American tendency to abbreviate terms, also seen in "coffee an' " or "He's collecting unemployment" for " . . . unemployment insurance" or "Have a happy" for "Have a happy day." Yet in Jewish speech there are similar short-cuts like "the Joint" for "the Joint Distribution Committee" or "enjoy" for "enjoy yourself" (see "enjoy" as an intransitive verb) and "entitled" for "entitled to" (see "entitled" without the "to it"). A sentence like "They have wonderful Danish"—which I seem to have heard only in the speech of American Jews—has to my ear a Yiddish ring. It seems pertinent that the term appears in ads in American Jewish weeklies, like the one of Dugan's bakers which headlines "Great Danish in the morning."[3]

Declarative Form in Questions

Yiddish is of course not the only force at work here, but the use of this type of question in popular journalism often strikingly reflects Yiddish intonation. Witness: "This is moral decadence?" (reader in Billy Graham's syndicated column questioning Graham's appraisal of American morality); "TV's Topmost—*This* is America?" (critical evaluation of TV programming in the *New York Times*); "It took somebody all this time to figure *that* out? Sheer brilliance . . ." (Xerox Corp. ad in *Time*); "This is Art?" (*Reader's Digest* heading for an item on a Londoner's technique of throwing tubes of paint on a large canvas on the floor and then driving a sports car over it); etc.

Such sentences sometimes begin with "So," as in an editorial head in my local newspaper: "So We Have a Permanent Acting Postmaster?" (*See* "so" at beginning of sentence.)

See also end of "Inverted Sentence Order" and " . . . no?"

Do me something.

This blithe defiance, which is a translation of TU MIR EPPES (Chap. II, Ann. and Arg.), is being picked up generally. Psychiatrist Eric Berne, in *Games People Play*, uses it to designate a "second-degree hard form" of the game "Why Don't You—Yes But." ("The patient refuses to do the housework, for example . . . .")

The expression is of course a companion to "Sue me!"—which has had a wider impact, chiefly through entertainers. The related "do me" for "do to me" is sometimes heard in "What can he do me?"

See IIIB, "Call me PISHER."

Don't ask!

This translation of FREG NISHT! (Chap. II, Exclam.) has

been showing up lately in newspaper and TV advertising copy. Notice the Ezra Brooks whiskey ad: "Have we got troubles? Don't ask! There we were, minding our business and . . . SUDDENLY THE ROOF FALLS IN! Overnight, everybody discovers our rare old Sippin' Whiskey. We're a hit! We're also way behind in our orders." Or witness the Chesterfield TV commercial which starts with a woman talking incessantly about why she likes Chesterfield King cigarettes and follows with: "Why does everybody like the taste of Chesterfield King? Don't ask!"

Double Negative

Although frowned upon by English teachers, the double negative has a natural drive in many languages, including English and Yiddish. The Yiddish occasionally bolsters the tendency in English, as in "He don't know from nothin' "—which *see*.

drek, dreck (taboo)

In the blunt shop talk of garment manufacturing, this means shoddy merchandise, junk. But it's not a word for polite company. It's a Yiddish equivalent of the four-letter word for excrement. Interestingly enough, it appeared in the term DREK-APOTEK, assigned to the class of medieval medical remedies involving animal excrement. (Jewish opinion was critical of such practice.) The word comes from German but in that language means merely "dirt."

Cf. IIIB, "A.K."

Drop dead!

My guess is that this originated in Jewish circles. It reflects the spirit of Yiddish imprecation and is very close to several Yiddish forms, for which it is a common translation: DI PTIRE ZOLSTU AYN-NEMEN and ZOLSTU KRIGN DEM TOYT (May you catch—or get—death) as well as the double-barreled SHTARB A TEYTE (Die a dead one).

The expression was widely used in the 1940's—I even remember it in a form of pun and super-climax: D.D.T. (Drop Dead Twice)—and is still heard and seen occasionally. A striking instance was the AP dispatch on Dec. 18, 1968, headed " 'Dear Santa, Drop Dead!' Says Methodist Minister."

dynaschmo

Variety coined this term, which is a combination of "dynamo" and "shmo" (which *see*). It was offered as a description of an operator who "makes like a whirling dervish, acts as though he knows everything, but in the final showdown always comes up blank."

"enjoy" as an intransitive verb

Though previously a rare form, this has become fairly common in recent years—largely encouraged, I believe, by the usage of American Jews.

"Enjoy yourself" was abbreviated to the simple "Enjoy" by the solicitous Jewish mother. Harry Golden, editor of the *Carolina Israelite,* made it popular around 1960 with his collection of reminiscences entitled *Enjoy, Enjoy!* In July 1964 the magazine *Prevention* carried an ad of *Quinto Lingo* urging: "Just read, enjoy, absorb!" and some months later a bank advertising on my local Pennsylvania radio station advised: "Save now, enjoy later."

In June 1966, over New York's radio station WQXR, Murray Shumach reported an interview with famed violinist Mischa Elman, quoting the musician's denial of being bitter: "I get a great kick out of life. I know how to enjoy." And several months later my local paper quoted Harry Balmer, a New Jersey sculptor, as saying: "Some people live to enjoy. I enjoy to live."

"entitled" without the "to it"

Harry Golden called attention to this ethnic English with his volume *You're Entitle'!* It has since been picked up in sundry quarters, such as the Congress of Racial Equality (CORE), which in 1964 offered a "Freedom Hat" in a circular which declaimed, "Yes, we changed it a little.[4] We're entitled, it's our idea." Or witness the women's-store ad for Mother's Day in my community in 1965: "She Baked Your Birthday Cakes . . . She Held Your Hand in the Dark . . . She Jollied Away Unhappiness . . . She's Your MOM . . . SHE'S ENTITLED!"

eppis

This term was reported in 1966 from carnival lingo on the West Coast as meaning "nothing" and being spoken with a shrug to indicate poor business. It may be an ironic use of Yiddish

EPPES (Chap. II, Exclam.), perhaps influenced too by the some-what similar Pennsylvania German *ebbes*.

"fall in" for "drop in"
From Yiddish ARAYNFALN, this is heard in both the present tense ("Straighten up the living room in case company falls in") and the past tense, as in a description of a family who chose the wrong time to stop by: "They fell in on us—just at suppertime!"

finif, finnif; fin
These slang terms for a five-dollar bill are from the Yiddish number five, FINIF (from German *fünf*).

"fire" for "firebrand" or "hothead"
"She's a fire" is a common second-generation description of a teenage daughter. It's from ZI'Z A BREN.

"first" for "just" or "just begin to"
This is common in the speech of American Jews, reflecting the impact of Yiddish ERSHT. Witness: "Here it was eight o'clock, and she first began to get dressed" (account of a daughter who does everything at the last minute); "They work till ten o'clock, and then they first go out for a good time till three in the morning" (a woman telling me of her son's experience in a camp job). Molly Picon in her autobiography quoted her grandmother as saying, "If a person can't have that feeling to joke any more, then it is first really serious." Even in literary usage, notice this line: "After the novel was published, I first realized that the main character, Yankel, must have come from a great hidden affection for my father. . . ." (Jerome Charyn, quoted in a review of his novel, *Once Upon a Droshky*).
See also end of III *re*. unconscious absorption of Yiddish syntax.

"from" for "of"
The often-heard "What do you want from me?" is a direct translation of the exasperated VOS VILSTU FUN MIR (HOBN)? (Chap. II, Ann. and Arg.). The more normal English would of course be, "What do you want of me?" Yiddish FUN means either "of" or "from," as does German *von*, and it is likely that German has had some influence too.

The slang "from hunger" is probably from Yiddish ER SHTARBT FUN HUNGER (He's starving from hunger; hence, is in need, inadequate), where the "from" again takes the place of "of." Other phrases from the entertainment world, like "strictly from borsht," referring to the style associated with the borsht circuit (IIIB), may be related.

See also "know from" for "know,". . .

from hunger *See* "from" for "of."

ganef

This Yiddish word for "crook" or "sharpie" (Chap. II, Char. and Des.) turns up in a variety of spellings in England and the U.S.: "gonnif," "gonoph," "gunnif," "gunef," etc. There is also the short-form "gun," presumably from the latter pronunciation and unrelated to the fire-arm. In South Africa there's an old cant term "goniv" for a buyer of stolen diamonds, as well as "goniva" for such a diamond—presumably from Yiddish GANEYVE (theft).

"Ganef" derives from Hebrew *ganov* (thief)—not, as was suggested over a hundred years ago, from English "gone off"! In English cant it has usually meant a pickpocket. In the United States it is a more general synonym for "crook" or "robber," though it has also been applied of late to a male homosexual. In the 1940's it was reported in use by carnival men for "fool."

England also has a somewhat similar term for simpleton, "gnof" or "gnoffe," which goes back to Chaucer's time. It too is credited to Hebrew *ganov* (having spread at a time when the Jews themselves were officially banned). The two terms appear to have reinforced each other. (*See* middle of III.)

"Ganef" has been used as a verb both here and in England, but in Yiddish the verb has different forms from the noun.

The Yiddish plural, GANEYVIM, has cropped up in science fiction as the name of the police (spelled "Ganavim") on a corrupt trans-galactic planet.

gelt

This underworld term for money has a long history in international thieves' slang. It was originally German, meaning tribute, payment. Its currency in the United States—sometimes as "geld" (Dutch)—has been at least partially bolstered by the Yiddish form. (*See* incident in beginning of III.)

According to Sholem Aleichem, GELT is something that everyone wants and nobody has.

Get lost.

From the Yiddish VER FARLOREN (Chap. II, Ann. and Arg.), this has been used for years in the comics and on radio and TV. In 1964 I noticed a sign in front of Alitalia Airlines on Fifth Avenue in New York urging, "Get lost! Get lost!" In November 1968 a foldout page in *Life* contained just two words: "Get lost." The inside page elaborated: "Get lost where you've always wanted to get lost. Anywhere in the Americas. Cut out the Del Monte items in grocers' ads, and get a free family vacation."

See also "Verlier."

Give a look.

Equivalent to the normal English "Take a look," this comes from the Yiddish GIB A KUK. It's been picked up in popular journalism and dialogue, and has led to the popular "Give a listen" on radio and TV. Recent variations are "Give it a listen"—which I saw in *Dig*, a teenage magazine in 1964 ("That record is so full of warmth and feeling, I can't believe it. Give it a listen.")—and "Give a little listen"—which Altec Lansing used for promoting its hi-fi equipment in a 1967 *Harper's* ad.

"Give a listen" seems quite parallel to the long-established "give an ear." When I heard the Englishman David Frost say on his New York TV show in August 1969, "Take a listen . . . ," I thought it sounded odd, even though it derives from the normal idiom "Take a look."

The catchiness of GIB A KUK has also invaded modern Hebrew, which now has the equivalent *naton mabat*.

In first-generation speech, "Give a . . ." takes still other forms, like "Give a run over" for "run over." This is often "Give a run over by" for "Run over to." (*See* "by" for "to" above.)

Give me a call.

This appears to have developed from "Give me a ring," the Yiddishism of an earlier generation. The announcers on several Pennsylvania radio stations invite comment with "Give us a call" and one of them often acknowledges listeners' responses with the awkward "Thank you for giving us a call." A local florist advertises "Just give Merwarth's a call; they'll do it all."

give toco; give toks *See* "tokus."

"Go" as an ironic substitute for "Try and," "You just can't," etc.

This is from Yiddish GEY and has been used for years on TV in such expressions as:

"Go be nice to people!" (See what it gets you!)

"Go know." (GEY VEYS—Chap. II, Resig.)

"Go fight City Hall." (A lot of good it'll do!) The more normal English is "You can't fight City Hall." The expression has been played on in picture squibs of an American Jewish weekly, the *American Examiner*: "Go Fete City Hall" (a presentation to New York City's Mayor) and "Go Light City Hall" (a Chanuka menorah being lighted at City Hall). These of course change the irony of the Yiddish and are more in the class of the normal English "go" seen in the heading of an ad for a marble-frying kit in *Mechanix Illustrated*: "Go Fry a Marble!" That in turn has elements of humor, from its similarity to the negative "Go fly a kite!" (*See* IIIB, "GEY fight. . . .")

"Go figure it out!" (I'll be darned; can you match that?) This is a frequent heading for oddities presented in the *Jewish Digest*. It has appeared in other places, sometimes cut to "Go figure," as in the conclusion of a recent *New York Times* article on culture in Indianapolis: "It might be added that the new Clowes Hall is . . . one of the best sounding halls in the United States. Its acoustic properties, with clouds and everything, were designed by the same Bolt, Beranek & Newman who were responsible for Philharmonic Hall. Go figure."[5] (As music lovers know, the acoustics of Philharmonic Hall were for some time less than ideal.)

See Chap. II, CHAZEN, ALEH YIDDEN KENEN ZAYN CHAZONIM . . . *re.* "GEY ZAY A SHAMMES."

goniv; goniva *See* "ganef."

gonnif, gonoph *See* "ganef."

Good goods!

This smiling judgment of a fellow Jew's new wearing apparel —accompanied by a fingering of the material—is apparently derived from GUTTE S'CHOYRE (Chap. II, Char. and Des.), and is heard in both the United States and Canada.

In England, "good goods" and "best goods" have been informal characterizations, as in "He was rather good goods."

gun; gunef, gunnif *See* "ganef."

gunsel, gunzel, guntzel, etc.

This underworld and hobo term for an inexperienced young boy is probably from German *Gänsel* (gosling), reinforced by the same Yiddish form. The term may also mean a sneak or crook, and it is possible that it was also influenced by "ganef" (which *see*).

Among carnival men, "guntzel" has reportedly been used for "fool."

In England, the low "go the guntz"—which means "go all the way"—may have borrowed from this term as well as from Yiddish GANTS (whole).

Cf. Chap. II, Food and Drink, GANZ.

guy

This slightly derogatory U.S. slang for "fellow" may have been influenced by Yiddish GOY (Chap. II, Tribalism), as suggested a generation ago. In England there are a number of other uses of the word, though a nineteenth-century cant one meaning a Christian ruffian, as against a Jewish one, may also have been related to Yiddish.

hame

In jazzmen's lingo, this is the place where a musician is working. It would seem to be from the Yiddish word for home: HEYM.

He don't know from nothin'.

This is the form in which ER VEYST NISHT FUN GORNISHT made its entry a generation or more ago. It has since been showing up in more sedate forms like "He doesn't know from nothing"; "He knows from nothing"; "He doesn't know from anything." (But note, all use the extra "from." *See* "know from" for "know, . . .")

As is common in Yiddish, the idiom has also been appearing with the pronoun "I." Witness the recent widely quoted statement by Attorney Dean Andrews, convicted of perjury in connection with his conflicting testimony regarding President Kennedy's assassination: "I don't know from nothing. What I got is a vivid imagination." Indeed, a character in the comic strip *Dr. Kildare* by Ken Bald[6] combined this kind of usage with that noted under "know from" for "know, . . .": "Don't pull the 'too proud to fight' bit on me, Kildare. I don't know from all this noblesse oblige."

hole in the head

One of the most common of recent Yiddish borrowings, this comes from ICH DARF ES (AZOY) VI A LOCH IN KOP, which is often fully translated, "I need it like a hole in the head" or "I need that the way I need a hole in the head." It appeared in Saul Bellow's *Herzog*: " 'I need this outing like a hole in the head,' he thought as he turned the key." In a Connecticut hospital in 1967, I heard a Gentile nurse comment on hearing an ambulance siren: "More business—like we need a hole in the head!" On the other hand, a Gentile Pennsylvanian soon to undergo the special skull-drilling operation for Parkinson's disease smilingly informed his friends that he *needed* a hole in the head!

See also "I need it like I need. . . ."

The term was used as the title of a Broadway show and a movie (*A Hole in the Head*; *Hole in the Head*) and also showed up in lyrics for a television marionette show: "Wise men in fact/ Are just a little cracked,/ So be glad there's a hole in your head." Even cigar companies have made use of it. The Roi-Tan firm, which pioneered in the punctured "head," originally used the slogan "The Cigar with the Hole in the Head"; but as other cigar makers picked up the idea and emphasized it with such text as "Notice the Hole in the Head," Roi-Tan changed the wording on its boxes to: "No biting off ends. The Hole in the Head Draws Easily."

J. D. Salinger's *Catcher in the Rye* used the variation "as much use as a hole in the head" in the irreverent sentence: ". . . the Disciples . . . were about as much use to Him as a hole in the head." A recent book on language puts the expression in the plural: ". . . if any of these people were here in this room, and instead of writing I were to start creating, with my tongue and my teeth and the holes in my head, the intermittent sounds which we call speech, they would know immediately what I am thinking."

In the comics, it has come through in the plural and in a question: "Ya think I got holes in my head?" (*Kerry Drake* by Alfred Andriola); as well as in a strange Russian-Cockney: "Before he hexpired, Ian Flemm *Tried* to tell me . . .'is publisher's haddress in Hamerica—But 'e couldn't remember the ZIP CODE—due, I Hassume, to th' 'ORRIBLE 'OLE IN 'IS 'EAD!" (*Li'l Abner* by Al Capp).

Finally, the phrase has become an adjective, in such copy as that offered by a Chevrolet dealer on Philadelphia TV: "How about those hole-in-the-head prices?"

hoo-ha

In Yiddish an exclamation (Chap. II), this has become an English noun meaning "to-do," "issue," "argument," as in this London dispatch to the *Nation* regarding current English and American satire: "The great hoo-ha has been the American scene."

The term has been bandied about in other ways. *Time* has made it a verb in " 'He's got to be joking!' hoo-ha'd Elizabeth Taylor, 34." My local radio station made it into an adjective, closer to the Yiddish meaning of "Oh boy!" when it featured week-end comedians on the "Hoo-ha Theatre" and musical selections from the "Hoo-ha Library." One less-than-decorous use occurred on the TV "Tonight" show, when Phil Ford and Mimi Hines described the laying of a square egg by a "Hoo-Ha Bird": When the egg was part-way down, the bird said "Hoo," and after the egg was out, the bird said "Ha." The scriptwriters may have been aware that in England the term can also mean an artillery demonstration or even a water closet. (Eric Partridge, in his *Dictionary of Slang and Unconventional English*, lists the additional spellings of "hoohah" and "huh-hah.")

T. S. Eliot used the term as a plural noun to refer to the difficulties of middle age: "You've had a cream of a nightmare/dream and you've got the hoo-ha's coming to you."

How sweet it is!

This famous line of TV's Jackie Gleason is reminiscent of OY, IZ DOS ZIS! (Chap. II, Endearment), which may have been in the mind of a Jewish scriptwriter. The Yiddish itself may have been inspired by the Biblical "Behold, how good and how sweet it is for brethren to dwell together in unity" (Psalm 133).

The line appeared in a *New York Times* headline several years ago, above an article reporting untoward friendliness in certain political circles: "Suffolk Politics: How Sweet It Is!" A pictorial history of television by A. Shulman and R. Youman is entitled *How Sweet It Was.*

ich! *See* "ickle."

ickie, icky, ikky

This old adjective of distaste—which became a noun in jazz lingo for someone who didn't like or understand swing music, and which has since been an occasional synonym for "cornball" or "square"—may have been influenced by Yiddish IKKEL (nausea) and perhaps by English "sticky," the old description of sentimental music.

See also "ickle."

ickle, ikkle

This verb "to upset" or "to gripe" seems to have come from Yiddish IKKELEN (to make nauseous). Rabbi Samuel Silver, who digests the Yiddish press for the *Jewish Post and Opinion,* tells me he once heard a girl in Texas say "That ikkles me," quite oblivious, he was sure, of the Yiddish origin of the term.

Some American Jews remember the pronunciation of EKKELEN rather than IKKELEN; others may have heard ICHELEN. This last form, I would guess, is related to the old playful expression of distaste, ICHEL-PICHEL (Chap. II, Exclam.). This same ICHEL may partly account for the slang "ich!"—variation of "ugh!"

In England, "ickle" is baby-talk for "little" and is probably unrelated.

if not higher

This is a translation of the title and last line of a famous story by I. L. Peretz about the Rabbi of Nemirov, who used to vanish Friday morning at the time of the Penitential Prayers (Chap. II, Rel. and Cul., SLICHES) and who, his disciples said, ascended into heaven. A skeptic decides to get the facts and hides himself in the rabbi's quarters. He discovers that the rabbi, disguising himself as a peasant selling wood, visits the cottage of a sick Jewish woman and not only offers her the wood on credit but puts the wood upon her fire, reciting the Penitential Prayers as he does so. Thereafter, when the rabbi's disciples boast of his annual ascension to heaven, the skeptic no longer scoffs but quietly adds, "if not higher."

Jews familiar with the story may quote the line in reference to well-deserved praise.

If you'll excuse the expression   *See* "You should excuse me."

I need it like I need . . . ; I need this the way I need . . . .

These ironic responses to an unwelcome situation are related to "I need it like a hole in the head" and have been picked up by many non-Jews. The Dannon Yogurt Co. has used the first form in New York radio advertising: A haughty millionaire states, "I need yogurt like I need a rich relative"; or a slim girl comments, "I need Dannon Yogurt like I need a parking ticket. Why do I eat it? I *like* it!"

See also "I need it very badly" *and* "That's all I need."

I need it very badly.

This translation of the ironic ICH DARF ES ZEYER HOBN[7] has been used on TV and elsewhere but seems, as yet, less widely adopted than "I need it like I need. . . ."

Inverted Sentence Order

The usual order of words in an English sentence puts the subject first and then the predicate. In oldest English, the opposite was often true. There are still many types of sentences in which the old inverted order is naturally used, as in questions ("Where did they go?"), quotations (" 'Not at all,' replied our visitor"), etc. However, in recent years the inverted order seen in popular advertising and journalism seems strongly related to Yiddish with its characteristic intonation and irony. Notice the banana ad in *McCall's*: "Mistakes we make. But we don't label them 'Chiquita.'" Or the Beaunit Fibers ad in the *New York Times*: "Maybe a great drummer he's not, but he looks so gorgeous in his Mr. Wrangler, Jr.'s, who cares?" Or the small-college ad in *Time*: "Viterbo College: Berkeley we ain't."

Witness further *Time*'s comment on Julie Andrews: "A Liz Taylor she's not." Or Douglas E. Kneeland's discussion of pigs in the *New York Times*: "But for all the things hogs are, he conceded, returning to his wife's adamant contention, humorous they are not."

A striking use of this order appeared in Earl Wilson's Broadway column, when he discussed the divorce plans of David Susskind, quoting Susskind's wife of twenty-five years as saying: "Pneumonia I will give him . . . divorce, NEVER!"[8]

Most popular, perhaps, is the smiling irony: "On you it looks good." This even appeared as the title of a novel in 1963.

My husband tells the story of a newspaper ad asking for a physicist who is unmarried and free to travel. A little Jewish man answers the ad and is asked, "Are you a physicist?" "No. I'm a tailor." The interviewer proceeds, "Are you single?" "No. I have a wife and seven children." "Are you free to travel?" "Of course not. How could I be, with a wife and family?" "Then what," the interviewer explodes, "are you doing here?" "I just came to tell you," the applicant replies, "on me you shouldn't count."

In Jewish speech, the word "maybe" also often appears in an abnormal position, sometimes in a declarative question,[9] and such usage has already turned up in magazine ads ("You were expecting maybe another get-tough-with-Avis ad?"—Hertz Rent-a-Car) and in the comics: "You were expecting maybe a BRASS BAND?" (*Batman*, by Bob Kane).

Ish Kabibble

Several theories have been offered about the derivation of this old slang term, which was a nonchalant rejoinder meaning "I should worry." The most likely is that it came from Yiddish IZ NISHT GEFIDELT. (*See* Chap. II, Resig., NU, IZ NISHT GEFIDELT under NU, IZ NISHT.) Polish pronunciation tends to slur NISHT to NISH, from which ISH is just a step.

"Abe (*or* Abie) Kabibble" was presumably a derivative. I've seen this as an adjective: "Abe Kabiblish."

I shoulda (should have, should've, should of) stood in bed.
This clowning expression of self-disgust at "one of those days" comes from the immigrant generation's confusion of "stood" and "stayed"—due to the fact that Yiddish SHTEY means both "stay" and "stand." Boxing promoter Joe Jacobs is supposed to have been responsible for spreading it around the country a generation ago. In recent years, it's been heard a good deal on TV, as in Art Carney's comment on seeing the sorcerer's apprentice: "I should have stood in bed," followed by a song which poked fun at the expression itself: "I'd Still Be Standing In Bed."

On radio, I heard a Pennsylvania announcer berate his slips of the tongue with, "Better I should have stood in bed." This combines the expression with another Yiddishism, "Better . . . should" (which *see*).

In 1962 *Time* used the expression with "could" instead of "should" and without the usual implied element of failure. Noting that Arkansas Governor Orval Faubus had gone sleepless on election night, it observed: "As it turned out, Faubus could have stood in bed: he pulled in about 52% of the votes, more than the combined total won by . . . also rans."

Associated with "stand" are Yiddish SHTEY's further meanings of "say" or "state," as in ES SHTEYT GESHRIBN (*lit.*, It stands written, it says in writing)[10] or VU SHTEYT ES GESHRIBN? (Where is it written?—Chap. II, Ann. and Arg.). Swedish-American speech has a similar use of "stand."

Is it good for . . . ? *See* Chap. II, Tribalism, 'SIZ GUT FAR DI YIDDEN?

It can't hurt.
This is from SHATN, KEN ES NIT (*lit.*, Hurt, it can't). It's common in the speech of American Jews, who also use a number of variations like "It wouldn't hurt," "Would it hurt?" etc. All are showing up in advertising. Witness the sign on a New York automat: "Have a bagel. It can't hurt" or the subway poster: "Bagel lovers—Would it hurt to try Lender's for a change?"

The approach isn't limited to bagel barkers. Nestle's Chocolate uses "It couldn't hurt" on TV: "Well, it's no substitute for a mother's love or a big bankroll, but it couldn't hurt . . . Nestle's Crunch! Have one! It couldn't hurt!" And the firm of A. B. Dick, in *Time*, uses ". . . won't hurt," substituting two words for the "it" ("Knowing this won't hurt") in an ad which begins with the English idiom, "What you don't know about copying and duplicating won't hurt you" and ends with the Yiddish-inspired usage: ". . . you only need to know one thing: in copying and duplicating, we have more answers than anyone else. . . . Knowing this won't hurt."

It could always be worse; could be worse.

Whether this came directly from Yiddish, which has the equivalent s'KEN ALTS ZAYN ERGER, is hard to say, but it must have been bolstered by the latter, for the philosophical acceptance of fate that is mirrored here is thoroughly Jewish. A classic story tells of the Jew who is relating his family troubles to an old friend: his wife has had a lengthy illness and is going into the hospital for a risky operation and he doesn't know whether she'll live or die. "Could be worse," the friend comments. "But you haven't heard anything yet," the man continues. "Last month my daughter ran off with a traveling salesman and I don't even know where she is." "Could be worse," the friend repeats. "It's TAKEH worse," the man declares. "With all my worrying about my wife and daughter, the doctor tells me I've developed an ulcer. Just what I need!" "It could be worse," his friend assures him. "OY," the man goes on, "I'm not through. On top of everything, business is terrible. I owe so much I'm afraid my creditors are going to foreclose on me any day." The friend clucks sympathetically but insists, "It could still be worse." "What do you mean?" the man complains; "how *could* it be worse?" "Easy," the friend replies; "it could have happened to me!"[11]

A cartoon by Jim Berry in 1966 showed two bums sitting on a step, one looking worried and the other saying: "Things could be worse—if you were a pensioner, you'd be the REAL victim of inflation!"

It shouldn't happen to a dog.

This popular denunciation of fate is of course directly from

TSU A HUNT ZOL ES NIT TREFN.[12] It began infiltrating American slang at least a quarter-century ago and has become quite common in recent years, in newspaper headlines and on TV. A late-summer brochure from a department store recently utilized it: "August—the Indians called this Season of the year 'Dog Days' —but what happened to us—'Shouldn't happen to a Dog.' We looked thru our books and find that this month—YOU DON'T OWE US A CENT!"

The expression was used in the affirmative, *It Should Happen to a Dog*, as the title of a wry little play by the English writer Wolf Mankowitz.

See "should" and "shouldn't". . . .

"It's just to . . ." for "It's enough to make you . . ."

This Yiddishism cropped up in a song which Sophie Tucker sang on the Ed Sullivan TV show in 1964: "There's so much to do in so little time . . . There's so much to do, that it's just to cry. . . ."

Cf. "What's to. . . ."

It's their America.

A translation of 'SIZ ZEYER AMERIKE, this is still heard in comment on the success of the younger generation. It mirrors the same immigrant view of the United States as that in AMERIKE GANEF! (Chap. II, Exclam.).

Joe Smoe *See* "shmo."

"Joosh" for "Jewish"

This is a good-natured in-group pronunciation, poking fun at the first generation's Yiddish-tinged English speech. Several years ago at a Bar Mitzvah celebration a woman who was greatly enjoying the refreshments grinned at me as she picked up a tiny KNISH and asked, "Aren't you glad you're Joosh?"[13]

But note, when used by outsiders, as in "Joosh pipple," the term is resented. (*Cf.* Chap. II, introduction to Tribalism.)

keek

A manufacturer's look-out man, especially in the garment industry, who spots what competitors are doing—presumably from German *kieken,* to peek or peep, reinforced by the Yiddish verb to look, KUKEN or KIKEN and the noun KUK or KIK. (Cf. "Give a look.")

The term also appears in English, Scotch and Irish dialect for "look" or "see." A "keeker" in Scotch coal mines is the man who checks on the quality of coal sent up the shaft.

kibitzer

This expressive term for someone who is looking on at others' activity and occasionally putting in his two cents' worth—often at cards—is generally credited to Yiddish, which probably drew on both German and Hebrew. In German, *Kiebitz* or *Kibitz,* a pee-wit, lapwing, or plover has reportedly long been applied to an onlooker at cards, especially one who offers advice. In Hebrew, there is the verb *kibeytz,* to gather.

A movie of the 1930's, *The Kibitzer,* featuring an innocent Jewish meddler, did much to diffuse the term.

Bilingual verbal forms like "kibitzing" and "kibitzes" are common. In 1955, when Margaret Truman substituted for Edward R. Murrow in covering the Presidential family on his *Person to Person* TV show, her mother was at one point walking from one room to another murmuring to herself. Margaret admonished her with: "No kibitzing, Mother, no kibitzing. No kibitzing." *Time*'s account carried a picture of the Trumans with the caption: "No kibitzing allowed." In 1942 the title of an article in *Word Study* by Julius G. Rothenberg was "A Devoted Reader Kibitzes the Lexicographers." That made the verb transitive. A similar use appeared in a recent issue of the *Las Vegas Israelite,* in the caption for a picture of comedian Jackie Mason looking over the shoulder of card-playing *Sun* columnist Ralph Pearl: "Mason Kibitzes Pearl."

The root of the word is sometimes used to mean "chew the rag" or "shmoose" (which was the original Yiddish meaning), as in the old popular song "My Baby Just Cares for Me": "She don't like a voice like Lawrence Tibbett's,/She'd rather have me around to kibitz." In this sense it's sometimes heard as a noun, as in "a good kibitz." But note, this is different from Hebrew *kibbutz,* a cooperative settlement, which is accented on the last syllable. Someone once wrote me she was sorry I was away; she was "in the mood for a good kibbutz"!

kike

This pejorative word for a Jew is supposed to have originated among German Jews in the United States who used it to refer to the lower-class Jewish immigrants from Eastern Europe.

One explanation, suggested by Prof. Gotthard Deutsch over a generation ago, is that it came from the Yiddish term for "circle," KAYKEL, which an immigrant peddler he knew used in various ways to mark his account books. A refinement of this theory, attributed to Philip Cowen, an old United States immigration inspector, is that the circle was first used by Jewish immigrants on Ellis Island, when they signed their names with this mark in lieu of an "X," which had Christological associations for them, the inspectors thenceforward speaking of such signers as KAYKEL, KAYKELE or KAYKI and finally KAYK or "kike."

Though at least one writer has objected that KAYKEL is not the Yiddish word for "circle" (which is more properly ROD or KRAYZ), the term appears in the Harkavy dictionary (1910). Peter Tamony has suggested two additional influences: the German *kieken*, to peep (*see* "keek" above) and the diminutives of Isaac, "Ike" and "Ikey"—the latter pejoratives, according to his account, having been common among German and Austrian Jews who were displaced in U.S. clothing manufacturing by the newer immigrants. (The terms have a history in English cant, where they have presumably been limited to the "out-group.")

Leo Rosten reports that the peddler was also known among Gentiles as the "kike man." In structure, at least, this is reminiscent of the term "Jew peddler," reported from Nevada speech over a generation ago, as well as of the common slur "Jew boy," which may well have begun as simple description.

Cf. Chap. II, Tribalism, YEKE.

klutz *See* "cluck."

"know from" for "know," "know of," "know about"

This influence from Yiddish is seen in various ways. First, there is the extra "from" where English would normally use only "know," as in the popular "He don't know from nothin'" and its derivatives discussed above. Among Jews, a similar

usage shows up in the variations of "not to know from BORSHT"
(IIIB).

As a substitute for "know of" or "know about," it is common
in Jewish speech, as in the exclamation of a character in Jerome
Charyn's fiction, recalling a poor childhood: "Who knew from
school!" A line like this came through on TV in the *Beverly
Hillbillies* in 1964, deprecating someone's acquaintanceship with
English actors: "What does he know from English actors?"
(Here the usual English meaning would be quite different.)

Also common among Jews are expressions like "You
shouldn't know from such things" (*see* end of "should" and
"shouldn't" . . .).

kosher; not so kosher

These figurative uses of the dietary term, to mean respectively, "on the up and up" and "unreliable," have become fairly
common in detective fiction and journalism and in the speech
of many Gentiles. Among the last-named a generation ago,
"kosher" was sometimes used slurringly as a synonym for "Jewish," as in "a kosher cutie" for an attractive Jewish girl. (*Cf.*
"motsa.") Today, it's generally more respectable. The late Senator Everett Dirksen, interviewed about his union membership
after he made a bestselling phonograph record, remarked
in 1967: "This I can tell you. Everything seems to be kosher."
In 1964 on TV's *McHale's Navy*, McHale stated: "There's
something about all this that just doesn't smell kosher to me."

In the dietary sense, "kosher" is also being used as a noun
meaning "kosher products" or kashruth, the system of kosher
observance. Witness the booklet issued by the public-relations
firm Joseph Jacobs Organization, "What You Should Know
about Kosher," which states: "In line with the general Spiritual
Revival, more Jewish people are paying more attention to their
religion—and this means more attention to 'kosher.'" In accordance with such advice, Dugan's bakers advertise that they
are "Finest for Kosher."

Jews also speak of "keeping kosher" and "eating kosher,"
and kosher butchers advertise the advice to "buy kosher."

See early part of III; Chap. II, Rel. and Cul., KASHRES.

lox *See* Chap. II, Food and Drink, LAKS.

"make with" for "give out with"

This translation of MACH MIT has been heard on the radio ("These famous voices make with 'What's the Use?' ") and in popular journalism, where it has led to "making with" as in a book review by John Barkham: "Having uttered his gripe, Smith moves into pleasanter pastures and begins making with the gags."[14]

matzo, matzoh

This unleavened bread of Passover is being used at times by some Christian clergymen as a communion wafer[15] and by many other Americans as a low-calorie cracker (being so advertised on the radio). Even the Air Force, if it didn't before, now has a pretty good idea of what matzo is, for a New Jersey woman reported an Unidentified Flying Object as looking like a big matzo, with tiny holes around the edge!

The word has shown up in a number of quips. *Time* has referred to Sam Levenson as a "matzo-barrel philosopher" and "matzo-barrel humorist." Velvel, ventriloquist Ricky Lane's dummy, has commented on TV, "That's the way the matzo crumbles." And poet Louis Untermeyer has described his wife, a singer, as a "matzo soprano."

Cf. "motsa."

maven

This spelling of the Yiddish term for connoisseur or expert, MEYVEN, has been used in a number of special ads by Vita Herring concerning the "Herring Maven," which elicited a surprising response from readers of the *New York Times*. Thousands of these proved willing to pay for Herring Maven forks or to copy a detailed drawing for the prize of a fork and an "I Am a Herring Maven" button. Canada Dry has been touting its product as "Maven's Choice" in American Jewish weeklies, where Switzerland Emmentaler cheese announces itself with: "Calling all Mayvinim!"

See Chap. II, Ann. and Arg., OYCH (MIR) A . . . , OYCH MIR A MEYVEN; Passing Judgment, ZINGN KEN ICH NIT, OBER A MEYVEN BIN ICH!

mazel tov

This Hebrew and Yiddish expression of congratulations and good wishes is being more and more widely used and understood. Ten years ago I heard a female radio m.c. say, "Well congratulations and mazel tov." About the same time it appeared in the movie *Please Don't Eat the Daisies*, where the characters were of course not Jewish. Since then, a Philadelphia radio station has been carrying a musical program for young people entitled *Mazel Tov* ("the Show with Young Ideas"), and a pop group has been organized in England ("new" in 1966) calling itself "Mozzle Toff." (According to the *London Jewish Chronicle*, only the drummer was Jewish.) When former Secretary of State Dean Rusk's daughter married a Negro in 1967 the comment for publication by Negro leader Bayard Rustin was: "Mazel tov." And in January 1968 a Pennsylvania radio announcer reported on the temperature: "We got to 23—mazel tof."

A silver bracelet charm on sale at jewelers' in recent years has a four-leaf clover on one side and engraved good wishes in many languages on the other, including MAZEL TOV.

As a private joke, in Raeburn Van Buren's comic strip *Abbie an' Slats,* a wealthy dowager bent on marrying off her daughter was named "Ma Zeltov." To celebrate said daughter's decision to marry "a man of character instead of cash," she "planned her specialty—fresh fish a la Ma Zeltov!" It took a certain corn-oil producer to advertise: "MAZOLA-TOV; Congratulations, you've found our 10¢ off Coupon .. . !" Appropriately enough, a dating bureau for Jewish singles, advertising in the *Nation* in 1969, is "Operation MAZEL TOV."

mazuma, mezuma, mazoomy, etc.

This old slang term for money or cash comes from Yiddish MEZUMEN, which derives from Aramaic *m'zumon*. It has sometimes been shortened to "mazoo" or lengthened to "mazoola" (combining with another slang term for money, "moola").

metsieh, metziah, mitsia, etc.

Reported a generation ago to mean, in jewelry auctioneers' lingo, a flashy but defective diamond, this is from the ironic Yiddish A GANTSE METSIEH (Chap. II, Char. and Des.).

Jewish residents of Great Neck, New York, have been smiling at the name of the new automobile dealer in their area selling Toyota, the Japanese car: "Mitsia Motors."

mish mash, mish-mash, mishmash; mish mosh, mish-mosh, mish-mosh

Another example of a foreign word adopted by English and later given impetus from the Yiddish which had also borrowed it. German *misch-masch* came into English about five hundred years ago as "mishmash," with a short "a." In recent years it has become common in the entertainment world, pronounced with a broad "a" as in Yiddish and accordingly sometimes spelled with an "o."

In 1964 when Governor Scranton of Pennsylvania used the term on TV, pronouncing it with the short "a," he received a letter from comic actor Groucho Marx, advising him that if he planned any campaigning in Jewish neighborhoods, he had better change his pronunciation to rhyme with "slosh." The Associated Press quoted Scranton as saying, "Ever since then, I've been trying to do that for Groucho." This incident was capitalized on immediately in TV's Dick Van Dyke show. Two writers were discussing a script in process. "What have we got? A mish mosh," said one. "So we've got a mish mash," replied the other. And the first one exclaimed, "Mish mash? It's mish *mosh*. Can't you speak English?"

Composer Leonard Bernstein, writing in *Vogue* a decade ago, made a verb of it: "There was Gothic melodrama with dancing girls in tights, and comedy songs, and long speeches by Stalacta, Queen of the Golden Realm; there were gnomes and demons and Zamiel the Archfiend, and Swiss peasant maids—all mishmashed together."

See Chap. II, Rel. and Cul., MEDRESH.

mishugge; mishuggene

These Yiddish terms for—respectively—"crazy" and "crazy one" have been picked up in the entertainment world and have been heard on Broadway, in movies and over radio and TV. An old lively radio musical group was called "The Mishuggenes" (The Nuts). A recent book by comedian Henny Youngman was described in a *New York Times* ad as "Mishugah!"—the spelling being based on the Hebrew from which the term derives.

In Yiddish, MISHUGGE is a predicate adjective and knows no gender (ER IZ MISHUGGE, He's crazy; ZI IZ MISHUGGE, She's batty), while MISHUGGENE is the feminine form of the adjective when it precedes a noun (A MISHUGGENE MEYDEL, a dizzy girl) and also the feminine form of the noun (OT KUMT DI MISHUG-GENE, Here comes the nut). The masculine form of the latter term is MISHUGGENER (A MISHUGGENER MENTSH, a wacky person; ER IZ A MISHUGGENER, He's a nut). However, as usually heard in American slang, MISHUGGENE applies to either sex.

See Chap. II, Char. and Des., MISHUGGE *and* MISHUGGENER.

mitsia *See* "metsieh."

"mix in" for "butt in" or "get mixed up in"

"Don't mix in" is common in the speech of the second generation and sometimes shows up in the patter of Jewish comedians. It seems to derive from MISH ZICH NIT (ARAYN)—Chap. II, Advice.

mockie

My hunch is that this old slurring term for a Jew came from Yiddish MAKEH (Chap. II, Imprec., A MAKEH IM!). I would also guess that the parallel slur "Makalairy," which Maurice Samuel reports from the England of his childhood, is a combination of Yiddish MAKEH and CHALERYE (Chap. I, Imprec., ZOL DIR CHAPN A CHALERYE!). The term "moggy," in English dialect, means cow, calf, or ass, and this may conceivably have been involved too.

Cf. "sheeny."

Money is round.

This homespun observation that money is undependable and can roll away is common among second-generation American Jews, often as an equivalent of "Money isn't everything," particularly with regard to a prospective suitor. It comes from the Yiddish GELT IZ KALECHDIK—A MOL IZ ES DO, A MOL IZ ES DORTEN (Money is round—sometimes it's here, sometimes it's there).

See also Chap. II, Advice, MIT GELT KEN MEN NIT SHTOL-TSIREN. . . .

motsa, motser, motzer

Although I have never heard it myself, "motzer" is listed in Berry and van den Bark's *The American Thesaurus of Slang* as a slurring term for a Jew. I would guess it comes from MATZO (Chap. II, Food and Drink), as did presumably the old, relatively rare, derogation "motsy."

"Motsa" and "motser" have been reported as Australian slang for a large sum of money, as in "He made a motsa."

mouchey

Another relatively rare derogatory term for a Jew, this is believed to derive from the Yiddish name MOYSHE (Moses). German has a somewhat similar verb, *mauscheln*, to speak with a Jewish accent or intonation or to speak in Yiddish.

nash, nasch *See* "nosh."

nebbish

This term for a poor fool, from NEBBECHEL (Chap. II, Char. and Des.) has shown up on TV ("He's a nebbish"), in newspaper columns ("Kovacs, who played a noble nebbish, turned the piece into a personal gambado"), in the comics (Fearless Fosdick's "Shhh!!—This is direct from the Nebbish Desert" in Al Capp's *Li'l Abner*), etc. It was popularized in the retail trade in the 1950's with the "nebbish" gift items "for the man who has nothing." (The line even included a "nebbish bank" for children, advertised on TV, from which the money came right out at the bottom.)

Note that some of these uses make the word an adjective. It's been used this way to describe a humble approach in advertising copy. Witness the statement by Norman B. Norman quoted in *Harper's* regarding the approach of Doyle Dane Bernbach, who directed the Avis Rent-a-Car campaign: "It's always *nebbish*, always apologetic."

As a noun the term is often shortened to "neb": "He's such a neb!"

The verb "to neb," meaning to be inquisitive, was reported a generation ago for southwestern Pennsylvania and West Virginia, but this may be from German and unrelated.

-nik *See* IIIB, "nogoodnik."

Nisht Amool

This is the name of a horse that was reportedly running in 1967 races. It is Yiddish for "Not Sometime" (but Now!).

. . . no?

Asking a question by tacking "no?" onto a statement is common in the speech of first- and second-generation American Jews. The practice presumably came from German, which influenced both English (the usage appears in Shakespeare) and Yiddish, with Yiddish helping to intensify it in the United States.

Note that this "no" is different from Yiddish NU (Chap. II, Exclam.). The editorial writer in my local paper once confused the two: "Esoteric, Shmesoteric—It's interesting, NU?"

nosh

This form of Yiddish NASH, snack (Chap. II, Food and Drink) has appeared in various places: in a cracker named "Nosh-o'-Rye" (a pun on NASHERAY)—with its rhymed advertising slogan "By gosh, what a nosh!"—and in the title of a cookbook *A Rage to Nosh*. In Florida a hotel snack bar is "Ye Noshery" (which I've heard pronounced like the cracker), and in the nation's capital a fancy Chinese restaurant was named "Chinese noshery."[16]

An establishment specializing in KNISHES has been dubbed "Nish Nosh." Isaac Gellis packages a "Salami Nosh" (chunks of salami for snacks). Stuff to nibble on has been called "noshables" in a food column; and Earl Wilson has quoted Burl Ives in a restaurant asking for "just a little something to nosh on," the column being headed "Burl Ives Takes Off Weight, but Noshing Puts It Back On."

On TV, the term has been used in various forms for over a decade now—from the line of Richard Willis the beauty expert to a stocky woman, "I'll bet you nosh all the time"; to the fancy chef on a Steve Allen show named "Neville Nosher"; to Danny Thomas's comment on a $70 bill for luncheon at the Plaza, "Somebody must have been doing some noshing."

On the radio, a food product has been recommended as "a posh nosh." And a recent ad for frozen BLINTZES in the *New York Times* read: "Nosh-niks of the world, unite! Join the Golden Blintz Revolution!" As mentioned previously in III,

paper napkins are available with the invitation "Have a Nash."
I have also seen "nasch time," in publicity for a holiday celebration of a synagogue sisterhood.

A distinction between "nosh" and "nibble" was made in an
ad in the *Hadassah Magazine* for Dromedary Date-Nut Roll,
in which two slices were shown, one with a large bite in it, the
other with a smaller one, the text reading: "NOSH or NIBBLE
it . . . Stack it HIGH . . . keep it handy to serve when
guests drop by!"

nudj, nudje   *See* Chap. II, Char. and Des., ER NUDJET.

nudnik

This popular Yiddish term for a bore or pest (Chap. II,
Char. and Des.) has been turning up in various places—from
an author's pseudonym, to the *Li'l Abner* character "Liddle
Noodnik," to the punning "nudenik" in a Broadway column for
a photographer persistently urging undraped posing. It has even
been misused in a series of animated cartoons about a pathetic
little character for whom everything seems to go wrong. The
poor fellow is really a SHLIMAZEL (*see* Chap. II, Char. and
Des., SHLEMIEL).

of beloved memory

The *Ellery Queen Mystery Magazine* has been wont to attach
this phrase to the name of any person departed or thing defunct.
This is of course common usage among Jews, who get it from
ZECHER LIVROCHO and OLEV 'A SHOLEM (Chap. II, Death).

"only" for "just"

English sometimes uses "only" for "just," as in "If I could
only. . . ." The impetus from Yiddish NOR, which also has
both meanings, is most colorfully seen in such a statement as
"He should only break a leg!" (*Cf.* "should" and "shouldn't"
. . . .)

On you it looks good   *See* "Inverted Sentence Order."

oonshick

This term for "a person of low intelligence" is reported from
Newfoundland usage by Eric Partridge, who wonders whether

it may be of Amerindian origin. I suggest it is a snappy short-form of Yiddish UNSHIKENISH, a dire happening. The exclamation AN UNSHIKENISH! (Chap. II, Ann. and Arg.) gives vent to annoyance at the person who is a calamitous pest, and this might often be a boring nincompoop or "imbecile."

out of this world
    Yiddish has the counterpart of this expression—Chap. II, Char. and Des., AN OYS NEM (FUN DER VELT)! It may have had something to do with the American slang expression.

shamus, shammes, shammus, shommus
    This term is well-known to readers of detective fiction as a synonym for a cop, a flatfoot, or more frequently a house detective. Though some observers have related it to the Irish surname "Seumas," noting that there are many Irishmen connected with police work, it seems much more likely to have come from Yiddish SHAMMES, the synagogue beadle (Chap. II, Rel. and Cul.), who was the keeper of the premises and object of a certain deprecation. (Hebrew *shamosh* means keeper, guardian or servant.)
    The short form "sham" is believed to be a derivative, though some argue that this is short for "shamrock," symbol of the Irish. It's also been suggested that this is the standard word "sham," implying a lack of police integrity. It could also conceivably be a short form for the old Indian word for medicine man, *shaman*, which had disparaging connotations.
    Leo Rosten has decried the absence of the term in the latest edition of Mencken's *American Language,* but it does appear there, as it did in that work's Supplement II of 1948.

sheeny
    An old derogatory term for a Jew, this probably came—as A. A. Roback suggested back in 1938—from the Yiddish imprecation A MISE MESHINNE (Chap. II), and as I believe other anti-Semitic slurs came from different commonly heard Yiddish imprecations (*see* "mockie").

shemozzel, shemozzle, shimozzle, schlemozzle, etc.
    In British and Canadian slang, this means a misfortune, difficulty, or "row," hence an affair of any kind. It's also used as a

verb, to mean "make tracks," "get moving." In the United States, it's occasionally seen as "schlemozzle" for "uproar." The origin would seem to be Yiddish SHLIMAZEL (Chap. II, Char. and Des.)

shice *See* "shyster."

shick *See* IIIB, "shikkered."

shickser, shikster, shakester, etc.
Yiddish SHIKSE, Gentile girl (Chap. II, Tribalism) is believed to be the source of these low terms used in England to mean, at various periods, a lady or a not-too-respectable female.

shlag, shlak *See* "shlock."

shlemiel
In retail jargon, this may mean a sucker. In general slang, its use is increasing, reflecting its Yiddish meaning of poor fish, dope (*see* Chap. II, Char. and Des.).
Contrary to Leo Rosten's assertion, the term is included in the 1963 edition of Mencken's *American Language*. It also appeared in Supplement I in 1945.

shlep, schlep
This root of the verb SHLEPPEN, to drag, is common in American Jewish speech ("Why should you shlep all those packages if you can have them sent out?) and has been spreading. The term was reported two decades ago among retail furniture salesmen, for the act of moving furniture around on the floor. I recall an S. J. Perelman play on TV in 1959, in which a Jewish psychiatrist remarked: "If I want an orange, I don't have to go shlep myself to some supermarket." A New York department store recently used the term as both verb and noun, advertising a new shopping bag in three sizes: "Schlep!," "Son of Schlep" and "Super-Schlep."
I've also heard "shlep" as an abbreviation of SHLEPPER (Chap. II, Char. and Des.), as in the statement actor Walter Mathau made to radio interviewer Arlene Francis: "I like to go around looking like a SHLEP." Asked to explain, he said a SHLEP was a guy who went around wearing an old lumber jacket.

Also common are a number of bilingual forms, like "shlepped," "shlepping," "shlep along," "shlep around" and "shlepping around." A much-quoted pun about a week-end when former President Lyndon Johnson went to the Catskills was: "LBJ shlepped here." An old Mickey Katz musical parody was "Schleppin' My Baby Back Home." In 1957 the New York *Post* reported: "Queen Elizabeth will schlep along 95 pieces of baggage on her trip here." A year before, it reported that a truck driver had found a purse in the road, noting that there was "$11 in it and the usual trifles that a woman—in this case Mrs. John B. Kelly, Grace's mother—might *schlep* around." In 1962 Earl Wilson's syndicated column used the verb intransitively: "While schlepping around Waikiki in my swim trunks, I met Debbie Reynolds . . . ."—the item being headed in a Pennsylvania paper: "Schlepping at Waikiki Becoming a Popular Sport"! Similarly, in 1967 society columnist Suzy (Aileen Mehle) noted in the New York *Daily News* that "Charlotte Ford Niarchos has been schlepping around the Greek islands with her ex-husband, Tanker King Stavros Niarchos . . . ." Apparently neither Earl Wilson nor Suzy was aware that in Jewish usage, "shlepping around" usually connotes a pointless courtship (*see* Chap. II, Family, ARUMSHLEPPEN).

The program for the 1967 musical burlesque "P.D.Q. Bach" in New York featured a "Schleptet."

In England, a "shlepper-in" is a barker, i.e., a person who drags in the customers.

In underworld cant, "make the shleps" means "get the bundle."

shlimazel *See* Chap. II, Char. and Des., SHLEMIEL.

shlock, schlock, shlak, shlag, schlag, shlog
    This current slang term, seen and heard mostly in "shlock-shop," for a store with third-rate merchandise and without fixed pricing, seems to have been influenced by several Yiddish words: SHLAK, a stroke (*see* Chap. II, Imprec., A SHLAK ZOL IM TREFN!); SHLACHT, slaughter, as in SHLACHT-HOYZ, slaughter-house; and SHLOGN, to hit. Back in the 1920's it was reported in the retail shoe business, as "schlach-joint." "Shlock" has also been used to mean an overcharge or a junky bit of merchandise or, as in theatre box-office lingo reported over a generation ago,

a brutal situation, a very poor ticket sale. Among circus people the term appears (along with "slum," "junk," "garbage") for the cheap wares sold by concessionaires. In underworld cant it's also used as a synonym for "junk," but there "junk" means narcotics.

In TV lingo, a "shlock-meister" is a hander-out of junk or shlock: i.e., a fellow who arranges for indirect commercial "plugs" to be used in TV scripts and who passes out gifts from the companies whose products are so mentioned. In the radio trade, a "shlock-minister" is a preacher who exhorts his listeners to send in contributions.

The word has also appeared as an adjective, e.g. in "shlock job" for a fill-in or pot-boiling assignment in the theatre, and as a verb, meaning to overcharge.

In Australia and Britain, to "shlog (*or* slog) it on" means to up the price.

shlub (shluhb)

This recent synonym for slang "jerk" is being used by many a Gentile. It has appeared on TV and in popular journalism, as in the following line in the New York *Daily News* over a decade ago: "Telvi had a contract for $500 . . . to punch some shlub around." It is apparently from Yiddish ZHLOB, a yokel, a big dope, a "lumbering idiot."

shlump, schlump

Probably from Yiddish SHLUMPER (slut, slattern), this usually means "slob." But it has been used in the comics for "jerk" ("So you admit you were a shlump?") and has appeared in a *Time* movie review as a verb indicating something like "laze" or "slink" ("Spirited performers also lend *Sylvia* a sorely needed touch of class, and Actress Baker schlumps through the role at a wry deadpan pace, obviously enjoying her buildup as Hollywood's sex queen pro tem.").

shm- *See* IIIB, "fancy-shmancy, etc."

shmaltz, schmaltz, schmalz, etc.

This musicians' term for sentimental music is of course the Yiddish word for poultry fat, so commonly used in the Old Country recipes. It has appeared in reference to greasy hair dressing and also as an adjective, as in *Time*'s reference to "Schmalz Pianist Liberace." Usually, though, one sees the bilingual adjective "schmaltzy," as in the 1968 Barton's candy ad: "This Valentine's Day, women are longing, waiting to be wooed the schmaltzy way."

To "shmaltz it up" in music or writing means to make it more sentimental. Maurice Samuel has spoken of the Broadway hit *Fiddler on the Roof* as "a shmaltzification of Jewish life."

shmaychel, shmeikle

This verb to con or fast-talk is from the Yiddish verb SHMEY-CHLEN or SHMAYCHLEN, to smile. As with the English "gladhand," the ideas of pleasure and deception are combined.

Cf. IIIB, "SHMAY around."

shmear, schmear, schmeer

In 1930, this term was reported as being used by furniture salesmen to mean to flatter a customer. It's believed to come from the Yiddish SHMIREN (from German *schmieren*), to smear or grease, hence "butter up" and thence to "tip" or even "bribe."[17]

The term may also denote to win dramatically against, as an intensified form of "smear," particularly with respect to football: i.e., when you shmear a player from the opposite team, you knock him over, hence "wipe the ground with him" or "smear" him.

The word also appears as a noun ("It was a real shmear"). An interesting extension is seen in the statement which a New York chemist told me he had heard from a Gentile salesman: "I've got the whole shmear." Apparently this means, "I've got the complete line; it'll outclass any competitor's." This usage has become more generalized, so that in February 1969 WOR's John Wingate employed it in the sense of "shebang" when he said of the play *The Wrong Way Light Bulb*: "Everything that's happening in New York is in that play . . . the whole shmear . . . ."

shmecken, schmecken

Dope addicts mean by this "narcotics." It's the Yiddish word to smell, from the German word to taste. Dope may of course be either sniffed or tasted, and both languages are probably involved.

Among Chicago addicts as reported a generation ago, "smecker" meant one of their kind.[18]

shmegegge *See* Chap. II, Char. and Des.

shmeikle *See* "shmaychel."

shmo

From the widespread use of this slang term, you might never guess that it comes from a taboo Yiddish word (SHMOK—from German *Schmuck:* ornament—denoting the male organ and, figuratively, fool). Indeed, the popular "Don't be a shmo" seems to be a direct rendering of ZAY NIT KEYN SHMOK (Don't be a fool). With the dropping of the last letter, the word was cleaned up a bit, but it's always been unsettling for me to see it in children's TV films (a potentate, "The Shmo of Shmoland"; "The Schmohawk Indians") or to hear it in the spot announcement on racial intolerance: "Don't be a shmoe, Joe,/Be in the know, Joe"—to say nothing of the jingle appearing on the box of a family type of puzzle, "What's Your Hi-Q?":
> "If you take a week,
> You're an average Joe.
> If you give it up,
> You're just a schmoe."

The height—or depth—of this trend was reached with Remco's "Shmo" game, about which TV ad copy proclaimed, "It's fun to play Shmo, to watch a shmo, to *be* a shmo!," but whose box carried a more accurate message: "I'm a shmo, and that ain't good!"

Vulgar terms of course frequently travel up the scale of acceptability. Slang like "snafu," "all bollixed up" can similarly trouble those who are sensitive to the terms' origins.

In World War II "Joe Shmoe" was common American Army slang, producing an alternate form, "Joe Smoe." This same dropping of the "h" I think explains the vulgar term "smock," which in England is used in many phrases of a licentious nature and is doubtless related to the Yiddish and German terms (as is the low English "schmock," a fool). Similarly, I assume that the English slurring term for a Jew, "shmog," with the same derivation, was the source of two epithets reported by Maurice Samuel from his childhood in England: "smoggy" and "smoggy Van Jew." The process was obviously known to the writer of advertising for Smucker's jams, which had a man with a knowing look saying: "With a name like this, it *has* to be good!"

The pronunciation "shmuck," as noted in Chap. I, Vulgarity, has been heard in a recent Broadway play. I have since heard it in the 1969 movie *Good-bye, Columbus* and recall it earlier in the Broadway musical *West Side Story*. It has appeared in several recent novels, spelled "schmuck," even being quoted in an advance review by the Kirkus Service: " 'Everything is itch and scratch, skin, surface, and advertising copy,' declares the narrator, a 'Jewish schmuck,' who memorializes the world of drugs. . . ." In modern fiction from England, I've seen the spelling "shmook" (*see* "shnook").

The outright term may well be supplanting "shmo." I have even heard the bilingual adjective "shmucky" in teen talk, voiced without any awareness of the taboo nature of the word.

Cf. "shmoo" and IIIB, "fancy-shmancy, etc.," *and* Chap. II, Char. and Des., SHMEGEGGE.

shmoo

This imaginary animal created by cartoonist Al Capp which lays eggs, gives milk, provides meat, and in its author's words "represents the earth in all its richness" has been the subject of speculation by several linguists. Capp himself once indicated the term came to him on a cross-country trip as a symbol of the lushness of our countryside, but two pertinent observations have been made: *Shmu* was used by German Jewish businessmen a generation or two ago to mean somewhat illicit profit, and SHMUE is taboo Yiddish for the female organ. The satirical Mr. Capp, who has gone on suggestive capers before, even without the protective screen of Yiddish (and been taken to task for them by the New York Board of Regents), has had his own big joke—topping it with a 1963 sequence about the Shmos of Outer Shmongolia, in which he gaily pointed out the difference between a "shmoo" and a "shmo."

Franklin D. Roosevelt, Jr., was quoted in 1966 as using the phrase "the old schmoo" to describe turning on the charm.

shmoose, shmooze

This slang term for "chat" or "chew the rag" can be a verb or noun and comes from Yiddish SHMUS (from Heb. *sh'muoth,* news or tales). It's often heard in the bilingual "shmoosing."

Several South African colloquial terms have a similar origin: "smouse," "smouch," and "smouser" for a peddler; and "smousing," peddling. (A peddler is an itinerant, who would bring news of other places.)

In England, opprobrious terms for a Jew in the eighteenth century were "smous(e)" and "smou(t)ch."

shnook

This recently popular synonym for "sucker" or "fool" *could,* as Thomas Pyles has suggested, be a minced form of taboo "shmuck"—perhaps through its occasional form "shmook" (*see* "shmo"); but I wonder whether the Yiddish SHNUK for "snout" or "trunk" may have been involved, in a further association with the sexual organ.

Over a generation ago, both SHNUK and SHNUKEL reportedly meant an easy mark to retail salesmen, and H. L. Mencken thought they might be related to German *Schnucke* (small sheep). I always heard the word as SHNUKEL in first-generation speech and have assumed that "shnook" was an American shortening of the term. But if the more licentious origin is truer, the suffix was of course added.

I have a gift apron, purchased at Lord & Taylor, New York, which proclaims: "Any shnook can cook!" (I think it would be more appealing if it said "I'm no shnook; I can cook!") The comic-strip *Mary Worth,* by Kevin Ernest and A. Saunders, over a decade ago had the line: "If I weren't a blind, rock-headed jingle-brained charter member of the 'Schnook-of-the-month club,' I'd be married to September Smith." In 1962 a pre-Christmas AP Newsfeature for children was titled "Mr. Shnoo's Zoo," and I wondered whether the name was from "shnook" or "shmoo" (which *see*) or both. It may even have involved a variation of SHM- play on the children's character "Mr. Magoo"—I recall a TV line, "Magoo, Mashmoo, I'll kill the miserable wretch!" (*See* IIIB, "fancy-shmancy, etc.")

shnorrer   *See* Chap. II, Char. and Des.

shofel, shofle, shoful

A cant term for counterfeit money, this came into English from German *schofel* (worthless), which in turn is supposed to have come from the Yiddish form of Hebrew *shaphal* (low, base).

In 1929 it was reported as an adjective in the speech of borax-house salesmen: "If business is bad, it's shofle."

shon, shonk, shonky, shoncker, shonnicker

These opprobrious terms for a Jew in England are supposed to have come from Yiddish SHONIKER (petty trader or peddler).

"should"—ironic

This Yiddish influence is seen in popular ironies like "I should worry" or "I should tell him he can't do it!"—the implication being "Why should I?" Sources are the ironic HOB ICH A DAYGE (I've got a worry) and MAYN DAYGE (Chap. II, Resig., 'SIZ MAYN DAYGE). An old popular song, "I Should Care," built on the expression: "I should care,/I should let it upset me . . . ."

The irony of this "should" was coupled with another Yiddish-derived "should," that of wishing, in the defiant children's rhyme of my generation: "I should worry, I should care,/I should marry a millionaire." (*See* "should" and "shouldn't". . . .)

"should" and "shouldn't" for "may" and "may not"

This translation of the Yiddish particle ZOL shows up in a number of expressions popular among Jews and fast infiltrating general speech: "I should live so long" (Chap. II, Life and Health, ICH ZOL AZOY LANG LEBN!); "So it shouldn't be a total loss"; "We should be so lucky"; "That should be your biggest worry" (Chap. II, Advice, ZOL DOS ZAYN DAYN ERGSTE DAYGE); "You should only be well"; etc.

An aquarium sticker being sold and used by pet shops declaims: "It Should Knock in Your Head like You Knock on the Glass." On WQXR, Murray Shumach in 1966 quoted a violinist's comment about his fellow artist Mischa Elman: "God should keep him a long time." (Elman was seventy-five at the time.) Going a step further, a Miami Beach hotel has advertised: "You should live to 120." This is of course a good-natured rendition of BIZ HUNDERT UN TSVANTSIK YOR (Chap. I,

Superstition). The added statement was: "If you know how to live, you'll live longer. If you don't know, you'll learn at the Sans Souci." A caption in *Time* under a picture of Joseph M. Katz, leading gift-paper manufacturer, was: "Santa? He should live forever."[19]

On a recent *Tonight* show on TV, a young singer presented a song about the trials of film stars, ending with the line: "It ain't easy—it should happen to me!" This is a direct translation of AF MIR GEZUGTGEVOREN (Chap. II, Destiny). Several years ago, when I was in a restaurant with husband and children, we all knew just what we wanted, and the waitress exclaimed: "All my orders should be given this easily!" Chiquita Brand bananas, advertising in a recent issue of the *Reader's Digest,* detailed its care in packing the product, "otherwise known as the Special Delivery Banana," and added: "The U.S. Mail should have it so good."

I've also heard "You shouldn't know (from) such things" and "You shouldn't know it" in the speech of a young Jewish woman who grew up with Gentile friends and married a Gentile. These are of course from ZOLST NIT VISN FUN AZELCHE ZACHEN (Chap. II, Destiny). Closely related is the title of a book prepared by a volunteer group in New York listing sources of help for various citizens' problems: *The Book You Shouldn't Need.*
See "You should excuse me, ..."

shtarker
"Strong one" in Yiddish, this term has been used in Vita Herring ads for a large hero sandwich including a number of other fillers in addition to herring.

shtik, shtick
Yiddish for "routine" or "bit" (Chap. II, Char. and Des.), this has been picked up in show business. Note entertainer Sammy Davis's comment in 1966, quoted in the *New York Times,* about his projected TV show: "The show won't be for hippies only. That inside *shtick* is not for me." Some months later, Harry Belafonte on the Joey Bishop show explained how hard it was to substitute for m.c. Johnny Carson: "They see right through your SHTIK."
The popular use of "bit" in this sense—as in the comic strip

Mark Trail by Edd Dodd: "You mean you're going to do the scout bit? . . . Birds and bees *and* leaf collecting?"—may be a derivative.

shtunk, shtoonk

This word for "stinker," often heard in "He's a shtunk," comes from Yiddish FARSHTUNKENER (a stinky one). Al Capp has used it in *Li'l Abner* as the name of an animal, the "Slobbovian Shtoonk," which "is not only sneaky, smelly, and surly, but—yak! yak!—just try to EAT one! !"

shyster

In both the United States and England, this adjective or noun usually refers to an unethical lawyer, but may mean any worthless person. Its source appears to be the taboo German term for a defecator *(Scheisser)*, with at least some help from the related Yiddish SHAYS, which is supposed to have been responsible for the vulgar eighteenth-century adjective "shice." Another possible Yiddish influence may have been SHAYKER (falsehood, liar).

slog it on   *See* "shlock."

smecker   *See* "shmecken."

smouse, smouser   *See* "shmoose."

snide and shine

In England, this used to denote a Jew, particularly a Jew of East London. One theory has connected "shine" with slick-looking hair and another with SHAYN, a variant of SHEYN (pretty, beautiful), as in a merchant's statement, DOS KLAYD IZ SHAYN (The garment is beautiful). My own hunch is that the phrase came from the exclamation SHNAYD UN SHOYN (*or* SHAYN) !—Cut and done already!—which a Jewish tailor might voice regarding the length of time it would take to make something, *equiv.,* "Before you can say Jack Robinson."

"so" at beginning of a sentence

This characteristic of first-generation American Jewish speech probably was influenced by Yiddish TSI, which in formal Yiddish is often used at the beginning of a question. In recent years it has been showing up in popular journalism, often before a declarative question (*see* "Declarative Form in Questions").

See also "So what else is new?"

so it shouldn't be a total loss *See* "should" and "shouldn't". . . .

So what?

This has been credited to the shrugging Yiddish IZ VOS (So is what?). It's been used in popular journalism and advertising in England as well as the United States. Indeed, it appeared as the title of a book by Charles Landery published in London in the 1930's.

So what else is new?

Among American Jews, this is an ironic way of changing the subject after unpleasant matters have been discussed, a kind of Americanized form of LO'MIR REDN FUN FREYLICHER ZACHEN (Chap. II, Exclam.).

The expression is so common, it has appeared on a comic paperweight made in Israel, a little bronze figure of a man with a humorously pathetic look, a sort of nebbish made in Israel. It's been appearing in general use, too, from TV commercials to newspaper ads,[20] to Hy Gardner's joke book with that title, to a recent novel by James Stevenson in which a television show is named SWEIN, short for "So What Else Is New?" My local electric company used it in a mail brochure, but stuck in an unnecessary comma: "So, what else is new?" (This is just the opposite of the situation with the ironic "yet," where Yiddish seems to need the comma (*see* "Yet" as Ironic Intensive).

The variant "What Else Is News?" appeared in a recent ad in the *New York Times Magazine*: "What Else Is News at Nat Sherman's?" (the "what else" being "Pink cigarettes for weddings—Blue for Bar Mitzvahs").

Sue me. *See* "Do me something."

Talk to the wall!

This ironic expression of exasperation means "I might just

as well be talking to the wall" and comes from Yiddish RED TSUM VANT! (Chap. II, Ann. and Arg., under RED TSUM LOMP!).

A rather sedate version was quoted from an anonymous European diplomat, in comment on General Charles de Gaulle's intemperate statements in Canada in the summer of 1967: "You might as well speak to a wall. The man is getting old—he is nearly seventy-seven." Other forms, like "We're tired of wasting our time talking to the wall," have appeared in advertising[21] and on TV. A guest on WNBC radio's Long John Nebel Show criticized Columbia University's attitude during the student protests of 1968: "The University has no means for student redress. The students can talk to the walls." (This use of the plural "walls" appeared also in the Israeli cartoon mentioned under RED TSUM VANT! referred to above.)

That's all I need.

From the ironic NOR DOS FEYLT MIR, this is fast invading popular speech, along with the other ironic complaints about fate that Yiddish is replete with (*see* "I need it like I need . . ."; "I need it very badly"; "Who needs it?"). John Wingate exclaimed on WOR radio in February 1969, "Another snowstorm? That's all we need!"

The apple doesn't fall far from the tree.

This common observation among Jews, noting that children are usually not too different from their parents (either good or bad), comes from the Yiddish DER EPL FALT NIT VAYT FUN BEYM. The same thought also appears in German and Dutch proverbs.

"The end was" for "The result was"

From DER SOF IZ GEVEN, this is common in first-generation American Jewish speech, and the second generation often quotes it smilingly.

"to" for "against"

"What do you have to him?" in first-generation speech comes from VOS HOSTU TSU IM?—in which the Yiddish TSU, which sounds so much like "to," means "against." One even hears it in

the bilingual "I have a TAYNE to you," from ICH HOB TSU DIR
A TAYNE (Chap. II, Ann. and Arg.).
   Cf. IIIB, "TSU whom . . . ?"

tocker
   This underworld term for a murderer may be related to
Yiddish TOCHES. *See* the concluding discussion under "tokus."

tokus, dokus, tokis, tukis, tookis, tuckus, tochas
   These are all variations of Yiddish TOCHES, rump (Chap.
II, Char. and Des.), which has been heard in one form or another in various parts of the country for over seventy-five years.
Among Gentile Germans in the West over a half-century ago,
the spelling was "tookis" and "tukis" and the meaning was
reportedly "anus." One modern slang dictionary lists a current
taboo meaning of "rectum." About fifteen years ago, a young
Jewish New Yorker teaching in a southern private school heard
the headmaster tell a group of boys that they had better buckle
down to work or they would get it in the "tokus." Playing dumb,
he asked the headmaster about the word and was told it was
just a localism!
   Several children's diminutives have developed in the United
States. One is "tush" (which was used a number of times in
Noah Gordon's best-selling novel *The Rabbi* as well as in mystery parodist Sol Weinstein's series on the war between Israel
and TUSH—Terrorist Union for Suppressing Hebrews!). On
Art Linkletter's TV program, a young boy who was asked what
he wanted to be when he grew up replied: "A doctor." When
Linkletter asked "Why?" the boy replied: "So I can give people
shots in the tush." Unaware, Linkletter asked "What's a tush?"
and the boy spread his arms and shrugged, saying: "It's a
tush." Still unknowing, Linkletter asked: "Do I have one?"
and the audience howled. Understandably, the name of British
actress Rita Tushingham has been cause for snickering among
American Jewish children!
   Another diminutive is "tushie." This spawned "tushie slide,"
which a Gentile social worker in the Midwest told me over a
decade ago meant to her Jewish charges "a slide down a slope
on your bottom."
   Pre-teens and teenagers have in recent years been using the

comment "tough tukis" to mean "tough luck," "too bad." And Jewish adults have been using a playful word-and-motion to express "How stupid of us": a repeated jabbing of the index finger at the temple, with the spoken word TOCHES, which is short for "It TOCHES (took us) a long time to figure it out!" (In conversation with me at a Connecticut hospital in 1967, a Gentile nurse used this same finger motion at her temple and commented about herself: "No kidneys." *Cf.* IIIB, "No KOP and no TOCHES.")

Apparently England's Eric Partridge did not recognize the term when spelled "tochas." Note his theorizing in his *Dictionary of the Underworld*, 1950:

> Tochas. Testicles (?): 1938, James Curtis, *They Drive by Night:* "I could do three months on me tochas. How'd you like to be hung?" extant. Origin? If we can alternatively spell it *tockers*, we obtain the following: Tockers suggests tick-tockers, reminiscent of a clock pendulum, which swings; therefore compare slang danglers (testicles).

Indeed, his "tick-tockers" might seem more pertinent to the underworld term "tocker," a murderer, for the latter truly "does time." But it would seem more likely that "tocker"— which Partridge indicates is American in origin—relates directly to TOCHES, because a murderer is a "lifer," or someone who sits on his TOCHES or tocker. Unwittingly, however, Partridge has come close to a meaning for TOCHES which is sometimes implied in Yiddish, as in the phrase A KALTER TOCHES, a cold fish.

I suspect that Yiddish TOCHES may also help explain the expressions used in England, to "give toco" or to "give toks," denoting a thrashing.

See also IIIB, introduction, "tochi"; "T.L."; "T.O.T."

tough tukis   *See* "tokus."

tsuris

A common alternate for TSORES (*see* Chap. II, Char. and Des., TSORE), this was given wide circulation by a full-page *New York Times* ad in July 1969 which presented El Al airline's "Cure for Terminal Tsuris"—a new waiting room at the Kennedy Airport.

Harrison D. Horblit, well-known book collector, likes to use the bilingual adjective "tsuritic" for "troubling" or "worrisome." This is a joking pronunciation of Yiddish TSURIDIK and is similar to the humorous pronunciation of REBBITZEN mentioned in the note to that item (Chap. II, Rel. and Cul.).

tumeler, tumuler

This Yiddish designation for a real fun-guy is now part of American slang—chiefly through its application to the staff member of Jewish resort hotels assigned to livening things up among the guests. (*See* Chap. II, Char. and Des., TUMEL.) Danny Kaye and other entertainers got their starts as tumelers in the Catskills. Among the second and third generations, one may hear, "Boy, is he a tumeler!" Cutting up or clowning is "tumeling around."

In underworld cant the word has been reported to mean a rough criminal.

tush, tushy, tushie   *See* "tokus."

Use it in good health. *See* "Wear it in good health."

Verlier.

A generation ago, this term was reported as common among furniture salesmen when they had a customer on the hook and wanted another hovering salesman to go away and leave them quiet waters. The meaning is "Lose"—short for "Lose yourself"—and suggests both German *Verlier zich* and the related Yiddish FARLIR ZICH, the latter being the active form of VER FARLOREN (*see* "Get lost").

"Lose yourself" has of course been heard in general slang for some time.

Wear it in good health; Wear it well.

Reported in 1943 as common among second-generation Jews, these two translations of TROG ES GEZUNTERHEYD (Chap. I, Concerns about Life and Health)[22] have been making steady inroads in American usage. From Ann Sothern on TV to Elizabeth Taylor in films, to Gentile merchants who have picked it up from former Jewish employers, a bevy of sources have been transmitting the sentiment to American ears. At a testimonial dinner for Pennsylvania's State Senator Jeanette F. Reibman in 1967, I heard a Gentile officer of the State Democratic Committee present pearl and diamond earrings to the senator with the words: "Wear them in good health."

The eyes too are being exposed. A New York maker of pulpit robes and academic gowns prints on the little envelope containing spare buttons: "All of us here at Bentley & Simon who made your robe wish you to enjoy Your Robe and wear it well"; and a well-known maker of raincoats attaches a label to its products saying: "Misty Harbor wishes you health to wear this. . . ." To top it all, a 1966 series of ads of the Chiquita banana company showed young people with the paper seal of the banana pasted onto their foreheads, in line with the advice: "Look for the seal on the peel and wear it in good health." (This stimulated a fad.) But my favorite was the installment of the comic strip *Miss Peach* by Mell Lazarus in which Ira, having broken his arm, was showing off his new sling with wooden splint and plaster cast, and his friend answered: "Wear it in good health."

Related is "Use it in good health"—said to someone who has acquired new furniture and sometimes put in the hybrid "Use it GEZUNTERHEYD."

The variation "Eat it in good health" appeared in a recent editorial in my local paper which commented on the raise in Congressional salaries from $30,000 to $42,500 a year after Senator Everett Dirksen reported picking up a luncheon tab for $160: "That's $1,500 to cover the (5 per cent) cost-of-living increase and $11,000 for lunch. Eat it in good health, boys."

"What . . . need with" for "What . . . need . . . for"

Molly Picon, in *So Laugh a Little*, quotes her grandmother as saying, "What do I need with a mirror?" The same idiom has been creeping into the speech of TV performers, as in a recent line of Jackie Gleason's: "What they need with that I'll never know."

"What's to . . . ?" for "What is there to . . . ?"

This showed up a few years ago in a lengthy ad for Heinz ketchup on the back cover of the *National Jewish Monthly*: "What's not to like about calf's liver?" and in a recent one for ZBT baby powder in *My Baby*: "How can there be this much to know about Baby Powder? . . . What's to know? Just this . . . ."

I also heard it in a sentence where normal English would, in addition, use a participle after the "to": two professional women were discussing their summer plans, and one projected graduate study, noting that her younger daughter could keep house; the other responded, "Keep house? What's to keep house? The other kids are away, and you'll be home half the day!"

What's with . . . ?

In *Hamlet*, the question is put, "What's the news with you, Laertes?" In Yiddish, the same question is reduced to, "What's with you?" (VOS IZ MIT DIR?), and this elliptical form has been appearing in various places. Note the 1962 cartoon *Carnival* by Dick Turner showing a man who has just come out of the shower and grabbed the phone, answering: "Oh, just catching a little pneumonia. What's with you?" Or witness the advertising flyer: "What's with fashion? A wardrobe of Garay belts!"

Even the sense of "What's the matter with," which is common in Yiddish, has been showing up in general use. A 1958 AP dispatch about the Burlington Liars Club quoted the club's president: " 'What's with Alaska?' Hulett demanded. 'They're bigger than Texas, but we didn't receive a lie from them in '58.' " A 1962 editor's note in the Nationwide Insurance magazine *Minutes* asked: "Whatever became of rest? What's *with* people, anyway? Always on the go. . . ."

"What's with . . . ?" is combined with "What's this?" in a cartoon mail-insert distributed by the Bell Telephone Company of Pennsylvania, in which a woman asks her husband, "Harry, what's this with the telephone directory?" Indeed, some of the recent popular uses of "What's with . . . ?" seem to be a breezier form of "What's this with . . . ?" A 1963 instalment of Ken Bald's comic strip *Dr. Kildare* had a waitress say to a nervous young man: "Something's wrong with you, mister. What's with the shakes?"

Who needs it?

Especially popular in recent years has been this cheerfully defiant Yiddish question (VER DARF ES?)—strikingly used in the title of an April 1969 cover article in the *New Republic*:

"The ABM: Who Needs It?"[23] It is closely related to "Who asked for . . . ?" (VER HOT GEBETN . . . ?), which as suggested earlier, reflects the Old World Jew's difficult situation and his daily round of blessings and prayers. Constantly asking God for help, he naturally assumed, when he came up against something that did not suit him, that someone else had asked for it. That is, Who would have asked for this? Who *needs* it?

Other words or phrases have been substituted for the "it" as in the book title *Who Needs a Road?* or the radio ad "Who needs a can-opener now that Carling Black Label Beer comes in the tab-opener can?" The expression is sometimes preceded by "so" and even by an entire sentence as in this real estate ad in the New York *Post*: "So tell me. Who needs Miami with a view like this?"[24]

Many other variations are dressing up current advertising and journalism. Notice these uses of introductory clause or phrase: "If this is Acrilan, who needs wool?"; "With Dylan Thomas and Richard Burton, Who Needs Stereo?" As it often does in Yiddish, the expression has also been appearing as an exclamation. A Union Oil Company ad asked "Profit? Who needs it!" Mutual of New York advertised "I could hit it big with beavers. Who needs life insurance!" Another MONY ad retained the question in the first part but put the exclamation in negative form: "Health insurance? *There's* an expense I don't need!" (*Cf.* "That's all I need.") The whole expression was used as a noun in the TV line: "I've been thinking about what you said about school being a waste of time and who needs it. Well, I'm going to drop out too."

A related question common among Jews is, "With a friend like him, who needs enemies?" It's sometimes a statement: "With a friend like him, you don't need any enemies." These have also been appearing in the comic strips and on TV in such forms as "With such friends (*or* "With neighbors like this), who needs enemies?"[25]

Seemingly stimulated by "Who needs . . . ?" is the growing use of a similar "Who wants . . . ?" Witness the *Harper's* filler presenting statistics on the overwhelming number of psychiatrists in the District of Columbia: "Who Wants an Explanation?" or the Lear Jet stereo ad in *Time*: "At times like this who wants to hear football scores."

See Chap. II, Advice, 'SIZ NIT NEYTIK.

Who's counting?

This humorous question is popular among American Jews and comes from an old joke about the woman who is being offered a tray of tidbits and tells her hostess, "I've already had three, but they're so delicious I'm going to have another"—to which the hostess replies, "You've had five, but who's counting?"

The idea was used on TV's *Ozzie and Harriet* show, when a visitor remarked, "This is about the third time I've happened to be in the neighborhood around suppertime" and the reply was, "Well, it's the fourth time, but who's counting?"

The joke may be subtly related to the superstitious avoidance of counting discussed in Chap. I.

Who sent for *him*?

This translation of VER HOT FAR IM GESHIKT? is common in American Jewish speech, *equiv.,* "Who asked for him?" (*See* "Who needs it?")

Who's minding the store?

This is the punch line of an old Yiddish joke about the storekeeper on his deathbed who asks for his wife, then for each of his children. When the last one responds, "Yes, Pop, I'm here," the old man exclaims, "Then who's minding the store?"

The ironic line has been widely used in recent years—from the title of a movie with Jerry Lewis, to newspaper and radio political commentary. In 1960, Washington columnist George Dixon complained: "While Ike is away on his amiability amble who's minding the store?" Several years earlier, a WQXR announcer had asked: "Who's minding the store at the White House?"

The verb was slightly changed in "Who Minds the Store?"— a heading for a 1962 column by Howard Taubman in the *New York Times* which noted that long theatre runs go stale without supervision. It was further changed in a *Times* article squib in 1968: "ORGANIZATION-ANTIORGANIZATION MAN—To attract today's college students into business and industry, all signs indicate that the campus recruiter is going to have to get with it. Otherwise, who's gonna mind the proverbial store?" A recent movie with Milton Berle and Joey Bishop changed the last word: "Who's Minding the Mint?"

Substitute verbs have shown up too. A 1959 column by Victor

Riesel, deploring a Supreme Court decision against the employee-screening of the Industrial Personnel Security Program, ended: "Okay, they won. Now who watches the store?" And a *Life* editorial in 1964, discussing what might be happening in the Communist Party while Khrushchev was in Cairo, was headed: "Who's Running the Red Store?"

The comment has also appeared as a statement in various forms. Presidential aspirant Adlai Stevenson, in a famous Madison Square Garden speech, declared: "Someone has to mind the store." TV's "Chief Half-Town" on the Popeye Theatre explained to his young viewers in 1962: "Sally Star has a vacation for the entire month of January. I'm here trying to mind the store for her." In the society page of the Philadelphia *Sunday Bulletin* in 1963, a picture of a couple who were keeping an eye on a horse-racing stable in Palm Beach for the absent owner was headed "Minding the Store." Here too the verb has sometimes been changed, as in the statement in the 1961 novel *The Scar* by Eric Rhodin: "Such was the way for a saloonkeeper; you always had to have somebody taking care of the store—life, death or high wind."

"with" for "of"

This influence of Yiddish idiom is seen in the common exclamation, "Enough with the nonsense!" in place of "Enough of your . . . !" or "Enough of that!"

Cf. "again with the . . . !" above.

Would it hurt to . . . ? *See* "It can't hurt."

"Yet" as Ironic Intensive

One of the most popular Yiddish borrowings in recent years, this has shown up on TV and in a variety of newspapers and magazines. A translation of NOCH (Chap. II, Exclam.), it is often equivalent to the ironic ". . . no less," as in the article heading in *Consumer Reports*: "another vegetable peeler (electrically powered, yet)." It has even appeared in a comic "superclimax" on containers of the confection halvah: "With NUTS YET" and "Without NUTS YET."[26]

The usage is also common in the speech of Pennsylvania Germans, but Yiddish appears to be the dominant carrier. Notice that sometimes the "yet" is preceded by a comma, other times not. For me, the comma helps convey the Yiddish intonation.

yock, yok, yog
  In England, "yock" is an alternate form for "yog," which is East London back-slang for GOY, a Gentile or a fool. (*See* discussion in introduction to Tribalism, Chap. II.)
  In the United States, "yock" is an old vaudeville term for "a loud laugh"—sometimes pronounced "yak" or "yuck"— and apparently unrelated to Yiddish.

You should excuse me; You should excuse the expression; If you'll excuse (*or* pardon) the expression; etc.
  The first of these is a direct translation of the Yiddish ZOLST MIR ANTSHULDIKEN! (Chap. II, Exclam.). It was a popular bilingual joke a generation ago to ask at a party, "Would you like—you should excuse me—a cocktail?" This punned on the Yiddish KAK (*see* IIIB, "A.K.").
  The locution has fanned out beyond American Jewish speech, appearing in a variety of lighthearted forms. Notice the simple extension to "You should excuse the expression," which Zero Mostel used in a monologue years ago: "I walked down to Delancey Street for—you should excuse the expression—a breath of fresh air" and which appeared in a recent Stanley and Janice Berenstain cartoon in *Look*: "This—you should excuse the expression—is my room."
  That form has also joined with more idiomatic English to popularize "if you'll excuse the expression," as in the 1956 radio broadcast by a pet expert listing meats for dogs: ". . . and, if you'll excuse the expression, pork." The latter form—which was given wide circulation around 1930 by the old radio comic Ursul Twing—later became ". . . an expression . . ." in one of the lyrics for Broadway's *South Pacific*: "If you'll excuse an expression I use, I'm in love . . . ." A 1964 AP dispatch helped widen the possibilities of who or what might do the excusing: "The American Institute of Hypnosis, in a burst of Thanksgiving spirit, has some advice that should make turkeys grateful until they die—if turkeys will excuse the expression."
  The "if" version (probably influenced by the idiom "if you

will pardon my saying so") also became "if . . . pardon the expression," in more than one way. First there was the simple "if you'll pardon the expression," as in the George Clark cartoon of a wife who has opened up a pile of cans and announced to her husband, "Dinner, if you'll pardon the expression, is ready." Then greater variety was given to the person or thing doing the pardoning. A 1967 *Commentary* review by Walter Goodman noted: "The 'careful analytic neutrality' to which the doctor lays claim turns out to be pure benevolence toward Hiss and a hatred of Chambers so relentless that, if everybody will pardon the expression, it seems unconscious." A 1959 *Harper's* article by William S. White went further, using the whole expression as a substitute for "with apologies to": "This experience produced (if the *Reader's Digest* will pardon the expression) some of the Most Unforgettable Characters I ever met. . . ." And another *Harper's* article, by Russel Lynes, in 1965 used the form with "they" and "forgive": "The new volume introduces two chroniclers of the suburbs who have emerged in the last decade, Charles Saxon and James Stevenson, both sociologists at heart (if they will forgive the expression), both extremely able. . . ." In addition, "expression" has been replaced, as in the song sung in the 1968 Miss Pennsylvania Pageant on TV: "Sometimes, if you'll pardon the word, I sweat."

In further variety, the "pardon" version has sometimes dropped the "if," as in Pulitzer Prize winner Relman Morin's AP feature: "Are we all heading straight toward (you'll pardon the expression) togetherness?" It has also taken on "me" as in the *Time* letter writer's "Thank God (and I hope the people of Venice will pardon me the expression). . . ." It took Harry Golden to combine "pardon me" with the original "should" in: "Most of the folks in the South, reflecting the attitudes of the dominant society, would like to have a rabbi (you should pardon me) who does not look 'too Jewish'. . . ." Intriguingly enough, a 1963 installment of the cartoon *Brother Juniper* by Fr. Mac uses the "should" with "pardon": The good Brother is coaching a children's baseball game and yells: "'STEAL!' . . . you should pardon the expression."

Finally, we've been hearing the brief "excuse the expression," as in the TV disc jockey's "That sounds like garbage—excuse the expression," and the similarly brief "pardon the expression," as in the 1963 UPI feature quoting a woman about to embark on a weight-losing fast: "I see no reason why my upcoming fast can't be, pardon the expression, a huge success." And I'm sure we ain't (you should pardon the slang) heard nothin' yet.

IIIB. How Well They Go Together (Bilingualisms)

In Chapter I we explored various ways in which Yiddish reflects a Jewish sensitivity to words, their meanings and sounds. Further evidence of this sensitivity is seen in the many bilingual terms, phrases and quips that have developed in the United States and England. Some of these, as you will already have noted, are merely good-humored, often irreverent, plays on sounds, as in "Yisgadoll" for *Yisgadal* or "pig-in-the-pen" for PIDYENABEN. Some put the English diminutive endings onto Yiddish words, as in "sukie" for SUKE or "shandie" for SHAND or SHANDE. In some cases, an English diminutive is substituted for the Yiddish one, as in "keppy" for KEPPELE.

In other cases, the new terms may also contain additional particles, as in "Mrs. McKenzie" for ME KEN ZI. Or they may involve sardonic twists of meaning, as in "Yiddified" for YIDDEN FAYNT. Still other expressions intensify their meaning by offering it in two languages, as in "EFSHER, maybe." In American English, a common joke has it that a girl at a co-ed college is studying for her "M.R.S. degree." The jokes noted here about Ph.G. and Ph.D. degrees go a little further, using two languages.

A few expressions cover up vulgarity by using English abbreviations for Yiddish words, as in "A.K." and "T.O.T." Others do it in manufactured bilingual forms, like the smiling Latin plural for TOCHES, "tochi." (The actual plural is TECHESER.) Still others combine Yiddish and English in partial translation like "Stop DREYing me a KOP" or in coined terms like "direc-

354

toren" for "wife of a director." In addition, there is bilingual rhyme, which in combination with incongruity provides such ticklers as "GUT YONTIFF, Pontiff." Or witness the old bilingual parody of the western song "I'm an Old Cow Hand from the Rio Grande": "ICH BIN AN ALTER buck/FUN Old Kentuck;/ MIT DI MEYDELACH,/HOB ICH NIT KEYN luck;/ICH GIB A TSUP AF MAYN BERDELE/UN GIB A SHPRING AF MAYN FERDELE,/UN SHIK DI VELT IN D'RERDELE; Yippie yi-yo ki-yay!" (I'm an old buck/From Old Kentuck;/With the girls I have no luck;/I give a tug at my little beard/And give a spring onto my little steed,/ And send the world to little ol' hell; Yippie yi-yo ki-yay!)

Jews obviously enjoy poking fun at their own mixtures of speech. There's a story about the English traveler in New York who stops to ask directions: "I say there, chappie, VU GEFINT MEN DO ERGETS Delancey Street?" (. . . where can I find Delancey Street around here?)— an incongruous coupling of upper-class British terminology and tone with the question, in Yiddish, about the whereabouts of the Lower East Side neighborhood of Delancey Street.

Listed here is a sampling of bilingual expressions which—in addition to those sprinkled throughout this book—have been common in American and English Jewish speech. A number have had an impact on general slang.

a big shmeal
    A little stronger than the ironic "a big deal," from which it comes. (*See* "fancy-shmancy.")

A.K.
    These letters stand for the good-naturedly vulgar ALTER KAKER (Old Crapper)—not, as *Variety* once said with tongue in cheek, "Antediluvian Knight"! It is roughly equivalent to "Old Goat" and is sometimes spoken in full or in the bilingual euphemism "ALTER Coyote."
    One Connecticut family some years ago slyly named its cocker spaniel "Alter." (ALTER is also a boy's name. *See* Chap. I, Superstition.) But recently when a race horse was named "Alter Kocker," the Jockey Club, which registers horses' names, barred the animal until its name was changed (to "Cubist")! I recall a letter to "Dear Abby" in 1963 which was signed, "Stuck with an A.K." Some months ago I saw a Connecticut license plate

"AK902" and remarked to my companion that the owner probably wasn't Jewish: if he were and these were his initials, he would certainly not have asked for them for his car!

According to a recent slang dictionary, "A.K." is now commonly substituted for the taboo "a-- kisser," but I doubt that Jews would ever use it that way. For that meaning, there is the slightly more acceptable "T.L." (which *see*). To some refugee Jews, "A.K." has a more ominous association: the Polish *Armia Krajowa*, a military group that was guilty of anti-Jewish crimes.

The word KAKER is sometimes used in rough men's talk for "half-pint," "ingrate," or "bum," as in, "Why, you little KAKER" —which I was surprised to hear comedian Jackie Leonard say to song-writer Sam Cahn on the Johnny Carson show. But one can never be sure what will be said on that TV show. (*Cf.* Chap. II, Rel. and Cul., MOYEL.)

See Chap. II, Char. and Des., A KNAKER ON A NUN, under A GANTSER KNAKER.

The crude "KAKcited" is sometimes used for "excited," somewhat reminiscent of the coarse "Hold your water" in place of "Hold your horses."

Some years ago, "cacked out" was reported from the speech of Jewish schoolboys for "physically exhausted, tired, played out," and "to have no cack" for being without strength or energy. These are reminiscent of "pooped out," the term "poop" also having reference to defecation in children's speech. In England, the noun and verb "cack" and noun "cacky" are vulgar references to excretion, now particularly among children. Eric Partridge traces them to Latin *cacare*, but Yiddish may have been a more direct influence.

See IIIA, "You should excuse me . . ."; Chap. I, Rhyme, MENDEL, MENDEL, . . .; Chap. II, Ann. and Arg., KAM OYSGE-KAKT!, under KAM OYSGEKRATST!

ALTER Coyote   *See* A.K.

A.M.

A visiting colleague of my husband's recently spoke of someone as an "Able MAMZER"[1]—i.e., an S.O.B. with ability. I suggested the description, "He has his A.M. degree." (*Cf.* Ph.G.)

a whole MEGILLE

A partial translation of A GANTSE MEGILLE (*see* Chap. II, Rel. and Cul., MEGILLE), this is used by many non-Jews who are quite unaware of the religious reference involved. A Pennsylvania broadcaster, completing a list of school closings one stormy day, noted: "That includes the whole megille." A popular song on jukeboxes several years ago, "Blow Your Horn," contained the line, "I'll give you the whole megille." And Lucille Ball, appearing on TV as a Mrs. McGillicuddy, quipped, "My mother was a Cuddy and my father was a Megille."

The children's TV character "Magilla Gorilla" is of course well known. He's the basis of a book as well as a game. And for a while there, a certain record stimulated a dance craze, "Making with the Megilla."[2]

balabairian

This coined word was suggested by a Nevada woman as a combination of BALABOSTE (her sp. for BALEBOSTE) and BAIRIA (her sp. for BERYE) to denote "a true household engineer." To me, the spelling as well as the "n" at the end is too reminiscent of "barbarian." A better combination of the two words would be BALEBERYE, and that would be all-Yiddish.

See "berry" for BERYE.

"berry" for BERYE

This good-natured term for the efficient housekeeper is a double pun, matching the similar sounds and also suggesting the old slang "She's the berries."

bialys

Here we have a short bilingual plural for BIALYSTOKER PLETSEL, a type of roll made in Bialystok (a city which was at times part of Russia and other times part of Poland).

The dough is softer and chewier than that of the popular bagel (*see* Chap. II, Food and Drink, BEYGEL) and has a floury finish. Also, the center is a depression rather than a hole and is filled with onion flakes.

blintzkrieg

A mixture of Yiddish BLINTZE and German *Blitzkrieg*, this

was jokingly applied to the lightning action of the Israeli Army in June of 1967.

See Chap. II, Food and Drink, BLINTZES.

BLONJE time
   This is the extra time my husband allows for getting lost in highway travel.
   As a back-seat driver, I have sometimes asked, "Will you please stop BLONJE-ing and ask directions?"
   See Chap. II, Ann. and Arg., VER FARBLONJET!, under VER FARLOREN!

BORSHT belt
   Just as certain portions of the fundamentalist South are known as the Bible Belt, particular portions of New York state which contain Jewish resort hotels—the Catskill Mountains— make up the Borsht Belt: the area where BORSHT is served. (*See* Chap. II, Food and Drink.)
   See also "BORSHT circuit."

BORSHT circuit
   This is show-biz lingo for bookings in the Borsht Belt, where entertainers are always in demand.
   About a decade ago, when the Catskill resorts began fancying up their entertainment facilities with nightclubs and theatres (as a graduation from the porch, from which so many of the old tumelers' antics were originally performed), comic Georgie Price commented that the borsht circuit should be renamed the Vichysoisse Circuit!
   Cf. IIIA, "from" for "of," *re.* "strictly from borsht"; Chap. II, Char. and Des., KOCHALEYN.

"Bubby" for BOBBE or BUHBE, Grandma
   Like "keppy" for KEPPELE and "Hupy" for CHUPE, "bubby" is an Anglicized diminutive. But Grandma's Americanization has been proceeding, and she is now more often called "Nanna."
   See Family, BOBBE.
   Cf. "Buby"—Chap. II, Endearment, under BUBELE.

Call me PISHER.
   As noted in Chap. I, this is a bilingual form of the casually

defiant RUF MICH PISHER (Call me pisser). It's a smilingly vulgar relative of "Do me something" (IIIA)—*equiv.*, "NU, so what can you do, shoot me?" It is usually limited to men's talk. Jerome Weidman, however—anticipating the antics of Al Capp (*see* IIIA, "shmoo")—back in 1942 published a story in *Stag* with this title, for which the following "definition" was provided: "pish-er (noun) a Good Late Amer. Colloquialism Denoting a Guy Who Gets Caught Between Two Other Guys, Usually With Muscles."[3]

"canary" for KEYN EYN HORE[4]
This is jokingly used in both negative and positive forms: "Don't give me a canary" or "No canary," meaning "No evil eye, please"; and "I'll give him a canary," meaning "I'll treat him so he'll have to get deliverance from the evil eye; I'll fix him but good."[5]

cheap like BORSHT
This comes from BILLIG VI BORSHT (Chap. II, Char. and Des.), *equiv.*, "cheap as anything," "cheap as dirt."

"Charlie" for SHAYLE
A lighthearted "Engdishism" quoted to me by a young Conservative rabbi in New England: "I have a Charlie for you." (*See* Chap. II, Rel. and Cul., PASKENEN A SHAYLE.)

directoren
This term for the wife of a director, as in "Hillel Directoren" (wife of a director of a Hillel Foundation, Jewish college-student organization), was coined over twenty years ago by Kathy Zigmond, wife of Rabbi Maurice L. Zigmond, director of the New England region of the Hillel Foundations. It is of course smilingly patterned after REBBITZEN (Chap. II, Rel. and Cul.).

Don't give it a GUT OYG!
Lit., Don't give it a good eye! Don't put a hex on it! (*See* Chap. I, Superstition.)

DREYing a KOP
This is commonly heard in such expressions as "Stop DREYing

me a KOP" (from DREY MIR NISHT KEYN KOP!—Ann. and Arg.) or "I keep DREYing myself a KOP." The latter has led to "I keep bothering my head."

Dr. Poonim
This name of a plastic surgeon appeared in the comic strip *Joe Palooka* by Ham Fisher. PUNIM is an alternate of PONIM (face).

Everyone has his own MISHUGAS.
A bilingual form of YEYDER HOT ZICH ZAYN MISHUGAS (Everyone has his own wackiness), an alternate for ITLECHER MENTSH HOT ZICH ZAYN SHIGOYEN (Chap. II, Passing Judgment).

"FA'MISHT" for "famished"
FARMISHT (Chap. II, Char. and Des.) means "mixed up." Obviously, when you're famished, your head feels light and you're therefore FARMISHT. Al Capp used this pun in *Li'l Abner*: "Breeng Food; I am Fameeshed."

fancy-shmancy, etc.
This handy formula of deprecation has been going strong for over a generation. Coming out of the Yiddish SHM- idiom (Chap. I, Twin Forms), it was worked to the hilt in the Bronx characters of Arthur Kober (e.g., *My Dear Bella*, 1937), and has been picked up on many levels of the general language:[6] comic strips, cartoons, greeting cards, magazines, books, films, TV, and even official Washingtonese. A 1956 issue of the *New Yorker* contained two different ads which used the formula, one by the conservative book publisher Macmillan crying: "Sibling Schmibling! You need *Baby Makes Four*"; the other by a Philadelphia camera company that declaimed a tongue-twisting: "Gadgets, Schmadgets . . . as Long as It Takes Pictures!" The second of these comes from the old "Cancer, shmancer, ABI GEZUNT." That popular irony was picked up some years earlier by Herblock in a pointed cartoon on the Atomic Energy Commission: "Mutations, Shmutations—Long as You're Healthy."
A recent variation is the psychiatric quip, "Oedipus, Shmoedipus, so long as he loves his mother"; and a greeting card even

introduced rhyme in the second part: "Freud, Schmoid, As Long as It's Enjoyed—Happy Anniversary!" A clever use of the formula was Al Capp's "shmoseblossoms," in which the play on "roseblossoms" also provided a pun on "shmo" (IIIA). The expression has also shown up in a somewhat new version in the recent TV disagreement on whether a wizard or a lizard was eating mosquitoes: "Wizard, lizard, as long as it eats mosquitoes." Here the second term did not SHM-, but supplied a true rhyme.

Another variation, in a letter to the *New York Times*, retained the SH but changed the M to W, to fit the letter in the first half: "My husband spotted Gwen Verdon as a potential star . . . so we have followed her career with interest, but Gwen, Schwen, the play's the thing, and 'Redhead' is an obvious, silly little story."

Further variations have involved omitting the first syllable in the second word, as in my local newspaper's editorial disputing David Susskind's evaluation of Jack Paar: " 'Deliciously Irreverent'? Irreverent Schmeverent!" (The classical form would have been "Irreverent, Irshmeverent!") In a *New Yorker* comment, "Oh confusion schmooshun," we see not only the dropping of the first syllable in the second half, but also a change in the spelling.

A still further variation is the dropping of the "h" in the second half, as in the Hallmark get-well card: "Penicillin, Smenicillin! I want a barber!" This also appeared in the recent stage play *Thumby* by Jerry Blatt: "Princess, smincess, do you want to get out of here or not?" These examples reflect the same process involved in "Joe Smoe" (IIIA, "shmo"). Contrariwise, in the comic strip *Abbie an' Slats*, the "m" was dropped and the "h" retained: "Contract, shontract! It's what's in my heart that counts. . . ."

Notice the difference in emphasis from one use of the formula to another, expressed in different punctuation. In "her fancy-shmancy friend," for instance, the compound adjective requires a hyphen. But if, on being told that a certain young lady is pretty, you respond with a scorning of the fact's importance, as someone did on TV with "pretty, shmetty, . . ." then obviously, the comma is needed. Sometimes, as in the Macmillan ad and *New Yorker* comment quoted above, the printed form comes through with no punctuation at all. These instances, for me, lack the YIDDISHEN TAM. The omission of the comma leaves little room for the proper intonation—just as the ironic "yet" seems different without the preceding comma (*see* IIIA, "Yet" as Ironic Intensive).

SHM- has been subtly used in the toy market: a construction set named "Krazy Ikes" provided a brochure illustrating many human and animal figures to be made with its plastic pieces, the models being given humorous names like "Crocodike," "Ikestrich," etc., including "Shmike," a pathetic little creature without arms.

We can doubtless expect many other uses of and variations on this twin-form theme. And I'll wager that all of these, like the examples already quoted, will be offered with little awareness of the suggestive element involved. (*See* reference cited in Chap. I, Onomatopoeia.)

filet MINYEN

A popular pun on filet mignon. (*See* Chap. II, Rel. and Cul., MINYEN.)

first-cut BRUST

The lean end of brisket, popular cut for roasts among Jewish housewives. To a kosher butcher, this is the usual term employed by the first and second generations.

GEY fight. . . .

A shortened bilingual version of the resigned "Go fight City Hall," *equiv.* "Waddaya gonna do. . . ."
See IIIA, "Go" as an ironic substitute. . . .

Grease the folks.

This light-hearted parting means "Give my regards to the folks" and puns on GIB A GERIS . . . (Give regards to . . .).

HAD'YADUDEL!

This warm greeting is a combination of the informal English "How d'ya do" and the Yiddish diminutive -EL.
Cf. Chap. I, Endearment, "Helloele."
Somewhat similar types of word formation appear in American Italian: *siriollo* from "city hall"; *sanemagogna* from "son of a gun."

HAVAYE for "Hawaii"

HAVAYE is Yinglish (which *see*) for "How are you." It is so much like the correct pronunciation of the fiftieth state that it is an inevitable pun among second-generation American Jews greeting someone returning from Hawaii.

Hit 'em in the KISHKES!

Old boxing fans will recall this partisan cheer, which means "Hit 'im in his guts," or "Knock his stuffings out." According to Harry Golden, it was coined by the father of the old prize fighter Joe Bernstein. This father, Golden says, would be in Joe's corner wearing a derby hat (covering a YARMULKE) and would call out this encouraging line to his son. Golden remembers hearing the same line from the balcony at other fights like that between Slattery, an Irishman, and Sharkey, a Pole.

Cf. Chap. II, Food and Drink, KISHKE.

"Holly" for CHALLE

Reflecting the same tendency seen in "Bubby" above, this popular term for Sabbath bread (Chap. II, Rel. and Cul., CHALLE) has been picked up by many a Gentile—food clerk, gourmet, and others. The term is printed on the labels of some commercial bakeries' product, one company even using the redundant "Holly Bread."

This word exchange is used in reverse in the parody of the famous Christmas carol, "Deck the halls with boughs of CHALLE" (*see* Chap. II, introduction to Tribalism).

ipsy-pipsy

Very fancy (a rung above "fancy-shmancy").

This may have developed from a deprecation of HIPSHE— i.e., HIPSHE-PIPSHE (*see* Chap. II, Char. and Des., A HIPSHE MEYDEL, *and* Chap. I, Twin Forms). English slang ironic "pip" may also be involved.

keppy

This is a bilingual rendering of Yiddish KEPPELE (little head). I know a Pennsylvania pediatrician who was so used to using the term with his own young children that he found himself saying to all his young patients (including Negroes): "Now, turn your keppy."

See Chap. II, Life and Health, A LEBN AF DAYN KEPPELE!

KRATS around

This is commonly heard in "before he KRATSes around"—meaning, before he gets moving. (*See* Chap. II, Exclam., EYDER ME KRATST ZICH OYS.)

KRECHTSing; KRECHTS'd; KRECHTS sessions

Three statements I heard in recent months are typical of second- and third-generation American Jewish speech: "When he doesn't feel well, he won't go to bed, but he walks around KRECHTSing" (i.e., groaning); "When I was married, I wore a size two shoe but I KRECHTS'd up to four and a half"; "They just meet for KRECHTS sessions" (of oldsters who have not found outside interests and merely exchange accounts of their aches and pains). (*See* Chap. II, Ann. and Arg., NOR ME KRECHTST!)

KVELL, to; KVELLing

These hybrid forms of the Yiddish verb KVELN, to feel proud (*see* Chap. II, Family, ER KVELT) are often heard with reference to children's accomplishments: "You've got reason to KVELL"; "Is he KVELLing!"

One of the singing Barry Sisters explained in a recent interview that there are four sisters all together: "Two sing and two KVELL."

"Michíganer" for "Michigander"

The proper term for a resident of Michigan is of course "Michigander," but Jews whose relatives go to the University of Michigan or otherwise move to the state can't resist this ready bilingual pun. (*See* Chap. II, Char. and Des., MISHUGGENER.)

MISHUgothic

A smiling criticism of the architectural style of some new synagogue buildings—based on MISHUGAS, craziness. (*See* "Everyone has his own MISHUGAS" above.)

Moishian

Novelist John Barth coined this ethnic designation for the human progenitor of his hero in *Giles Goatboy* (1966). It combines the Yiddish word for Moses, MOYSHE, and English "ian."

"MOYSHELE" for "Mosholu"

New York's Mosholu Parkway in the Bronx was dubbed "MOYSHELE (Dear Moses) Parkway" by second-generation students in the 1930's.

Mrs. McKenzie

An ironic title that Jewish retail salesmen applied a generation or two ago to the customer who looked and looked but never bought: from ME KEN ZI (*lit.*, One knows her; I know her kind).

The term "McKenzie" was also applied by adolescent Jewish boys in Connecticut during the 1920's to refer to a girl who was free and easy, as an abbreviation for ME KEN ZI TAPN (You can feel her up). As might be expected, the Tappan Zee Bridge near the Westchester Expressway in New York has evoked a smile from many a Jewish driver.

nogoodnik

This Yiddish-American synonym for slang "bum" has found its way into comic strips and popular journalism. The -NIK suffix, which Yiddish borrowed from the Slavic tongues, has for years provided a wealth of popular bilingual terms for American Jews: "allrightnik" (someone who's doing all right for himself); "realestatenik" (a dealer in real estate); "cruisenik" (someone who goes on cruises); etc. These were prevalent among Jews long before the launching of the Russian sputnik in the fall of 1957 brought "-nik" into widespread American use.[7]

See Chap. II, Rel. and Cul., LAMEDVOVNIK; Chap. IV, discussion of suffixes; *and* "Phudnik" below.

no KOP and no TOCHES

Lit., no head and no behind—comment on the person who doesn't use his head and doesn't lift a finger, i.e., shows no initiative whatever. I heard it recently applied to the quality of sales help available these days.

not to know from BORSHT

This is reminiscent of the English "not to know beans" (for

which there is a closer *equiv.* in Chap. II, Char. and Des., ER VEYST FUN BOPKES). BORSHT, like beans, was simple fare, and relatively cheap. (*See* Char. and Des., BILLIG VI BORSHT.) I've heard "I don't know from BORSHT" from the mouths of third-generation American Jews who don't know Yiddish.

See "Oh, BORSHT!" *and* "BORSHT belt"; IIIA, "know from" for "know," . . . .

NU, DARF MEN GEYN IN college?

When Cousin Izzie, who quit school at thirteen, became a rich man, this was the natural wry comment of the older generation (So, do you have to go to college?), and it's still quoted with a laugh in similar situations. The Jewish emphasis on education is thus wryly pricked. The same tone appears in the famous story of an immigrant who applied for a job as SHAMMES of a SHUL and was turned down because he couldn't write. He went into business and later made a fortune. One day he was at the bank signing an "X" to a check, and the teller remarked, "Just think, Mr. Ginsberg, what you might have done with an education!" "With an education," he replied, "I would still be the SHAMMES of the SHUL!"

See Chap. II, Rel. and Cul., SHAMMES.

Oh, BORSHT!

This exclamation of disgust—a kind of kosher version of "oh, bosh!"—is a by-word of a certain Pennsylvania manufacturer. His Gentile secretary told him one day that she had heard "that word" of his on TV. She had thought it was a cuss-word!

OYS holiday; OYS vacation; etc.

No more holiday; the vacation's over; etc. ("Back to the grind.")

patsky, patshky *See* "potsky around."

Ph.G.

This pharmacy degree has been transmuted into a comment on marital qualifications: "Papa HOT GELT" (Papa Has Money). The quip probably derives from the fact that many Jewish pharmacy students have expectations of going into Papa's existing business or into one he will set up for them.

Phudnik

Fifteen or twenty years ago, Jewish college students jokingly defined a Phudnik as "a NUDNIK who is working for his Ph.D." But the degree has become more common every year, as has the -NIK suffix (*see* "nogoodnik" above), and today the term is just a good-natured description of a doctoral candidate. It may be the source of the short-form nickname by which a group of Cornell undergraduates studying in a special pre-doctoral program are known: "The Phuds."

Pig-in-the-Pen

A humorous duplication of the sounds in PIDYENABEN (Chap. II, Rel. and Cul.).

This is similar to the process involved in some English quipping terms like "hickery-pickery" for Latin *Hiera picra*, a purgative drug.

See Chap. I, Acronyms, *re.* the phrase *yagt den has* for *yaknehaz;* Chap. II, Death, ZITSEN SHIVE, *re.* the similar "sit 'n shiver."

plotzed, plotzing

These come from Yiddish PLATSEN, to burst, to split one's seams, and are often used to mean "howling" or "dying" in the sense of laughter, as in "OY, I'm plotzing!" A recent ad for a Yiddish revue read: "In Miami they're plotzing"—meaning, "They're still howling over the preview."

Recent journalistic borrowings are making of it a transitive verb, as in this *Time* line about Woody Allen: "Last year he wrote a wacky feature *(What's New, Pussycat?)* that plotzed so many people that it has already grossed more than $10 million."

Among teenagers, "plotz" is becoming a noun, as in the comment on some great party plans: "That'll be a real plotz!"

Cf. Chap. II, Ann. and Arg., ME KEN PLATSEN!

potsky (patsky, potshky, patshky) around

This verb for "putter" or "mess (with)," as in "Quit potskying around," comes from PATSHKE and is sometimes heard more accurately as "PATSHKE around" and "PATSHKE-ing around." (*See* distinction between PATSHKE and PATSH, Chap. II, Ann. and Arg., VILST A PATSH?)

schnozzle

This humorous word for "nose" was once thought to be a combination of Yiddish SHNOBEL (beak) and English "nozzle." Wentworth and Flexner (*Dictionary of American Slang*, 1960) suggest it is from German *Schnauze*, snout, reinforced by the Yiddish term, which they spell SCHNUBBL. Webster's Third Edition (1966) credits a different Yiddish term, SHNOYTSL, diminutive of SHNOYTS, from the same German *Schnauze*.

The famous label for comedian Jimmy Durante's proboscis, "schnozzola," is of course "schnozzle" or its short form, "schnoz," with the added comic "-ola."

An underworld term for an addict whose drug-taking method is exclusively sniffing is "schnozzler" or "snozzler."

schnozzler, snozzler *See* "schnozzle."

schnozzola *See* "schnozzle."

shicked; shickered; on the shikker *See* "shikkered."

shikkered, shickered

Yiddish SHIKKER (Chap. II, Char. and Des.), from Hebrew *shikkor*, is also an adjective and accounts for this word for "soused," which is probably influenced too by FARSHIKERT (soused up).

Related is the slang phrase "on the shikker," meaning "drunk" or "habitually tipsy." The short form "shicked" is common in Australia, where the noun "shick" also means a drunk.

SHMAY around

Presumably from the Yiddish verb SHMAYCHLEN (to smile), this is used to mean to enjoy oneself, to pass the time away, to browse. The grandmother of a teenager visiting my daughter once said to me: "If the girls want to SHMAY around town in the afternoon, I can pick them up later and take them over to the house." Recently a woman with whom I was exchanging chatter in a local store during a sale ended the conversation with: "You go SHMAY around. I'll see you later."

Cf. IIIA, "shmaychel, shmeikle."

such a TSIMMES; to make a whole TSIMMES

These popular terms regarding a fuss are outgrowths of MACHEN A GANTSEN TSIMMES (Chap. II, Advice, MACH NIT DERFIN KEYN GANTSEN TSIMMES). I remember hearing Perry Como ask on TV, "What are you making such a TSIMMES over it for?"

Such uses are reminiscent of "getting into a stew over it." A TSIMMES, like a stew, takes time to prepare. It's the procedure of long cooking that seems to be involved, of "simmering," "cooking," "boiling"—all expressions which are used figuratively in both languages for a state of annoyance.

That doesn't hurt *my* PUPIK!

Lit., That doesn't hurt *my* belly-button! It doesn't have to concern *me!*

See "Wallenpupik" for "Wallenpaupack."

That's not BOPKES!

That's not beans! That ain't hay!

See Chap. II, Exclam., BOPKES!

There's MAZEL in SHLIMAZEL.

This takes note of the fact that MAZEL (luck) is contained in the word for bad luck and also suggests that there may be some good in the bad luck, as in "Every cloud has a silver lining." (The English "misfortune" is similar, carrying "fortune" within it.)

A recent item being sold in Jewish gift shops is a little ceramic man with YARMULKE and TALIS, named "Mr. Mahzel."

See Chap. II, Destiny, TSUM SHLIMAZEL DARF MEN OYCH HOBN MAZEL.

Cf. Chap. II, Char. and Des., SHLEMIEL.

T.L.

The old euphemism for TOCHES LEKER is sometimes used as a

participle, as in the remark a mother made to me about her son:
"He's T.L.-ing me, so I'll be nice to his girl." (*See* Chap. I,
end of Acronyms; Chap. II, Char. and Des., TOCHES.)

T.O.T.

This old catch-phrase stands for TOCHES OYFN TISH (Arse
on the Table), which was a businessman's snappy rendition
of "Cash on the line." (OYFN is a variant of AFN.) A Pennsylvania proctologist likes to tell his Jewish patients: "Get your
TOCHES on the table." The chuckle puts the patient at ease, and
is actually less vulgar than it may seem in print.[8]
See Chap. II, Char. and Des., TOCHES.

tsuritic *See* IIIA, "tsuris."

TSU whom are you talking, TSU whom?

This humorous question was used by the second generation
to spoof the speech of their parents, who were capable of
coupling super-correctness with a disconcerting retention of Yiddish particles. I was reminded of this when a TV comedian
picked up the careful question that had been addressed to him—
"To whom do you think you're talking?"—and replied, "To
whom? To youm, that's whom."
Cf. IIIA, "to" for "against."

Vat's DI MERE MIT you?

First-generation bilingual rendering of "What's the matter
with you?" (Yiddish vos IZ DER MER MIT DIR?)—often quoted
good-naturedly.

"Very FONYE" for "very funny"

This ironic comment puns on the Russian *fonye* (soldier),
which is also a humorous Yiddish appellation for a Russian.
Two facts encourage the pun: an alternate for *fonye* is *foni*,
and a common pronunciation of "funny" by the first generation
was "fawny." The irony is fed by the fact that a soldier was
anything but funny to the Russian Jew—not only because of
Judaism's emphasis on peace and learning, discussed in Chap. I,
but because the Russian army snapped up young Jewish boys
and kept them in service for years. A famous story by Mendele

jokes about the army's rapacity, telling how two simple-minded
Jewish married men are handed over to the military for a price.
(*See* Chap. II, Char. and Des., ER FIRT IM IN BOD ARAYN.)

    Cf. Chap. II, Char. and Des., FONYE GANEF, under GANEF.

    Similar pronunciation comes through in the joking "My little
honye bonye" for "my little honey bun."

"Wallenpupik" for "Wallenpaupack"

The latter is the name of a large lake in Pennsylvania, which
some of the state's residents and visitors like to call "Wallenpupik." (*See* Chap. II, Food and Drink, PUPIK.)

What are you BALEBOSTEVin' about?

This good-natured question uses a hybrid verb from Yiddish
BALEBOSTEVEN, to bustle, which comes from BALEBOSTE (Chap.
II, Char. and Des.) That noun, by the way, is the feminine
form of BALEBOS, boss, so that it is akin in spirit to "bosslady."

What can you MACH?

    What can you do? (good-natured resignation)

    Cf. Chap. II, Greetings, VOS MACHT IR?

"woof-woof" for OYF-RUF

A young Conservative rabbi told me of the puzzling telephone call in which a congregant spoke of his projected "woof-
woof." The rabbi finally realized he meant OYF-RUF, the calling
up to the Torah. (*See* IIIA, "called up. . . .")

YENTZing (taboo)

This noun meaning a swindle or "trimming" is from the
Yiddish equivalent of the four-letter verb to fornicate, YENTZEN.
It is chiefly heard in businessmen's talk, as in "He gave him a
yentzing." A swindler is a "yentzer"—which is the same as the
Yiddish form.

    The verb is thought to have been spread by rum-runners dur-
ing the days of Prohibition. It was reported from jewelry auctioneering as "yinceth" in 1928. That would seem to be a garbled
rendering of the third-person singular.

Yiddified

An ironic in-group joke is this term for "anti-Semitic" among

English Jews. It puns on Yiddish YIDDENFAYNT (Jew-hate) and dates to the 1930's.

Yiddishbord
This term was used by Las Vegas Hadassah for its gourmet Jewish smorgasbord in 1967.

Yidgin English *See* "Yinglish."

Yinglish
This coined term describes English that contains Yiddish idiom, pronunciation and/or intonation. Witness a parent's expostulation at talkative children: "So enough with the TSHAYNIK HAKing, already! Quiet you can't be for a minute? On Mother's Day, yet!"

Another such term is "Yidgin English"—a play on "Pidgin English."

IV. And Vice Versa: How Yiddish Responds to English

In his introduction to *Royte Pomerantsen,* Immanuel Olsvanger expressed a lovely theory about the "melody of living speech." Each language, he suggested, has its characteristic cadence, which should really be submitted to musical notation to convey its true melody to foreign readers. In *L'Chayim!* he added the observation that an immigrant "soon catches the speech melody of his new surroundings and quickly begins to preconstruct the expression of his thought according to the new rhythm, but in the familiar words of his mother tongue; wherever the old words do not fit the new rhythm, he substitutes words of the new language."

This at least partly explains what has happened to Yiddish in its encounter with American English. There has been, first, a tendency toward translation of American phrases into the mother tongue—i.e., CHAPEN A KOLT (to catch a cold), MACHEN A LEBN (to make a living), UPRUFN (to call up), KURTZ IN GELT (short in funds), etc. Over thirty-five years ago this tendency toward translation had already shown rather striking effect. Dr. Max Weinreich pointed out in the *Forward* that the idiom VOS MEYNT DOS (What does that mean?) had replaced VOS HEYST DOS? and VOS IZ DAYN NOMN? (What is your name?) had supplanted VI HEYSTU? (Indeed, as he reported, these changes were then even evident in European Yiddish, picked up from the American.) Other changes were noted by Dr. Judah A. Joffe in *YIVO BLETER* and the *Universal Jewish Encyclopedia*, such as ICH BIN HEYS (I am hot) for MIR IZ HEYS;

EYB IR ZET IM (if you see him) for EYB IR VET IM ZEYEN; A VOCH FUN MONTIK (a week from Monday) for IBER A VOCH MONTIK; etc.

The translations have sometimes been incomplete, as in "FARN benefit FUN" (for the benefit of), "NEMEN A VOK" (to take a walk), "MACHEN A SPITSH" (to make a speech), "MACH UP DAYN mind" (make up your mind). In some of these, there is no exact equivalent for the English word that has been retained—just as there are none for the numerous adoptions like "subway," "movies," "politician," "campaign," etc. But with NEMEN A VOK the speaker is forsaking not only the Yiddish GEYN SHPATSIREN (to go walking) but the possibility of NEMEN A SHPATSIR. This new hybrid NEMEN A VOK may be explainable by Olsvanger's theory of the "old words not fitting the new rhythm," but it is the kind of usage that hurts the ear of a purist—almost as much as does the hybrid-slang "GEBN A call" when it displaces the colloquial translation UPRUFN!

In some instances, as Dr. J. H. Neumann has noted, the existent Yiddish may not be clear-cut, offering a choice of various terms from Hebrew, German, Russian, etc., which may not have quite the same tone as the American (as with the word "jail," for instance), and the American term may simplify matters. But in many other cases of American terms displacing Yiddish ones, no explanation is likely to satisfy a conscientious Yiddishist. Take EFN DI VINDE for "Open the window." Is not FENSTER, we are asked, still a good word? Or take BETVIN (between), which so often replaces TSVISHEN, or APSTEZ (upstairs) in place of OYVN or AROF, or HET and HETKE (hat) instead of HUT, etc. Are these "really Yiddish"?

Milton Berle is supposed to have been asked some years ago for the Yiddish equivalent of "disappointed" and to have called his mother long distance to find it out. He told her that his planned trip from California to New York would have to be postponed, and she exclaimed, "OY, MILTELE, ICH BIN AZOY disahpointet!" Yiddish does have a word that Mrs. Berle could have used—ANTOYSHT—but like most American Jewish speakers of Yiddish, she was more inclined to use the American term.

When Harry Kemelman's best-selling mystery story *Saturday the Rabbi Went Hungry* ran in translation in New York's Yiddish daily *The Day-Journal*, I was surprised to see that the title was given as *SHABBES HOT DER RABAY GEHUNGERT*.

Why, I wondered, wasn't it . . . *DER ROV* . . . or . . . *DER REBBE* . . . ? If Yiddish already had two words for "rabbi," why should the American term be borrowed? But the explanation is not really hard to find. First of all, there is a world of difference in the connotations of ROV, REBBE and "rabbi," as noted earlier (Chap. II, Rel. and Cul.). Secondly, "rabbi" is itself derived from the same Hebrew root as ROV and REBBE and so the three terms have a HEYMISHE relationship linguistically. Thirdly, Yiddish has been doing this kind of thing for ages—just as have other tongues. English has a palmful of terms for an ecclesiastic, from Greek and Latin: "minister," "pastor," "cleric," "clergyman," etc.

Why not, then, a new term for ROV or REBBE, especially when it refers, as in the book in question, to the new American species of the rabbinical breed?

This kind of borrowing—frowned upon though it may be by purists—represents an inevitable linguistic process, from which at least some examples usually become "acceptable" in time. Whether the motivating influence is one of "speech melody" or merely the frequency of usage in the new language, or any other factor or combination of factors, probably does not matter. The lack of logic involved is well illustrated by "boy" and "girl." While "boy" has for some time been taking the place of INGEL *or* YINGEL (Chap. II, Family), "girl" has shown no signs of competing with the still general MEYDEL—perhaps, as has been suggested, because MEYDEL is reinforced by English "maid."

You may have noticed that in a number of borrowings mentioned, the pronunciation changes: "walk" becomes VOK; "window" becomes VINDE; "upstairs" becomes APSTEZ. One such transformation that the third generation has a certain fondness for is that of "Yankee" to YENKE. A young Conservative rabbi in Connecticut told me chucklingly of the comment that an elderly member of his congregation made at SHUL when the early morning MINYEN was breaking up and the "second MINYEN" was arriving: "OT KUMEN DI YENKES!" ("Here come the Yankees!")[1]

Besides the outright borrowing of words, Yiddish is prone to the partial loan: an English word is taken and added to in some way. With nouns, it may add an extra letter, as in PEYNTNER from "painter." (This term has been subject to much reminiscing, from *Commentary* magazine to Alan Sherman's parodying folk song, "When the Paintners Come Marching In.") In some instances, as in the fondly quoted HENGLISH—a kind of Yiddish Cockney for "English"—it adds a letter while also changing the vowel sound. In PRETSENT for "per cent," it transposes the "e" and "r" and changes the "c" to "ts." (The former interchange, which turned "per" into "pre," is presumably the kind of thing that inspired the joking VATS DI MATTRE, mentioned in Chap. I, Twin Forms.)

Yiddish freely tacks on suffixes like -TSHIK (MILYONTSHIK: a millionaire); -NIK (feminine, -NIKE) in such terms as B'NEY B'RISNIK (a person active in B'nai B'rith) or "nogoodnik," discussed in the preceding chapter; -KE (DRESSKE); -IGE or -IKE (NEKSDORIGE—the lady next door); -L or -EL (VEYSTEL—waist, blouse); -LE or -ELE (BEYBILE — little baby).[2]

In plurals, the English "s" may be drawn out, as in TOYESS. In other cases, a Yiddish plural ending is utilized in the adopted word, as in FORLAYT for "foremen" or POLI(T)SLAYT for "policemen"—the latter also occasionally containing an extra letter.

Or see what is done with verbs. Yiddish may take an English root and tack on an ending, as in ER MUZ STAPN SMUKN (He must stop smoking). In the future tense, it also adds the appropriate verbal auxiliary, as in ZI VET ES TSHARJEN (She will charge it). In the past tense, it may retain an English word unchanged, as in "ICH BIN GEGANGEN shopping" (I went shopping), or it may attach a Yiddish prefix to the English past form, as in ICH HOB GEVATSHT TV (I watched TV). It may even tack on two prefixes, as in ZI HOT ZICH OYSGEFIKST (She fixed herself up; i.e., She's feeling better).

This last usage gives new meaning to the English "fix." A similar change occurs with the term "boy," which takes on the meaning of "unmarried" in ER IZ NOCH A BOY (He is still a boy). Or notice the change in the adjective "next," which becomes a noun, equivalent to "turn," in VART FAR DAYN NEKST (Wait for your next).[3]

Delightful are the occasional verbs that grow out of adopted nouns, like BIZNEVEN from "business" or SPITSHEVEN from "speech." (ZEY HOBN GESPITSHEVET means "They made speeches," i.e., There were speakers on the program.) Especially charming are formations like OYSGEMITINGT, which means "all meetinged out"—i.e., how you feel after four days in a row of PTA, Girl Scouts, Hadassah and Sisterhood! An element of good nature seems to creep into these new terms—something distinctively Yiddish. In a small way it is like the flavor of the irreplaceable verbs like FARBLONJEN ("to lose one's way" seems so pale beside it!) or BURTSHEN, which somehow connotes a little more than "mutter," or FONFEVEN, for "talking through the nose."

More colorful, perhaps, is the practice of bilingual punning, discussed in Chap. I. A typical quip is the characterization of a demanding wife as "Mrs. VANTZ (Bedbug)," because NOR ZI VANTS (She only wants—i.e., "All she knows is 'Gimme' ").

The whole process of Yiddish borrowing from American English began over two hundred years ago. The mid-eighteenth-century business letters of the Gratz brothers, earliest published examples of written American Yiddish, contained such expressions as ICH HOB GETRAYIT (I tried). (This is still heard and doesn't seem to conflict with the fact that GETRAY and GETRAYE have other meanings.)

In 1938, a study of the usage of New York's then three leading Yiddish dailies showed how widely English loans were being made in modern Yiddish. In the advertising pages about twenty per cent of the words were loans, and in the smaller types of ads usually placed by individuals—reflecting quite informal usage—as many as twenty-eight per cent of the words were English loans. In the years since then, the borrowing has certainly continued and if anything would seem to have increased, as any listener of New York's Yiddish station WEVD can testify. With the immigration of Yiddish-speaking Jews remaining virtually cut off, the existent Yiddish-using population is more and more exposed to American English. The first part of H. B. Wells's prediction in *American Speech* over thirty-five years ago may possibly be in process: ". . . American Yiddish will within a very few years lose its identity, at least as Judeo-German" and "will turn into Judeo-English. . . ."[4]

Small wonder, then, that American Yiddish journalistic writing—as well as speech—should so often give one a feeling of breakage. As Yiddish itself puts it, ER TSUHARGET DI SHPRACH (He's murdering the language). What is fascinating, though, is that this very Yiddish comment makes use of a hybrid verb, combining a Hebrew root and German prefix and suffix! Contrariwise, I once heard a Brooklyn woman speak a fascinating broken English, which appeared to develop chiefly from adding Yiddish endings to English verbs, as in "Vy you dunt taket a nap? Di baby sleepet already." (Pennsylvania German shows similar effects in forms like "outen the light.")

Whatever be the future of Yiddish in America—one recent prediction gave it another hundred years[5]—it is certainly not doomed because of its linguistic borrowings. Borrowings alone do not kill off a language, as evidenced by the heavily hybrid character of the American language itself. In the late nineteenth century Yiddish writers in this country attempted to "purify" the language by Germanizing it. Their efforts never took root. As linguists have often pointed out, no living language can be "ruled" by decree. It is what "comes naturally" that guides human speech; what one generation considers unforgivable usage may be the accepted standard of another. This does not imply that any concern about standards in Yiddish is not warranted; but rather that the application of standards, in Yiddish no less than in English, requires an eye with a long view. And for the Jew, accustomed to thinking in terms of millennia, that is perhaps only to be expected.

V. For More than a Taste:
Selected Reading and Records

ABOUT THE PEOPLE WHO MADE THE
LANGUAGE WHAT IT IS

Life Is with People. Mark Zborowski and Elizabeth Herzog, New York: International Universities Press, 1952; Schocken Paperback, 1962. A re-creation of life in the East European SHTETL, from the viewpoint of anthropology, on the basis of nostalgic interviews with SHTETL graduates and their descendants in New York.

Voices of a People; the Story of Yiddish Folk Song. Ruth Rubin, New York: Thomas Yoseloff, 1962. A documented history, presenting individual songs as a reflection of Jewish life.

A Treasury of Jewish Folklore. Nathan Ausubel, New York: Crown, 1948.

The Jews: their History, Culture and Religion. Louis Finkelstein, ed., New York: Harper, 1949, 4 vols.; 1960, 2 vols. Due out in paperback.

Introductions to *A Treasury of Yiddish Stories* and *The Golden Tradition* (both listed below under "Yiddish in Translation"). These summarize the religious and intellectual currents among European Jewry of the eighteenth and nineteenth centuries.

Yiddish Literature: Its Scope and Major Writers. Charles A. Madison, New York: Frederick Ungar, 1968. A comprehensive survey, including a brief account of the development of the language and two bibliographies.

The World of Sholem Aleichem. Maurice Samuel, New York: Alfred A. Knopf, 1943; New York, Schocken Paperback, 1965. An appreciative discussion of the characters and their setting, and the language of the Yiddish writer.

The Ghetto. Louis Wirth, Chicago: University of Chicago Press, 1928, 1956; Chicago, Phoenix Books Paperback, 1956. A famous and highly readable sociological study of American Jewish immigrants, with special reference to Chicago and in relation to their European roots.

The Spirit of the Ghetto. Hutchins Hapgood, illus. by Jacob Epstein, Cambridge, Mass.: Harvard University Press, 1902; ed. and with introd. and notes by Moses Rischin, 1967. This informal study of the early immigrant Jews of New York's Lower East Side represents the sympathetic and colorful observations of a resident "outsider." A somewhat similar study was made of Polish Jews at about the same time, by a Gentile woman in their midst (Beatrice C. Baskerville, *Polish Jews*, New York: Macmillan, 1906), but that study was far from sympathetic.

Another new edition of Hapgood, with preface and notes by Harry Golden, New York: Funk and Wagnalls, 1965, is also available as a Schocken Paperback.

YIDDISH IN TRANSLATION

Short Fiction

A Treasury of Yiddish Stories. Irving Howe and Eliezer Greenberg, eds., illus. by Ben Shahn, New York: Viking, 1953; New York: Compass Books, 1965; abridged edition, Greenwich, Conn.: Fawcett, 1968.

The Old Country. Sholem Aleichem, trans. by Julius and Frances Butwin, New York: Crown, 1946; reprinted in large measure in *Selected Stories*, Sholem Aleichem, with introd. by Alfred Kazin, New York: Modern Library, 1956; incl. as vol. 1 of boxed *Collected Stories of Sholem Aleichem*, illus. by Ben Shahn, Crown, 1965, vol. 2 being *Tevye's Daughters*, trans. by Frances Butwin, Crown, 1946. A selection from both these volumes makes up *The Tevye Stories and Others*, New York: Pocket Books, 1965.

Some Laughter, Some Tears. Sholem Aleichem, trans. by Curt Leviant, New York: G. P. Putnam's, 1968; Paperback Library, 1969.

The Travels and Adventures of Benjamin the III. Mendele Mocher Sforim, trans. by Moshe Spiegel, New York: Schocken, 1949, 1968.

In This World and the Next; Selected Writings. I. L. Peretz, trans. by Moshe Spiegel, New York: Thomas Yoseloff, 1958. Includes an appendix of essays about Peretz by Sholem Asch and others.

Restless Spirit; Selected Writings. Zalman Shneour, trans. by Moshe Spiegel, New York: Thomas Yoseloff, 1963. Includes selections from his novel *Noah Pandra*.

Items in *A Treasury of Jewish Humor*. Nathan Ausubel, Garden City, New York: Doubleday, 1951; New York, Paperback Library, 1967.

Short Friday and Other Stories. Isaac Bashevis Singer, New York: Farrar, Straus & Giroux, 1966.

The Book of Paradise; the Wonderful Adventures of Shmuel Aba Abervo. Itzik Manger, trans. by Leonard Wolf, illus. by Mendel Reif, New York: Hill & Wang, 1965. A merry spoof by a famous Yiddish poet of the legend that babies inhabit Paradise before they are born. (In prose, with some light verse.)

Short Fiction: Records

Stories of Sholem Aleichem. Read by Menasha Skulnik, trans. by Charles Cooper. Caedmon (TC 1173). Includes "Happy Millionaire," "A Matter of Advice," "It's a Lie," "Chanukah & Pinochle" and "High School."

I. B. Singer Reading "Gimpel the Fool" and "The Man Who Came Back" Caedmon (TC 1200). The first story is from Singer's *Gimpel the Fool and Other Stories*, trans. by Saul Bellow, New York: Farrar, Straus & Giroux; the second from *The Spinoza of Market Street*, trans. by Mirra Ginsburg, New York: Farrar, Straus & Giroux (both collections available in paperback, Avon Books).

See also *The World of Sholem Aleichem* under "Plays: Records" below.

Novels, Plays, Poetry

Fishke the Lame. Mendele Mocher Sforim, trans. by Gerald

Stillman, illus. by Ahron Gelles, New York: Thomas Yoseloff, 1960.

Adventures of Mottel the Cantor's Son. Sholem Aleichem, trans. by Tamara Kahana, illus. by Ilya Schor, New York: Henry Schuman, 1953; New York: Collier Books, 1961.

Three Cities. Sholem Asch, trans. by Edwin Muir, London: Macdonald, 1933, 1955.

The Brothers Ashkenazi. Israel Joshua Singer, New York: Alfred A. Knopf, 1936; Cleveland: World Publishing, Forum Books, 1963; New York: Grosset, Universal Library, 1967.

The Family Moskat. Isaac Bashevis Singer, trans. by A. H. Gross, New York: Alfred A. Knopf, 1950; Noonday Press Paperback, 1965.

The Well. Chaim Grade, trans. by Ruth Wisse, Philadelphia: Jewish Publication Society, 1967.

See also selections from *Noah Pandra* in *Restless Spirit* under "Short Fiction" above.

The Dybbuk and Other Great Yiddish Plays. Ed. and trans. by Joseph C. Landis, New York: Bantam Books, 1966. Contains an introduction dealing with the spirit and scope of Yiddish literature generally and with the development of the Yiddish theatre.

Nine One-Act Plays from the Yiddish. Bessie White, Boston: Humphries, 1932; Boston, Crescendo, 1968.

A Treasury of Yiddish Poetry. Irving Howe and Eliezer Greenberg, eds. New York: Holt, 1969.

Siberia. Abraham Sutzkever, trans. and with introd. by Jacob Sonntag, with a letter and drawings by Marc Chagall, New York: Abelard-Schuman, 1961. (UNESCO Collection of Contemporary Works.)

See also poems in *Restless Spirit* under "Short Fiction" above, items containing translations under "Yiddish in Transliteration" below, and bilingual items under "To Learn the Language, To Read and Write" below.

Plays: Records
The World of Sholem Aleichem. Tikva (T-28). Dramatic versions, written by Arnold Perl, of Sholem Aleichem's "High School," of Peretz's "Bontshe Shvayg" and of a famous Chelm tale. With musical background.

Tevya and His Daughters. Columbia (OL 5225). A play by Arnold Perl, first produced in New York in 1957, based on Sholem Aleichem's stories. This play in turn provided the basis for the more recent musical production, *Fiddler on the Roof*.

Non-fiction

The Golden Tradition; Jewish Life and Thought in Eastern Europe. Lucy S. Dawidowicz, ed., New York: Holt, 1967; Beacon Press Paperback, 1968. Memoirs and letters, most of them translated from Yiddish by the editor and others.

Nationalism and History; Essays on Old and New Judaism. Simon Dubnow, ed. and with introd. by Koppel S. Pinson, Philadelphia: Jewish Publication Society, 1958; New York: Meridian Books; Cleveland: World, 1961.

The Inner Eye; Selected Essays. Hayim Greenberg, New York: Jewish Frontier Association, 1953, 1964, 2 vols.

One Destiny; an Epistle to the Christians. Sholem Asch, trans. by Milton Hindus, New York: G. P. Putnam's, 1945.

Homecoming at Twilight. Jacob Glatstein, trans. by Norbert Guterman, foreword by Maurice Samuel, New York: Thomas Yoseloff, 1962. A beautifully written account, with undertones of prophetic sadness, of a visit to Poland on the eve of World War II. (The only translated volume of a Yiddish trilogy.)

Anthology of Holocaust Literature. Jacob Glatstein, Israel Knox and Samuel Margoshes, eds. Philadelphia: Jewish Publication Society, 1968. An important, comprehensive collection of writings about the Nazi holocaust, under the following headings: Occupation, Actions, Selections; Life in the Ghettos; Children; Concentration and Death Camps; Resistance; The Non-Jews. Includes prose and poetry from other languages, though Yiddish is the major source, trans. by Moshe Spiegel, Joseph Leftwich and other well-known hands. Contains a glossary and brief biographies of the more than fifty authors.

See also bibliographies in *Yiddish Literature* by Madison under "About the People . . ." above or *Yiddish Literature in English Translation* (Books Published 1945-67), comp. by Dina Abramowicz, YIVO Institute for Jewish Research, 1048 Fifth Ave., New York 10028. Valuable guides to the many English translations of Sholem Aleichem and Peretz are to be found in "Literary Bibliographies," Pts. 2 and 3, by Uriel Weinreich, in *The Field of Yiddish*, Linguistic Circle of New York, 1954, pp. 285-88 and 292-96.

YIDDISH IN TRANSLITERATION
(in English—i.e., Roman—Alphabet)

ROYTE POMERANTSEN. Immanuel Olsvanger, New York: Schocken Books, 1947.

L'CHAYIM! Immanuel Olsvanger, New York: Schocken Books, 1949.

Two little volumes of Yiddish wit, reflecting the characteristic irony, intonation and "super-climax" of Jewish humor.

Yiddish Proverbs. Hanan J. Ayalti, ed., New York: Schocken Paperback, 1963. Rendition of selections from the monumental Yiddish compilation of Ignaz Bernstein (Frankfort on the Main, 1908), with translations by Isidore Goldstick.

Onions and Cucumbers and Plums (poetry anthology). Sarah Zweig Betsky, Detroit: Wayne State University Press, 1958. (With translations.)

Selected Poems. Isaac E. Rontch, illus. by Marc Chagall, with translations by Ira Mark, Max Rosenfeld and Ruth Rubin, New York: Alliance Books, 1961.

GUT YUNTIF, GUT YOHR (light verse). Marie B. Jaffe, New York: William-Frederick Press, 1966; Citadel Press, 1969.

Songs of Our People. Samuel Bugatch, New York: Farband Book Publishing Association, 1961.

Jewish Folk Songs in Yiddish and English. Ruth Rubin, ed., with guitar accompaniments by Ethel Raim, New York: Oak, 1965. (With English adaptations.)

See also *Voices of a People* and Part Six, "Songs and Dances," of *A Treasury of Jewish Folklore*, both listed under "About the People . . ." above.

TO LEARN THE LANGUAGE

To Speak

Invitation to Yiddish (2 records and 111-page manual). Yudel Mark, New York: Commission on Jewish Affairs, American Jewish Congress, 1962. Instruction from a world-renowned authority. Presents a conversation of four family members, utilizing everyday vocabulary but also giving insights into Jewish history and culture. Manual contains alphabet and pronouncing guide, and gives Yiddish, transliteration and English.

Say It in Yiddish (phrase booklet). Uriel and Beatrice Weinreich, New York: Dover, 1958. Common expressions classified for easy reference, chiefly for travelers. Booklet contains alphabet and pronouncing guide, with English, Yiddish and transliteration. Though the late Dr. Weinreich worked closely with YIVO (see his books under "To Read and Write" below), the spelling system used here differs from YIVO's (and Mr. Mark's in the preceding item) for several sounds.

Yiddish; Conversa-phone's Round-the-World Language Record Course (record and 16-page booklet). New York: Conversa-phone Institute (CX-156), 1961. The spelling system in the booklet is a little inconsistent and does not properly differentiate between certain sounds, but listening carefully to the record, repeating its phrases, and marking the booklet for your own guidance could possibly overcome these defects. Booklet contains the alphabet, with English, Yiddish and transliteration.

Instant Yiddish. Fred Kogos, New York: Tikva (T 114), undated. Similar in coverage to the Conversa-phone record, offering simple vocabulary for travelers, this uses two voices. The accompanying booklet (published before the record) has a number of inaccuracies. This means you would have to spend a good deal of time listening and marking the booklet to conform with the record before you could use it properly.

To Read and Write
Manual in *Invitation to Yiddish* under "To Speak" above.

Yiddish for Beginners. Jean B. Jofen, New York: Committee for Yiddish in the High Schools, Jewish Education Committee, 1960; 2d edition 1962, available from the author, 1684 52nd St., Brooklyn, N. Y. 11204 ($1.50).

College Yiddish. Uriel Weinreich, New York: YIVO Institute for Jewish Research, 1949; 4th revised edition 1966 ($4.75).

Modern English-Yiddish Yiddish-English Dictionary. Uriel Weinreich, ed., New York: McGraw-Hill and YIVO, 1968 ($18).

When you think you are ready, try reading some of the publications that provide both Yiddish and English, so that you can help yourself when you get stuck. A simple place to start is the inserts provided with some of the Yiddish records listed below, under "To Enjoy in the Original." Begin with an easy one like that in Theodore Bikel's *More Jewish Folksongs*, and go on to harder ones like that in the *Sholem Aleichem* record read by Gustav Berger. Then you can try some like the one in the *Jewish Classical Literature* record read by Chaim Ostrowsky, which omits the translation and provides only a brief English preface to the Yiddish text. You also can practice on text in some of the song books published by the Metro Music Company, available in most music stores.

Another useful item at this stage is *Gleanings from Yiddish Literature*, a new experimental reader developed at Brandeis University (available from Brandeis's Department of Contemporary Jewish Studies, Waltham, Mass., $2).

Several recent books containing Yiddish plus English are: *Symbol and Substance* by Leibush Lehrer, trans. by Lucy S. Dawidowicz, with an appreciation by Aaron Zeitlin, New York: 1965 (31 pp.); *An Anthology of Modern Yiddish Poetry*, trans. by Ruth Whitman, New York: October House, 1966; *Ghetto Factory 76*, poem by Rachmil Bryks, trans. by Theodor Primack and Eugen Kullman, foreword by I. B. Singer, illus. by Raphael Soyer, New York: Bloch, 1967.

Two earlier books providing both languages, and available in libraries, are: *Modern Yiddish Poetry*, ed. by Samuel J. Imber, New York: East and West Publishing Company, 1927 (with translations in prose); *Peretz*, ed. and trans. by Sol Liptzin, New York: Yiddish Scientific Institute-YIVO, 1947.

If you can manage some of these, you can handle a Yiddish newspaper like *DER TOG-ZHURNAL* (*The Day-Journal*, 183 East Broadway, New York 10002) or *DI FORVERTS* (*The Forward*, 175 East Broadway, New York 10002). For magazines, try *YUGNTRUF*, a quarterly journal addressed to high-school and college students (3328 Bainbridge Ave., New York 10467) or *TSUKUNFT* (25 East 78th St., New York 10021), a monthly sponsored by the Congress for Jewish Culture and the Central Yiddish Culture Organization (CYCO).

Other Yiddish magazines reflect the variety of occupation

and ideology to be found in the first generation, involving different conceptions of religion, peoplehood and even of Zionism. Most of those in the United States and Canada are listed in the annual *American Jewish Year Book* (New York: American Jewish Committee; Philadelphia, Jewish Publication Society). Others, on this continent and elsewhere around the globe, are listed in the *Jewish Press of the World*, comp. by Josef Fraenkel (World Jewish Congress, 15 East 84th St., New York 10028, $1.25). Of particular quality are Argentina's *DAVKE* (Montes de Oca 1275, Buenos Aires) and Israel's *DI GOLDENE KEYT* (P. O. Box 303, Tel Aviv), both quarterlies.

TO ENJOY IN THE ORIGINAL

Books
ANTHOLOGIE FUN DER YIDDISHER LITERATUR FAR DER YUGNT. Y. Zilberberg and Yudel Mark, eds. Congress for Jewish Culture (25 East 78th St., New York 10021), 1969 ($5). A useful anthology for the new reader.

MOTTEL PEYSE DEM CHAZENS. Sholem Aleichem, *ALEH VERK*, vols. 18-19, New York: Folksfond, 1917-25; abridged edition, 1946.

MOTKE GANEF. Sholem Asch, New York: FORVERTS, 1916; *GEZAMELTE SHRIFTEN,* vol. 11, New York: Sholem Asch Committee, 1921.

MAYNE KINDER YOREN. Peretz Hirshbein, Warsaw; LITERARISHE BLETER, 1935; *VERK,* vol. 1, New York, Los Angeles: Peretz Hirshbein Books Committee, 1951.

VEN POYLEN IZ GEFALEN. Joseph Opatoshu, New York: Central Yiddish Culture Organization (CYCO), 1943.

YIDDISHER HUMOR UN YIDDISHE LEYTZIM. B. J. Bialostotzky, New York: CYCO, 1963.

See also *GEKLIBENE YIDDISHE BICHER FAR AYER BIBLIOTEK* (*Selected Yiddish Books for Your Library*), Jewish Book Council of America (145 East 32d St., New York, 1954, 5¢) and subsequent issues of the *Jewish Book Annual* (published by the same Council) or reviews in the Literary Section of the monthly *JWB Circle* (National Jewish Welfare Board, same address). Catalogs of the Bloch Publishing Company (31 West 31st St., New York) or Farlag Matones (22

East 17th St., New York) list current items of various publishers.

A recent extensive compilation of books and periodicals is *100 YOR MODERNE YIDDISHE LITERATUR (100 Years of Modern Yiddish Literature)*, Workmen's Circle (175 East Broadway, New York 10002), 1965.

An intriguing place to browse is the several volumes issued to date of the all-Yiddish dictionary edited by Judah A. Joffe and Yudel Mark, *GROYSER VERTERBUCH FUN DER YIDDISHER SHPRACH*, New York: Yiddish Dictionary Committee, 1961-. Also worth while for language buffs are Nahum Stutchkoff's thesaurus *DER OYTSER FUN DER YIDDISHER SHPRACH*, New York: YIVO, 1950, and the magazine *YIDDISHE SHPRACH,* issued irregularly by YIVO.

If your public library does not have what you want, ask the librarian to get it through inter-library loan. Most good-sized city libraries have at least some Yiddish titles. In a number of cities Yiddish works are also available at college and university libraries (which also have inter-library loan systems)—in New York, for example, Columbia University and City College; in Boston, Harvard and Brandeis; in Philadelphia, Gratz College and Dropsie College. Cincinnati has the library of the Hebrew Union College, which has branches in Los Angeles and New York. New York also has collections of other Jewish bodies: YIVO, Jewish Education Committee, Jewish Teachers' Seminary, Yeshiva University, Jewish Theological Seminary. Yiddish books are also available at some campus Hillel Foundation libraries and at some synagogues and Jewish community centers.

Yiddish books may be purchased from the Educational Department of the Workmen's Circle (175 East Broadway, New York 10002) as well as from the publishers noted above.

See also note at end of Records list below *re.* recordings of Yiddish books available to the blind.

Magazines   See "To Learn the Language, To Read and Write" above.

Records: Songs
Jewish Folk Songs. Mark Olf, accompanying himself on the

guitar. (With texts and trans.) Folkways 10″ (FP 6826).

Theodore Bikel Sings More Jewish Folk Songs. (With texts, transliterations and translations.) Elektra (EKL 165).

Jewish Folk Songs of Europe. Raasche, folk singer, with mandolin, balalaika and guitar accompaniment. (With texts and trans.) Folkways (FW 8712). Also includes some Hebrew and Ladino songs.

Jewish Melodies. The famed Sidor Belarsky, basso. (With English synopses.) Artistic Enterprises (B 106).

Mordecai Hershman Sings Folk Songs of the SHTETL. (With texts.) Collector's Guild (CG 614). A reissue of selections from old 78's by the famous cantor.

Songs of the Baal Shem: Chasidic Melodies. Collector's Guild (CGL 637).

Lazar Weiner Songs, Musical Settings of Yiddish Poetry. Bianca Sauler, soprano, with composer at the piano. Available from Naomi Smith, 310 West 97th St., New York 10021 ($5.50). Choice art songs by a distinguished musicologist, utilizing work of sixteen Yiddish poets.

Isa Kremer Sings Yiddish Folk Songs. Collector's Guild (CGY 604). (With texts and transliterations.) Reissue of an old disc by a renowned interpreter of Yiddish folk song.

Nekhama Lifshitz Sings the Songs of Her People in the U.S.S.R. Collector's Guild (CG 634). (With explanatory notes.) The famous song bird of the Soviet Union, now an Israeli, who recently toured the United States.

Jewish Children's Songs and Games. Ruth Rubin, accompanied by Pete Seeger on the banjo. (With texts.) Folkways 10″ (FC 7224).

DOS GOLDENE LAND. Workmen's Circle (WC 004). A warm documentary in song of American Jewish immigrant experience, comp. by Joseph Mlotek, narrated by Himan Brown, sung by Miriam Kressyn, Louis Danto, Mort Freeman and others.

Songs of the Ghettos. Louis Danto, tenor. Da Vinci (D 201).

See also *A List of 55 Recommended Yiddish Records* compiled by Eleanor G. Mlotek, Educational Department of the Workmen's Circle (address given at end of Books listing above).

Records: Stories, Theatre, Poetry

Isaac Bashevis Singer Reading His Stories in Yiddish: "Big & Little," "Shidda and Kuziba," "The Man Who Came Back." Caedmon (TC 1202). The first of these appears in English in Singer's *Short Friday* listed under "Yiddish in Translation, Short Fiction" above; the last is read in English on the record in the same category, "Short Fiction: Records."

SHOLEM ALEICHEM. Read in Yiddish by Gustav Berger: "Mr. Green HOT A Job," "A MAYSE MIT A Greenhorn," "DER DAYTSH." Folkways (FL 9907).

SHOLEM ALEICHEM DIR, AMERIKE. Molly Picon and Jewish People's Chorus of New York, Tikva (T 44). A folk-operetta based on *MOTTEL PEYSE DEM CHAZENS* listed under Books above.

FIDLER OYFN DACH. Samuel Rudenski and others, Columbia (OL 6650). A Yiddish version of Broadway's *Fiddler on the Roof*, recorded in Israel. (See *Tevya and His Daughters* under "Yiddish in Translation, Plays: Records" above.)

Ida Kaminska and Her Yiddish State Theatre of Poland. Bruno (BR 50196). Selections from *DER DIBBUK* by S. Anski, *MIRELE EFROS* by Jacob Gordin, etc. An old recording of a new American.

Jewish Classical Literature. Read by Chaim Ostrowsky: "NACHES FUN DI KINDER" by Sholem Aleichem; "ALEF BEYZ" by Sholem Stern, "CHASSIDIM" by A. Lutzky, "DER KUNTSEN MACHER" by I. L. Peretz, "DER AMERIKANER" by Sholem Asch. (With Yiddish texts and brief English introductions.) Folkways (FL 9945).

Poetry of Abraham Sutzkever. Folkways (9947). The eminent "Vilna Poet," editor of Israel's *DI GOLDENE KEYT*, reading thirteen of his poems. (With Yiddish texts and commentary by Ruth Wisse.)

See also current issues of the Schwann LP catalog, available from large record dealers (60¢) and catalogs of Bloch Publishing Company or Farlag Matones (mentioned under Books above). Discontinued discs can often be obtained from Metro Music Company (54 Second Ave., New York 10003).

A word of caution: Try to hear a record if possible before purchasing it. In some cases neither the title nor the jacket is a proper representation of its contents. One offering is billed as

Sholem Aleichem: If I Were Rothschild, but it is essentially a collection of Yiddish art songs with this one monologue thrown in. The jacket misleadingly carries a picture of a young boy, for whose age group both the songs and the monologue seem inappropriate. (The same can be said of translations: Howard da Silva has a disc entitled *An Evening with Sholem Aleichem*, but it is a recording of a performance which also includes—as though Sholem Aleichem could not stand by himself—modern comic material, which jars the mood.) Be wary especially of the cheap and vulgar productions that are dressed up with misleading titles like *Twentieth Century Yiddish Humor*. 'SIZ AZ ACH UN VEY.

Note: The Jewish Braille Institute (48 East 74th St., New York 10021) has Yiddish recordings which it mails on loan to the blind on request. (These travel in postage-free containers.)

For other useful information on Yiddish materials, organizations, camps, etc., see *Guidelines for a Yiddish Club* by Maurice M. Rosenthal (P. O. Box 637, Corrales, New Mexico 87048), 1968 ($3).

Notes

PREFACE

[1] The Yiddish expressions discussed in Chap. I are not listed under the classifications of Chap. II unless there is some additional comment to be made about them.

[2] Cross-referencing is not as complete as it would be in a dictionary. Within the same section, if two expressions are related, the cross-reference usually appears at only one of the terms, on the premise that you will be reading the entire section and would not welcome repetition.

[3] *See* Chap. II, Life and Health.

Chap. I: THE YIDDISH *TAM*

Familiarity with God; Irony

[1] *See* Chap. II, Food and Drink, MILCHIK, *re.* the humor involved in the name.

[2] *See also* Chap. II, Destiny, FUN ZAYN MOYL, IN GOTS OYER.

[3] *See* Chap. II, Family, CHOSSEN, KALEH *and* SHADCHEN.

I was fascinated to notice, at the Jewish Museum in New York, an eighteenth-century inscription for certain Torah headpieces (silver ornamental coverings for the wooden spindles of the scroll): "Presented in honor of the Torah. . . ." Such presentations are usually in honor of or in memory of human beings.

[4] *See also* Chap. II, Rel. and Cul., story under MESHIACH.

[5] The popular "Jehovah" came from *Yhvh* (the original pronunciation of which is uncertain, though it's often rendered as *Yahveh*) plus the vowels from the substitute *Adonoy* or *Adonay*.

[6] The lengths pursued in avoiding God's name may be seen in the name of Hebrew "Arbor Day," *Chamisho Oser b'Shvat*—the fifteenth day of the month of Shvat, the first two words meaning "ten" and "five." The name of this holiday is often rendered as *Tu b'Shvat*. Why? If you take the tenth and fifth letters of the Hebrew alphabet, you get *yod* and *hey,* which are the first two letters of the ancient tetragrammaton for God, *Yhvh.* Therefore, to avoid this, the ninth and sixth letters, *tes* and *melupm-vov* (u), were substituted for the same total of fifteen, making *tu.*

[7] *See* the similar story in Chap. II, Rel. and Cul., DAVENEN.

[8] SHIL is a variant of SHUL.

[9] These words from Psalm 22 were the last words of Jesus.

Concerns about Life and Health; Destiny

[1] *Chayim* is a plural form. The singular is *chay* and is often represented by the letters *ches* and *yod*—as in the gold necklaces and bracelets sold by synagogue gift shops. The numerical values of these letters total eighteen (Hebrew had no numbers but assigned values to the letters of the alphabet), and Jews will frequently make special charitable contributions of $18 to wish a person or a cause well. (But *cf. "chay* KAK" under Vulgarity.)

[2] *See* reference to such use of the latter two terms under Vulgarity.

[3] *See* Chap. II, Exclam.

SUPERSTITION

[1] Such practice, it has been suggested, is reminiscent of the ancient Egyptian custom of confessing sins by denying them.

Realism

[1] *See* Chap. II, Family.

[2] *See* the text under AZ ME KEN NIT ARIBERGEYN, GEYT MEN ARUNTER in Chap. II, Advice.

[3] "Is it such a fast that I have chosen—a day for a man to afflict his soul? . . . Is not this the fast that I have chosen—to loose the bonds of wickedness, to undo the heavy burdens, and to let the oppressed go free, and that ye break every yoke? Is it not to deal thy bread to the hungry, and that thou bring the poor that are cast out to thy house?" Isaiah 58:5–7.

Endearment

[1] The degree of littleness did not end with "nothing." *See* Chap. II, Char. and Des., A KLEYN GORNISHT.

[2] *See also* Chap. IIIB, HAD'YADUDEL!

Word-consciousness

PUNNING

[1] A period of separation for man and wife was specified for the duration of menstruation plus seven days, after which the woman was to visit the ritual bath for purification before coitus (*see* Chap. II, Rel. and Cul., MIKVE). This timed the major coital contact at approximately mid-cycle, which we now know is the fertile period—a fact which the ancient Hebrews may have been able to figure out, to implement the injunction to "be fruitful and multiply." We know too that in many women one of the natural peaks of desire occurs at mid-cycle, so that something can still be said for the discipline, even with contraception. One rabbi-author espouses it as a sure means of preserving the glow of a "marriage made in heaven." However, the formula does not take account of the other common peaks of desire just before and just after the menstrual period. (Orthodox authorities usually advocate that separation begin at least a day before the expected menstruation.)

What is especially fascinating, though, is that in spite of the presumable intention of utilizing sex for propagation, Jewish tradition sanctioned the continuation of sexual relations beyond the menopause and even in cases of infertility. (Divorce could be granted on the grounds of long-term barrenness but it was not prescribed therefor. A precious story tells of the childless woman who visits a rabbi, expressing her concern that she owes her husband a divorce. The rabbi advises her to arrange a party in anticipation of the divorce, and to take home with her from the party her most precious possession. When the time comes, the woman plies her husband with wine until he is in a stupor. She then takes him—her most precious possession —home again with her!)

2 See Chap. II, Rel. and Cul., BRIS.

3 This concerned a YESHIVE BOCHER who wrapped his sexual organ in a page of Talmud. See Chap. IIIA, "I shoulda stood in bed."

4 For a Yiddish-Japanese pun, see Sid Caesar's use of TAKEH METSIEH, under A GANTSE METSIEH, Chap. II, Char. and Des., as well as the somewhat similar "Mitsia Motors" under IIIA, "metsieh."

5 See the similar type of bilingual pun in "Tappan Zee" noted under Chap. IIIB, "Mrs. McKenzie."

6 See last note to Acronyms.

TWIN FORMS

1 In English "egg" of course has slang uses too: "a good egg," "a bad egg," etc. Re. the merged form, cf. Chap. II, Char. and Des., SHMEGEGGE.

RHYME

1 ALEF, AN ADLER—AN ADLER FLIT; BEYZ, A BOYM—A BOYM BLIT; GIMEL, A GALECH— A GALECH KNIT; etc. (ALEF, AN ADLER—an eagle—flies in the air; BEYZ, A BOYM— a tree—blooms so fair; GIMEL, A GALECH—a priest—kneels in prayer; etc.)

2 See Chap. II, Rel. and Cul., MAMME LOSHEN.

ONOMATOPOEIA

1 See A. A. Roback, "Shmoo and Shmo: the Psychoanalytic Implications," Complex, Spring, 1951, p. 5. This article also appears in Roback's Destiny and Motivation in Language (Cambridge, Mass., 1954).

ACRONYMS AND OTHER SHORT-CUTS

1 The making of acrostics is the direct obverse of another practice very common to the rabbis of the Talmud, that is, the finding of words within words. For instance, the Bible speaks of the woman of valor, in Proverbs, as eyshes chayil; and the Talmud notes that the Hebrew letters in chayil represent: ches for chesed, compassion; yod for yira, faith; lamed for limud, learning; hence the valorous woman has compassion, faith and learning.

Or to cite another type of word manipulation: the blessing recited before reading from the Torah contains the word bochar, chosen. The rabbis mused that the same letters put into different positions (anagrams) would yield chaver, friend (in Hebrew "b" and "v" are the same letter) and cherev, sword. Their conclusion: man must choose between the sword and friendship with his fellow man. This sort of thing was carried to great lengths by the adherents of KABOLE (Chap. II, Rel. and Cul.).

2 These forms are close relatives of the earlier term PEY-TSADIK, which reduced the taboo word POTZ or PUTZ to its two consonants. (The euphemism was carried a step further in the term ACHTSIK-NAYNTSIK (eighty-ninety), the numerical equivalents of PEY and TSADIK.)

Taste

1 English puts this positively, in the approving "salt of the earth"—which goes back to the ancient Hebrews. Jesus is quoted as using it in Matthew 5:13.

Learning

1 *See* Chap. II, Char. and Des.

2 *See also* Chap. II, Char. and Des., ER SHRAYBT *Noach* MIT ZIBN GRAYZN, and other expressions under Passing Judgment.

3 *See* the discussion of self-mockery under Tribalism in Chap. II.

4 Another example of a joke with a "super-climax."

Psychological Insight

1 *See also* Chap. II, Family, DI TOCHTER SHTROFT MEN, DI SHNUR MEYNT MEN, under SHNUR.

2 The latter proverb is discussed in the introduction to Passing Judgment, Chap. II.

3 *See also* Chap. II, Rel. and Cul., AFIKEYMEN, *re.* psychological insight involved in holiday observances.

Vulgarity

1 *See also* the compliment on a soup quoted in the introduction to Food and Drink, Chap. II. This was written in Dutch.

2 Two variants are ME TRACHT UN TRACHT/ UN NOCHER BAMACHT MEN (You meditate and speculate,/ Then on yourself you defecate) and M'IZ KLIG UN KLIG, UN AZ S'KUMT TSU EPPES, BAMACHT MEN ZICH (You're smart and smart, and when it comes to something, you do a job on yourself).

3 *See* Eric Partridge, *Dictionary of Slang and Unconventional English,* Fifth Edition (New York, 1961), pp. 877–78.

4 English of course has "sh-t on him" as well as "piss on him." Notice how the former verb is weakened in the bilingual pun quoted in Chap. II, Food and Drink, note to ME SHIT ARAYN.

5 *See also* Chap. II, Food and Drink, ER DREYT ZICH VI A FORTS IN ROSSEL, under ROSSEL.

6 A brother of mine, while writing a recent book, was offered the professional editing services of a New Jersey firm. When he asked what these services would cost, the Jewish executive smilingly answered, "*Chay* KAK."

Russian Jews were of course prone to punning on the innocent Russian adverb *kak* (how).

7 *See* Chap. IIIA, "tokus."

8 *See* Nathan Ausubel, *A Treasury of Jewish Humor* (New York, 1961), p. 381. The term is SHVANTZ or SHVUNTZ, which is referred to by A. A. Roback in "Shmoo and Shmo . . ." cited earlier.

⁹ This is a Germanic spelling (as is that of *"mensch"*). *See* preceding note for a more accurate Yiddish form.

Humor
1 Other self-critical jokes are discussed in Chap. II under Tribalism.

Chap. II: POPULAR TERMS AND EXPRESSIONS

Advice
1 This story pokes fun at the Jews' cosmopolitan tastes in food and recreation (cha-cha, Chinese food, mahjongg). Similar ribbing occurred in an earlier quip about the Chinese restaurant in Chicago that had so many Jewish customers, it started serving pizza and hired a Latin-American band!. It is interesting that Chinese and Italian restaurants often advertise in American Jewish weeklies, and that in most suburban communities with a large Jewish population, the shopping-restaurant areas include one or two Chinese restaurants and a pizza parlor. Indeed, chow mein is commonly served at Bar Mitzvah buffets, particularly by kosher caterers. New York City even has a kosher Chinese restaurant—Schmulka Bernstein's! (In Jerusalem, too, at least one restaurant serves Chinese-Jewish cuisine.) A striking sign of the phenomenon is the recent series of kosher-Chinese, kosher-Italian and kosher-French cookbooks. (*See* Food and Drink, NASH, *re.* "Chinese noshery.")

The Chinese note was climaxed in a *Dayenu* cartoon by Henry Leonard which showed a Chinese restaurant with a sign on its window, "Eat Here during Passover. No bread served." (*See also* Chap. I, Punning, for Chinese-Yiddish anecdotes; stories in notes for Food and Drink, BEYGEL ("BIST OYCH FUN BIALYSTOK?") and Tribalism, introduction ("You don't *look* Jewish!"). It is intriguing that Max Dimont, in his best-selling *Jews, God and History,* suggests that China may be the next center of creative Jewish life if western civilization declines. The folklore is already there!

My own guess, though, is that Japan rather than China may fulfill such a prophecy. Japanese interest in Judaism has been notable in recent years, involving a number of conversions, and there is already at least one congregation led by an American-educated rabbi. Indeed, a fascinating organization in Tokyo is the "Third Civilization Society," which sees an emerging civilization in Japan which will combine the best characteristics of the material civilization of the West and those of the spiritual civilization of ancient Japan, the synthesis to be brought about by the "return" of Jewry to Japan, where, according to the Society's historical studies, both Moses and Jesus had occasion to sojourn in earlier times.

2 SHLAFN and SHLUFN are variants of SHLOFN.

3 *See* Char. and Des., ME FARGINT NIT YENEM.

Annoyance and Argument
1 *See* Char. and Des., ER HOT IM GEGEBN A MISHEBEYRACH.
2 *See* Chap. IV for quip *re.* "MRS. VANTZ."
3 Here is another variety of "super-climax."

Characterization and Description

1 For similar coinings, *see* Chap. I, Special Names.

2 For other deprecating use of the name Jacob, *see* Tribalism, YEKE.

3 *Cf.* Chap. I, Punning, *re.* "putz."

4 *See* Destiny, note to AF MAYNE ERGSTE SONIM . . . *re.* reference to enemies.

5 *See* Rel. and Cul.

6 *See* Chap. I, end of Taste.

7 *See* Chap. I, Superstition.

8 *See* Chap. III, note 4.

9 The spelling used in this book would of course have made it ZEYDE.

10 This is reminiscent of the observation under Destiny, ICH ZOL HANDLEN MIT LICHT, VOLT DI ZUN NIT UNTERGEGANGEN.

11 A similar ironic use of French ending on a Yiddish word is SHAYTÈL (Rel. and Cul.).

12 *See* Family.

13 In each case the blessing would begin as in the HA-MEYTSI (Rel. and Cul.), the last phrase being changed to fit the kind of food being eaten.

14 Another example of the rhyming doublets discussed in Chap. I, Twin Forms.

15 *See* A HIPSHE MEYDEL above.

Death

1 *See* Life and Health, ABI GEZUNT; Chap. I, end of Superstition *and* beginning of Twin Forms.

2 *Cf.* Life and Health, ICH ZOL AZOY LANG LEBN!

3 *See* Rel. and Cul., YONTEF.

Destiny

1 The consciousness of enemies—seen in several expressions in this section—goes back at least to the Twenty-third Psalm: "Thou preparest a table before me in the presence of mine enemies. . . ."

Endearment

1 *See* Chap. I, Famil. with God.

2 *See* Tribalism.

3 As noted in Chap. I, Special Names, this was also a girl's name.

Exclamations and Catch Phrases

1 *See* Ann. and Arg., OYCH (MIR) A. . . !

2 DU is a variant of DO.

3 *See* Chap. I, beginning of Concerns about Life and Health.

4 P. 30.

5 *See also* Chap. I, Rhyme, MENDEL, MENDEL,/ KAKT IN FENDEL.

6 Translation by Emanuel S. Goldsmith.

Family

1 KLOP is a variant of KLAP.

[2] *See* Char. and Des., TSORE.

[3] Samuel has expounded on this phrase in *Prince of the Ghetto* (New York, 1948), pp. 265–66, and also in his review of Saul Bellow's *Herzog*, "My Friend, the Late Moses Herzog," in *Midstream*, April 1966, pp. 12–13.

[4] P. 375.

[5] P. 46.

Food and Drink

[1] *See* Advice, note at end of AZ ME KEN NIT ARIBERGEYN. . . .

[2] *See*, for instance, Advice, CHAP NIT DI LOKSHEN FAR DI FISH *and* MISH NIT OYS KEYN KASHE MIT BORSHT; Passing Judgment, AZ AN OREMAN EST A HUN . . . *and* GIB A BEHEYME A ZAROZE; etc.

[3] *See* Passing Judgment, ZINGN KEN ICH NIT, OBER A MEYVEN BIN ICH.

[4] This is similar to the humor of the question whether Abraham wore a YARMULKE. *See* Rel. and Cul., YARMULKE.

[5] *See* Char. and Des., FUN MELECH SOBIESKIS YOREN.

[6] The invitation on the El Al booklet for interested "bagel scholars" to write to the "Bagel Research Center" of the airlines brought hundreds of letters and thousands of bagel jokes, so that a second edition of the treatise has been issued. A million copies of the first edition had been distributed to passengers by the end of 1965.

[7] *See also* Char. and Des., ZI VEYNT UN BAKT BEYGEL.

[8] This chuckle over the fact that Jews and their influence are to be found everywhere is the basis for many other jokes (including the one about Christmas and Chanuka under Life and Health, A LEBN AF DAYN KEPPELE!). Typical is the story of the Jew from Bialystok who comes to visit the United States and is taken around town by some American co-religionists. They first take him to the top of the Empire State Building, thinking he will be greatly impressed. But he comments, "This we have in Bialystok." They take him to Philharmonic Hall in Lincoln Center, and he declares, "This we also have in Bialystok." The American hosts finally hit on something they think will surely make a dent: a Chinese restaurant. As they sit down, the visitor looks around and remarks, "You know, this we don't have in Bialystok." And the Chinese maitre d', hovering nearby, comes over and asks enthusiastically, "BIST OYCH FUN BIALYSTOK?"—You're from Bialystok too? This joke also refers to the Jewish adoption of Chinese food, *re.* which *see* note to Advice, AZ ME KEN NIT ARIBERGEYN, ...

A Spanish locale appears in the story about the Jewish tourist in Madrid who wants to watch a bullfight but finds that the tickets are sold out. As he wistfully stands near the entrance to the ring, he sees a man go up to the gatekeeper and announce himself: "Picador"; whereupon the gatekeeper waves him in: *"Adelante, adelante!"* (Come in, come in!). In a few minutes he sees a second man approach and present himself: "Matador"; and he too is waved in with *"Adelante, adelante!"* Still a third man appears at the gate and announces: "Toreador"; and the gatekeeper again waves him in with *"Adelante, adelante!"* The tourist then boldly walks over to the attendant and proclaims: "Isidore." The response is: "KUM SHOYN ARAYN!" (Come right in!). In addition to the Jews' ubiquity, this joke further illustrates the "super-climax."

[9] The reference to "navel" is a translation of PUPIK, which *see.*

[10] This is the German spelling.

[11] *See* Rel. and Cul.

12 P. 59.

13 *The American Language,* Supp. I (New York, 1945), p. 607, n. 2; Abridged Edition, Raven I. McDavid, Jr. (New York, 1963), p. 373, n. 3.

14 Slightly easier to say is the conscious punning on the same term in the playful 'SIZ SHVER UN SHITTER for 'SIZ SHVER UN BITTER . . . (Resig.). SHITTER means "loose."

15 For Tevye's complaints about his station in life, *see* Chap. I, Famil. with God.

16 This spelling for TAM is closer to the Hebrew.

17 A character in one of Isaak Babel's stories, noting that God sometimes makes mistakes, asked why the Jews had to be settled in miserable Russia, when a place like Switzerland would have been so much nicer, with fresh air, charming scenery and Frenchmen for neighbors! I suppose he could have added the attractions of good cheese!

Greetings and Partings

1 *See also* story in note to Food and Drink, BEYGEL ("BIST OYCH FUN BIALYSTOK?").

2 *See* the similar incident at end of BEYGEL, Food and Drink, including note.

Imprecation

1 P. 61.

2 P. 34.

Life and Health

1 *Cf.* story in last par. under BEYGEL, Food and Drink.

2 Contrast this with the withholding of compliments on the home-made offerings, under Food and Drink, ES *DARF* ZAYN GUT.

Passing Judgment

1 *See also* Family, A SHLECHT VAYB IZ NOCH TOMID GERECHT.

2 TSAR derives from the same Hebrew word as TSORE (sorrow, trouble). By coincidence the TSAR (czar) of Russia was also a source of sorrow, but the words are unrelated.

3 *See* Rel. and Cul., SHULCHEN-ORUCH.

Religion and Culture

1 More and more Christians are attending Bar Mitzvah services, and I have had several calls the past few years asking whether one should give a gift to the boy and if so what type of gift is customary. I've even been asked by a gift-store proprietress whether Bar Mitzvah and Confirmation are the same thing. She had read about our temple's impending Confirmation service at Shevuoth and was wondering whether one of the three types of Bar Mitzvah card or the one of Bas Mitzvah they stocked would serve as a Confirmation greeting. The answer was no. *See* the rest of this discussion.

2 *See* Passing Judgment.

3 This is the beginning of a prayer for the dead: "God, full of mercy, Who dwells on high, bind up the souls of our departed in the bond of eternal life. . . ."

4 I am indebted for documentation of this incident to Cantor Baruch J. Cohon.

5 P. 28.

[6] P. 277.

[7] P. 291.

[8] *See* Chap. I, beginning of Taste.

[9] *See* MESHIACH; Char. and Des., CHOCHEM, A CHELMER CHOCHEM.

[10] *See* Char. and Des., AF EYN FUS.

[11] The symbol of the fish is of course very old. *See* Chap. I, Acronyms, *re.* Greek acrostic.

[12] *See* Chap. IIIA, "mish mash."

[13] E.g., the problem of aesthetics or of possible male infections, particularly for the uncircumcised.

[14] This is often spelled "rebbitzin" or (theoretically more correctly) "rebbetsin"; but the pronunciation of the vowel in the second syllable usually seems like an "i"—dramatically evident in the jocular form "re-bít-sin," with which I used to be addressed by a dear congregational president in the South.

[15] *See* Chap. I, Acronyms.

[16] P. 43.

Resignation

[1] This second half of the ironic judgment illustrates the "superclimax" discussed in Chap. I.

Tribalism

[1] *See* Chap. I, Twin Forms, p. 47.

[2] In Passing Judgment, a proverb noted that every Jew has his own SHULCHEN-ORUCH and his own kind of lunacy. This recognized the fact that each Jew, in studying religious law, felt free to interpret it according to his own understanding, and also that each Jew had his own idiosyncrasies and was perhaps entitled to them.

[3] *See also* Passing Judgment, VEN ALEH MENTSHEN ZOLN TSIEN AF EYN ZAYT, VOLT ZICH DI VELT IBERGEKERT.

[4] This motif even appears with a Chinese setting. An American traveling in China goes to the synagogue and meets the rabbi, who has a long braid of hair hanging down his back, his head capped with a YARMULKE and his shoulders covered with a TALIS. The visitor tells the rabbi how wonderful it is to find a synagogue in China, and the rabbi asks, "Are you Jewish?" "Of course," the American replies. And the Chinese rabbi exclaims, "You don't *look* Jewish!"

[5] KOYACH is a variant of KEYACH.

[6] *See* song mentioned in Endearment, -ENYU, and story in Food and Drink, FLOMEN.

[7] *See* Char. and Des., BOBBE MAYSE, *re.* "Buber-MAYSES."

[8] *See* the similar incident under Greetings, SHOLEM ALEYCHEM! Also *cf.* note to that item.

[9] *See* Char. and Des., PASKUDNE.

[10] There are of course black Jews, in the United States and elsewhere. Some trace their ancestry to Solomon and the Queen of Sheba.

[11] It may even partly account for the Cockney soldiers' rhyming slurs for a Jew, "four-by-two" and "three-by-two."

[12] *See also* Food and Drink, end of introduction, *re.* "S. S. MAYN KIND!"

[13] *See* Rena Smith Blau, "In Defense of the Jewish Mother," *Midstream*, Feb., 1967, pp. 42–49.

[14] *See* Chap. I, end of Taste.

Chap. III: HOW ENGLISH IS AFFECTED

[1] I am indebted for an account of this incident to Dr. Irving Babow.

[2] *See* Chap. II, Char. and Des., ER VEYST FUN BOPKES.

[3] *See* Chap. II, Rel. and Cul., CHANUKA.

[4] In 1952 Professor Leo Spitzer noted that a secretary at Johns Hopkins had been using this formula constantly in such phrases as "moon-shmoon," "Plato-Shmato" and that after influencing the speech of certain Hopkins faculty and students, she moved to Texas, presumably passing on the lingo in the academic South.

[5] *See* the incident reported in Chap. II, Food and Drink, TSIMMES.

[6] *See* IIIA, "ganef."

Chap. IIIA: THE YIDDISH IS SHOWING

[1] In the fall of 1966, attending the Helen Hayes Theatre in New York, I discovered I had no program and asked a female usher if I could have one. Her response—"Why not?"—was especially striking because of its intonation, which was equivalent to the notes La, Sol. Most Americans, I think, would use the opposite intonation, more closely approximating Fa, Sol. Though I did not inquire into the lady's background, she looked as though she might be Irish, and that might support the statement of Mr. Doyle; but it is also possible that an Irish person in New York would have picked it up from Jewish speech, in which intonation is often La, Re, Fa (Why no-ot?).

Perhaps Pennsylvania German was at work. That dialect tends to start questions on a high note and to end them on a lower one; but whether the questioning reply itself could also be Pennsylvania German I am not certain. (Susan Sontag has reported "Why not?" to be a common response in Sweden.)

[2] *See* Chap. II, Char. and Des., A POR KLUHTZIM.

[3] *Cf.* Chap. IV, note *re.* "I'm an Orthodox. . . ."

[4] This was presumably changed from the YARMULKE which the freedom riders had previously used. *See* Chap. II, Rel. and Cul., YARMULKE.

[5] I am indebted for the clipping to Dr. Marshall D. Berger.

[6] Whether this name is a pseudonym I don't know, but the two words in Yiddish mean "Can Soon" or "Know Soon."

[7] *See* Chap. I, Famil. with God.

[8] This is reminiscent of the cussing in Chap. II, Imprec., A MAKEH IM! as well as of the story under Family, GET.

[9] *See* "Declarative Form in Questions."

[10] *See* Chap. I, Punning, *re.* pun on ALLES SHTEYT IN TALMUD.

[11] This line is related to some extent to the concern about destiny, as in "It should happen to me!" *See* "should" and "shouldn't". . . .

[12] *See* Chap. I, Famil. with God.

[13] This sentiment has shown up in advertising, as in the picture of a gloved and monocled Englishman exclaiming, "By Jove, it's great to be Jewish and enjoy Rokeach Gefilte Fish." Lest the Gentile feel left out, the makers of Levy's Rye Bread have for some time been pointing out: "You don't have to be Jewish to

enjoy Levy's rye. . . ." (The poster noting this with a picture of an Indian has been reproduced and sold in the recent craze-market for posters!) Indeed, the opinion advanced of late by the communications industry, through both Jewish and Gentile performers, is that "When you're in love, the whole world is Jewish."

[14] *See also* IIIB, end of "a whole MEGILLE."

[15] The wafer is of course based on the unleavened bread of the Last Supper. (*See* Chap. II, Rel. and Cul., SEYDER.)

[16] For other examples of such cultural syncretism, *see* Chap. II, Advice, note to AZ ME KEN NIT ARIBERGEYN. . . .

[17] *See* Chap. II, Passing Judgment, AZ ME SHMIRT DI REDER. . . .

[18] *Re.* the dropping of the "h," *see* discussion under "shmo."

[19] Note the different wish for Santa under "Drop dead!" above.

[20] Particularly intriguing was the 1966 ad in the *New York Times:* "So what else is new for Christmas? The Hamilton Beach Oral Hygiene Center, that's what."

[21] This appeared in a recent ad of Weyenberg Massagic Shoes in the *New York Times,* along with "knocking our heads against the wall" ("For months now, we've been knocking our heads against the wall trying to convince you that Weyenberg Shoes are better than Portage shoes"). *See* Chap. II, Ann. and Arg., KLAP KOP IN VANT!

[22] P. 31.

[23] I am indebted for the clipping to Prof. James Macris.

[24] The clipping was kindly provided by Dr. Marshall D. Berger.

[25] As may be seen in Chap. II, Destiny, a number of Yiddish expostulations at fate call up a relationship to friend or enemy, and these are often heard in translation. *See also* Char. and Des., last par. under FINSTER.

[26] These halvah designations were reported to me from California by Dr. Irving Babow.

Chap. IIIB: HOW WELL THEY GO TOGETHER
(Bilingualisms)

[1] *Cf.* Chap. II, Family, AZ DI MUTER SHRAYT AFN KIND 'MAMZER'. . . .

[2] *Cf.* IIIA, "make with" for "give out with."

[3] Weidman earlier wrote a story entitled "Chutzpa" (*see* Chap. II, Char. and Des.).

[4] *See* Chap. I, Superstition.

[5] The latter is reminiscent of ICH'L IM GEBN A MISHEBEYRACH (*see* Chap. II, Char. and Des., ER HOT IM GEGEBN A MISHEBEYRACH).

[6] *See* Chap. III, p. 293, reference to effect of mobility.

[7] A striking adoption is the Sears, Roebuck "neatnik," prominently featured in 1968 and 1969 catalogs and sales flyers ("Be a Neatnik," etc.).

[8] *Cf.* Chap. I, end of Vulgarity, "TSORAss" for TSORES.

Chap. IV: AND VICE VERSA: HOW YIDDISH RESPONDS TO ENGLISH

[1] Humorous reports of Yiddish dialect have often used what seems to be a direct exchange of sounds between the English long "e" (eel) and short "i" (in), words

like "piece" and "pill" becoming "piss" and "peel." Yale's Robert J. Menner theorized years ago that this is not exactly as it may sound, that in actuality Yiddish employs for both these English vowels the very same sound, which is midway between the English "ee" and "ĭ" and therefore creates for the hearer a contrast with whichever English sound it is attempting to produce. This same explanation has been advanced for the apparent interchange between other vowels such as "a" and "e."

In a loan like APSTEZ, there is a further change of vowel sound plus a dropping of consonant, also seen in "Cooney Islan' " for "Coney Island" or "lendler' " for "landlord."

² Colorful bilingual uses of -ELE, as in "Helloele" or the name Raouelele, have been mentioned earlier, as have such uses of the diminutive -ENYU (sweet).

³ This last process even shows through in first-generation English, as in "I'm an Orthodox, and my son is married to a Reform." *Cf.* similar effects in IIIA, "dairy" for "dairy products" *and* "Danish" for "Danish pastry."

⁴ The rest of his prediction: the language would then "expire quietly, and finally become as delightfully musty and passé a subject for doctor's theses as Anglo-Saxon is today." *Cf.* note below concerning forecasts about the Yiddish theatre.

⁵ The accuracy of such forecasts in the past may be gauged by two sample statements about the Yiddish theatre in the United States. Back around 1898, in his *History of Yiddish Literature in the Nineteenth Century,* Professor Leo Wiener of Harvard questioned whether the Yiddish theatre could last in America for another ten years. And over a half-century later, in 1958, Howard M. Sachar, in *The Course of Modern Jewish History,* reported: "In 1945 the Second Avenue Yiddish Theatre closed its doors for the last time. . . ." Even as Sachar's book was being published, Molly Picon was making plans for a new opening. As noted before, the Yiddish theatre is currently in another upswing, both here and abroad. In New York it is not confined to Second Avenue—both because the neighborhood has changed and because some shows are presented on Broadway. As Leon Spitz put it back in 1930, "Yiddish . . . is currently designated as a dying language gasping for a last breath. But it may be observed that it seems to take a phenomenally long breath. It appears quite likely that, as the case was with Mark Twain, the death of Yiddish has been slightly exaggerated."

Index of Words and Phrases

Index

427